Dryden and the Traces
of Classical Rome

Dryden and the Traces of Classical Rome

PAUL HAMMOND

OXFORD
UNIVERSITY PRESS

PR
3427
.R65
H36
1999

OXFORD
UNIVERSITY PRESS

Great Clarendon Street, Oxford OX2 6DP

Oxford University Press is a department of the University of Oxford.
It furthers the University's objective of excellence in research, scholarship,
and education by publishing worldwide in

Oxford New York

Athens Auckland Bangkok Bogotá Buenos Aires Calcutta
Cape Town Chennai Dar es Salaam Delhi Florence Hong Kong Istanbul
Karachi Kuala Lumpur Madrid Melbourne Mexico City Mumbai
Nairobi Paris São Paulo Singapore Taipei Tokyo Toronto Warsaw

with associated companies in Berlin Ibadan

Oxford is a registered trade mark of Oxford University Press
in the UK and in certain other countries

Published in the United States
by Oxford University Press Inc., New York

British Library Cataloguing in Publication Data

Data available

Library of Congress Cataloging in Publication Data
Hammond, Paul.
Dryden and the traces of classical Rome/Paul Hammond.
Includes bibliographical references.
1. Dryden, John, 1631–1700—Knowledge—Rome. 2. Latin poetry—
Translations into English—History and criticism. 3. Translating
and interpreting—England—History—17th century. 4. Dryden, John,
1631–1700—Knowledge—Literature. 5. Classicism—England—
History—17th century. 6. English poetry—Roman influences.
7. Great Britain—In literature. 8. Imperialism in literature.
9. Rome—In literature. I. Title.
PR3427.R65H36   1999   821'.4—dc21   98–39756
ISBN 0–19–818411–5

1 3 5 7 9 10 8 6 4 2

Typeset in Bembo
by Cambrian Typesetters, Frimley, Surrey
Printed in Great Britain
on acid-free paper by
Bookcraft Ltd
Midsomer Norton, Somerset

Doubt wisely; in strange way
To stand inquiring right, is not to stray;
To sleepe, or runne wrong, is. On a huge hill,
Cragged, and steep, Truth stands, and hee that will
Reach her, about must, and about must goe;
And what th'hills suddennes resists, winne so.

PREFACE

THIS book examines the uses which Dryden makes of Latin in his poetry and his critical writing, firstly through quotation and allusion, and secondly through formal translation. In the first part I explore the ostensible paradoxes that Dryden's sense of himself as an English writer, and as a modern, is characteristically articulated by means of a turn to classical Latin; and that his understanding of the contemporary English nation is repeatedly conceptualized through references to ancient Rome. In the second part I offer readings of Dryden's translations from Horace, Juvenal, Lucretius, Ovid, and Virgil—culminating in a long essay on the *Aeneis*—in which I show how Dryden used translation from the Latin poets as a way of exploring new terrain: in the public sphere, empire and its loss, and in the private world, selfhood and its dissolution. I hope that in following the varied traces of Rome in the texture of Dryden's writing, and by emphasizing his continual engagement with mutability and metamorphosis, this book will counter some of the commonplace assumptions about Dryden's stolidly conservative or merely opportunistic engagement with life, and will make a case for the subtlety, rigour, and variety of his poetic imagination, and the searching compassion of his humanism.

I am grateful to the editors of *The Modern Language Review* and *The Seventeenth Century*, and to Cambridge University Press, for allowing me to adapt some material which appeared first in their publications; these adaptations are acknowledged at the appropriate points. I am also grateful to the Trustees of the National Gallery, and to the Librarian of Leeds University Library, for permission to reproduce images from their collections. I owe special thanks to Dr David Hopkins, Dr Paulina Kewes, and Dr Nigel Smith, firstly for the pleasures of their friendship, but more

particularly for their kindness in reading a draft of this book at a busy time of year, and providing both invaluable criticism and welcome encouragement. That the book exists at all is a tribute, once again, to Nick.

Dryden and the Traces of Classical Rome is dedicated to the memory of my best teacher, Dr Carl Baron, who introduced me not only to Dryden, but to a way of life.

P.F.H.

CONTENTS

LIST OF PLATES

(between pages 164 and 165)

A NOTE ON TEXTS AND ABBREVIATIONS

Unless otherwise stated, Dryden is quoted from *The Poems of John Dryden*, edited by James Kinsley, 4 vols. (Oxford, 1958), as this is currently the only complete old-spelling edition of his poetry. This edition is cited by short title as '*Poems*', with line numbers for verse texts and page numbers for prose. Writings not included in that edition are quoted from the California edition, *The Works of John Dryden*, edited by H. T. Swedenberg *et al.*, 20 vols., in progress (Berkeley, 1956–), cited by short title as '*Works*', with act, scene, and line numbers for plays, and volume and page numbers for prose works. Occasionally texts which are not available in either of these editions have been cited from other sources. Reference is also made to my own edition in the Longman Annotated English Poets series, *The Poems of John Dryden: Volume 1: 1649–1681* and *Volume 2: 1682–1685*, edited by Paul Hammond (London, 1995), cited by short title as '*Poems*, ed. Hammond'.

The principal Latin poets are cited from editions approximating to those which Dryden is known to have used (marked in the bibliography with an asterisk). For other classical writers the editions in the Loeb Library have been used, unless specific editions are listed. Virgil's poem is cited as *Aeneid*, Dryden's translation of it as *Aeneis*.

All translations are my own, unless otherwise attributed.

The following abbreviations have been used:

OED   *The Oxford English Dictionary*
OLD   *The Oxford Latin Dictionary*

LIMEN

I

In his *Landscape with Aeneas at Delos*,[1] painted in Rome in 1672, Claude Lorrain depicts one of the originary sites of the European imagination. Delos was the birthplace of Apollo, and contained his oracle. Apollo is the ideal type of manly beauty, the radiant sun-god, the god also of music, prophecy, and medicine, the one who approves codes of law, inculcates moral and religious principles, and promotes philosophy. It is with the birth of Apollo that our civilization begins.

Delos had once been a floating island, until it was fixed by Apollo as an act of reverence to the place of his birth.[2] (Eden, by unhappy contrast, becomes an unfixed, wandering place after the fall of man.[3]) It was to Delos that Leto came, pregnant with the child of Zeus, to find refuge from the anger of his consort Hera, who had jealously forbidden sea or land to shelter her. Delos, the wandering place, neither earth nor ocean, was conceptually scandalous, confounding two categories; a suitable place, perhaps, to receive the scandalous Leto, but a curiously labile site to be the origin of the arts of clarification and order. Here Leto clung during her labour to two trees, the olive and the palm, which we see dominating the centre of Claude's painting.

The name of the place, Delos, means 'clear, visible' (*delos* in Greek); before it became fixed, this wandering island had been *adelos*, obscure and difficult to see. At Delos the oracle of Apollo

---

[1] London, National Gallery. Reproduced as Plate 1. For discussions of Claude's handling of architecture, time, and space see particularly I. G. Kennedy, 'Claude and Architecture', *Journal of the Warburg and Courtauld Institutes*, 35 (1972) 260–83; and Marcel G. Roethlisberger, 'The Dimension of Time in the Art of Claude Lorrain', *Artibus et Historiae*, 20 (1989) 73–92.

[2] For the classical legends see Williams, *ad Aeneid*, iii. 75–6.

[3] Alastair Fowler *ad Paradise Lost*, x. 296 and xi. 829 in *The Poems of John Milton*, ed. John Carey and Alastair Fowler (London, 1968).

is asked to prophesy the future and provide advice, but oracles
notoriously do not make things clear.[4] The god is not himself visible, and speaks only through an intermediary; he speaks in riddles
and paradoxes, or in ostensibly clear pronouncements which turn
out later to have a double sense. The meaning of the oracle often
becomes clear only after a lapse of time, after errors have made it
apparent that the questioner's original interpretation was a misin-
terpretation. Oracular speech—the primary form of authentic,
original language, being the words of a god—is already displaced
from its source as we hear it; oracular speech invites misconstrual,
setting in motion a chain of interpretation and error, prompting
Oedipus to flee Corinth for Thebes, and Aeneas to lead his
companions to disaster in Crete instead of safety in Italy. Oracles
speak the truth, but impede our recognition of that truth. And
now oracles are ceased.

In Roman fable Delos provides a temporary haven for Aeneas
as he wanders the Mediterranean after his escape from the burning
ruins of Troy. He is greeted by Anius, who in Roman fashion is
both the king of the island and the priest of Apollo. Claude's
painting shows Anius, in white, addressing Aeneas and his father
Anchises, with Aeneas' son Ascanius standing slightly apart from
the group, attentive to what his elders are doing, but not intrud-
ing. Anius gestures towards the two trees which are almost at the
centre of the painting—not exactly at the centre, but displaced
sufficiently to keep the eye in motion, so that we locate the centre
in the space between the natural form of the trees and the architectural solidity of Apollo's temple on the right-hand side. The
olive and the palm are growing so closely together that at first
glance they seem to spring from a single trunk, forming a bifur-
cated tree, half-palm, half-olive. (Indeed, in Claude's drawing of
the painting in his *Liber Veritatis* they clearly do share a single
trunk.[5]) The painting teases us to construe this apparently unnatural sight. To understand it we have to read it not as a natural form
but as a sign, as the trace of an event: we can only comprehend

---

[4] Servius *ad Aeneid*, iii. 73 makes the connection between the island's name and the
character of the oracles: *Servianorum In Vergilii Carmina Commentariorum Editionis
Harvardiana*, vol. 3 (Oxford, 1965), p. 36.

[5] Michael Kitson, *Claude Lorrain: Liber Veritatis* (London, 1978), pl. 179.

this strange sight by recalling a narrative. Indeed, to understand the painting as a whole we have to recall more than one narrative: the arrival of Aeneas at Delos is related by Virgil in *Aeneid* III and by Ovid in *Metamorphoses* XIII, while the birth of Apollo is related in *Metamorphoses* VI. Details in Claude's painting show that he consulted both writers.[6]

There is a marvellous serenity about Claude's scene, in the poised attention of the figures, the calm embrace of the ships by the harbour, and the morning light which suffuses sky and sea. There is no tension. Yet spatially there are anomalies. The temple of Apollo is perched awkwardly on the edge of the water, only just fitting onto the rock and leaving no space for one to walk around it. Buildings of refined conception and deft workmanship sit directly on rough, unpaved ground. A wall and a ditch separate the principal group of figures from the ground in front of the sacred trees. Anius gestures across this gulf, directing the attention of Aeneas and his companions to the trees themselves, but also prompting our gaze to attend to the fissure which separates the humans from the trace of the divine. As in much of Claude's work (especially in his frequent paintings of harbours, with their scenes of embarkation or landing) we realize that this is liminal ground. It is not an integrated space in which it would be easy to move around: in spite of the bridge, the landscape has not been fashioned into a coherent public milieu. The sacred, the civic, and the natural are juxtaposed, not combined. The actual classical remains in seventeenth-century Rome would have presented something resembling this spatially incoherent relationship to Claude's eyes, though without the clarity and cleanliness of his depiction: the buildings on the Campo Vaccino, for example, would have appeared jumbled in a semi-rural setting, with cattle grazing among the stones and little impression of imperial orderliness; by this date the temples would have lost the ceremonial forecourts which most of them had originally possessed and which separated them off from common ground. Claude's painting takes just such a mingling of the rustic and the imperial, but instead of this being a sign of decay and ruin, it has been purified into the constituents of a scene of uncorrupted origins, bracketing the intervening period of imperial history.

---

[6] Humphrey Wine, *Claude: The Poetic Landscape* (London, 1994), p. 96.

As the space is complex, so too is the implicit time of the scene. The temple of Apollo is recognizably modelled on the Pantheon, a building which (in the narrative time implied by the presence here of Aeneas) does not yet exist. Rome has not yet been founded, and yet here is one of its principal temples transposed to Apollo's island, with golden eagles at its corners symbolizing the Roman empire. An imperial structure inhabits—and shapes our perception of—a pre-imperial location. The island is the site where Aeneas will receive the prophecy of Rome's great destiny, a destiny which is already promised in this displaced building, paradoxically the trace of a future rather than a past, gesturing towards *telos* rather than *archē*.[7] The connection between the time of Aeneas and the time of historical Rome is itself fabular, for the syntax in which they can be linked is provided only by the *Aeneid*, in which Virgil included references to monuments, people, and customs which have no place in the supposed time of Aeneas, but are contemporary with himself and his readers.[8] In Claude's painting the model for the temple is not the building which Virgil would have known—built to commemorate the victory of Augustus at the Battle of Actium—but the second temple built by Hadrian on the same site, retaining the same name and (confusingly) the same inscription recording its construction by Agrippa.[9] Agrippa's original building had an important dynastic function: he wanted to name it after Augustus, and placed a statue of him inside it, but Augustus would not accept either honour. Nevertheless, Agrippa did manage to make the same compliment more subtly by substituting a statue of the deified Julius Caesar.[10] Augustus meanwhile particularly associated himself with Apollo, and integrated his house on the Palatine with the Temple of Apollo.[11] The Pantheon was subsequently the first temple in Rome to be adapted as a Christian church, and was variously decorated and vandalized

---

[7] In Greek, *telos*: 'completion, consummation'; but also 'supreme authority'. *archē*: 'origin, beginning'; but also 'sovereignty, empire'.

[8] Catherine Edwards, *Writing Rome: Textual Approaches to the City* (Cambridge, 1996), p. 31.

[9] William L. MacDonald, *The Pantheon: Design, Meaning, and Progeny* (Harmondsworth, 1976), p. 13.

[10] Karl Galinsky, *Augustan Culture: An Interpretive Introduction* (Princeton, 1996), p. 318; MacDonald, *The Pantheon*, p. 77.

[11] Galinsky, *Augustan Culture*, pp. 146, 213–24.

by successive popes, so Claude's structure is an idealized version of the building which he was actually able to see. Claude's use of the Pantheon displaces it from history and purges it of the traces of ideological change, but the resulting image is located at the intersection of several lines of signification, each of which has a temporal dimension. As the temple of Apollo it refers back to the birth of the god in Greek myth; as a building which is Roman rather than Greek in style it is part of the Roman appropriation and adaptation of Greek culture; as an element within Virgil's narrative it has a place in the foundation myth of Rome; as an approximately recognizable historical edifice it is an element in the painter's or viewer's experience of modern Rome, an experience which is itself partly an act of imaginative reconstruction on the site of a ruined civilization. Hadrian's Pantheon replaced and reconstructed a previous building, but Claude's version of this temple has no such historical depth; it has lost the memory that it was made and remade. Such are mythic forms: 'le mythe est constitué par la déperdition de la qualité historique des choses: les choses perdent en lui le souvenir de leur fabrication.'[12] Our recognition that Apollo's temple derives from, but does not quite belong to, these various cultural narratives—that is to say, our recognition of its partial but multiple displacement, its scandalous status—is itself an acknowledgement of its special significance as a holy site.

The several disjunctions—spatial, temporal, semantic—which this painting offers, call our attention to the mobility of meaning, the instability of signs, the fictive status of narrative; and in particular we are led to apprehend the complex construction of those sites which we think of as originary. But if this semantic mobility in Claude's painting is a deconstructive play, a challenge to our conceptual structures, this is not a destructive decomposition of form and meaning. The painting itself both initiates and circumscribes the play of signification: though we are conscious of the anomalies which attend the principal objects and the relations between them, we are also aware that the painting has evoked these anomalies with intelligence and wonder. Technically this scene which assembles buildings from different sites is a *caprice* or

---

[12] Roland Barthes, *Mythologies* (Paris, 1957, 1970), p. 230: 'Myth is constituted by the loss of the historical quality of things: in it things lose the memory of their making.'

capriccio, but there is nothing capricious about the rhythmically asymmetric composition, the grace and strength of the individual forms, or the beauty of the light. It is a self-consciously accomplished painting which attends to the strangeness of human artistry as it contemplates the point of origin of its own artistry and values, the site where Apollo was born. To fix a floating island is the work of a god, and belongs to mythology. When art, repeating Apollo's act of reverence to his birthplace, fixes time and space in a painting or a poem, it cannot altogether arrest the movement of the signifier and abolish the traces of other times, other places, other narratives; but by making us attend to those traces the work of art can help us to apprehend something of the complexity and fragility of our thinking, the strangeness of the human world.

II

The historical city of Rome was a space which it was difficult to read. Livy records that the Romans themselves recognized that the building of their city had been haphazard, and had not resulted in a readily intelligible space.[13] The imperial city retained traces of its rudimentary past, as Propertius observed,[14] and displayed nothing like the clarity of plan which would be devised for London by Wren or for Paris by Haussmann. And partly because of the work of Renaissance scholars such as Pirro Ligorio,[15] who explored the archaeology of Rome, the maps which Dryden's contemporaries found in their handbooks of Roman antiquities presented a confusing jumble of buildings (Plate 2). The city was a palimpsest: architecturally, in that buildings stood on the sites of earlier buildings, reusing whatever materials were at hand, so that groundplans and boundaries preserved the lines of vanished structures, while ancient masonry and ornament appeared in new and often incongruous places; and conceptually, too, since the idea of Rome was an intricate patchwork of republican, imperial, and papal ideologies, each of which selectively appropriated and rewrote those texts which gave imaginative shape to the eternal city.

Classical Rome traced its origins to Romulus, but in another

---

[13] Livy, *Ab urbe condita*, v. 55.   [14] e.g., Propertius, iv. 1A.
[15] See *Pirro Ligorio: Artist and Antiquarian*, ed. Robert W. Gaston (Milan, 1988).

sense its founder was Aeneas, the exiled Trojan prince. Rome is therefore a second city, a substitute for the original home. The idea of origin is a necessary fiction for a culture, but our myths of origin are complex and even contradictory, shaped as they are from diverse viewpoints and competing needs. Dumézil points out that the accounts of early Roman history bear the impress of a common mythic pattern whereby a nation needs three types of skill, the king, the warrior, and the farmer.[16] Livy's narrative accordingly provides three founding figures after Romulus, each of whom initiates one of these areas of life. Romulus himself laid out the physical foundations of the city, with supernatural assistance. Then Numa (combining in his kingly role legal and religious functions) established religion and the law; Tullus developed the arts of war; and Ancus presided over the geographical and economic expansion and consolidation of the city. Origins are multiple; foundation is necessarily repeated. Such was Rome's need to cultivate its origins that the supposed house of Romulus was rebuilt several times, and there were even two such houses, rival shrines on opposite hills.[17]

The point of origin is, it seems, never single and unitary; there is a tendency to make it fissured or doubled. In his essay *Das Unheimlich*[18] Freud explores the relationship between the *heimlich* (homely, familiar) and its ostensible opposite, the *unheimlich* (strange, uncanny). The primary meaning of *heimlich* is 'belonging to the house or family', like the Latin *familiaris*, but the semantic field of the word is strangely fractured and folded back on itself. Tracing the mobility of its definition, Freud shows that *heimlich* is used for that which is familiar and agreeable, but also for what is kept secret and out of sight: the homely, our domestic realization of self-presence, is not out on display but hidden away, hidden even from ourselves. A displacing movement within the semantic field of *heimlich* traces a path—'withdrawn from knowledge, unconscious . . . that which is obscure, inaccessible to knowledge . . . something hidden and

---

[16] Georges Dumézil, *Mythe et épopée: l'idéologie des trois fonctions dans les épopées des peuples indo-européens* (Paris, 1968), pp. 262–72. He discusses Propertius, iv. 1A on pp. 304–36, and on pp. 337–422 argues that the *Aeneid* replicates the tripartite structure of the legendary birth of Rome. [17] Edwards, *Writing Rome*, pp. 34–5.

[18] Sigmund Freud, *Gesammelte Werke*, ed. Anna Freud *et al.*, 18 vols. (London and Frankfurt, 1940–68), xii. 227–68. Translated as 'The "Uncanny" ' in *The Standard Edition of the Complete Psychological Works of Sigmund Freud*, trans. James Strachey *et al.*, 24 vols. (London, 1953–74), xvii. 217–52.

dangerous'—which approaches its opposite, *unheimlich*, that which arouses dread and horror because it ought to have remained secret and hidden but has come to light. There is an undoing of the stability of meaning already at work within what we had taken to be the site of origin. Similarly Benveniste charts an etymological (and thus a conceptual) connection between the ideas of self, host, guest, and enemy in the Indo-Germanic languages.[19] To illustrate this by citing the Latin forms of these words, *ipse* which signifies 'one's self', is linked to *hospes*, which means 'host' (*OLD* 2) but also 'guest' (*OLD* 1), and as an adjective 'foreign, alien' (*OLD* 3); and these are linked to *hostis*, which is 'stranger' (*OLD* 1) but also 'enemy' (*OLD* 2). Several aspects of this chain of connections are immediately striking: that an idea of selfhood seems to require one to entertain others, and is thus predicated upon accommodating strangeness; that the roles of host and guest seem, at some level, to be the same; that the guest may also be the enemy, the strange may become a threat. The integrity of the self is dependent upon strangeness, and yet that strangeness may undo it. From several perspectives, the self, the homely, the point of origin, seem to be disconcertingly unstable concepts.

Language carries within it the traces of its past, quasi-archaeological remains from structures of thought which have crumbled away; and literary language, with its heightened self-consciousness, is especially aware of the origins from which its present culture springs, or claims to spring. To write is to be engaged in a passionate relation to the origin, says Derrida:

«*Écrire, c'est avoir la passion de l'origine*».

Mais ce qui l'affecte ainsi, on le sait maintenant, ce n'est pas l'origine mais ce qui en tient lieu; ce n'est pas davantage le contraire de l'origine. Ce n'est pas l'absence au lieu de la présence mais une trace qui remplace une présence qui n'a jamais été présente, une origine par laquelle rien n'a commencé.[20]

---

[19] Émile Benveniste, *Le Vocabulaire des institutions indo-européennes*, 2 vols. (Paris, 1969), i. 87–101.

[20] Jacques Derrida, *L'Écriture et la différence* (Paris, 1967, 1994), p. 430: '*To write is to have a passion for the origin.* But what affects writing in this way, one now knows, is not the origin, but that which takes its place; which is not, moreover, the opposite of the origin. It is not absence instead of presence, but a trace which replaces a presence which has never been present, an origin from which nothing has begun.' (For Alan Bass's translation of this see his p. 295.)

So what we take to be the origin is likely to be only a simulacrum of origin, a fiction which is constructed as part of a culture's essential mythology of itself. The fictive status of the origin weighs heavily upon the writer, since he carries the responsibility for his culture's understanding of its roots. Meanwhile, he has his own origins, those ancestral texts which have the power to awe him into silence or inspire him into words of his own.

For Dryden, the origins of his culture lie partly in Rome, and in Latin, but origins are to some degree invented *ex post facto*, and those Latin texts which he pored over as a boy and translated and quoted as an adult are traces which take the place of the origin, overlaying the historical fabric of Rome with a text which is the creation of Renaissance scholars. In Dryden's own writing Rome is recreated yet again. Virgil had written of Rome as *Imperium sine fine*,[21] and Ovid had seen Rome and the world as co-extensive: *Romanae spatium est Urbis & orbis idem.*[22] In the textual field which Dryden creates there is, by contrast, a vital boundary—a line running between English and Latin, between England and Rome, present and past, although each of these terms is generated and defined by its partner, and thus finds its identity by reflection, its stability by the movement between itself and its opposite. Each carries the trace of the other.

III

> Well then; the promis'd hour is come at last;
> The present Age of Wit obscures the past:
> Strong were our Syres; and as they Fought they Writ,
> Conqu'ring with force of Arms, and dint of Wit;
> Theirs was the Gyant Race, before the Flood;
> And thus, when *Charles* Return'd, our Empire stood.
> Like *Janus* he the stubborn Soil manur'd,
> With Rules of Husbandry the rankness cur'd:
> Tam'd us to manners, when the Stage was rude;
> And boistrous *English* Wit, with Art indu'd.
> Our Age was cultivated thus at length;
> But what we gain'd in skill we lost in strength.

[21] Virgil, *Aeneid*, i. 279: 'an empire without end'.
[22] Ovid, *Fasti*, ii. 684: 'The world and the city of Rome occupy the same space.'

> Our Builders were, with want of Genius, curst;
> The second Temple was not like the first:
> Till You, the best *Vitruvius*, come at length;
> Our Beauties equal; but excel our strength.
> Firm *Dorique* Pillars found Your solid Base:
> The Fair *Corinthian* Crowns the higher Space;
> Thus all below is Strength, and all above is Grace.[23]

Writing in 1693, after the Revolution had dispossessed him of the laureateship, Dryden addresses his young friend William Congreve as the architect of the long-awaited edifice which heralds a new style. The achievements of the present finally obscure the past, a past inhabited by intimidating giants, ancestors who had strength if not grace. This 'Gyant Race, before the Flood' was the generation of Jacobean playwrights led by Shakespeare, Jonson, and Fletcher, and only now does Dryden see their achievement being eclipsed by a new literature; in the 1660s, when he was writing *Of Dramatick Poesie, An Essay*, they had seemed uncomfortably close and potent. Congreve is 'the best *Vitruvius*', a second version of the great Roman architect, and his building combines the strength of the Doric mode with the grace of the Corinthian. Here is an art which replicates and perfects the past, while being fully appropriate to the present, and inaugurating the future.

But this account of apparent progress and refinement, this celebration of the present, is fraught with tensions, silences, doublings, evasions. Though the opening line of the poem greets the present, this is a present in which Dryden himself hardly participates. The elegant structure raised by Congreve is the achievement of a younger generation, and actually contrasts with Dryden's own work. It is a building which Dryden has not designed or constructed, though he modestly effaces his own contribution to Congreve's success, and later casts himself in the role of master turned pupil. Though the references in this poem are principally to the drama, and Dryden may be thinking that Congreve has brought about a purer neo-classical dramaturgy than his own, the connections between the two men up to this point had chiefly

---

[23] 'To My Dear Friend Mr. Congreve, On His Comedy, call'd *The Double-Dealer*', ll. 1–19; published in Congreve's *The Double-Dealer* in Dec. 1693, dated 1694. This is also the starting-point for Eric Griffiths's thoughtful and perceptive lecture 'Dryden's Past', *Proceedings of the British Academy*, 84 (1994) 113–49.

been concerned with classical translation. Congreve's poem 'To Mr. Dryden, on his Translation of Persius' had appeared in October 1692 in the collected translation of Juvenal and Persius published by Tonson, to which Congreve contributed the version of Juvenal XI; *Examen Poeticum*, the third volume of the Dryden–Tonson miscellanies, published in March 1693, included translations from Horace and Homer by Congreve, whom Dryden singles out for special praise in his preface;[24] Dryden was indebted to Congreve for reviewing his translation of the *Aeneid*, perhaps as early as 1693; and Congreve's translations from Ovid's *Metamorphoses* and *Ars Amatoria* may also belong to the period 1692–3.[25] Displaced from the laureateship, he has no prospect of regaining that position, and now hopes only that Congreve will succeed him. That succession has not yet occurred, so in this respect the promised hour has *not* come, and indeed the tense in which Dryden writes of this hypothetical succession locates it in an unrealized past:

> Oh that your Brows my Lawrel had sustain'd,
> Well had I been Depos'd, if You had reign'd![26]

If this ever does occur, a parenthesis will inevitably have fallen between the two men, for the heir cannot simply and smoothly fill up the place once held by the ancestor. Succession to the laureateship is not within Dryden's gift, but depends on the will of the country's rulers. The poem acknowledges the power of such men, while mocking it by turning the results of their patronage into a mere parody of true government: '*Tom* the Second reigns like *Tom* the first.'[27] Dryden asserts the power of the literary text to shape

---

[24] 'Mr. *Congreve* (whom I cannot mention without the Honour which is due to his Excellent Parts, and that entire Affection which I bear him.) . . . I wish Mr. *Congreve* had the leisure to Translate him [Homer], and the World the good Nature and Justice, to Encourage him in that Noble Design, of which he is more capable than any Man I know' (*Poems*, pp. 797–9).

[25] This account of Dryden and Congreve's connections as classical translators is derived from D. F. McKenzie, *The Integrity of William Congreve: The Clark Lectures for 1997* (Privately Printed, 1997), pp. 6–10. I am grateful to Professor McKenzie for his kind permission to cite this material.

[26] 'To My Dear Friend Mr. Congreve', ll. 41–2.

[27] 'To My Dear Friend Mr. Congreve', l. 48. '*Tom* the first' is Thomas Shadwell, Dryden's successor as Historiographer Royal, and '*Tom* the Second' is Thomas Rymer, who succeeded Shadwell in 1692.

cultural spaces by suggesting that the intervention of government in the world of letters can only produce a hiatus between two genuine writers; it can displace true genius but not replace it with adequate substitutes. But while Dryden makes Congreve his heir and the guardian of his reputation, he is choosing to acknowledge one form of displacement rather than another. His own work is only a second temple, second best, lacking the strength of his giant ancestors' work and the combined strength and grace of his successor's new Vitruvian structure. Dryden felt himself to be 'betwixt two Ages cast, | The first of this, and hindmost of the last'.[28] But he had written those lines back in 1675: the sense of displacement was not generated simply by the Revolution, but was a recurring condition in Dryden's writing.

Contemporaries noticed this characteristic, and some mocked it. One described Dryden in 1693 as 'a famous *Abdicating Poet*',[29] while George Powell, writing in 1698 about Dryden's verses on George Granville's *Heroick Love*, said:

This Poem, though designed a Caress to the Honourable Author, however, makes the top Compliment at home; the main flourish upon himself: when with his own long and laudable Vanity, all true *Drydenism*, he gives the Reader to understand, That *J. Dryden* is the very Father of the Muses, the Source, Fountain, and Original of Poetry, nay, the *Apollo* himself; when all the Address he has to make this Ingenious and Honourable Author, is, the Resignation of his own Lawrels.

But here, I am afraid, he makes him but a course Compliment, when this great Wit, with his Treacherous Memory, forgets, that he had given away his Lawrels upon Record, no less then twice before, *viz.* once to Mr. *Congreve*, and another time to Mr. *Southern*. Prithee, old *Oedipus*, expound this Mystery: Dost thou set up thy own *Transubstantiation* Miracle in the Donation of thy Idol Bays, that thou hast 'em Fresh, New, and whole, to give 'em three times over?[30]

Touché: Dryden had indeed told Granville that 'With less regret, those Lawrels I resign, | Which dying on my Brows, revive on

---

[28] 'Prologue to *Aureng-Zebe*', ll. 21–2.
[29] *An Humble Remonstrance of the Batchelors, in and about London* (London, 1693), p. 1.
[30] Preface by George Powell to *The Fatal Discovery; or, Love in Ruines* (London, 1698), sig. A2ʳ.

thine'.[31] But he nowhere suggests that he is himself the original, the source, the father, Apollo—that is Powell's fantasy, and his inadvertent tribute. There is indeed a characteristic 'Drydenism' here, but it is self-displacement rather than self-assertion. By 1698 he had abandoned the stage for the field of translation. Two years later he would be dead. And according to one contemporary, after Dryden's death Apollo found no one worthy to succeed him.[32]

Although the poem to Congreve had opened with a gesture ('Well then . . .') which is as close to the speaking voice as writing can come, giving a strong simulation of Dryden's own authorial presence in the text, by the end of the poem Dryden represents himself retiring from the stage, and even about to retire from life:

> Already I am worn with Cares and Age;
> And just abandoning th' Ungrateful Stage:
> . . . .
> Be kind to my Remains; and oh defend,
> Against Your Judgment, Your departed Friend![33]

It is ironic, but (as this book will argue) wholly typical, that Dryden should displace himself from the very poem in which he celebrates the present.

This is one of the awkwardnesses in this poem, the way it locates the poet in the present, both the present of the written text and the present which that text celebrates. Another is the way it locates the past and fashions a narrative of recent cultural history. Four ages seem to be described. The first is the age of Shakespeare and his contemporaries. The description of them as the giant race before the flood suggests two possible allusions, either to the Bible

---

[31] 'To Mr. Granville, on his Excellent Tragedy, call'd *Heroick Love*', ll. 5–6. Dryden had written three prologues to plays by Southerne, but in none of them does he speak of resigning his laurels to Southerne. Southerne himself, however, had written of Dryden as Apollo, and of Congreve as his eventual successor: '*Dryden* has long extended his Command, | By Right Divine, quite through the Muses Land, | Absolute Lord; and holding now from none, | But great *Apollo*, his undoubted Crown: | (That Empire settled, and grown old in Pow'r) | Can wish for nothing, but a Successor:' (Thomas Southerne, 'To Mr. Congreve', ll. 18–23, in *Comedies by William Congreve*, ed. Bonamy Dobrée (Oxford, 1925), p. 18). Southerne's poem, prefixed to Congreve's *The Old Batchelor* (1693), may have given Dryden a hint for his own poem a year later.

[32] *A New Session of the Poets, Occasion'd by the Death of Mr. Dryden* (London, 1700).

[33] 'To My Dear Friend Mr. Congreve', ll. 66–7, 72–3.

or to Ovid.[34] Or perhaps the poem invites us to hold both myths
in our minds, and thus to create momentarily a new temporal field
from these two myths of origin.[35] In the biblical myth the giants
are part of a wicked race which God destroys through the flood;
in Ovid they inhabit the earth after Astræa the goddess of justice
has left in disgust, and they rebel against the gods. Although
Shakespeare's generation is being praised for its strength, neither of
these allusions is complimentary if pursued to its source, and so the
compliment half-undoes itself. The second period is 'the Flood',
the Civil War and Republic, a crucial stage in the nation's history
which is almost elided here by being characterized so briefly.
However, it is also doubly characterized, because in line 6 it is
called 'our Empire', and so the years of flood are simultaneously
years of empire, albeit an empire which was in need of renovation.
Paradoxically, then, this age is figured simultaneously as structure
and destruction. But since this is primarily a cultural rather than a
political history, we may also read 'our Empire' as a reference to
the empire of the Muses, the state of English letters. The third age
is the period after 1660, when the arts of cultivation were learnt,
but when skill was acquired at the expense of strength. It was
presided over by Charles II as Janus, the god of new beginnings.
But Janus was also a god with two faces, and so Dryden's allusion
suggests that renewal was combined with—and perhaps undone
by—the King's duplicity. Charles's encouragement of the arts did
not ultimately extend to paying his laureate's salary on time, or to
creating the conditions in which Dryden could write the epic
which might have been a Carolean *Aeneid*. This is the period
which was Dryden's time, the time of the second temple.

The allusion is to the temple in Jerusalem which was rebuilt
after the Exile, but was thought to be poor in comparison with the
glory of the original structure; moreover, God was no longer
present with his people in the same way, for the Holy of Holies
which had contained the Ark of the Covenant was now empty.[36]

---

[34] Genesis 6: 4; Ovid, *Metamorphoses*, i. 151–62.

[35] For differing modes of interpreting classical and biblical myths of prehistory see
Arthur B. Ferguson, *Utter Antiquity: Perceptions of Prehistory in Renaissance England* (Durham,
NC, 1993).

[36] Ezra 5–6, Haggai 2: 3. See W. Jackson Bate, *The Burden of the Past and the English
Poet* (London, 1971), pp. 21–7, for a discussion of this image.

Yet because of the references to Janus and Vitruvius, this second temple is implicitly a quasi-Roman structure as well, and this fusion of Jewish and Roman is appropriate in that Solomon's temple was thought to have used the classical orders. The second temple featured variously in seventeenth-century culture as an image of glory and purity recovered. In the reign of James I there had been designs for Whitehall Palace to be rebuilt along the ground-plan of Solomon's temple, as the Escorial palace had been.[37] Milton remarked that the Presbyterians who were mourning Charles I had once regarded him as the wicked King Ahab, but now saw him as the pious Josiah who rebuilt the temple.[38] Bunyan made Solomon's temple the allegorical form by which his followers were to build their own inner spiritual temple.[39] Stillingfleet saw the time of the second temple as a period when the text of the scriptures was preserved more faithfully than during the subsequent diaspora, when the Jews 'were *discarded* by *God* himself from being his people, when he broke up *house* among them at the *destruction* of *Jerusalem* and the *Temple*'.[40]

There had, therefore, been several second temples, actual or projected, literal or symbolic, as the modern tried to predicate itself upon the ancient and to make its modernity classic, and the complication of temporal references within Dryden's poem emphasizes the imaginary status of this structure. Each of these three periods is over-written, characterized by images and allusions which do not fit together into a coherent whole, and even jar against one another: thus each period is mythologized, yet— inevitably—the mythology is not ultimately coherent. But it is clear that for Dryden the second temple, his own structure, is already in the past, for there is a marked shift of tenses with the arrival of Congreve. The fourth period is the present age, the one which obscures the past. But which past does it obscure? Does the present eclipse only Shakespeare's generation, or Dryden's as well?

---

[37] Roy Strong, *Britannia Triumphans: Inigo Jones, Rubens, and Whitehall Palace* (London, 1980), pp. 55–64.

[38] *The Complete Prose Works of John Milton*, ed. Don M. Wolfe *et al.*, 8 vols. (New Haven, 1953–82), iii. 365.

[39] John Bunyan, *Solomon's Temple Spiritualiz'd* (London, 1688).

[40] Edward Stillingfleet, *Origines Sacrae* (London, 1663), p. 557.

Understanding the cultural history of the seventeenth century is made more difficult through these elisions and ambiguous allusions, and the second temple itself stands awkwardly within this already dislocated and dislocating narrative. It seems to be a rebuilding of early seventeenth-century culture, but because of the Roman references it is also seen as a rebuilding of antiquity: a double achievement of reconstruction, then, but also therefore doubly impoverished in comparison with its predecessors. Perhaps the second temple is already obscured by the Doric strength and Corinthian grace of Congreve's new building. By contrast with such a clearly articulated structure, Dryden's account of his own lifetime is strikingly unclassical, mixing Roman and Jewish allusions, and producing a macaronic space in which different times and different languages jostle. This conceptual structure is, unlike Congreve's building, not easily read, but troubled by contradictions. Because two of the major influences on Dryden's career—the Civil War and the Revolution—are almost elided from the narrative, this poem about large cultural transformations becomes partly a poem about building personal structures of thought in spite of all the building and demolition taking place around one in the public domain. It is therefore an intensely personal poem, but one which almost makes Dryden disappear from the cultural scene and from his own text, as his 'Remains' are handed over to someone else.

IV

This poem raises various issues which will be the subject of this book. It registers an ambition to be classical, to build structures which have both elegance and strength, and which can be understood through a language inherited from the ancient world. But inheritance is difficult. Perhaps it is impossible to inherit, to take full possession of something which the ancestor once owned. The inheritance may instead bring with it an uncanny possession of the heir by the ancestor. Culture is built upon—or perhaps we should say that culture can only think itself through—the traces of the ancestors. As Derrida observes:

Il n'y a pas de culture sans culte des ancêtres, ritualisation du deuil et du sacrifice, lieux et modes institutionnels de sépulture . . . Pas de politique . . . sans organisation de l'espace et du temps de deuil, sans topolitologie de la sépulture, sans relation anamnésique et thématique à l'esprit comme revenant, sans hospitalité ouverte à l'hôte comme *ghost* qu'on tient aussi bien qu'il nous tient en otage.[41]

Mourning therefore is central to culture, which is founded on reverence for ancestors, even (perhaps especially) when they are mythic. Absence inescapably shadows our apprehension of presence; alterity becomes the ground of our fiction of self-definition. But the great figures of the past may be ghosts who come unbidden to haunt us, as much as honoured guests whom we set out to entertain.

During the period of Dryden's second temple, the times and spaces of mourning were contested. The first ritual surrounding the execution of Charles I was a sacrificial street theatre, but this was succeeded by private mourning among royalists conducted through reading the *Eikon Basilikē* in separate, multiple secrecies linked by a shared grief and a shared text; later, the King's death was written into the liturgical calendar, while the body of Cromwell, once ruler now regicide, was dug up from Westminster Abbey, dismembered, and scattered across London to form a set of miniature and already decaying monuments. Such rapid shifts in the sites and languages of mourning created strange transformations of the nation's symbolic geography, with sudden absences and silences, anamnesic acts of oblivion. And there were textual monuments too: in 1662 the royal bookseller Richard Royston published *Basilika: The Workes of King Charles the Martyr*, which collected the King's writings, reordered history through an account of his life, his negotiations with Parliament, and his trial,

---

[41] Jacques Derrida, *Apories: mourir—s'attendre aux «limites de la vérité»* (Paris, 1996), pp. 83, 112: 'There is no culture without a cult of ancestors, a ritualization of mourning and sacrifice, institutional places and modes of burial . . . There is no politics . . . without an organization of the time and space of mourning, without a topolitology of the sepulcher, without an anamnesic and thematic relation to the spirit as ghost (*revenant*), without an open hospitality to the guest as *ghost*, whom one holds, just as he holds us, hostage' (trans. Thomas Dutoit, pp. 43, 61–2). I assume that 'topolitologie' is Derrida's coinage, a portmanteau word fusing *topos, polis*, and *litē* ('prayer') to suggest that the city locates itself (literally and conceptually) around a place of ancestral burial.

and prefixed to this handsome folio a title page which placed an image of Charles at the centre of a classical temple (Plate 3). While these transformations of the spaces of mourning and vengeance were taking place, Dryden reorganized for himself the times and spaces of mourning through his own texts, partly by sacrificing to the ghosts of Latin literature, welcoming them as guests in his poetry. And so his English verse became a field of traces which lead back to the originary site of Rome, an origin created by traces.

Dryden writes as the heir to the Romans partly to avoid (or as a way of carrying) the burden of being heir to the Jacobeans, and to avoid (even to have to avoid ignoring) that *aporia*, both flood and empire, which in retrospect he saw as an interregnum, a period betwixt two ages cast. His engagement with classical Rome allows him to shape an imagined world which follows its own distinctive contours in time and space, displacing the weight of Roman and of Jacobean culture, but also displacing the burden of contemporary anxieties, the exigencies of the present. The present (particularly for a writer who earned his living chiefly as a dramatist and political controversialist) could be a labile time, and in the face of such time Dryden's poems fashion their own kinds of time and space which are translations from a Restoration language via Latin back into a metamorphosed present; they thus effect a translation within Restoration English in which the language is made to work against itself so as to expel its crassness, and to move beyond its mere temporality—made, therefore, to renounce its temporizing.

Dryden builds his own structures,[42] but within these structures there are faultlines. One of these is created by his use of Roman allusions and Latin phrases. How do we read such traces? What relationship is there between the Latin and the English, the imaginary past and the invented present? What happens at the boundary between the two languages? At these faultlines a movement

---

[42] For Dryden's interest in architecture, and in fashioning quasi-architectural forms in his own poetry, see Richard Luckett, 'The Fabric of Dryden's Verse', *Proceedings of the British Academy*, 67 (1981) 289–305; and Robert W. McHenry, 'Dryden's Architectural Metaphors and Restoration Architecture', *Restoration*, 9 (1985) 61–74; and cp. Howard Erskine-Hill, 'Heirs of Vitruvius: Pope and the Idea of Architecture', in *The Art of Alexander Pope*, ed. Howard Erskine-Hill and Anne Smith (London, 1979), pp. 144–56.

begins which prevents the second temple from being a homogeneous fabric. When we see repetition we recognize difference; when we see quotation we register disjunction as well as admiring the new tessellation. In acknowledging the role of the past in defining the present we cannot always remain untroubled, for when articulating the homely by means of the foreign we become less sure about where to locate those two ostensibly opposite sites, less sure about how the distinction between them might be sustained, since the 'foreign' is notoriously produced partly by our unrecognized and irresolvable anxieties about the home. We displace ourselves as we make such readings, no longer quite in possession of our home ground. Such a movement in the text calls into question the singleness of the poet's voice, and the presence-to-itself of that culture and nationhood which the poem is helping to fashion; it displaces the presence of the present.

Complete self-presence would make signification redundant, and it is only some form of displacement in time and space which makes the work of signs necessary and possible. Dryden's writing refigures time and space to effect a movement away from illusions of presence. In its temporality it may often appear to be obsessively timely, addressing theatre audiences on particular days, intervening in political crises as they are developing, marking births and deaths, commending publications. But the poetry complicates the kind of time into which it draws us. In *Absalom and Achitophel* or *The Hind and the Panther* the time in which the poem's narrative is set is an invented, displaced and multiple time, not altogether removed from history or contemporary events but making an intermittent translation of past and present into a discontinuous narrative, a myth whose fabric is full of strange overlapping folds and unexpected fissures. Often the poet's utterance is belated (*Threnodia Augustalis* on the death of Charles II begins 'Thus long my Grief has kept me dumb') or the poet's grasp is defeated by an untimely occasion ('To the Memory of Mr. Oldham' begins 'Farewel, too little and too lately known'). Belatedness haunts Dryden's writing, as if any modern writing must inevitably be late. He has been born too late to be a colleague of Shakespeare, and now it is too late in his career for him to be a colleague of Congreve. More generally, belatedness haunts writing itself, but to acknowledge this (to build this recognition into the way that writing functions as

a mode of knowledge) is to rethink the relationship between the text and its contemporary occasion, for the present time passes into the text of the poem and so into its textuality, being translated into a language which is recognizing the traces of its distant Latin past. The textual presence of Latin is one means by which Dryden separates, absents, himself from the present in order to write the complexities of presence.

But the relationship in which Dryden stands to the texts of the past is not a negative one: the past is not simply a burden, nor is influence only a source of anxiety.[43] As it is separation which makes a semiotic system possible, so it is the distance from the writers of the past which provides the stimulus and the resources for the creation of a contemporary literature. Dryden's poems reuse classical materials in complex ways, breaking and reassembling the Roman fabric, and fashioning a textual space which translates past and present. Meanwhile, his critical prefaces re-describe the writers of classical Rome, differentiating them and defining their characteristics.[44] Through this comparative criticism which separates Virgil from Ovid, Horace from Juvenal, Dryden makes the Roman inheritance anything but monolithic. And by tracing patterns of resemblance and filiation between Roman and Renaissance writers, he reconfigures the classical heritage on his own terms.[45] Belatedness is not simply a post-lapsarian condition, for it is such a recognition of separation which allows him to make his own space and his own time.

Quotation and translation are two methods by which Dryden gives himself space. When Latin writers are quoted in epigraphs to

[43] As argued by Bate in *The Burden of the Past*, and Harold Bloom in *The Anxiety of Influence: A Theory of Poetry* (New York, 1973).

[44] Dryden compares Virgil and Ovid in the 'Account of the Ensuing Poem' prefixed to *Annus Mirabilis* (1667); offers a critique of Ovid in the Preface to *Ovid's Epistles* (1680); analyses the characteristics of Virgil, Lucretius, Horace, and Theocritus in the Preface to *Sylvæ* (1685); compares Juvenal, Persius, and Horace as satirists in the 'Discourse Concerning the Original and Progress of Satire' prefixed to the translation of Juvenal and Persius (1693), but also branches out there into a discussion of heroic poetry, comparing Homer and Virgil with Spenser and Milton; provides a sustained critical account of Virgil as an epic poet in the Dedication of his *Aeneis* (1697); and in the Preface to *Fables Ancient and Modern* (1700) compares Chaucer, Ovid, and Boccaccio.

[45] For analyses of Dryden's representation of lines of literary inheritance see particularly David Bruce Kramer, *The Imperial Dryden: The Poetics of Appropriation in Seventeenth-Century England* (Athens, Ga., 1994), and Jennifer Brady, 'Dryden and Negotiations of Literary Succession and Precession', in *Literary Transmission and Authority: Dryden and Other Writers*, ed. Earl Miner and Jennifer Brady (Cambridge, 1993), pp. 27–54.

the poems or in the critical essays and prefaces, their authority is both deferred to and deferred. They carry authority, but in a text which has been made epigrammatic, so that the value of Virgil or Horace lies not in narrative, in structure, in variety, or in tone, but in the lapidary shape of an utterance. Thus the structure of the Roman poem is dismantled, its thought made into a portable commonplace. Such quotation confers authority on the English poet and provides him with an imagined licence to write. But there is another form of quotation, the deployment of allusions, the imitation of images, and the activation of the Latinate roots of English, through which Dryden gives his verse a quasi-Roman texture, shaping a macaronic space which is an imagined world composed from both English and Roman materials, a space which he can shape to his own satisfaction.

In other cases Dryden writes a poetry in which the Roman poets are not guests but ghosts: in his translations from Virgil, Horace, Ovid, and Lucretius he is remaking poems from the Roman period which have a strong hold over him because of the wit or the philosophy of the original. To translate is, literally, to carry over, but the impossibility of translation is a commonplace. Nothing can be carried over, but something new can be built on a similar ground-plan. In quotation the Latin text enters the English in fragments, as a sign of an authority elsewhere but at the same time testifying to the power of the modern author. In translation the Latin text is banished from the page, but haunts every line as we hear echoes of the ghostly original. Impossible but necessary, translation provided Dryden with the ground which he could fashion for himself, a territory where he was free to explore Roman insights about the gods, and sexuality, and death, and the loss of the homeland: it facilitated the fashioning of a self, the discovery of a voice through the suspension of a proud insistence on originality and selfhood. Rome as the point of origin is both fractured and doubled: fractured as its texts are broken into quotations, doubled as they are repeated through translation. And this happens particularly to the *Aeneid*, which in so many ways is for Dryden the dominant, foundational pre-text.[46]

Quotation and translation are the two themes of this book.

---

[46] It is what Genette would call the 'hypotexte': Gérard Genette, *Palimpsestes: La littérature au second degré* (Paris, 1982), p. 13.

PART I

QUOTATION

I

LATIN AND THE ENGLISH WRITER

THE TEXT AS A WORLD OF TRACES

—Non deficit alter
Aureus; & simili frondescit virga metallo.[1]

This quotation comes from the Sibyl's instructions to Aeneas on how to find the golden bough which will give him access to the underworld and the ghosts of the dead. When he has broken off the golden bough, she says, a second one will arise in its place. As chosen by Dryden and Tonson as the epigraph for their collection *Sylvæ: or, The Second Part of Poetical Miscellanies* (1685), the quotation has a double implication. It promises a second instalment of poetry as glittering as the first collection of *Miscellany Poems* (1684), a second golden bough offered to potential readers as a sequel worthy of its predecessor; but because the collection is dominated by translations from Virgil, Horace, and other Latin poets, it also suggests that Dryden and his fellow translators form a second group of golden poets worthy of comparison with their Roman ancestors, their Latin originals. They are a second branch from the sacred tree. It offers the reassurance that to be second is not to be secondary, not reduced to being a mere supplement.

When Dryden came to translate these lines for his complete *Aeneis* of 1697, he rendered them thus:

a second will arise;
And the same Metal the same room supplies.[2]

---

[1] 'Another golden one is not lacking; and a branch of a similar metal sprouts' (Virgil, *Aeneid*, vi. 143–4).   [2] *Aeneis*, vi. 215–16.

This replaces Virgil's *simili* ('similar') with the repeated word 'same', shifting the emphasis from similarity to identity; it supplements Virgil's text by adding the idea of the gap ('room') which is created by the plucking of the first golden bough, but then by adding 'supplies' it imagines the second branch perfectly filling up that gap ('supplies' comes from the Latin *supplere*, to fill up), a supplement which fully takes the place of the original. And yet a counter-movement within Dryden's translation undoes this assurance, for there is a slippage between future and present as we move between the rhyme words 'will arise' and 'supplies'. There is no rhyme of tenses here as there is in Virgil (his *deficit* and *frondescit* are both in the present tense), but instead an uncertainty as to the kind of time in which this miraculous replacement of one bough by another can be imagined as happening. The dream of perfect repetition and repletion surfaces here as a miniature private myth slipped into his translation of the *Aeneid*, Dryden's brief, wistful supplement to Virgil's text. But the imperfect rhyme of tenses troubles this attempt to fill up the gap, for Dryden's poetry is too intelligent to present such a myth of recovered wholeness without some gesture of demur, some tremor of *différance*.

Derrida's neologism '*différance*'[3] is not strictly definable, since it operates as the gap which makes definitions possible, and yet at the same time the movement which makes them unstable. For it is the difference between signifiers which allows them to function as semiotic elements ('Virgil' as distinct from 'virgin'; 'Ovid' not 'avid' or 'ovoid'); and it is the difference between signifier and signified (the sound or the written form of the word, and the idea which it signals) which makes a sign both possible and necessary. Pure self-presence has no division, and so neither permits nor needs signs: it would be outside language. But, says Derrida, '*il n'y a pas de hors-texte*'.[4] *Différance* combines 'difference' and 'deferral'. Language works by differing and deferring, for each signifier takes its place in a network of differences across which a ripple of signification passes as we pursue meaning. Although we may imagine

---

[3] See Jacques Derrida, *Marges de la philosophie* (Paris, 1972), pp. 1–29.

[4] 'There is no outside-text': Jacques Derrida, *De La Grammatologie* (Paris, 1967), p. 227; original italics.

some point of origin which acts as a guarantor of the authenticity of meaning (Derrida's 'signifié transcendantal'[5]), this origin is never attainable. It is always already lost. While language is a supplement to originary presence, writing is classically thought of as a supplement to speech, since speech is a more direct product of the body, and is perhaps also prized for its very evanescence, as if its immediate loss and irrecoverability were marks of its originary character and special value. There is, consequently, always some semiotic movement within a text, or rather some movement or play ('jeu') which disturbs the text's semiotic capacity, the clarity and coherence of the signs which it constructs. The deconstructive play is set in motion by each intelligent text, where language under the full pressure of its poetic responsibilities places its own principal terms 'sous rature', under erasure,[6] bracketing them while keeping them mobile in a new 'jeu', a network of new connotations. Such play becomes integral to thoughtful literature, for as Paul de Man observes, 'a literary text simultaneously asserts and denies the authority of its own rhetorical mode . . . Poetic writing is the most advanced and refined mode of deconstruction.'[7] This is not to demolish the structure or to make it unworkable, but to advertise its structurality, to show something of the exclusions which make a particular literary form (and its underlying episteme) possible, and to register the otherwise unacknowledged tensions within those textual and conceptual structures. 'Ce mouvement du jeu, permis par le manque, l'absence de centre ou d'origine, est le mouvement de la *supplémentarité*.'[8]

We live, then, in a world of traces. 'La trace n'est pas seulement la disparition de l'origine, elle veut dire ici . . . que l'origine n'a même pas disparu, qu'elle n'a jamais été constituée qu'en retour

---

[5] 'transcendental signified': Jacques Derrida, *L'Écriture et la différence* (Paris, 1967, 1994), p. 411.

[6] This means that the term is deleted but still legible, a practice used by Derrida in *De La Grammatologie*, adopted from Heidegger. The force of the term is thereby called into question, but not actually abolished—suspended rather than erased.

[7] Paul de Man, *Allegories of Reading* (New Haven, 1979), p. 17.

[8] Derrida, *L'Écriture et la différence*, p. 423: 'this movement of play, permitted by the lack, the absence of centre or of origin, is the movement of *supplementarity*'. (For Bass's translation see his p. 289.) For an exploration of the idea of the supplement see Derrida, *De La Grammatologie*, pp. 203–34, and *L'Écriture et la différence*, pp. 423–5.

par une non-origine, la trace, qui devient ainsi l'origine de l'origine.'⁹ Language is restless, and seems to be seeking a world elsewhere. Sometimes explicitly, and always implicitly, its ultimate
point of reference is some *archē* or *telos*, not necessarily conceived
of as an origin or apocalypse remote in time, but more often as a
conceptual source, remote from human reach, which would give
coherence to our thinking: some 'signifié transcendantal' such as
truth, or reason, or nature, or God. But the work of poetic
language is also a recollection (a collection in the form of traces,
so also a fragmentation) of other texts, drawing along with them,
sometimes quizzically, their own cultural values and unacknowledged tensions. In some works such intertextual allusiveness may
be prominent and self-advertising, in others submerged and awaiting the skilled reader. Seneca, Erasmus, and Petrarch thought that
one should conceal one's borrowings,¹⁰ whereas Ovid prided
himself on his borrowings from Virgil being noticed,¹¹ and Virgil
himself often uses a vocabulary which invites us to hear echoes of
Ennius or Lucretius. Such allusiveness may appear to be making a
movement backwards in time, but the new text is creating its own
temporality; it may appear to invoke origins and foundational pre-
texts, to yearn nostalgically for an unerring guide and an abiding
city; but such *archai* are themselves textual fictions, made in and for
the present: the trace is the origin of the origin. These sources of
power are never quite the same on each occasion that they are
named, even within the same text. 'Rome' never stands in the
same place.¹²

---

⁹ Derrida, *De La Grammatologie*, p. 90: 'The trace is not only the disappearance of the
origin, it means here . . . that the origin has not even disappeared, that it was never constituted except retrospectively by a non-origin, the trace, which thus becomes the origin of
the origin'. (For Spivak's translation see her p. 61.)

¹⁰ G. W. Pigman III, 'Versions of Imitation in the Renaissance', *Renaissance Quarterly*,
33 (1980) 1–32, at pp. 4–11. For Petrarch see also Philip Hardie, 'After Rome: Renaissance
Epic', in *Roman Epic*, ed. A. J. Boyle (London, 1993), pp. 294–313, at p. 296.

¹¹ Seneca, *Suasoriae*, iii. 7.

¹² Rather than develop any further a theory of intertextuality and imitation, and the
kinds of reading which they require, I leave the close readings offered in this book to function as practical demonstrations. The critical and scholarly literature on intertextuality and
imitation is considerable, and I shall simply cite as invaluable the following studies: Jay
Clayton and Eric Rothstein, 'Figures in the Corpus: Theories of Influence and
Intertextuality' in *Influence and Intertextuality in Literary History*, ed. Jay Clayton and Eric
Rothstein (Madison, 1991), pp. 3–36; Gérard Genette, *Palimpsestes: la littérature au second
degré* (Paris, 1982); Thomas M. Greene, *The Light in Troy: Imitation and Discovery in*

Classical Rome existed for Dryden only as a set of traces which pointed back to an originary culture which could never be recovered, but only reimagined, translated. As he read the Latin texts and their accompanying apparatus of editorial commentary (made up of paraphrases, glosses, and parallel passages) Dryden rebuilt 'Virgil' or 'Ovid' out of these materials. The original Latin text was itself a Renaissance reconstruction, and came surrounded by supplements, traces of other writers. The act of reading follows the traces, weaving them together into a new texture. For the trace is not simply a reference back to some actual or supposed origin: it is an invitation to the reader to construct a semantic field. Much of Dryden's own work recognizes that it stands in the position of a supplement to the classical corpus, but this condition of displacement from the origins is made into a source of creativity—not just theoretically, in that language can only operate through displacements, but also practically, in that Dryden's poetry is composed as a fabric which repeatedly explores its own double displacement from the present and from the source. Dryden's writing confesses *différance*, troubling any illusions of presence. The time of writing is made strange, its 'now' made complex; the poetry moves away from the Restoration present into what one might call a macaronic time.[13] As with time, so with space. By weaving Latin into the texture of his English, Dryden shapes not a coherent classical terrain, but his own macaronic space. It is the fragmentary character of its elements that enables the engendering of a multiply-dimensional space.[14] This movement between English and Latin signals that the movement between present and past, between Restoration England and classical Rome, is not, as some would

Renaissance Poetry (New Haven, 1982); Pigman, 'Versions of Imitation in the Renaissance'; and Christopher Ricks, 'Allusion: The Poet as Heir', in *Studies in the Eighteenth Century III*, ed. R. F. Brissenden and J. C. Eade (Toronto, 1976), pp. 209–40.

[13] Thomas Pavel similarly uses the term 'hétérochronie' for the time fashioned by French classical literature as it responds to a need to inhabit different epochs simultaneously (Thomas Pavel, *L'Art de l'éloignement: essai sur l'imagination classique* (Paris, 1996), p. 24).

[14] Cp. Paul de Man's comment on Rilke's 'Archaic Torso of Apollo': 'The observer is . . . being observed by the fragmentary statue . . . The reversal is possible only because the sculpture is broken and fragmentary . . . The absent eye allows for an imaginary vision to come into being, and it makes the eyeless sculpture into an Argus eye capable of engendering, by itself, all the dimensions of space' (de Man, *Allegories of Reading*, p. 44). For an analysis of the ways in which place has been imagined philosophically see Edward S. Casey, *The Fate of Place: A Philosophical History* (Berkeley, 1997).

have it, a rhetorical confirmation of the present and its ideological forms; rather, the movement is a deconstructive solicitation. This is not to suggest that Dryden's work intends or accomplishes a demystification or subversion of ideological structures: rather, the solicitation is precisely a troubling (from the Latin *sollicitare*, to disturb, shake)[15] of our structures of thought, a poetic rethinking of the language of the present by means of a turn towards those very foundations (linguistic, cultural, political) which contemporary culture had claimed for itself. And the way in which those origins are brought into play in the text creates a collocation of the classical and the modern which is one of reciprocal definition, and reciprocal enstranging.

What arrests the movement of *différance*, the solicitation of structure, and the pursuit of the trace? What prevents this from being an unending and destructive movement, and its philosophical consequences from being merely nihilistic? Theoretically, perhaps, nothing may; but in the practical sphere of reading, where men ponder texts for knowledge and pleasure, a community of readers with shared experiences and at least mutually intelligible assumptions may decide to suspend both totalizing truth claims and ultimate scepticism. This is the world of Rorty's liberal ironist.[16] When such an interpretative community grows smug, and fails to perceive the unravelling, then it becomes the duty of a writer to startle it into such a perception. But the writer's own textual voice will also arrest the decomposition of his text to some degree, so that for the duration of the work a temporarily coherent world is created, and within that space the opportunity for the reader to experience a new form of subjectivity. And the text itself also contains the play of traces through its selection and ordering of material, through the mapping of its terrain, the use of allusion and connotation, through the italicization which it thereby imparts to its own structuring principles: for when one text brings another into play and includes traces of it within its own textual field, the mode of incorporation will limit, or at least seek to limit, the outward movement of traces even as it sets that process in motion. And so each text invites a particular mode of reading, and

---

[15] Derrida, *Marges de la philosophie*, p. 22.
[16] Richard Rorty, *Contingency, Irony, and Solidarity* (Cambridge, 1989).

opens up a form of self-solicitation. Neither text nor author can control a whole terrain; the most that they can do is to juxtapose figures and so stake a claim for truth within that territory. This is the work of a contingent epistemology rather than a noumenal one;[17] surprisingly, perhaps, in that a noumenal epistemology based on divinely sanctioned truth claims is what Dryden's readers might suppose him to have espoused. But a longing for that truth did not blind him to the contingency of human language and the comedy of human authority.

The kind of text which is allusive in this manner, the linguistically or conceptually macaronic text, is very human in its anxiety about coping with difference and with *différance*, as it seeks with some courage both to own contradiction and to assert values. The humanism which such texts depend upon, and which they in their turn re-empower, is not imperialistic and homogenizing, but a mode of thought whose confidence depends upon its ability to manage loss and separation from origins. This is the kind of anxiety which Petrarch experienced at the origins of Renaissance humanism, and which Dryden experiences at its close.

The play between English and Latin opens up the interval—the fracture worked by *différance*—between the present and its supposed origins (those origins which, we are accustomed to imagine, allow us to grasp the presence of the present), which is also an interval within the apparent wholeness of the present, a self-division within the structures of selfhood and nationhood which assume presence and self-substantiality. As Dryden's writing turns back towards Latin, it turns particularly to the *Aeneid* as the primary text which encounters the primary loss, to that literary structure which is built upon the destruction of Troy, the city which was mythologically the origin of both Rome and London. The summoning of the *Aeneid* into the texture of Dryden's writing is not a recovery of origins but a recognition of separation. The necessity of acknowledging the impossibility of return to Troy had already been recognized by Horace, for in one of the *Carmina* Juno warns:

[17] I draw here on Richard W. F. Kroll, *The Material Word: Literate Culture in the Restoration and Early Eighteenth Century* (Baltimore, 1991), p. 17.

> Dum longus inter saeuiat Ilion,
> > Romamque pontus: qualibet exsules
> > In parte regnanto beati.
> Dum Priami, Paridisque busto
> Insultet armentum, & catulos ferae
> > Celent inultae: stet Capitolium
> > Fulgens, triumphatisque possit
> > Roma ferox dare iura Medis
> .   .   .   .
>
> Sed bellicosis fata Quiritibus
> > Hac lege dico, ne nimium pij:
> > Rebusque fidentes, auitae
> > Tecta velint reparare Troiae,
> Troiae renascens alite lugubri
> Fortuna, tristi clade iterabitur.[18]

The second city will only flourish so long as the originary city remains in ruins, for ever a site of mourning. To seek to rebuild it would court a repetition of its first destruction. Excessive or misplaced piety to the past may lead to one's own current home not fulfilling its potential: there are dangers, it seems, in pursuing the supposed origins of one's culture. And so the origin cannot be recovered, only reconstructed on a different site, which is to say, misconstructed:

la différance n'implique nullement que la présence différée puisse toujours se retrouver . . . mais la différance nous tient en rapport avec ce dont nous méconnaissons nécessairement qu'il excède l'alternative de la présence et de l'absence.[19]

To hold together Latin and English in this necessary misconstruction of origins is to exhibit the irresolution of the two

---

[18] Horace, *Carmina*, III. iii. 37–44, 57–62: 'So long as the wide sea rages between Troy and Rome, let the exiles be happy ruling in whatever part they please; so long as cattle trample over the burial place of Priam and Paris, and the wild beasts hide their young there unpunished, let the Capitol stand glittering, and fierce Rome give the law to the conquered Medes . . . But I prophesy such a future for the warlike Romans on this condition: that they should not, through an excess of piety and confidence, wish to repair the roofs of their ancestral Troy. If Troy should be reborn, with grim omens her fortune will be repeated with bitter ruin.' There is another warning against rebuilding Troy in *Aeneid*, xii. 826–8.

[19] Derrida, *Marges de la philosophie*, p. 21: '*Différance* in no way implies that the deferred presence can always be found again . . . Rather, *différance* maintains our relationship with that which we necessarily misconstrue, and which exceeds the alternative of presence and absence' (trans. Bass, p. 20).

languages, fashioning an unstable synthesis which never accomplishes a return to presence but has to rest in the incomplete:

> La structure du retardement . . . interdit en effet qu'on fasse de la temporalisation (temporisation) une simple complication dialectique du présent vivant comme synthèse originaire et incessante, constamment reconduite à soi, sur soi rassemblée, rassemblante, de traces rétentionnelles et d'ouvertures protentionnelles. Avec l'alterité de «inconscient», nous avons affaire non pas à des horizons de présents modifiés—passés ou à venir—mais à un «passé» qui n'a jamais été présent et qui ne le sera jamais, dont l' «a-venir» ne sera jamais la *production* ou la reproduction dans la forme de la présence.[20]

And so a literary work cannot simply weave traces together into a synthesis which refers back to a past, consolidates a present, and promises a future. The structure of the text is labile, and its complexities place the ostensibly secure notions of past, present, and future under erasure. And in Dryden's work it is particularly the jostling of Latin against English which alerts us to the wonderful mobility of these forms of time.

Différance troubles—though to trouble is here to complicate and so to enrich—the very core of whatever we take to be immediate, present, homely, and its solicitation becomes particularly apparent in Dryden's texts at those moments when he approaches figures of origin and presence, and recognizes his inevitable displacement from both. A dislocation of ordinary English, taking the form of a Latin quotation or an unnaturalized Latinate vocabulary, often signals an approach to this threshold. To address the present, to open a poem, to reflect on the poet's role, these are repeated minor crises which require a turn to Latin, often a turn to Virgil. But a turn to Virgil risked returning to a greater crisis, that primal scene in the second book of the *Aeneid* where Pyrrhus crosses the threshold of Priam's palace, violates the sacred hearth by slaughtering the

---

[20] Derrida, *Marges de la philosophie*, pp. 21–2: 'The structure of delay . . . in effect forbids that one make of temporalization (temporization) a simple dialectal complication of the living present as an originary and unceasing synthesis—a synthesis constantly directed back on itself, gathered in on itself and gathering—of retentional traces and protentional openings. The alterity of the "unconscious" makes us concerned not with horizons of modified—past or future—presents, but with a "past" that has never been present, and which never will be, whose future to come will never be a *production* or a reproduction in the form of presence' (trans. Bass, p. 21).

king's son in front of his eyes, and then kills the father on the altar
which is dedicated to his household gods. When approaching that
threshold, whenever he touched threads which led back into this
locus of ultimate horror, Dryden stuttered and stumbled; but he
could not keep silent. Aeneas told Dido that his grief at the fall of
Troy was *infandum*, unutterable, but Dryden omits that idea from
his translation.[21] He knew that this grief had to be uttered, and to
confront this loss of origin and separation from presence required
a move across the linguistic threshold.

THE PLACE OF LATIN IN DRYDEN'S CULTURE

'Wir selbst Fremdsprachige sind', said Freud in his meditation on
the uncanny: we ourselves speak a language that is foreign.[22] What
does it mean to speak a language that is foreign, to turn to another
tongue to articulate and define that which is most intimately one's
own? Trained in an educational system where Latin was the
primary object and medium of knowledge, Dryden would hardly
have regarded that language as foreign, but it could never quite be
his native language. The 'I' which was formed through this education would always be a form of identity which recognized a home
elsewhere:

Il se serait alors *formé*, ce *je*, dans le site d'une *situation* introuvable,
renvoyant toujours ailleurs, à autre chose, à une autre langue, à l'autre en
général . . . il n'y avait pas de *je* pensable ou pensant avant cette situation
étrangement familière et proprement impropre (*uncanny*, *unheimlich*)
d'une langue innombrable.[23]

As Dryden grew into a professional writer, the authorial 'I' would
often be voiced through Latin, not in the sustained form of Latin
verse or prose composition, but through quotations and allusions

---

[21] *Aeneid*, ii. 3; *Aeneis*, ii. 3–4.

[22] Sigmund Freud, *Gesammelte Werke*, ed. Anna Freud *et al.*, 18 vols. (London and
Frankfurt, 1940–68), xii. 232.

[23] Jacques Derrida, writing of his own early relation to French as an Algerian Jew, in
Le Monolinguisme de l'autre (Paris, 1996), p. 55: 'It would then be *formed*, this *I*, in the site of
a undiscoverable *situation*, always sending us off elsewhere, to something else, to another
language, to the other in general . . . there was no *I* which was thinkable or thinking before
this strangely familiar and properly improper (*uncanny*, *unheimlich*) situation of a language
which cannot be reckoned.'

which defined him by reference to the Latin poets. And the texts of these poets provided him with alternative ways of imagining his selfhood, some of which he would explore through translation.

Latin was the language over which Dryden attained mastery in the privileged setting of Westminster School under the rod of Richard Busby.[24] Boys would translate daily from Latin into English and *vice versa*, and learnt to compose with equal facility in each language. Sometimes they would put a Latin poem or speech into English, and then translate the translation back into Latin, or on into Greek. Through this discipline the languages became intricately linked, and one's sense of the character and resources of each separate language was shaped by the recognition of how it related to others: English was Latin *in potentia*. And Latin was the key to power, the way into the symbolic order. When Dryden signed the Trinity College admissions book as a scholar—the moment when he became a member of the foundation—he wrote his name in Latin, and Latinized his origins: 'Johannes Dryden Northamptoniensis'.[25]

But the symbolic order of mid-century England was being broken and remade, and with it the place of Latin. In earlier times the language which Dryden mastered at school would have given him access to a body of literature and of scholarship which connected with (and provided a way into) the public discourses of the arts and sciences and government. Latin had a place in a reasonably coherent symbolic order. But during the Commonwealth the nature and location of authority were being disputed, and sectarians suspicious of classical learning demanded the abolition of colleges where Latin and Greek were studied, while a divinely inspired English became the correct mode of

---

[24] For Dryden's schooling, including his early study of Latin, see James Anderson Winn, *John Dryden and his World* (New Haven, 1987), pp. 36–57. The typical school curriculum and methods of study are described in Charles Hoole, *A New Discovery of the Old Art of Teaching Schoole* (London, 1660). The importance of Latin as a cultural medium in the 16th and early 17th cents. has been amply demonstrated by J. W. Binns in *Intellectual Culture in Elizabethan and Jacobean England: The Latin Writings of the Age* (Leeds, 1990); while the place of Latin in early 17th-cent. English literature is explored by Judith H. Anderson in *Words that Matter: Linguistic Perception in Renaissance English* (Stanford, 1996).

[25] Trinity College Cambridge, Muniments: 'Admissions 1645–1659', p. 84; reproduced as pl. IV in Paul Hammond, 'Dryden's Employment by Cromwell's Government', *Transactions of the Cambridge Bibliographical Society*, 8 (1981) 130–6.

discourse. A series of displacements fractured the symbolic order to the point where it becomes dubious whether such a notion—at least in the singular—is still appropriate. Competing authorities and rival tongues arose within incompatible (and even mutually incomprehensible) discursive communities.[26] Dryden himself underwent a series of displacements, as he moved from a puritan family to a royalist school and on to a puritan college; then into the service of the Protectoral government before greeting the returning King, embarking upon the life of a dramatist, and becoming Poet Laureate. In these changes—both ideological and pragmatic—he was changing his relations to the changing language around him. Perhaps it was the breaking of the symbolic order which helped or required Dryden to establish his own particular relation to Latin, and made Latin a foundational language for him, the medium in which he thought about his own originality, and the invented home to which he kept returning.

Latin gave him access to the poets, historians, and philosophers of ancient Rome, and provided him with a second homeland all the more potent for being internal and imagined; it was a terrain whose contours he had mapped for himself, a structure which he built from his own favourite texts. The boundaries of this territory did not run where other people's boundaries ran, nor coincide with the dividing lines between past and present, or between Latin and English. Latin lurked within English. Etymologically the English language carried traces of its Latin origins, as the English landscape was still traversed by Roman walls, now defending unnecessary emplacements, often half-ruined and put to new uses, but still reminders of other ways of inhabiting the land. Dryden could activate the half-hidden Latin roots of the language, relying on readers who had shared his kind of education to pursue the traces and recognize the Roman lexical values in these words. This Latinate vocabulary carried traces of the cultural values of Rome, and so could bring into play highly charged fields of signification. The word 'pious', for example, could set against the obnoxious piety of the puritans a different set of values derived from the *pietas*

---

[26] See Nigel Smith, *Perfection Proclaimed: Language and Literature in English Radical Religion 1640–1660* (Oxford, 1989).

of ancient Rome,[27] that combination of reverence for the gods, the homeland, and the family which linked religious observation with respect for the state in a way which contrasted sharply with Nonconformist principles. Indeed, one of the attractions of the Latin word may have been that it encoded just that intimate association of filial, patriotic, and religious duties which had been rendered impossible by the upheavals of the mid-century. There is, therefore, a potential for translation within the semantic field of a single word—from one form of 'piety' to another— a movement between different cultural fields which can elide one form of the present by summoning an alternative set of values and aspirations into the presence of the text. 'Cette traduction se traduit dans une traduction interne . . . jouant de la non-identité à soi de toute langue.'[28] Cumulatively these movements into Latin weave through Dryden's writing a field of strangeness within the familiar, even for readers brought up on the classics as Dryden himself had been, since the process of selection and quotation brings English and Latin, past and present together in configurations which are quite distinctive. So much did this become a feature of his poetics that, as he admitted, some critics said 'that I latinize too much'. But he was unrepentant: 'I Trade both with the Living and the Dead, for the enrichment of our Native Language.'[29] What he wanted to avoid was the awkwardness which contemporaries such as William Wotton saw as characteristic of Jonson's use of a Latinized English: 'for want of reflecting upon the grounds of a Language which he understood as well as any Man of his Age, he drew it by Violence to a dead Language that was of a quite different Make.'[30]

Dryden was conscious that the English language carried the traces of its multiple origins, and to him that mixture was impure

---

[27] For this concept see James D. Garrison, *'Pietas' from Vergil to Dryden* (University Park, 1992); and Karl Galinsky, *Augustan Culture: An Interpretive Introduction* (Princeton, 1996), pp. 86–8.

[28] Derrida, *Le Monolinguisme de l'autre*, p. 123: 'This translation translates itself in an internal translation . . . playing on the non-self-identity of every language.'

[29] 'The Dedication of the *Aeneis*' (*Poems*, p. 1059).

[30] William Wotton, *Reflections upon Ancient and Modern Learning* (1694), p. 58; cited from *Ben Jonson*, ed. C. H. Herford, Percy and Evelyn Simpson, 11 vols. (Oxford, 1925–52), xi. 358.

and unstable.[31] In the Dedication to the Earl of Sunderland prefixed to *Troilus and Cressida* (1679), he remarks that even the language of the Goths and the Vandals 'had the fortune to be graffed on a *Roman* stock', whereas 'Ours has the disadvantage, to be founded on the *Dutch*'.[32] Two concerns animate Dryden's discussion, and are not always kept distinct. He is anxious to establish correct (grammatically exact) knowledge of the language, and also to establish a correct (socially elegant) language. Both projects require the collaboration of 'the Court, the Colledge, and the Town',[33] but it is not enough to imagine the language of the present as something which is shaped by and for present needs, and whose correctness may be determined by those who fashion and use it. The standard of correctness has to be sought elsewhere, in those languages which lie at its origins: 'as our *English* is a composition of the dead and living Tongues, there is requir'd a perfect knowledge, not onely of the *Greek* and *Latine*, but of the Old *German*, the *French* and the *Italian*.'[34] Such a turn back towards the origins in order to establish correct usage is not only the duty of the grammarian and lexicographer, it is Dryden's own day-to-day practice as a poet, for in the absence of any reliable contemporary English grammar he regarded translation into Latin as a necessary detour in order to establish the correctness of any English expression:

But how barbarously we yet write and speak, your Lordship knows, and I am sufficiently sensible in my own *English*. For I am often put to a stand, in considering whether what I write be the Idiom of the Tongue, or false Grammar, and nonsense couch'd beneath that specious Name of *Anglicisme*; and have no other way to clear my doubts, but by translating my *English* into *Latine*, and thereby trying what sence the words will bear in a more stable language.[35]

---

[31] Contemporaries were also worried about the inadequacy and instability of language in general, not just English: see (*inter alia*) Kroll, *The Material Word*; and Sidonie Clauss, 'John Wilkins' Essay toward a Real Character: Its Place in the Seventeenth-Century Episteme', *Journal of the History of Ideas*, 43 (1982) 531–53.   [32] *Works*, xiii. 223.

[33] Ibid. 222.   [34] Ibid.

[35] *Works*, xiii. 222. Though Dryden calls Latin a more stable language than English, he was well aware that it had changed in the classical period, and remarks that some of his contemporaries thought that since the days of Shakespeare and Jonson, English 'has been in a continual declination; like that of the *Romans* from the Age of *Virgil* to *Statius*, and so downward to *Claudian*' (*Works*, xi. 205).

Translation from English into Latin is the only way to identify the true native idiom, and to distinguish this from some embarrassingly idiosyncratic usage, an '*Anglicisme*' which merely betrays the oddity of English when compared with other tongues.[36] Similarly in 'To Mr L. Maidwell, on his New Method' (1684) Dryden remarks that Maidwell has provided a secure foundation for the English language by drawing up a new Latin grammar:

> Latine is now of equal use become
> To Englishmen, as was the Greek to Rome.
> It guides our language, nothing is exprest
> Gracefull or true but by the Roman test.[37]

The correct native form only becomes apparent, therefore, when translated into another tongue, and until that movement into strangeness has been accomplished, the truth or falsity of that which is familiar cannot be discerned.

Dryden brought Latin into play in his English partly to shape his own imaginative space, partly to contest the discursive spaces of others. It contributed to his inner dialogue with himself, enabling a movement of self-division in which he temporarily suspended the tropes (and even, perhaps, the epistemic structures) of his own day, feeling his sexuality with the help of Ovid, dreaming his death with the help of Lucretius; encountering the gods. Latin helped Dryden to shape a more complex form of selfhood, a richer kind of community, a more troubled history, enabling him to effect a translation and displacement of the contemporary world. The Roman tropes of contemporary political discourse become troubled through their co-option into Dryden's macaronic text, and readers who have grown accustomed to current political rhetoric have to rethink the way their language works as they encounter it afresh in Dryden's unfamiliar and often unwelcoming spaces. *Absalom and Achitophel*, for example, quotes from the current Whig

---

[36] The *OED*'s examples suggest that an 'Anglicism' is an idiom which reveals a gauche English idiosyncrasy when compared with other languages, and can distort the correct use of other languages by English writers.

[37] 'To Mr. L. Maidwell, on his New Method', ll. 1–4; quoted from *Poems*, ed. Hammond, ii. pl. 4; for a modernized annotated text see ii. 225–7. The poem is not included in *Works*, or *Poems*, ed. Kinsley. Dryden's authorship of this poem is not beyond dispute, but at this point the sentiments of the poem are precisely in line with his thinking elsewhere.

political vocabulary and turns it into uncomfortably new configurations.[38]

In what is only superficially a paradoxical habit, Dryden repeatedly turned to Latin at moments when he needed to express his understanding of England, the English language, and the role of the English poet in the present. Something more profound is at work here than what some readers have seen as Dryden mouthing the commonplaces of a neo-Augustanism, for he was not particularly interested in the specifically Augustan element in Roman culture, and did not see the Carolean period as an imitation of Augustan political or cultural order; indeed, it was often the contrast between the two periods which struck him. No application of Augustan imagery was unproblematic to him, for his sense of the complexities of the past and the present, and the intricacy of the movements between them, was too acute to allow him to be content with such an illusory coherence. Instead, by writing a poetry which makes us aware of the gap between English and Latin, between the Restoration present and the Roman past, he maps an alternative present. By evoking other ways of being, Dryden's Latin marks out the gap between possible cultures and the actual nation, and so mourns the failed promises of 1660 and the betrayals of 1688. Through his repeated recourse to Latin, Dryden dreams his own cultural space.

If this was partly a reply to the imagined England of godly communities which had been envisaged in the 1650s through a sectarian vernacular, and to the threat posed by their heirs after 1660, it was also a rejoinder to Milton. His defence of regicide and of the English republic had been made in Latin, or in an English which deployed Latinate vocabulary and Roman precedents: *Pro Populo Anglicano Defensio Secunda* (1654) echoes Anchises' prophecy of Rome's imperial destiny.[39] But when in *The Readie & Easie Way to Establish a Free Commonwealth* (1660) he writes of England as 'another *Rome* in the west', this is part of a bitter gesture of self-correction, epanorthosis on a grand scale, as he records the failure of this hope amid a confusion of languages:

[38] This is documented extensively in the notes to *Absalom and Achitophel* in *Poems*, ed. Hammond; and in Phillip Harth, *Pen for a Party: Dryden's Tory Propaganda in its Contexts* (Princeton, 1993).

[39] Milton, *The Complete Prose Works*, ed. Don M. Wolfe *et al.*, 8 vols. (New Haven, 1953–82), iv. 554–6; *Aeneid* vi. 679–892.

Where is this goodly tower of a Common-wealth which the *English* boasted they would build, to overshaddow kings and be another *Rome* in the west? The foundation indeed they laid gallantly; but fell into a worse confusion, not of tongues, but of factions, then those at the tower of *Babel*; and have left no memorial of thir work behinde them remaining, but in the common laughter of *Europ*.[40]

In *Paradise Lost* Milton used classical myth and rhetoric in an epic which countered and displaced much of the tawdry verse of Dryden's contemporaries, forcing Dryden himself to attend and respond. Furthermore, Dryden's use of Latin was also a gesture of self-correction, placing under erasure (rather than wiping out) that classical republican idiom which he had once shared: for this turn to Latin is, *inter alia*, a detour around the trauma of civil war and the destruction of a kingdom. In the Interregnum, that nameless time, that *aporia* which in the poem to Congreve seemed both flood and empire, the classical structures of the early Stuart monarchy were destroyed. James I's Banqueting House became the backdrop for his son's execution, while both the artefacts and the iconography of Charles's art collection were plundered. The language of classical Rome had been used to fashion images of Charles I in Van Dyck's equestrian portraits or Le Sueur's busts, and some of these tropes were appropriated by the Parliamentarian leaders, with Fairfax being painted on horseback, and Cromwell depicted on his coinage as a Roman emperor. But while there is a confidence (not to say *hubris*) in the Stuart adaptation of Roman forms and styles, an air of defensive imitation attends the Protectorate's quasi-royal, quasi-Roman iconography. The republic's Latinate style never attained sufficient force and cogency to be a new idiom for the nation.[41] Ironically, Dryden's own *Heroique Stanza's* on the

---

[40] Milton, *Complete Prose Works*, vii. 357. See Andrew Barnaby, ' "Another Rome in the West?": Milton and the Imperial Republic, 1654–1670', *Milton Studies*, 30 (1993) 67–84.

[41] But for discussions of various aspects of republican classicism see David Norbrook, 'Lucan, Thomas May, and the Creation of a Republican Literary Culture', in *Culture and Politics in Early Stuart England*, ed. Kevin Sharpe and Peter Lake (Basingstoke, 1994), pp. 45–66; Nigel Smith, *Literature and Revolution in England 1640–1660* (New Haven, 1994), esp. pp. 103, 203–7, 337–8; Sean Kelsey, *Inventing a Republic* (Manchester, 1997); Martin Dzelzainis, 'Milton's Classical Republicanism', and David Armitage, 'John Milton: Poet against Empire', in David Armitage, Armand Himy and Quentin Skinner (eds.), *Milton and Republicanism* (Cambridge, 1995), pp. 3–24 and 206–25.

death of Cromwell are one of the few truly confident expressions of a neo-Roman republicanism. Dryden's turn to Latin in the poems after 1660 is a movement of revision, a necessarily elliptical way of writing a poetry of loss which mourns both the lost kingdom of mid-century England and his own youthful part in its destruction.

The place of Latin in the literary culture of the Restoration was quite different from what it had been in the world of Dryden's mentors. The comparison with Milton exemplifies this change.[42] He was the last of the Renaissance humanist poets, multilingual, composing Latin verse for publication, exchanging letters with foreign poets and scholars to maintain a literary community across Europe, writing in Latin to defend his country to a Continental audience. Dryden, by contrast, wrote no Latin for publication,[43] and did not use the language to address a European readership: Latin was declining as an international language, and both Hobbes and Locke wrote their principal treatises in English. When *Absalom and Achitophel* was translated into Latin in Oxford (twice, by rival hands) it was more an exercise in donnish trivia than a bid to reach an influential public. Dryden's readership included many who had little or no Latin. Certainly there were those in his circle who shared his scholarship—Congreve's library is testimony to that[44]—and there were patrons with whom he would discuss the classics and from whom he could borrow the best editions. His poetry would always include the learned among its implied readership. But as a professional playwright and poet he was also writing for theatre audiences and for connoisseurs of poetry who had not necessarily had a university education but who were well-read, discriminating, and affluent—a metropolitan bourgeoisie who were powerful influences on literary taste and on politics. This constituency

---

[42] For Milton's relation to Latin see John K. Hale, *Milton's Languages: The Impact of Multilingualism on Style* (Cambridge, 1997); Charles Martindale, *John Milton and the Transformation of Ancient Epic* (London, 1986); and William M. Porter, *Reading the Classics and 'Paradise Lost'* (Lincoln, Nebr., 1993).

[43] The only Latin work which survives is his undergraduate 'Carmen Lapidarium' on the death of John Smith (*Poems*, ed. Hammond, i. 11–13; not in *Poems*, ed. Kinsley, or *Works*).

[44] John C. Hodges, *The Library of William Congreve* (New York, 1955).

included many women, and women were prominent among admirers of Dryden's work, perhaps being particularly receptive readers of his classical translations.[45] So for some of Dryden's readers his English verse substituted for Latin, the translations giving them an idea of the major Roman poets, with Dryden's whole *œuvre* increasingly taking on a classic, canonic force of its own. For others, Dryden's English was enticingly engaged in an intricate dialogue with Latin, a play which contributed importantly to the meaning and pleasure of the text. And it is the likely experience of this second group of readers which the present book seeks principally to recreate.

ENGLISH WRITERS AS HEIRS TO THE ROMAN HERITAGE

To begin then with *Shakespeare;* he was the man who of all Modern, and perhaps Ancient Poets, had the largest and most comprehensive soul. All the Images of Nature were still present to him, and he drew them not laboriously, but luckily: when he describes any thing, you more than see it, you feel it too. Those who accuse him to have wanted learning, give him the greater commendation: he was naturally learn'd; he needed not the spectacles of Books to read Nature; he look'd inwards, and found her there.[46]

This passage from *Of Dramatick Poesie* (1668) marks Shakespeare out as the original genius of English writing, the one to whom all the images of nature were present, unmediated by books. In this respect he stands to Dryden as Homer stood to Virgil, as the primary writer, the natural genius who is the origin of all later work.[47] Indeed, he may also surpass the ancient poets as well as the moderns in his 'comprehensive soul'. A decade later, in the 'Prologue to *Troilus and Cressida*', Shakespeare himself is made to boast of his untaught skill and unborrowed store of material:

---

[45] Evidence for women admiring Dryden's work is provided by the subscription lists for his Virgil, and by *The Nine Muses: Or, Poems Written by Nine Severall Ladies Upon the Death of the Late Famous John Dryden, Esq.* (London, 1700). See also James Anderson Winn, *'When Beauty Fires the Blood': Love and the Arts in the Age of Dryden* (Ann Arbor, 1992), pp. 378–436.

[46] *Works*, xvii. 55.

[47] For such 17th-cent. characterizations of Homer see Kirsti Simonsuuri, *Homer's Original Genius* (Cambridge, 1979).

Untaught, unpractis'd, in a barbarous Age,
I found not, but created first the Stage.
And, if I drain'd no *Greek* or *Latin* store,
'Twas, that my own abundance gave me more.
On foreign trade I needed not rely
Like fruitfull *Britain*, rich without supply.[48]

This claim goes further than Milton's characterization of Shakespeare as 'fancies childe' warbling 'his native Wood-notes wilde',[49] or Jonson's description of his learning as 'small *Latine*, and lesse *Greeke*',[50] for it asserts that Shakespeare stands entirely on native ground, without any reliance upon the classics. This, of course, is an exaggeration to the point of falsehood, but as a myth it indicates the need which Dryden feels for English poetry to have more than one point of origin—in the Latin poets and in Shakespeare.

But something curious happens when Dryden needs to distance himself from the way this original genius used the English language. To illustrate Shakespeare's excessively metaphorical style, he chooses a passage from the Player's speech in *Hamlet* which he says Shakespeare quoted from some other poet.[51] The founding father is therefore not criticized directly. Moreover, Dryden chooses a speech in which two themes are prominent which are crucial to his own imaginative reconstruction of Roman thought. This is a speech which denounces Fortune and exclaims, 'all you Gods, | In general Synod, take away her Power'.[52] Now, as we shall see later in this book, Fortune is one of the recurring classical motifs in Dryden's writing, signifying that power of chance which arbitrarily gives us good things and just as arbitrarily snatches them away, and it is used by Dryden to characterize the public arena which entices men like himself to betray their

---

[48] 'Prologue to *Troilus and Cressida*', ll. 7–12. See *Poems*, ed. Hammond, i. 206–8 for the context of Dryden's critique of Shakespeare here and in the 'Prologue to *The Tempest*'. The idea of a poet's rich store which has been provided by Nature is repeated in 'To the Memory of Mr. Oldham', ll. 11–12, where the store is incomplete through the poet's premature death; and again in 'To My Dear Friend Mr. Congreve', ll. 59–63, where Congreve is said to be the only poet since Shakespeare to whom Nature has given such a store. [49] John Milton, 'L'Allegro', ll. 133–4.
[50] Ben Jonson, 'To the memory of my beloved, The Author Mr. William Shakespeare: And what he hath left us', l. 31. [51] *Works*, xiii. 244–5.
[52] Ibid. 244.

own souls. The second topic which this speech addresses is the fall of Troy, summoning up a pathos-laden image of Hecuba lamenting the murder of her husband. Here, at the very point where Dryden has to criticize his father-figure, he backs away, criticizing instead someone else's work from which Shakespeare has already, it seems, distanced himself through ironic quotation; and choosing a passage which speaks of that primal scene of outrage, the killing of King Priam and the destruction of his city. Even in this elusive, elliptical way, the founding father of English poetry is linked to Rome.

Much more overtly, Dryden turns to Rome in order to define the literary achievement of his contemporaries, and establish the discursive space of modernity. We have already seen that in 'To My Dear Friend Mr. Congreve', Congreve's achievement is problematically located both in the present and in history. Verbal echoes between this poem and *Mac Flecknoe* (1676)[53] make the tentative and troubled exposition in 'To My Dear Friend Mr. Congreve' a further corrective to that facile self-confidence of Shadwell's which Dryden had mocked in the earlier poem. Among the issues which fuelled the controversy between Dryden and Shadwell in the decade before the composition of *Mac Flecknoe*[54] were questions about imitation, originality, and plagiarism, and specifically about the status of Ben Jonson. Dryden was all too sharply aware of the cultural difference between himself and Jonson, and envisaged the imitation of a predecessor as a noble struggle, a classic *agon*,[55] whereas Shadwell invoked Jonson as a transhistorical standard for the writing of comedy, calling him 'incomparably the best Drammatick poet that ever was, or, I

[53] In 'To My Dear Friend Mr. Congreve' there are repeated images of paternity and succession to empire which echo those in *Mac Flecknoe*; l. 48 ('For *Tom* the Second reigns like *Tom* the first') alludes to Thomas Shadwell; l. 53 ('High on the Throne of Wit') echoes *Mac Flecknoe*, l. 107 ('High on a Throne of his own Labours rear'd'). Southerne's poem to Congreve also echoes *Mac Flecknoe* when complimenting Dryden.

[54] 1676 is the probable date of the poem's composition and its first circulation in MS. For the context of *Mac Flecknoe* and the debate between Dryden and Shadwell see *Poems*, ed. Hammond, i. 307–10; Paul Hammond, *John Dryden: A Literary Life* (Basingstoke, 1991), pp. 74–81; id., 'Figures of Horace in Dryden's Literary Criticism', in *Horace Made New: Horatian Influences on British Writing from the Renaissance to the Twentieth Century*, ed. Charles Martindale and David Hopkins (Cambridge, 1993), pp. 127–47, at pp. 140–4; Richard L. Oden (ed.), *Dryden and Shadwell* (Delmar, 1977).

[55] See *Works*, xiii. 228, where Dryden cites Longinus and Hesiod for this view.

believe, ever will be'.[56] Moreover, Shadwell was unimaginatively repeating dicta from Horace to clinch his argument about the moral purpose of writing, without reflecting on either the historical circumstances of Horace's original remarks, or their applicability to modern conditions. Where Shadwell seemed to assume a homogeneous, ahistorical classicism, Dryden's meditation on Jonson and the Roman poets combined an awareness of historical difference with a self-conscious mythologizing, so forming a discourse which confessed the necessarily difficult relationship between a writer and his ancestors. Fascination with the trace and with its play does not entail an inability to tell true from false: indeed, the gesture which appropriates another man's terms and reapplies them in a corrective way is a repeated characteristic of Dryden's poetics.

Mac Flecknoe responds to Shadwell's lack of historical and mythological sophistication by making him a participant in a strange ritual of succession and coronation which is both bathetically contemporary and comically over-mythologized. Dryden's poem counters Shadwell's claim to be the heir and imitator of Jonson not only by casting him as the heir of Flecknoe, but also by grotesquely multiplying his origins. Shadwell is given a bogus Irish origin; he is made Flecknoe's son; he is made heir to Flecknoe's Augustus (but the poem's refusal to give him a name in that role suspends him between being the promising youth Marcellus, or the debauched tyrant Tiberius); he is made Elisha to Flecknoe's Elijah, and Christ to Flecknoe's John the Baptist; and he is Ascanius to Flecknoe's Aeneas in a travesty of that wonderful moment in *Aeneid* II when amid the chaos of Troy's destruction the boy is marked out as the destined heir by fire from heaven. His plays likewise have too many origins, since they use other people's work (passages are plagiarized from Etherege or contributed by Sedley), and yet at the same time they lack the necessary origin in art and nature. Meanwhile, of their much-vaunted origin in Jonson there is no trace, for as Flecknoe exclaims:

> Thou art my blood, where *Johnson* has no part;
> What share have we in Nature or in Art?[57]

---

[56]   Thomas Shadwell, *The Virtuoso* (London, 1676), sig. A2ᵛ.
[57]   *Mac Flecknoe*, ll. 175–6.

Shadwell's origins are both multiple and deficient. Ironically, his own presence is all too substantial, for the poem is oppressed by his body, huge, drunken, and sleepy. He is also the full embodiment of dullness and the perfect heir of Flecknoe:

> *Sh*—— alone my perfect image bears,
> Mature in dullness from his tender years.
> *Sh*—— alone, of all my Sons, is he
> Who stands confirm'd in full stupidity.[58]

Here is the writer who will easily fill the vacancy left by his predecessor. Shadwell is thus made into an impossible kind of writer, the antithesis to Dryden who knows that a writer's relation to his origins must be problematic, and that the writer's own presence in his writing is necessarily strange and imperfect. Shadwell's prefaces lacked any rhetorical acknowledgement of the provisional and relative character of literary judgement and the citation of authority, and this lack of a complex texture is remedied satirically in *Mac Flecknoe* through the fabrication of an impossibly complex discursive space, a jumble of Restoration, classical, and biblical persons, places, and times.

The historical processes by which the culture of the present emerges from the past, and the mythology by means of which that culture represents its own connections to its origins,[59] are both contemplated in 'To the Earl of Roscommon, on his Excellent *Essay on Translated Verse*' (1684). Here Dryden envisages culture as a series of translations, from the eastern Mediterranean to Greece to Rome, and so via Italy and France eventually to England.[60] But the actual origins of culture are made uncertain, for the poem begins with a hesitation:

---

[58] Ibid., ll. 15–18.

[59] For a discussion of the cult of origins see David Quint, *Origin and Originality in Renaissance Literature: Versions of the Source* (New Haven, 1983); and Kroll, *The Material Word*, p. 61; also Kroll, p. 34 for an account of the discussion of the origins of Stonehenge in Dryden's poem 'To my Honour'd Friend, Dr Charleton'.

[60] For the topoi of *translatio imperii* and *translatio studii* see Ernst Robert Curtius, *European Literature and the Latin Middle Ages* (London, 1953), pp. 28–30. Dryden is particularly indebted here to Sir John Denham's 'The Progress of Learning'. Vida had compared the poetic imitation of the ancients to Aeneas' transfer of the gods of Troy to Italy (*De Arte Poetica*, iii. 234–6; *The 'De Arte Poetica' of Marco Girolamo Vida*, ed. Ralph G. Williams (New York, 1976), p. 100).

> Whether the fruitful *Nile*, or *Tyrian* Shore,
> The seeds of Arts and Infant Science bore . . .[61]

And there is also a hesitation over Roscommon's own origins, as to whether this Irishman is originally English:

> Their Island in revenge has ours reclaim'd,
> The more instructed we, the more we still are sham'd.
> 'Tis well for us his generous bloud did flow
> Deriv'd from *British* Channels long ago;
> That here his conquering Ancestors were nurst;
> And *Ireland* but translated *England* first:[62]

Who is translating whom? Dryden's lines recall Horace's analysis of the cultural relationship between Rome and Greece: *Graecia capta ferum victorem cepit: & arteis | intulit agresti Latio*,[63] though Dryden urges that in this case the movement is circular, for the conquest is illusory, the foreign nation only a temporary detour through which we find Roscommon's true origin at home. And yet the wit of this argument makes it palpably a conceit, and we understand that the rhetoric of origins is a fiction, a contest for the possession (or for the successful invention) of the source.

The apparently linear progress of culture is complicated and to some degree reversed at the end of the poem, where contemporary English writers are said to rival or excel their precursors:

>   *Brittain*, last
> In Manly sweetness all the rest surpass'd.
> The Wit of *Greece*, the Gravity of *Rome*
> Appear exalted in the *Brittish* Loome;
> The Muses Empire is restor'd agen,
> In *Charles* his Reign, and by *Roscomon*'s Pen.
> . . . . . .
>
> *Roscomon* writes, to that auspicious hand,
> Muse feed the Bull that spurns the yellow sand.
> . . . . . .

---

[61] 'To the Earl of Roscommon, on his Excellent *Essay on Translated Verse*', ll. 1–2.
[62] 'To the Earl of Roscommon', ll. 43–8.
[63] Horace, *Epistulae*, II. i. 156–7: 'Greece the captive made her savage victor captive, and brought the arts to rustic Latium.'

Now let the few belov'd by *Jove*, and they
Whom infus'd *Titan* form'd of better Clay,
On equal terms with ancient Wit ingage,
Nor mighty *Homer* fear, nor sacred *Virgil*'s page:
Our *English* Palace opens wide in state;
And without stooping they may pass the Gate.[64]

Britain (or England, for Dryden hesitates between the Latin and the Old English versions of the name of his culture[65]) may have raised literature to new heights of sophistication, but those threads which are woven into a new fabric in the British loom are Greek wit (i.e. 'intelligence') and Roman gravity: though they 'appear exalted' in this new material, the elements from which this text is woven are not actually native. Moreover, the very terms in which this contemporary achievement is formulated are themselves derived from the Latin language and from Roman mythology, so that the present is apprehended only by being translated back into the past: the image of the bull prepared for sacrifice is adapted from Virgil[66] and associates Roscommon with the Roman poet and critic Pollio, while the final vignette of the reception of Homer and Virgil within the portals of a newly confident English culture is itself a return to Rome, since it is an adaptation of Virgil's description of Aeneas' entry through the gates of Evander's palace.[67] This is a potent allusion. In Book VIII of the *Aeneid* Evander and Aeneas walk the site of what will one day be Rome, and the landscape through which they pass is haunted by the structures of the future as Virgil describes the location in terms of the buildings which his contemporaries knew, ghostly traces of a *telos* which has now been realized. In stooping to enter through Evander's narrow doorway, Aeneas is repeating the theoxeny of Hercules.[68] This was a passage in which Virgil was particularly indebted to Lucretius,[69] so Dryden was turning to a textual site which had already been the ground where two great Roman poets had met.

[64] 'To the Earl of Roscommon', ll. 24–9, 66–7, 73–8.
[65] The hesitation continued: in l. 60 '*Brittish*' in the 1684 text was changed to '*English*' in the 1685 edition.   [66] Virgil, *Ecloga*, iii. 86–7.
[67] *Aeneid*, viii. 366–7.
[68] For the significance of theoxeny (when a god is received in a human dwelling) see Virgil, *Aeneid Book VIII*, ed. K. W. Gransden (Cambridge, 1976), pp. 26–9.
[69] Philip R. Hardie, *Virgil's 'Aeneid': Cosmos and Imperium* (Oxford, 1986), pp. 217–18.

It is impossible to know whether Dryden was unaware or
unconcerned that in reaching this climax his poem had slipped
from hortatory panegyric into uncritical flattery. But perhaps we
should stress the optative and idealizing mode of this ending, its
visionary promise of a culture based upon a meeting with the classical poets which, in the event, only Dryden himself was capable
of implementing. The tenses of the poem confess the paradox: the
English palace 'opens wide' in an uncomplicated present tense, but
the forms of the verbs which relate the encounter between
Roman and English writers locate their meeting in a permitted but
as yet unrealized future: 'Now let the few . . . ingage'; 'they may
pass the Gate'. Such a time and place can only be present in a
discursive space constituted as a collection of traces, the verbal
equivalent to Claude's *capriccio*, which joins a fictive Roman *archē*
and a fictive English *telos*.

The elusiveness of such a fully achieved English classicism
becomes evident again in a darker key in 'To the Memory of Mr.
Oldham' (1684), a poem which is shadowed by a sense of loss and
of belatedness.[70] Oldham is displaced by death, but Dryden himself
is displaced in the course of the poem. The opening lines are an
admission of the poet's inadequate and belated knowledge:

> Farewel, too little and too lately known,
> Whom I began to think and call my own;
> For sure our Souls were near ally'd; and thine
> Cast in the same Poetick mould with mine.[71]

Dryden's knowledge was too late; Oldham's talent was 'early ripe',
but his death too early. Dryden addresses the dead poet as
Marcellus, the lost heir to Augustus (always already lost before we
can know him) whom Aeneas glimpses on his visit to the underworld in Book VI. This allusion corrects the earlier suggestion of
Shadwell as the heir to Augustus/Flecknoe. Besides registering the
classical allusions in this poem, one hears the Latin language
informing the English lines:

---

[70] For details of this poem's sources and allusions see *Poems*, ed. Hammond, ii. 228–33;
for Dryden as Nisus see Dustin H. Griffin, 'Dryden's "Oldham" and the Perils of Writing',
Modern Language Quarterly, 37 (1976) 133–50; and for Oldham's own work see Paul
Hammond, *John Oldham and the Renewal of Classical Culture* (Cambridge, 1983).

[71] 'To the Memory of Mr. Oldham', ll. 1–4.

Once more, hail and farewel . . .[72]
in perpetuum, frater, ave atque vale . . .[73]

But Fate and gloomy Night encompass thee around.[74]
Sed nox atra caput tristi circumvolat umbra.[75]

In this lament for one who never quite managed to take his place as inheritor, and who never completely learned the numbers of his native tongue, the native English of Dryden's lines is scarcely ever self-sufficient, and is repeatedly almost overwhelmed by memories of Latin, and particularly of Virgil.

The dominant pre-text here is actually not Aeneas' meeting with Marcellus in *Aeneid* VI, but the episode in Book V where Nisus falls in a race and gives victory to his beloved friend Euryalus:

> Thus *Nisus* fell upon the slippery place,
> While his young Friend perform'd and won the Race.[76]

Commentators have noted the curious displacement which the use of this allusion sets moving through the poem, for the reader's initial expectation that the fall of Nisus parallels the death of Oldham is superseded (without ever quite being erased) by the subsequent recognition that Dryden sees himself as Nisus. Dryden-as-Nisus stumbles and falls on a slippery place. That place, the ground on which the poet loses his footing, has a multiple but indeterminate signification. Literally, in the episode from the *Aeneid* it is a patch of earth made wet with the blood from a sacrifice; symbolically, for English translators from Wyatt to Marvell the 'slippery' place is the dangerous ground (*aulo lubrico*) spoken of in the chorus from Seneca's *Thyestes*, which warns of the dangers of a life led wholly in the public domain without sufficient self-reflection. In Cowley's version,

---

[72] Ibid., l. 22.   [73] Catullus, ci. 10.

[74] 'To the Memory of Mr. Oldham', l. 25.

[75] *Aeneid*, vi. 866, of Marcellus.

[76] 'To the Memory of Mr. Oldham', ll. 9–10. Dryden translated the episode of Nisus and Euryalus for *Sylvæ* at around the same time as writing the poem on Oldham; for the translation see *Poems*, ed. Hammond, ii. 228–33 and 258–86, where verbal connections between the two pieces are noted.

Upon the slippery tops of humane State,
  The guilded Pinnacles of Fate,
Let others proudly stand . . .
  To him, alas, to him, I fear,
The face of Death will terrible appear:
Who in his life flattering his senceless pride
By being known to all the world beside,
Does not himself, when he is Dying know
Nor what he is, nor Whither hee's to go.[77]

These lines speak of the necessity for self-knowledge, so that death does not find one bewildered, and Dryden's subdued allusion to them effects a poignant variation on his opening confession that Oldham was 'too little and too lately known'. But the application of this commonplace to Dryden's own life and art, which his poem seems to require, is withheld from view. The poem itself stumbles as it makes this association, and all we grasp is that Dryden acknowledges that he has undergone some kind of death as a poet: he has made himself a ghost in his own text. There is an *aporia* here, an unapproachable site which cannot be represented directly but only made traceable through this fold in the text, the doubling of the allusion to Nisus. Oldham's race is completed, while Dryden is left behind to write a memorial poem which is replete with traces of Oldham's own poetry, but also with traces of other poems of love and loss by Catullus, Virgil and Seneca, Shakespeare, Milton and Cowley: two traditions fragmented and rebuilt into a new structure to mark the site of a perpetual absence, a tragic displacement. Having been, however briefly, the English Horace, Juvenal, and Ovid, the one Roman role which Oldham fulfils perfectly is that of the unfulfilled, unfulfilling Marcellus.

ROMAN ALLUSIONS AND THE AUTHORIAL PERSONA

Dryden turns most insistently to classical allusion and quotation in order to shape his own authorial persona, in a move which combines self-assertion with self-abnegation. The first person singular which weaves through his dedications and critical prefaces is itself a fabric which is fashioned in part by means of the citation

---

[77] Cowley, *Essays*, pp. 399–400.

of Latin predecessors. Langbaine remarked sourly: 'I cannot but observe that whenever the Criticks pursue him, he withdraws for shelter under the Artillery of the Ancients; and thinks by the discharge of a Quotation from a Latine Author to destroy their Criticisms.'[78] But Dryden's method is by no means as brash as Langbaine would have us believe, for the rhetoric of self-construction incorporates many gestures of hesitation and self-doubt, signals of the gulf between the ancient and the modern, as well as confident depictions of their imagined proximity.

The latter, the assertive mode, appears strikingly in the Dedication of *The Assignation* (1673) to Sir Charles Sedley, where Dryden fashions a protective classical space through a series of Roman allusions. He admits that the play fared badly on the stage, but against its appearance on the public scene he sets another, prior appearance before a more discriminating audience: 'It succeeded ill in the representation, against the opinion of many the best Judges of our Age, to whom you know I read it e're it was presented publickly.'[79] In this case Dryden recreates a sympathetic semi-public stage for the work, and behind this an altogether more powerful scene in which Dryden and Sedley are associated with the poets of classical Rome. For poets to name their contemporaries in their work as a protective gesture has, he says, impeccable classical precedent:

This was the course which has formerly been practis'd by the Poets of that Nation who were Masters of the Universe. *Horace* and *Ovid*, who had little reason to distrust their Immortality; yet took occasion to speak with honour of *Virgil*, *Varius*, *Tibullus*, and *Propertius* their Contemporaries: as if they sought in the testimony of their Friendship a farther evidence of their fame. For my own part, I, who am the least amongst the Poets, have yet the fortune to be honour'd with the best Patron, and the best Friend. For . . . I can make my boast to have found a better *Maecenas* in the person of my Lord Treasurer *Clifford*, and a more Elegant *Tibullus* in that of Sir *Charles Sedley*.[80]

As the comparison develops, Dryden evokes a scene in which the aristocratic wits of the Restoration equal Horace and his contemporaries in their civilized social intercourse:

[78] Gerard Langbaine, *An Account of the English Dramatick Poets* (Oxford, 1691), p. 174.
[79] *Works*, xi. 319. [80] Ibid. 320.

Certainly the Poets of that Age enjoy'd much happiness in the Conversation and Friendship of one another . . . We have, like them, our Genial Nights; where our discourse is neither too serious, nor too light; but alwayes pleasant, and for the most part instructive.[81]

The first person plural creates a social and literary grouping which includes Dryden but excludes his censurers, and does not even stretch to embrace his readers. Having said that he was the least among the poets, Dryden ends by associating himself squarely with Horace:

I am made a Detractor from my Predecessors, whom I confess to have been my Masters in the Art. But this latter was the accusation of the best Judge, and almost the best Poet in the *Latine* Tongue. You find *Horace* complaining, that for taxing some verses in *Lucilius*, he himself was blam'd by others, though his Design was no other than mine now, to improve the Knowledge of Poetry.[82]

It is the similarity of the accusations levelled against Horace and against Dryden that links the two poets, and so Dryden's detractors here implicitly become the authors of this association: they are made to produce the comparison which empowers him.

But when Dryden aligns himself with Horace or Virgil, it is rarely without some corrective gesture of distancing and demurral which holds the modern and the classical apart. In the Dedication of *Troilus and Cressida* to the Earl of Sunderland (in which one might have expected him to be comparing himself with Shakespeare) he compares himself with Horace, and then with Virgil, citing first the *Georgics* and then the *Eclogues*. The former quotation aligns Dryden with Virgil at the moment when he was praying for the success of his patron Augustus in 'raising up his country from the desolations of a civill war'.[83] Through the second quotation Dryden imagines being encouraged like Virgil to venture beyond his current style of poetry into writing epic. But between the two Latin quotations Dryden draws back to contemplate his own act of writing, and to examine his present state of mind: 'I know not whither I am running, in this extasy which is now upon me: I am almost ready to reassume the ancient rights of Poetry.'[84] To reassume the ancient rights of poetry would be to

---

[81] *Works*, xi. 320–1.   [82] Ibid. 322.   [83] *Works*, xiii. 221.
[84] Ibid.

take up and continue Virgil's work. But such a possibility is, in its very moment of articulation, deferred ('I am *almost* ready . . .') and ruefully characterized as the ecstatic, erring speech of one who is not quite himself. There is no consolidation of an authorial self here, but instead a movement between different personae as Dryden (ever the student of Montaigne) imagines himself in multiple roles and tries out different voices. The ideal of authorship is no longer attributed statically to the unattainable classical work, but enacted dynamically in the undulations of the present-day English text.

Such citation of his Latin predecessors not only helps Dryden shape a place for himself in the public world, it provides him with authority for his own freedom to innovate.[85] In 'The Authors Apology for Heroique Poetry; and Poetique Licence' prefixed to *The State of Innocence* (1677) Dryden commends Horace for his own bold use of metaphor. (Just as when introducing *Troilus and Cressida* Dryden stepped aside from discussing his confrontation with Shakespeare, and focused instead on his Latin predecessors, so here the engagement with Milton is transposed into a classically-based argument.) Horace and Virgil, he says, 'the severest Writers of the severest Age, have made frequent use of the hardest Metaphors, and of the strongest *Hyperboles:* And in this case the best Authority is the best Argument'.[86] Authority is supreme but also in this case limited, and while Dryden defends the poetic licence to develop tropes and figures by reference to Horace, he cautiously declines to be dogmatic in an area where Horace has not ventured: 'How far these Liberties are to be extended, I will not presume to determine here, since *Horace* does not. But it is certain that they are to be varied, according to the Language and Age in which an Author writes'.[87] Earlier, in the 'Account of the ensuing Poem' prefixed to *Annus Mirabilis* (1667), Dryden claims to have followed Virgil carefully as his model for the language of this poem, while also innovating, for which he claims Horace's licence:

---

[85] The following discussion of Dryden and Horace draws some material from my 'Figures of Horace'. [86] *Works*, xii. 90.

[87] Ibid. 96.

I have followed him every where, I know not with what success, but I
am sure with diligence enough: my Images are many of them copied
from him, and the rest are imitations of him. My expressions also are as
near as the Idioms of the two Languages would admit of in translation
... some words ... I have innovated (if it be too bold for me to say
refin'd) upon his *Latin*; which, as I offer not to introduce into *English*
prose, so I hope they are neither improper, nor altogether unelegant in
Verse; and, in this, *Horace* will again defend me.

> *Et nova, fictaque nuper habebunt verba fidem, si*
> *Graeco fonte cadant, parcè detorta*———[88]

The inference is exceeding plain, for if a *Roman* Poet might have liberty
to coin a word, supposing onely that it was derived from the *Greek*, was
put into a *Latin* termination, and that he us'd this liberty but seldom, and
with modesty: How much more justly may I challenge that privilege to
do it with the same praerequisits, from the best and most judicious of
Latin writers?[89]

This last sentence is a rough translation of the lines which follow
Dryden's quotation from Horace,[90] so Dryden is revoicing Horace
in defence of his practice of revoicing Virgil.

Many of Dryden's Latin quotations are misquotations; evidently
they were never verified by reference back to a written text.[91]
These 'misquotations' are not signs of an unscholarly carelessness,
but creative refashionings of texts which had long ago lodged in
his memory and become transposed into something new, for
when remembering them he sometimes imported into the texts
words from the accompanying glosses in Renaissance editions, and
he often adapted the syntax of the original to fit the new context.
These new lines of verse are made to fit the right metre, and so
become pieces of neo-Latin verse. Thus the quotation of an
ancient authority becomes a new text, slips from being Horace to
being Dryden's Horace: a new Latin phrase displaces the old, and
though the ostensible origins of the quotation are important to the
rhetoric of authorization, they are false origins, for the quotations
are *simulacra*; the Latin which we read is not exactly Horace's

---

[88] 'Words, though new and of recent make, will win acceptance if they spring from a
Greek fount, and are drawn from there sparingly': Horace, *Ars Poetica*, ll. 52–3.
[89] *Poems*, p. 48.   [90] Horace, *Ars Poetica*, ll. 53–8.
[91] See Hammond, 'Figures of Horace', *passim*.

Latin, but Horace edited and glossed by editors and then reworked by Dryden. Horace's text has receded into being the pre-text for Dryden's own piece of Latin, which is itself a pre-text authorizing Dryden's use of English. But it seems to be necessary that these quotations be stones recut to fit the second temple rather than simply relics from the first.

It is characteristically when Dryden wishes to assert his own originality as a poet that he turns to such Latin pre-texts: a claim for originality, it seems, rapidly becomes implicated in a discourse of origins, with the present becoming caught up in a chain of traces. In *Of Dramatick Poesie* his almost despairing meditation on the bankruptcy of the English literary inheritance leads him to assert the need to do something new and distinctly different himself, for imitation of his predecessors will not suffice:

> We acknowledge them our Fathers in wit, but they have ruin'd their Estates themselves before they came to their childrens hands . . . This therefore will be a good Argument to us either not to write at all, or to attempt some other way. There is no bayes to be expected in their Walks; *Tentanda via est quà me quoque possim tollere humo.*[92]

But this gesture is itself an imitation of an illustrious predecessor, for Cowley had used the same quotation as the epigraph for his address to the reader in his first adult collection of poetry, *The Mistress* (1647).[93] The quotation itself (whose grammar has been altered to fit its new context) comes from the *Georgics*, from a passage which is influenced by Lucretius.[94] In the passage from which Dryden is quoting, Virgil expresses his desire to achieve something new in Roman literature, saying that he intends to do this by appropriating and bringing home the culture of Greece, building a temple in his home valley:

> Tentanda via est, qua me quoque possim
> Tollere humo, victorque virum volitare per ora.
> Primus ego in patriam mecum (modo vita supersit)
> Aonio rediens deducam vertice Musas:

---

[92] 'A way must be attempted by which I too may raise myself from the ground' (*Works*, xvii. 73).

[93] Abraham Cowley, *Poems*, ed. A. R. Waller (Cambridge, 1905), p. 458.

[94] Hardie, *Virgil's 'Aeneid'*, p. 48.

> Primus Idumaeas referam tibi, Mantua, palmas:
> Et viridi in campo templum de marmore ponam
> Propter aquam, tardis ingens ubi flexibus errat
> Mincius, et tenera praetexit arundine ripas.[95]

As Dryden later rendered the lines:

> New ways I must attempt, my groveling Name
> To raise aloft, and wing my flight to Fame.
>   I, first of *Romans*, shall in Triumph come
> From conquer'd *Greece*, and bring her Trophies home:
> With Foreign Spoils adorn my native place;
> And with *Idume*'s Palms, my *Mantua* grace.
> Of *Parian* Stone a Temple will I raise,
> Where the slow *Mincius* through the Vally strays.[96]

Dryden's own Latin quotation breaks off at the point where Virgil begins to detail the work of appropriation, so that his readers are left to pursue and complete the allusion for themselves. On its own the sentiment is one of modest aspiration—'A way must be found by which I too may raise myself from the ground'—but as readers supplement and complete Dryden's quotation they make him the new Virgil. In this particular case, Dryden's Latin turn is a turn away from the overburdening inheritance of the early Stuart writers, a heritage which is both full and empty—full in that it permits no supplement from a latecomer, empty in that all the resources of the culture have been used up in its creation. Imitation of them is impossible—and Dryden makes that point by imitating Cowley imitating Virgil's proposal to imitate the Greeks. There is no escape from a chain of imitation. To be original, Dryden has to invent new origins.

Not all of Dryden's Latin tags are actual quotations. In the 'Account of the ensuing Poem' before *Annus Mirabilis* he emphasizes the rich subject matter with which the times have provided him; by contrast with those ruined estates of the preceding

---

[95] Virgil, *Georgics*, iii. 8–15: 'A way must be found by which I too may raise myself from the ground, and as a victor soar before men's eyes. I shall be the first to bring the Muses back with me from the Boeotian mount to my native land (if I only live long enough); I shall first bring the Idumaean palms back to you, Mantua: and I shall place a temple of marble on the green plain, on account of the water, where great Mincio wanders with slow curves, and shades the banks with slender reeds.'
[96] 'The Third Book of the *Georgics*', ll. 13–20.

generation, the events of Dryden's own day have furnished him with a plentiful harvest:

Omnia sponte suâ reddit justissima tellus.[97] I have had a large, a fair and a pleasant field, so fertile that, without my cultivating, it has given me two Harvests in a Summer, and in both oppress'd the Reaper.[98]

This English sentence describing the fruitful present is only a rewording of, a supplement to, the Latin tag. The terse Latin comes first; the leisured English sentence follows it as a copious but secondary gloss. Editors have failed to find a single Latin source for this line, which conflates phrases from Virgil and Ovid:[99] Dryden has made up his own Latin hexameter which has echoes of the great Roman poets but is not itself a direct quotation. At the very moment of celebrating the poetic fertility which this contemporary English subject has inspired in him—celebrating the fullness of England and English, and the spontaneity of its productions—he turns to Latin, and instead of borrowing a classical text he composes a new Latin verse of his own, a kind of quotation which bears traces of its ancestry but could not be put back into the corpus of classical texts without doing violence to that fabric. The *tellus* is no longer England but the imagined ground which Dryden himself has created.

Though such Latin quotations occur throughout Dryden's prefaces, they take on a special importance at moments of personal and professional crisis, and help Dryden to translate himself out of the vicissitudes of the present. This may be seen in two uncannily similar texts, his Dedications to *Aureng-Zebe* (1676) and to *Don Sebastian* (1690), where he is working out his position *vis-à-vis* his patron,[100] and reflecting on the unhappy state of the nation which is restricting his own creativity. In offering *Aureng-Zebe* to the Earl of Mulgrave, Dryden expresses his dissatisfaction with one kind of public life, that of the playwright, and his desire to devote himself instead to writing an epic. In the Dedication to *Don Sebastian* Dryden is negotiating another difficult situation, since he has been forced by his loss of public office at the Revolution to return to

---

[97] 'The most fertile earth has given me everything of its own accord.'
[98] *Poems*, p. 46.   [99] *Poems*, ed. Hammond, i. 118.
[100] For a study of Dryden's relations with his patrons, see Dustin H. Griffin, *Literary Patronage in England, 1650–1800* (Cambridge, 1996).

the stage in order to make a living. In both texts Dryden uses quotation, and particularly Latin quotation, to weave a text which forms a meditation upon the standing of the writer and his complex negotiations with power. But that is to put it too impersonally, for both these prefaces are also explorations of the transitoriness of life and the precariousness of selfhood—themes which also recur through Dryden's Latin translations.

The Dedication to *Aureng-Zebe* opens with an observation on princes attributed to Montaigne, to the effect that 'we ought not, in reason, to have any expectations of Favour from them; and that 'tis kindness enough, if they leave us in possession of our own'.[101] None of the possible sources which editors have proposed in Montaigne[102] quite matches Dryden's citation, and in particular none has his emphasis on princes leaving us in possession of our own. The need for secure possession of one's own goods and one's own self, and the dangers which threaten such security, echo through this Dedication: 'possession . . . ruine . . . secures . . . solid . . . solid . . . ruine . . . crush . . . safety . . . ruin'd . . . sav'd . . . inviolable . . . firmness . . . constant . . . steady . . . confidence . . . solid foundations . . . hazards . . . tranquillity . . . secure . . . unsettl'dness . . . changeable . . . accidents . . . change'.[103] In a world where security is impossible, it is necessary to have a philosophy which accepts change without requiring one to accommodate oneself too readily to those forces which would upset one's equanimity, and unravel the very text through which one has woven an identity. While Dryden assures Mulgrave that Charles II is far from being implicated in Montaigne's remark, later in the Dedication he recalls that he had been encouraged by the King to undertake an epic, but is still waiting for some solid guarantee of support, for 'the unsettl'dness of my condition has hitherto put a stop to my thoughts concerning it'.[104] And Dryden insists that Montaigne's observation applies to many of Charles's courtiers, who act like Fortune herself in handing out favours without any concern to reward merit: 'If good accrue to any from them, 'tis onely in order to their own designs: conferr'd most commonly on the base and infamous; and never given, but onely *hapning*

---

[101] *Works*, xii. 149.   [102] Ibid. 410.   [103] Ibid. 149–57.
[104] Ibid. 155.

sometimes on well deservers'.[105] How can a writer of integrity manage in such conditions?

The management of the self which this Dedication both discusses and exemplifies is conducted partly through the deployment of classical quotations. And this turns out to entail a management of power, at once delineating the writer's relationship to the ruler, and placing that ruler in a complex text whose weavings bring him within the scope of appraisal and criticism. Charles himself is described as

A Prince, who is constant to himself, and steady in all his undertakings; one with whom that Character of *Horace* will agree,

> Si fractus illabatur orbis
> Impavidum ferient ruinae.[106]

The Horatian quotation comes from *Carmina* III. iii, the poem (quoted earlier) in which the Romans are promised a glorious future so long as they do not seek to rebuild Troy on its original site. The solidity of Charles which is celebrated here is that equanimity and sang-froid in the face of adversity which had sustained him in exile and would soon stand him in good stead during the turbulent years of the Popish Plot and the Exclusion Crisis. There is no reason to suppose that Dryden was being ironic: his admiration for the King was genuine, but it was not unmixed. A little later in the Dedication, Charles appears as one who has commended to Dryden the project of writing an epic, but has forgotten that he would need money to live on while writing it. The King's solid unconcern begins to seem less like Stoic nobility and more like that stolid thoughtlessness which Dryden had earlier described as characteristic of some of his courtiers. Mulgrave, says Dryden, may need to refresh the King's memory:

As I am no successor to *Homer* in his Wit, so neither do I desire to be in his Poverty. I can make no Rhapsodies, nor go a begging at the *Graecian* doors, while I sing the praises of their Ancestors. The times of *Virgil* please me better, because he had an *Augustus* for his Patron. And to draw the Allegory nearer you, I am sure I shall not want a *Maecenas* with him.

---

[105] Ibid. 149; original italics.
[106] 'If the heavens should crack and fall, the ruins would strike him undaunted' (Horace, *Carmina*, III. iii. 7–8); *Works*, xii. 152.

'Tis for your Lordship to stir up that remembrance in his Majesty, which his many avocations of business have caus'd him, I fear, to lay aside: And, (as himself and his Royal Brother are the Heroes of the Poem) to represent to them the Images of their Warlike Predecessors; as *Achilles* is said to be rous'd to Glory, with the sight of the Combat before the Ships. For my own part, I am satisfi'd to have offer'd the Design; and it may be to the advantage of my Reputation to have it refus'd me.[107]

The analogies are precarious, the likenesses turn into unlikenesses as the sentence unrolls, and we see the wide gap (too wide, it seems, for allegory to bridge) between Charles and Achilles or Augustus. The multiple analogy which Dryden would like to fix, that between Augustus–Maecenas–Virgil and Charles–Mulgrave–Dryden is still held in suspense, awaiting the outcome of Mulgrave's good offices with the King. The epic was never written; indeed, the final sentence of this extract confesses the likelihood of disappointment. Characteristically, however, Dryden simultaneously recognizes that success in obtaining this commission would probably have meant failure of another kind, the revelation of his own incapacity to be a second Virgil. One hears blended together the regret that his age will not give him the opportunity to test himself against Virgil, and the acknowledgement that the ancient culture cannot be repeated.

The way in which Dryden's text undoes some of its earlier work, and loosens the threads which had attached the Latin quotations to the vernacular exposition, recalls the teasing, unsettling movement of an essay by Montaigne. So perhaps that opening citation was in part an intimation to the reader that he should prepare for similar ironic disjunctions. Montaigne is brought into play again towards the end of the Dedication, when Dryden reflects on the instability of our thinking:

As I am a Man, I must be changeable: and sometimes the gravest of us all are so, even upon ridiculous accidents. Our minds are perpetually wrought on by the temperament of our Bodies: which makes me suspect, they are nearer alli'd, than either our Philosophers or School-Divines will allow them to be. I have observ'd, says *Montaign*, that when the Body is out of Order, its Companion is seldom at his ease. An ill Dream, or a Cloudy day, has power to change this wretched Creature, who is so proud of a reasonable Soul, and make him think what he thought not yesterday.[108]

---

[107] *Works*, xii. 155.   [108] Ibid. 157.

Then Cicero is quoted, to the same effect: *Nos in diem vivimus; quodcunque animos nostros probabilitate percussit, id dicimus.*[109] But Dryden notes that this was an untypically modest utterance on Cicero's part, and recalls the paradox that it was Cicero's very thirst for fame—but fame on his terms—which compromised his reputation with posterity:

A Modern Wit has made this Observation on him, That coveting to recommend himself to Posterity, he begg'd it as an Alms of all his Friends, the Historians, to remember his Consulship: And observe, if you please, the odness of the event; all their Histories are lost, and the vanity of his request stands yet recorded in his own Writings.[110]

The 'Modern Wit' is not named, but it is Montaigne,[111] who once again appears in the role of the modern who understands how to manage man's labile life and fame. Montaigne and Cicero are helping Dryden to identify two forms of the first person singular. Cicero provides an example of the over-confident, over-ambitious and egotistical writer who wishes to manage public affairs, his own texts, and his posthumous reputation. Montaigne more modestly reminds us of our human inconstancy, and the intimate yet unpredictable relationship between the mind and the body which makes our selfhood so shifting and so strange.

Another writer much quoted by Montaigne, Lucretius, is cited here by Dryden as providing an attractive but unacceptable solution to the problem of the wise man's perspective on the world. Saying that he admires and covets nothing 'but the easiness and quiet of retirement', Dryden continues:

I naturally withdraw my sight from a Precipice; and, admit the Prospect be never so large and goodly, can take no pleasure even in looking on the downfall, though I am secure from the danger. Methinks there's something of a malignant joy in that excellent description of *Lucretius*,

> *Suave mari magno turbantibus aequora ventis*
> *E terrâ magnum alterius spectare laborem;*
> *Non quia vexari quenquam est jucunda voluptas*
> *Sed quibus ipse malis careas, quiâ cernere suave est.*

---

[109] 'We live from day to day; whatever strikes our minds with probability, that is what we say' (Cicero, *Tusculan Disputations*, v. xi. 33); *Works*, xii. 157.

[110] *Works*, xii. 151.   [111] Ibid. 402.

I am sure his Master *Epicurus*, and my better Master *Cowley*, prefer'd the
solitude of a Garden, and the conversation of a friend to any consideration, so much as a regard, of those unhappy People, whom in our own
wrong, we call the great. True greatness, if it be any where on Earth, is
in a private Virtue; remov'd from the notion of Pomp and Vanity,
confin'd to a contemplation of it self, and centring on it self:

> *Omnis enim per se Divum natura, necesse est*
> *Immortali aevo summâ cum pace fruatur;*
> ——*Curâ semota, metuque*
> *Ipsa suis pollens opibus*——[112]

The complacent perspective on the turbulent life of others is a
security which Dryden can happily forgo. Instead, he adapts the
lines which Lucretius had applied to the gods to describe his own
ideal of contentment and detachment, a stability centring on his
self which is implicitly contrasted with the stolid self-centredness
of the courtiers, and even of the King. But Dryden's humility and
self-knowledge (as well as his temporary position as a writer
addressing his patron) prevent him from advancing this as a stability which he personally possesses. It is distanced from the first
person singular by the syntax, which defines true greatness only
conditionally ('if it be any where on Earth') and by the subsequent
image of Dryden as 'a sufficient Theater to my self of ridiculous
actions'.[113]

At the end of this Dedication, Dryden avoids putting into his
own English the apologetic strain which he seems to feel ought to
inhabit the address of writer to patron, and instead quotes from
Cicero an extended passage in which he tells Brutus that he is not
writing in order to instruct him on a subject (philosophy) which he
understands better than Cicero himself, but to give his own work
the support of a superior critic's name. In quoting this passage (just
changing '*Philosophia*' to '*Poesi*') Dryden is both voicing and not

---

[112] *Works*, xii. 153–4. The first quotation is from Lucretius, *De Rerum Natura*, ii. 1–4:
'It is pleasant, when over a great sea the winds trouble the waters, to gaze from the land
upon someone else's great tribulation: not because for someone to be troubled is a delec-
table pleasure, but because it is pleasant to perceive the ills which you are free from yourself.' Dryden would translate these lines in *Sylvæ* (1685). The second quotation is from *De
Rerum Natura*, ii. 646–50: 'for the very nature of divinity must necessarily enjoy immortal
life in the deepest peace—remote from care and fear, mighty through its own resources.'
The phrase *Cura semota, metuque* ('remote from care and fear') is Dryden's alteration of
Lucretius, taken from ii. 19.   [113] *Works*, xii. 154.

voicing these sentiments. He pays Mulgrave the same compliment (with the additional compliment of assuming that the Earl can read Cicero's Latin fluently enough to understand that he is being complimented) but retreats behind the protection of words which he has only minimally co-authored, a language which makes Dryden's own 'I' disappear behind the first-person inflections of Cicero's verbs. The Dedication ends by inviting Mulgrave to apply the parallel to himself, adroitly appearing to return power to the patron, while appending Dryden's own signature to the whole performance:

Which you may please, my Lord, to apply to your self, from him, who is
Your Lordship's most obedient humble Servant,
DRYDEN.[114]

The Dedication to *Don Sebastian* fourteen years later, presenting that play to the Earl of Leicester, repeats several of the tropes and movements from the Dedication to *Aureng-Zebe*. But now, in January 1690, only months after the Revolution, Dryden's position in the state is precarious, his livelihood and perhaps even his life at risk; the writing of the self becomes more urgent, Rome a more ominous precedent. The example of Cicero is repeated, but now with quite different implications. First Dryden recalls that when Cicero addresses Atticus, 'knowing himself overmatch'd in good sense, and truth of knowledg, he drops the gawdy train of words, and is no longer the vainglorious Orator'.[115] The comparison of Leicester with Atticus is then elaborated to praise Leicester's choice of retirement in the face of a chaotic commonwealth:

What a glorious Character was this once in *Rome;* I shou'd say in *Athens*, when in the disturbances of a State as mad as ours, the wise *Pomponius* [i.e. Atticus] transported all the remaining wisdom and vertue of his country, into the Sanctuary of Peace and Learning. But, I wou'd ask the World, (for you, My Lord, are too nearly concern'd to judge this Cause)

---

[114] Ibid. 158. Malone noted that this is the only occasion on which Dryden signed himself in print solely by his surname, in the French fashion, writing his name as if he were Corneille or Racine (*The Critical and Miscellaneous Prose Works of John Dryden*, ed. Edmond Malone, 3 vols. (London, 1800) I. ii. 431). Normally in English only a peer (like Mulgrave) signs himself with his surname alone, so was this a quiet assertion of status by Dryden?

[115] *Works*, xv. 59.

whether there may not yet be found, a Character of a Noble *Englishman*, equally shining with that illustrious *Roman?* Whether I need to name a second *Atticus;* or whether the World has not already prevented me, and fix'd it there without my naming? Not a second with a *longo sed proximus intervallo;*[116] not a Young *Marcellus*, flatter'd by a Poet, into a resemblance of the first, with a *frons laeta parum, & dejecto lumina vultu*,[117] and the rest that follows, *si qua fata aspera rumpas Tu Marcellus eris:*[118] But a Person of the same stamp and magnitude; who owes nothing to the former, besides the Word *Roman,* and the Superstition of reverence, devolving on him by the precedency of eighteen hundred years: One who walks by him with equal paces, and shares the eyes of beholders with him: One, who had been first, had he first liv'd; and in spight of doating veneration is still his equal.[119]

Some curious twists mark this comparison of Leicester with Atticus. Dryden's rapid self-correction ('in *Rome;* I shou'd say in *Athens*') emphasizes the supersession of Rome by another site, as Atticus shifts not only himself but 'all the remaining wisdom and vertue of his Country' to an Athens which provides him with a sanctuary of peace and learning, an extreme form of *translatio studii*. (Was there such a sanctuary available to Dryden in 1690? Could it only be an Athens of the mind?) The idea that Leicester is a second Atticus is introduced with elaborate syntactical flourishes which absolve Dryden of the responsibility for the comparison by suggesting that the world may already have made it. And Dryden insists, with further convolutions, that if Leicester is a second Atticus, this is merely because he was born later, not because he is in any way secondary: he is 'of the same stamp and magnitude'. This point is made partly by summoning up, only to repudiate, the figure of Marcellus, that recurring sign of the unful-filling heir. Whereas, when writing of Oldham, Dryden had used Marcellus to suggest that it was impossible for a modern to possess the Augustan inheritance, the same figure is now used to signal that inheritance is no longer at issue: Leicester is not the heir to the Romans, he is not a secondary Atticus, but rather a living example of how to reject a Rome which has grown chaotic.

---

[116] 'Next, but by a long distance': *Aeneid*, v. 320, from the episode of Nisus and Euryalus, which Dryden had translated in *Sylvæ*.

[117] 'His brow far from cheerful, and his eyes downcast': *Aeneid*, vi. 862, describing Marcellus.

[118] 'If by any means you could break the harsh fates, you will be Marcellus': *Aeneid*, vi. 882–3.   [119] *Works*, xv. 60–1.

Leicester exemplifies that centred self which Dryden had also praised in the earlier Dedication: unlike the ambitious but short-lived meteors who seek fame in the public sphere because they have no sphere of their own,

how much happier is he . . . who centring on himself, remains immovable, and smiles at the madness of the dance about him. He possesses the midst, which is the portion of safety and content: He will not be higher, because he needs it not; but by the prudence of that choice, he puts it out of Fortunes power to throw him down.[120]

In thus complimenting Leicester, Dryden describes his own mode of freedom.

Like the Dedication to *Aureng-Zebe*, this Dedication concludes with another untranslated quotation from Cicero:

Me, O Pomponi, valdè poenitet vivere: tantum te oro, ut quoniam me ipse semper amâsti, ut eodem amore sis; ego nimirum, idem sum. Inimici mei mea mihi non meipsum ademerunt. Cura, Attice, ut valeas.[121]

This actually weaves together, with alterations, the endings of two letters which Cicero sent to Atticus in 58 BCE as he was about to leave for banishment.[122] We might translate Dryden's Ciceronian cento as: 'It pains me exceedingly to live, Pomponius: this much I beg of you, since you have always loved me for myself, that you preserve the same love; I am truly the same. My enemies have taken away from me my possessions but not my self. Take care of yourself, Atticus, that you may flourish.' Schoolboys were encouraged to compose Latin epistles to their friends reusing phrases from Cicero's correspondence.[123] This passage includes many first person pronouns, and these are juxtaposed emphatically in the penultimate sentence so as to bring out the important idea that Cicero's enemies may have robbed him of his goods but not his self: *Inimici mei mea mihi non meipsum ademerunt.* (The effect is not really repeatable in English, but is literally: 'enemies-my my-things

---

[120] Ibid. 60. With the last clause here cp. 'Enjoy the present smiling hour; | And put it out of Fortunes pow'r:' ('Horat. Ode. 29. Book 3', ll. 50–1; and also 'Horace Lib. I. Ode 9', ll. 20–2).

[121] *Works*, xv. 64. The phrase *quoniam me ipse* is likely to be Dryden's or a printer's error; Shackleton Bailey's text has *quoniam me ipsum*, which must be the correct reading grammatically.   [122] *Ad Atticum*, iii. 4 and 5; identified in *Works*, xv. 411.

[123] Hoole, *A New Discovery*, p. 151.

from–me not myself have–taken'.) These Latin pronouns speak for
Dryden and associate his insecurity as a Catholic and a supporter
of James II with Cicero's position as he faced exile for having
saved the state (at least in his own eyes) by taking swift (albeit il-
legal) action against Catiline. Dryden would have recalled as he
transcribed these lines that during Cicero's exile his house in
Rome and his villa at Tusculum were wrecked by thugs, depriv-
ing him of a home, but that after only a year in exile he was
recalled and fêted on his return. Dryden leaves that part of the
narrative unwritten: but he also leaves unwritten the gruesome
end which Cicero suffered. Murdered while trying to escape the
soldiers of Mark Antony, his body was dismembered, and on
Antony's orders his head and hands were nailed up on the rostrum
in the centre of Rome.[124] Dryden leaves us in the uncomfortable
state of recognizing a close but uncertain parallel, and not knowing how far to pursue it. In the quotation his own personal
pronouns have been transcribed into Latin, thus placing under
erasure his own self and his own authorial signature. The
Dedication is dated with a Latin formula which echoes the dating
of Cicero's letters: '*Dabam Cal.* | Jan. 1690'.[125] This was the first
day of a new year, no longer that guilty year of revolution, 1689.
Writing the date of the present in a Latin which can never be his
native language (and which at this point in history is perhaps
valued precisely for that reason, for its distance from the everyday
language of an England in which he felt adrift) Dryden poignantly
signals the necessary but elusive collocation of Rome and England,
a parallel which was beginning to look grim.

---

[124] Plutarch, *Cicero*, 48–9. For an earlier example of a meditation on the fate of Cicero
see the play *Marcus Tullius Cicero* (1651), and Dale B. J. Randall, 'The Head and the Hands
on the Rostra: *Marcus Tullius Cicero* as a Sign of its Time', *Connotations*, 1 (1991) 34–54.
[125] *Works*, xv. 64.

2

ROME AND THE ENGLISH
NATION

In the texts discussed in the previous chapter, the time of writing
and the culture of the present were made legible through a turn to
Latin. The standing and authority of the writer are established
through the citation of another time and another culture.
Quotation of Latin and allusion to Rome are also important strat-
egies in the poems in which Dryden addresses political issues and
significant moments in the nation's history. In such texts the turn
to Latin has the effect of translating the present and its debates into
a time and place which are no longer either contemporary or past,
home or foreign, but newly shaped conceptual spaces in which the
fluid and contested language of the present can be brought under
control, albeit a control which is often polemical and temporary
(Dryden's enemies would say 'temporizing'). The macaronic time
and space fashioned through these citations enable Dryden to
manage the discourse of the nation through an act of translation.
This is not translation into a single idiom, but translation into a
world made both *heimlich* and *unheimlich*, where the very juxtapo-
sition of English and Latin, past and present, compels us to see
each of those elements afresh, and to recognize that they are
bound in (or to observe them being bound by the poetry into)
connections of reciprocal definition and mutual qualification. It is
a further demonstration of *correctio*, Dryden's favourite rhetorical
move, which takes up the language of his literary or political
opponents and turns it against them, giving new and uncomfortable implications to the terms through which Shadwell or
Shaftesbury had represented themselves. In such a way Dryden
remakes the language of contemporary political debate.

ROMAN MOTIFS IN THE *HEROIQUE STANZA'S*
ON CROMWELL

The occasion on which Dryden first addressed public events in public verse[1] was the passing of Cromwell on 3 September 1658, which he marked with the *Heroique Stanza's,* | *Consecrated to the glorious memorie* | *Of his most Serene & Renowned Highness* | *OLIVER* | *Late Lord Protector of this Common=wealth. &c.* | *Written after the Celebration of his Funeralls.*[2] The occasion was in several respects an awkward one for a poet to put into words, and the *Heroique Stanza's* both deliberately remake the language of royal panegyric and ponder how to find an appropriate form of words to represent the Protector.[3] The opening subject of the poem is not Cromwell but the poem itself, the time of writing, as Dryden confesses that he has deferred writing, but claims that he is now breaking the silence at the right moment:

> And now 'tis time, for their Officious haste,
> Who would before have born him to the sky,
> Like *eager Romans* ere all Rites were past
> Did let too soon the *sacred Eagle* fly.[4]

Dryden insists on his command of the present. His deferral had been apt, not culpable, though the poem does not actually explain why it would have been premature to write earlier, why poetry needed to wait until after the state funeral. Indeed, by the time Dryden's poem eventually appeared in print, at some unknown date after January 1659,[5] the claim of that opening phrase would have seemed puzzling. This is but one of several gaps which open up as we contemplate this strange occasion. The funeral rites for Cromwell had themselves been delayed until 23 November, and since the body had begun to decompose an effigy had been used instead of the corpse. The event had been strikingly monarchical in its iconography, approximating more to Stuart ceremonial than

---

[1] If we omit the schoolboy verses on the death of Lord Hastings, and the undergraduate 'Carmen Lapidarium' on the death of John Smith.

[2] This is the title as given in the autograph fair copy, British Library MS Lansdowne 1045, fo. 101ʳ (*Poems*, ed. Hammond, i. 533).

[3] See further, Paul Hammond, *John Dryden: A Literary Life* (Basingstoke, 1991), pp. 16–20.　　　　　　　　　　　　　　　　　　　　[4] *Heroique Stanza's*, ll. 1–4.

[5] *Poems*, ed. Hammond, i. 17.

to any republican idiom which could have been derived from Roman precedent. Dryden's poem effaces the oddity of that occasion, providing the classical dignity which the ceremony itself had lacked through its sober style and by referring in the opening stanza to Roman rites, the ceremony for the deification of an emperor at which an eagle was released over the funeral pyre.[6] But this allusion is not sufficiently specific to bring into the visible texture of the poem a likeness between Cromwell and the deified emperors: the simile actually links the hasty poets and the eager Romans, so that the Romanizing of Cromwell is left suggestive, undetermined. It is a caution—a scepticism, even—about historical parallels which characterizes the poem, and contrasts with the confident though controversial Romanizing of Waller's earlier *Panegyrick*.[7] And it contrasts also with the flights of fancy in the anonymous poem *Anglia Rediviva: or, England Revived* (1658), which imagines Cromwell's coronation, complete with a procession through the streets of London under arches held up by classical columns, past an equestrian statue of Cromwell adorned with the triple Roman crowns, castrensic, muric, and civic.[8] This was an unrealized, and probably unrealizable dream, but the potency of this possible future for the nation survives as a shadow in Dryden's transposition of the funeral into this partially Roman form.

Dryden transforms the funeral ceremony again at the end of the poem, when in the final stanza he imagines Cromwell's resting place not in Westminster Abbey but in a Roman funeral urn:

> His Ashes in a peacefull Urne shall rest,
> His Name a great example stands to show
> How strangely high endeavours may be blest,
> Where *Piety* and *valour* joyntly goe.[9]

---

[6] For the ceremony see Basil Kennett, *Romae Antiquae Notitia: or, The Antiquities of Rome* (London, 1696, 7th edn. 1721), pp. 363–4, illustrated opposite p. 336, reproduced here as Plate 4. The Romans actually used a wax image instead of the body at such ceremonies, so this coincidence offered Dryden a fortuitous parallel, and may have prompted the comparison.

[7] Edmund Waller's *A Panegyrick to my Lord Protector* (1655) was parodied by several writers, including Lucy Hutchinson: see David Norbrook, 'Lucy Hutchinson versus Edmund Waller: An Unpublished Reply to Waller's *A Panegyrick to my Lord Protector*', *The Seventeenth Century*, 11 (1996) 61–86, discussing the Roman allusions on p. 66.

[8] *Anglia Rediviva: Or, England Revived. An Heroick Poem* (London, 1658).

[9] *Heroique Stanza's*, ll. 145–8.

Cremation was alien to the burial customs of seventeenth-century England, so the first line of this stanza transposes Cromwell into a quasi-classical world. The tense of the verb ('shall rest') imparts a tension to the idea of Cromwell's peaceful rest in this dignified urn, for it is not a simple future (which would be 'will rest') but a declarative one, assertive rather than calmly prophetic. That Dryden had difficulty with this final placing of Cromwell can be seen from his autograph manuscript, which preserves a reading which he apparently rejected for the printed text: 'In peacefull Urne his sacred Ashes rest'.[10] Second thoughts suggested to Dryden that this line was unhappy in its deification of Cromwell ('sacred Ashes'), and its bare, factual (and incorrect) present tense ('rest').[11] But Dryden had no second thoughts about his final line, 'Where *Piety* and *valour* joyntly goe', which in joining piety and valour joins two Latinate values, and is, more specifically, an echo of Propertius' explanation for the success of Rome:

> nam quantum ferro tantum pietate potentes
> stamus: victricis temperat ira manus.[12]

This final translation of Cromwell into an example of publicly necessary virtues brings England and Rome together with proud confidence; other juxtapositions and translations are less secure.

Such tensions in the placing of Cromwell (we might say, such self-solicitation by the poem of its own rhetorical and mythological procedures) are apparent earlier in the alignments of Cromwell with Roman precedents. In the lines:

> When past all Offerings to *Feretrian Jove*
> He *Mars* depos'd, and Arms to Gowns made yield,[13]

Dryden alludes to the custom whereby a Roman general who had personally captured arms from an enemy commander dedicated them to Jupiter Feretrius. This feat was first performed by Romulus, and was subsequently repeated on only two occasions.

---

[10] British Library MS Lansdowne 1045, fo. 103ᵛ; *Poems*, ed. Hammond, i. 538.

[11] One could read 'rest' as a subjunctive, meaning 'may rest', but the parallel verb 'stands' in the following line is in the indicative mood.

[12] Propertius, III. xxii: 'For we stand powerful as much through piety as through the sword: our anger stays its hand in victory.' Propertius' *stamus* probably explains Dryden's choice of 'stands' in l. 146.   [13] *Heroique Stanza's*, ll. 77–8.

Dryden's phrasing does not actually state that Cromwell joined such august company; the wording 'When past all Offerings' could imply that Cromwell surpassed such achievements, or merely that the time for making such offerings passed with the ending of the war. The poetry is evocative but not specific, holding out the possibility that Cromwell might be placed in a narrative of heroic emulation, but not actually constructing such a narrative. The suggestion that Fortune began to favour Cromwell at the same stage in life when she turned against Pompey[14] depends upon the unlikeness which the chronological coincidence reveals, so that we are asked to read against the parallel which the poem has found. The idea that Cromwell was weighed down by the greatness of his reputation as the Vestal Virgin Tarpeia was crushed under the weight of the shields of the Sabines to whom she had betrayed Rome,[15] is a comparison which is tenuous if not inept. The poem does not place Cromwell coherently in a typology which is defined through such Roman references, nor does it place him comfortably in time: apart from some allusions to our bribed ancestors and to his military victories,[16] British history is hardly visible here as a narrative within which we might locate and understand Cromwell.

Avoiding such emplotment, which would have raised difficult questions about providence, justice, and legitimacy at a juncture when these issues were about to be redefined yet again, Dryden more easily locates Cromwell within a new kind of space. This is part-Roman, part-English, but also coloured by the Renaissance Italy of Machiavelli and Guicciardini, with its ideas of statecraft.[17] It is geography rather than history which changes: the map of England has been remade by his conquests, the balance of power in Europe has been changed by his strength, the English lion roars in Belgian walks, and voyages of exploration and conquest extend the nation's influence across the globe.[18] And it is nature and heaven rather than history and its contingencies which most readily explain Cromwell: he is the 'confidant of Nature', with special insight into her mysteries, and his natural greatness preceded any

[14] Ibid. ll. 31–2.   [15] Ibid. ll. 135–6.   [16] Ibid. ll. 124, 41–8.
[17] See *Heroique Stanza's*, ll. 29–30*n*, 63–4*n*, in *Poems*, ed. Hammond, i. 20, 23.
[18] *Heroique Stanza's*, ll. 54–6, 85–92, 115–16, 121–3.

military glory which Fortune conferred on him.[19] Whereas
Marvell saw Cromwell as 'the Wars and Fortunes Son',[20] Dryden
sees him as their master. But the time of Cromwell is transposed
into an achronicity, at best an interval or halcyon moment
between two periods of storm,[21] his multiply-defined, macaronic
space finally transformed into the symbolic stasis of the classical
urn.

This is a point of singleness and stillness at the end of a poem
which had both registered movement and itself moved between
different mythological and historical planes, even if as a symbol the
urn cannot quite contain Cromwell within a coherent conceptual
space. Indeed, the memory of Cromwell was not to be confined
by this gesture, and returned at key moments in Dryden's career.
The *Heroique Stanza's* were themselves reprinted by Dryden's
enemies in attempts to make the public redefine him through this
memory of his past allegiance: this happened during the Exclusion
Crisis in 1681, with two further printings in 1682, and again in
1687 after the publication of *The Hind and the Panther*.[22] Cromwell
also stayed in Dryden's own memory, partly by means of another
poem.

Memory rarely works by constructing coherent narratives;
more usually it floods the past so as to leave just a few islands, sites
of special significance which one is compelled to revisit. One such
site for Dryden was Marvell's 'An Horatian Ode upon Cromwel's
Return from Ireland'. This was first printed in his *Miscellaneous
Poems* of 1681, though even then it was excised from most copies;
moreover, there is no evidence that it circulated in manuscript. In
having access to the 'Ode', particularly prior to 1681, Dryden was
therefore an exceptionally privileged reader. Marvell probably
showed the poem to Dryden when they were both working with
Milton in the Protectorate's Office for Foreign Tongues, and it

---

[19] *Heroique Stanza's*, ll. 99–100, 21–4.
[20] Andrew Marvell, 'An Horatian Ode upon Cromwel's Return from Ireland', l. 113.
[21] *Heroique Stanza's*, l. 144.
[22] Hugh Macdonald, *John Dryden: A Bibliography of Early Editions and of Drydeniana* (Oxford, 1939), pp. 5–7; Paul Hammond, 'The Circulation of Dryden's Poetry', *Papers of the Bibliographical Society of America*, 86 (1992) 379–409, at pp. 387–8. Some readers also copied the poem into their private manuscript miscellanies in the 1680s: see Peter Beal, *Index of English Literary Manuscripts*, ii: *1625–1700, Part 1: Behn–King* (London, 1987), pp. 403–4.

may have been this biographical connection back to a period in Dryden's life which ran counter to his mature political principles that helped to give the 'Ode' its nagging, recurrent fascination for him, making it a site which he could neither address directly, nor forget.[23]

Marvell's own handling of classical material in the 'Ode' is complex, deploying Horatian and Lucanic motifs along with other Roman allusions and colouration.[24] The poem deploys a Latinate vocabulary and philosophical framework: we are in a world of 'Temples', '*Gods*', 'Fortune', and 'Fate',[25] but this classicizing is problematic. Since it was in large measure Charles I's devout adherence to the Church of England which led him to the scaffold, to associate him with 'the *Gods*' is to traduce rather than translate, or is at best a tendentious translation. So too when Cromwell, who continually referred his military successes to divine Providence, is called 'the Wars and Fortunes Son',[26] this translation of English history into a Roman idiom is more than an elegant classicizing gesture, it calls into question the Christian Providential language through which Cromwell represented his motives to himself and to observers. Later we are told that Cromwell is 'still in the *Republick*'s hand',[27] but the word 'republic' is also problematic. From the Latin term *res publica*,[28] it could mean in English simply 'the state' or 'the common weal' (*OED* 1), as well as 'a state in which the supreme power rests in the people and their elected representatives' (*OED* 2). In which of these senses is Marvell using the word? How committed is the poem to the idea of an English republic in the second sense? After the

[23] The following discussion of Marvell's 'Horatian Ode' is adapted from my essay 'Classical Texts: Translations and Transformations', in *The Cambridge Companion to English Literature 1650–1740*, ed. Steven N. Zwicker (Cambridge, 1998), pp. 143–61.

[24] For divergent readings of the classical elements in Marvell's poem, see John Coolidge, 'Marvell and Horace', *Modern Philology*, 63 (1965–6) 111–20; R. H. Syfret, 'Marvell's "Horatian Ode" ', *Review of English Studies*, 12 (1961) 160–71; A. J. N. Wilson, 'Andrew Marvell: *An Horatian Ode upon Cromwel's Return from Ireland*: The Thread of the Poem and Its Use of Classical Allusion', *Critical Quarterly*, 11 (1969) 325–41; David Norbrook, 'Marvell's "Horatian Ode" and the Politics of Genre', in *Literature and the English Civil War*, ed. Thomas Healy and Jonathan Sawday (Cambridge, 1990), pp. 147–69.

[25] Marvell, 'Horatian Ode', ll. 22, 61, 113, 37.   [26] Ibid., l. 113.

[27] Ibid., l. 82.

[28] The term *res publica* also had a range of meanings in Latin: see Karl Galinsky, *Augustan Culture: An Interpretive Introduction* (Princeton, 1996), pp. 58–70.

execution of the King in 1649 England became a republic in that second sense, but the word itself was not commonly used to describe the new state, which was instead officially called the 'Commonwealth and Free State'.[29] It was far from clear, when Marvell was writing in 1650, who or what constituted 'the republic' in either of the available senses. The Roman term does not quite pass into modern English idiom, and so a crucial ambiguity blurs Marvell's definition of that public sphere to which Cromwell is still, apparently, subject. As with many of Dryden's Latinate usages, it is precisely because of the surrounding Roman allusions that we are more sensitive than usual to the word's Roman history and its incomplete naturalization, and so we hear a strangeness in its application, a strangeness which suggests that the new order is far from fixed. Moreover, there are unsettling associations if we trace the word back to Horace's time, for Augustus had, in effect if not in name, abolished the Roman republic with its liberties and instituted a monarchy, even while avoiding the hated name of king.

Marvell's use of allusions to particular figures from Roman history is also problematic. Cromwell's forceful rise unseated Charles,

> And *Caesars* head at last
> Did through his Laurels blast.[30]

Caesar here stands for Charles I, the point of comparison being (perhaps) that both rulers were killed because they were thought to pose a threat to the people's liberties. But later in the poem it is Cromwell who is now Caesar:

> A *Caesar* he ere long to *Gaul*,
> To *Italy* an *Hannibal*.[31]

Here Cromwell is the Caesar who expanded the Roman empire through his foreign conquests, and yet since Caesar's untimely end

[29] See Martin Dzelzainis, 'Milton's Classical Republicanism', in David Armitage, Armand Himy and Quentin Skinner (eds.), *Milton and Republicanism* (Cambridge, 1995), pp. 3–24, at p. 15; and Thomas N. Corns, 'Milton and the Characteristics of a Free Commonwealth', ibid., pp. 25–42, at pp. 27–8.

[30] Marvell, 'Horatian Ode', ll. 23–4.

[31] Marvell, 'Horatian Ode', ll. 101–2.

has already been alluded to, it is difficult to expunge that part of his story from our memory as we ponder this image. Yet Cromwell is also aligned here with Hannibal, the foreigner who invaded Italy to destroy Rome, but was himself destroyed in the attempt. What does that suggest about Cromwell's future? John Coolidge[32] sees a further alignment of Cromwell with Augustus in the lines:

> And has his Sword and Spoyls ungirt,
> To lay them at the *Publick*'s skirt.[33]

which recall the occasion in 27 BCE when Octavius resigned his various offices and powers, only for the Senate to hand him more. If we recognize the allusion, how far do we pursue the parallel? Do we see Cromwell as a potential Augustus, establishing peace and prosperity after years of civil war? Or, if we have read Roman history through Tacitus, do we become apprehensive about the loss of ancient liberties which an Augustan principate might entail? These various allusions appear at first to locate Cromwell in a clear narrative of military success, and yet if we remind ourselves of the original Roman contexts, they turn into narratives of *hubris* and *nemesis*. Nor are these allusions mutually compatible.

The parallels are fragmentary, inconsistent, and contradictory, suggestive rather than definitive, teasing and disturbing us, and through their interaction disturbing one another. The reader faces a complex interpretative problem, as no coherent narrative pattern is able to triumph, nor is any single parallel established between 1650 and a particular moment in Roman history. Reading the 'Horatian Ode' becomes a lesson in the complexities of reading history and reading the present, in reading the present through a history which is itself dismembered and remembered to serve the needs of the present.

Dryden in turn dismembers Marvell's poem, using it to reconfigure his own memory of the 1650s and to realign himself with the present. The first example of Dryden revisiting the 'Horatian Ode' occurs in 1662, in lines addressed to the Earl of Clarendon. Describing the close relationship between Clarendon and the

---

[32] Coolidge, 'Andrew Marvell', p. 115.
[33] Marvell, 'Horatian Ode', ll. 89–90.

King, Dryden remarks that it could not be changed without some breach occurring in the natural order:

> though your Orbs of different greatness be,
> Yet both are for each others use dispos'd,
> His to inclose, and yours to be inclos'd.
> Nor could another in your room have been
> Except an Emptinesse had come between.[34]

This passage echoes two couplets in which Marvell had figured first the relationship between Cromwell and his allies, and then that between Cromwell and Charles I:

> And with such to inclose
> Is more then to oppose . . .
> Nature that hateth emptiness,
> Allows of penetration less:[35]

While Dryden's lines take over Marvell's vocabulary, they present a radically different vision of politics and of nature. In the troubled cosmology of the 'Horatian Ode', Cromwell moves through the heavens like a shooting star or a bolt of lightning, destroying both rivals and enemies. In the new world of Restoration England the earth seamlessly joins the sky,[36] while Clarendon's orb is peacefully contained within the orb of Charles II in a version of the Ptolemaic cosmology. Violent movement has given way to harmonious structure. And whereas Marvell had explained the phenomenon of Cromwell by citing two kinds of impossibility (the first a vacuum, the second the simultaneous presence of two bodies in the same space), Dryden conceives of only one: no one could replace Clarendon without creating a vacuum. The second form of impossibility—the idea that two bodies might contest possession of the same regal space—finds no place, for it has become unthinkable even as an image of impossibility. The natural world now sustains the political order instead of permitting its overthrow. Enclosure is now a sign of the good subject, rather than an irritating restraint upon ambition. In Dryden's lines the proper political relationship between sovereign and subject

---

[34] *To My Lord Chancellor*, ll. 38–42.
[35] Marvell, 'Horatian Ode', ll. 19–20, 41–2.
[36] *To My Lord Chancellor*, ll. 31–6.

displaces that earlier violent displacement of Charles I by Cromwell. And so Dryden's text endeavours to place Marvell's text under erasure, and along with it that experience of the Civil War and the Commonwealth for which the 'Horatian Ode' is, it seems, Dryden's troubling mnemonic.

There is a second echo later in the same poem, when Dryden says of Clarendon's activity:

> How strangely active are the arts of Peace,
> Whose restlesse motions lesse than Wars do cease![37]

Compare:

> So restless *Cromwel* could not cease
> In the inglorious Arts of Peace.[38]

Dryden's repetition of 'restless' rewrites the energy of the mighty subject as a creative force: no longer does such a man urge 'his active Star',[39] for now it is the 'arts of Peace' that are 'active', and no longer can they be thought 'inglorious'. But there is also an unsettling self-echo in these lines, for Dryden's own *Heroique Stanza's* had concluded with the reflection that Cromwell's example showed

> How strangely high endeavours may be blest,
> Where *Piety* and *valour* joyntly goe.[40]

What links the two poems is the word 'strangely', used in both cases to mean 'in an uncommon or exceptional degree' (*OED* 4). Both Cromwell and Clarendon exhibit exceptional skills and energies, but now the exceptional man finds his proper sphere, at one with the political and the natural order.

That Cromwell was haunting Dryden's memory at this point in *To My Lord Chancellor* is evident in the passage which precedes these lines. Clarendon appeared at the Restoration,

> As new-born *Pallas* did the Gods surprise;
> When springing forth from *Jove's* new-closing wound
> She struck the Warlick Spear into the ground;
> Which sprouting leaves did suddenly inclose,
> And peaceful Olives shaded as they rose.[41]

---

[37] *To My Lord Chancellor*, ll. 105–6.
[38] Marvell, 'Horatian Ode', ll. 9–10.
[39] Ibid., l. 12.
[40] *Heroique Stanza's*, ll. 147–8.
[41] *To My Lord Chancellor*, ll. 100–4.

These peaceful olives are a retrospective erasure of Oliver Cromwell, for during the Protectorate writers had used the olive— traditionally a symbol of peace and prosperity—as an emblem for Oliver.[42] So Dryden's image is performing a corrective gesture. Another revision of Cromwellian history is made through the reference to Pallas Athene. Her miraculous birth from the head of Jove is (by contrast with the unnatural intervention of Cromwell in public affairs) a happy transgression of the natural order of things. Dryden's account of Athene here conflates the story of her birth with the story of the weaving contest between Athene and Arachne.[43] Challenged by the over-confident mortal, Athene wove a picture of herself among the gods, identifying herself by her spear turning into an olive tree and crowned with the fruits of victory. This image is surrounded by four others depicting the fate of mortals who challenged or rebelled against the gods. Athene is therefore weaving an admonitory text about *hubris* and rebellion, one which is aptly brought into play in Dryden's poem through this allusion. Like the echoes of Marvell, this serves to mark out the contrast between Cromwell's ambitious, destructive career and Clarendon's self-limiting, creative service.

Dryden was drawn back to the 'Horatian Ode' in the writing of *Absalom and Achitophel* (1681), at another moment in English history when subjects were challenging the rights of kings. The first echo occurs when Absalom is speaking to Achitophel about King David and his brother:

> His Brother, though Opprest with Vulgar Spight,
> Yet Dauntless and Secure of Native Right,[44]

This recalls Marvell's account of the dignified behaviour of Charles I on the scaffold:

> Nor call'd the *Gods* with vulgar spight
> To vindicate his helpless Right;[45]

---

[42] The punning emblem had been a commonplace, but one example which Dryden would have encountered was *Oliva Pacis*, the volume of commendatory poems on Oliver the peacemaker published by Cambridge University in June 1654, a few months after he had graduated.

[43] Athene's birth is related by Hesiod, *Theogony*, ll. 924–6; the weaving contest by Ovid, *Metamorphoses*, vi. 5–145. [44] *Absalom and Achitophel*, ll. 353–4.

[45] Marvell, 'Horatian Ode', ll. 61–2.

The half-rhyme of 'helpless' and 'Dauntless' points up the lack of rhyme between the circumstances of Charles I and his son James. Moreover, the right which in 1649 was 'helpless' has now become 'Native', as Dryden emphasizes that government is rooted in the hereditary principle. The words are spoken by Absalom at the moment when he is thinking of forcing a breach in the orderly succession, contemplating a violence which Dryden evidently considers analogous to the violence perpetrated upon Charles I by Cromwell. The second echo comes in a speech from Achitophel:

> But when shou'd People strive their Bonds to break,
> If not when Kings are Negligent or Weak?[46]

Compare:

> But those do hold or break
> As Men are strong or weak.[47]

Marvell's observation of what does actually happen in the political arena becomes translated in Achitophel's seductive argument into a reason for action: Marvell's verb 'do' has become Achitophel's 'shou'd', and that word 'shou'd' vacillates uneasily between meaning 'could' and meaning 'ought', between suggesting that the people have a golden opportunity to break their bonds, and suggesting that they have a moral obligation to do so. And along with that crafty ambiguity goes another, the uncertainty as to whether these are 'Bonds' in the sense of 'fetters', or 'Bonds' in the sense of 'legal obligations'. Dryden's transposition of Marvell's neutrally descriptive account into the slippery rhetoric of the opportunist suggests that he was reading Marvell's lines as promoting an amoral, Machiavellian attitude to power and right.

In the voice of the poem's narrator, Dryden later observes that

> To change Foundations, cast the Frame anew,
> Is work for Rebels who base Ends pursue:
> At once Divine and Humane Laws controul;
> And mend the Parts by ruine of the Whole.[48]

These lines recall Marvell's account of Cromwell's endeavour,

---

[46] *Absalom and Achitophel*, ll. 387–8.
[47] Marvell, 'Horatian Ode', ll. 39–40.
[48] *Absalom and Achitophel*, ll. 805–8.

> To ruine the great Work of Time,
>   And cast the Kingdome old
>   Into another Mold.[49]

Where Marvell sees the kingdom as old, and the work of time, Dryden sees it as a structure with foundations and a frame sustained by laws which are at once human and divine: for him the fabric exists in a timeless sphere, whereas for Marvell it is the product of time, and as such subject to change.

The third poem which weaves material from the 'Horatian Ode' into its fabric is *Threnodia Augustalis* (1685), Dryden's elegy for Charles II. Once again, the uncomfortable memory of Cromwell, and the uncomfortably memorable words of Marvell, surface as Dryden describes an exemplary relationship between subject and sovereign. The dying King entrusts the realm to his faithful brother:

> his own Love bequeath'd supream command:
> He took and prest that ever loyal hand,
>   Which cou'd in Peace secure his Reign,
>   Which cou'd in wars his Pow'r maintain,
> That hand on which no plighted vows were ever vain.
>   Well for so great a trust, he chose
>   A Prince who never disobey'd:
> Not when the most severe commands were laid;[50]

Several lines from Marvell have shaped Dryden's passage:

> How good he is, how just,
> And fit for highest Trust:
> Nor yet grown stiffer with command.
>
>   .   .   .
>
> How fit he is to sway
> That can so well obey.
>
>   .   .   .
>
> The same *Arts* that did *gain*
> A *Pow'r* must it *maintain*.[51]

This is the moment of inheritance, the transfer of power and of right from Charles II to James II, the peaceful succession which

---

49 Marvell, 'Horatian Ode', ll. 34–6.   50 *Threnodia Augustalis*, ll. 229–35.
51 Marvell, 'Horatian Ode', ll. 79–81, 83–4, 119–20.

very nearly did not happen, and the like of which had not occurred before within living memory. (The last such transfer had been the accession of Charles I in 1625, before Dryden was born.) This moment shared between the two brothers forms a poignant contrast with the death of their father. The echoes of Marvell's poem also point another contrast, between Marvell's advice to Cromwell that 'The same *Arts* that did *gain* | A *Pow'r* must it *maintain*', and the stress in Dryden's lines on 'right'. That word 'right' had also featured importantly in the 'Horatian Ode', but whereas Marvell had seen Charles I's right as 'helpless', Dryden sees Charles II's right as given by heaven.[52] Significantly, 'maintain' now rhymes with 'reign' not with 'gain', and power is secured by the hand of James (which is a sign both of military strength and of plighted trust) rather than by the Machiavellian arts of Cromwell. Above all, the emphasis at this point is on loyalty. Dryden's lines recuperate the vocabulary of trust and obedience which Cromwell had violated, or which Marvell had violated by using it of Cromwell.

Curiously, there is in the *Threnodia* another self-echo of the *Heroique Stanza's*, for the poem begins with Dryden's admission that he has been slow to break the silence: 'Thus long my Grief has kept me dumb.'[53] The *Heroique Stanza's* had also opened with an admission of lateness, in this case an assertion that the poet had waited until it was properly time to speak. Two times, two kinds of time, understood within incompatible political and imaginative structures, meet in this gesture of repetition. Dryden was not only correcting Marvell's 'Horatian Ode' in *Threnodia Augustalis*, he was momentarily recuperating his own past: and the echo between the two opening lines (probably an inadvertent one) offers a demonstration of the difficulty which Dryden had in placing himself in the time and narrative of public discourse. Far from being a poet who writes easily for the present moment, he arrives belatedly and awkwardly in the public domain.

These intertextual echoes of the 'Horatian Ode' are not allusions which a reader is expected to recognize: even after the publication of *Miscellaneous Poems* in 1681 the 'Ode' would not have been sufficiently well known for them to function as overt references.

---

[52] *Threnodia Augustalis*, l. 226.   [53] Ibid., l. 1.

Rather they are Dryden's private recollections of a private reading of a private poem, a poem which came to function as the site of a memory which could never be effaced, and which needed to be repeatedly revisited, repeatedly transformed. Dryden is therefore rewriting both his own past and that of the nation, and to do this he breaks up Marvell's poem into pieces, into significant words and phrases too small to be perceptible by contemporaries, but too insistently repeated for the connections to be coincidental. As Marvell's poem about the breaking and rebuilding of the national fabric is itself broken up and rebuilt into the fabric of Dryden's verse, so that *aporia* in the nation's existence is drawn into a troubled and troubling connection with the present. The 'Horatian Ode' is thus placed under erasure—not effaced, but bracketed and marked as a text which is both impossible and crucial, one which has no lodging in the discourse of the present, yet is too heavily charged with significance for it ever to be wiped away. As for its author, he was written out of the visible record, for nowhere in his critical essays and prefaces does Dryden give Marvell a place in the lineage of English poets from Chaucer to the present which he repeatedly charts.[54]

THE QUASI-AUGUSTAN MOMENT OF *ASTRÆA REDUX*

Dryden's deployment of Latin to define and control his poetic territory is particularly evident in his use of epigraphs, for he controlled the approach to his poems through Latin quotations which were placed on the title pages, meeting the reader on the threshold.[55] This superliminary Latin marks (and at the same time conceals) the point at which the poet's own territory begins, covering the awkwardness and presumption of the transition from emptiness to writing, from the blank page to the English verse. It does more than announce a theme, for by making us pause on the threshold and read a text which both is and is not part of the work, whose origins we may not be able to place, and whose significance remains to be disclosed, it advertises the way the poem positions itself (and positions its subject and its readers) in time and space.

---

[54] When Dryden does mention Marvell, in the Preface to *Religio Laici*, it is as a scurrilous political pamphleteer in the lineage of Martin Marprelate (*Poems*, p. 308).

[55] For the importance of prefatory gestures see Gérard Genette, *Seuils* (Paris, 1987).

In *Astræa Redux* a quotation from Virgil's *Eclogue* IV proclaims the poem's mythological premiss: *Iam Redit & Virgo, Redeunt Saturnia Regna.*[56] Astræa, the goddess of justice, and with her the Golden Age, are returning to the earth. This quotation appears to mark our point of entry simultaneously into the poem and into the new age, effecting a perfect coincidence of the writing and the present. But through this epigraph announcing a return and a restoration, both the poem and the time become implicated in a tradition which had taken Virgil's eclogue on the birth of a child and applied it variously to the birth of Augustus, to the birth of Christ, to Elizabeth I, and to James I.[57] The present seems to be part of a history which is perceived typologically,[58] and yet the way in which Dryden handles the epigraph begins the poem's task of making us apprehend the strangeness of the present even as we greet the return of Charles, and with him the return of a recognizable language and mythology and time. Moreover, the pre-text to which Dryden refers here is itself handling the idea of the Golden Age in a strange way. Virgil's idea that the Golden Age could be restored was idiosyncratic and tendentious, for the ancients believed that the Golden Age was irretrievably lost. Nor, for Virgil, is the Golden Age completely realized: it will attain perfection as the child develops, and this idea of the perfectibility of the Golden Age is also Virgil's innovation.[59]

The reader starts with the present as addressed by Virgil: *Iam* ('now'). Indeed, this is a present created by Virgil, since through the work of his poem the Golden Age was made present: this was a performative speech act which sought to make the Golden Age return through the very act of announcing it. We then pass immediately from the Virgilian present to the present announced by the poem's first English line: 'Now with a general Peace . . .'.[60] We expect there to be a match between *Iam* and 'Now', so we read Dryden's 'Now' as the translation and fulfilment of Virgil's *Iam*.

---

[56] 'Now the virgin Astræa [goddess of Justice] returns, the kingdom of Saturn returns' (Virgil, *Ecloga*, iv. 6).   [57] *Poems*, ed. Hammond, i. 37.

[58] For Dryden's use of typology in his political poems see Steven N. Zwicker, *Dryden's Political Poetry: The Typology of King and Nation* (Providence, 1972).

[59] Wendell Clausen, *A Commentary on Virgil, 'Eclogues'* (Oxford, 1994), pp. 121, 125. Clausen also notes Virgil's management of time through the oddity of *uenit* ('has come': perfect tense) in l. 4: 'strictly speaking, the last age has not yet come, but the poet eagerly anticipates it' (p. 131).   [60] *Astræa Redux*, l. 1.

'Now' is May 1660, when Charles II is returning to England and Dryden's poem is addressing its first readers, and this is the moment in which the Golden Age of Saturn is brought back. But this reading is soon shown to be a misreading, an over-hasty translation from Latin to English, from past to present. As we read on, it turns out that the period referred to in the opening line is actually the hiatus preceding the Restoration, when other countries had recovered a Saturnian peace but England had not. Let us complete the quotation:

> Now with a general Peace the World was blest,
> While Ours, a World divided from the rest,
> A dreadful Quiet felt, and worser farre
> Then Armes, a sullen Intervall of Warre.[61]

That 'Now' turns out to be a false, or at least a premature, translation of *Iam*. The misreading prompted by the over-hasty movement from *Iam* to 'Now' is educative, reminding us that such a translation between cultures is not so easy. By stumbling on the threshold, we are made to recognize the complexity of reading the times mythologically. The moment when the peaceful present of Virgil's *Iam* can be replicated in England and in English is deferred. First we have to make a detour through a re-reading of history and another Latin pre-text, this time Virgil's *penitus toto divisos orbe Britannos*,[62] which furnishes Dryden's second line, 'a World divided from the rest'. In its original context the line had signalled the remoteness of the Britons from the centre of Roman power and civilization, and had—poignantly for many readers of *Astræa Redux*—been part of a passage in which the shepherd Meliboeus, ejected from his farm after it had been appropriated by the victors in the civil war, laments that he faces a life of exile in remote places with little chance of seeing his home again. Although the words had been quoted as a proud boast on the Fenchurch arch in James I's coronation entry,[63] Dryden's translation reminds us that the capacity of the nation to fulfil Latin pre-texts has its tragic dimension too.

The teasingly premature 'Now' of the opening line leads us into

---

[61] *Astræa Redux*, ll. 1–4.
[62] 'Britons almost cut off from the whole world' (Virgil, *Ecloga*, i. 67).
[63] *Poems*, ed. Hammond, i. 38.

a detour through an account of the untimeliness of the 1650s. This takes various forms. The poem's first couplet echoes Sir Richard Fanshawe's 'An Ode Upon occasion of His Majesties Proclamation in the yeare 1630. Commanding the Gentry to reside upon their Estates in the Country', which opens with the line 'Now warre is all the world about', and presents Britain as a haven of peace, a 'world without the world', a land apt to breed a new Virgil.[64] The echo links the two poems across the gulf of civil war, momentarily joining 1660 and 1630. Then the phrase 'sullen Intervall' characterizes the period as a moment within war which is itself unnamed and undefined. Moreover, the word 'sullen' has connotations which range beyond 'gloomy, melancholy' (*OED* 3) to include 'baleful, malignant' (*OED* 1d, twice citing Dryden for this usage) and 'passing heavily, moving sluggishly' (*OED* 3). In this interval, it seems, the stream of time itself moves with unusual slowness. The usual rhythm of the ages of man is disturbed, as the young envy their elders, who at least have known the pleasures of youth, whereas they themselves possess no such joys;[65] indeed, in a proleptic echo of the essay *Of Dramatick Poesie*,

> We thought our Sires, not with their own content,
> Had ere we came to age our Portion spent.[66]

In a world where the heir to the throne has been deprived of his inheritance, no one else is able to possess their heritage either. Booth's premature rebellion is contrasted with Monck's perception that the providentially ordained moment for action had at last arrived.[67] As for the Parliamentarian side, they are displaced from a coherent historiography and inserted into multiple narratives, incompatible times, repeating various mythological versions of the past, as Typhoeus, as the Cyclops, and as primitive, uncivilized Britons before the arrival of the Romans:

> They own'd a lawless salvage Libertie,
> Like that our painted Ancestours so priz'd
> Ere Empires Arts their Breasts had Civiliz'd.[68]

---

[64] Sir Richard Fanshawe, 'An Ode . . .', ll. 1, 34, 75–6; the echo was noted by Michael Cordner, 'Dryden's "Astræa Redux" and Fanshawe's "Ode"', *Notes and Queries*, 229 (1984) 341–2.   [65] *Astræa Redux*, ll. 25–6.

[66] Ibid., ll. 27–8; cp. *Works*, xvii. 73.

[67] *Astræa Redux*, ll. 145–50.   [68] Ibid., ll. 37, 45, 46–8.

As the principal contrast to the untimeliness of the Interregnum
years, Charles himself is made perfectly in touch with the movement of time and of history: unlike the presumptuous Otho he
does not force events,[69] and uses his exile in order to prepare the
ground for a reign in which his actions will not be rash but duly
ripened and timely.[70] Charles is made the master of time.

So Dryden's movement away from the promise held out in his
epigraph is a caution against fixing the meaning of the present until
the untimeliness of the recent past has been acknowledged. It is a
movement which contests those assumptions about providential
guidance which had been the daily rhetoric of the republic. The
period before the promise held out by that first Virgilian quotation
can be implemented is a fraught silence:

> An horrid Stillness first invades the ear,
> And in that silence Wee the Tempest fear.[71]

Dryden's contemporary critics ridiculed that first line,[72] but its
awkwardness is exact: the silence (for us as readers, it is the silence
between *Iam* and the much-deferred 'now') is precisely 'horrid' in
the Latin sense of 'bristling'; the silence of expectation is threatening, bristling with terrifying possibilities,[73] and invasive in taking
possession of the ear until the time has come for it to be ousted by
that longed-for word. The *Iam* does not find its proper fulfilment
in English until later in the poem, in the first line of the second
section, when the poem seems to begin again after the typographical break provided by a line space: 'And welcome now (*Great
Monarch*) to your own'.[74] Here *Iam* and 'now' join; the embarrass-
ing near-redundancy of welcoming Charles to that which is
already his own emphasizes the unnaturalness of that long deferral,
the hiatus of the Interregnum. The line fuses different forms of
present and presence—the poem's performative utterance of
welcome, the arrival of Charles on the shore, the return of the
Golden Age—as the King takes possession of that which he had
always and never owned.

For the poem to locate itself in the present, to locate the

---

[69] *Astræa Redux*, ll. 67–8.   [70] Ibid., ll. 88–9.
[71] Ibid., ll. 7–8.   [72] *Poems*, ed. Hammond, i. 38.
[73] Milton has Satan break the 'horrid silence' in hell: *Paradise Lost*, i. 83.
[74] *Astræa Redux*, l. 250.

present, to allow readers to take possession of this new time, a detour in time and space has been necessary. Such a detour is characteristic of the work of a preface, as Derrida suggests:

Mais comme *notre temps* n'est pas tout à fait, tout simplement propice à cette élévation, comme ce n'est pas encore tout à fait le moment, comme le moment, du moins, est inégal à lui-même, il faut encore le préparer et le faire se rejoindre à lui-même par une didactique; et si l'on considère que le moment est venu, il faut en faire prendre conscience, introduire à ce qui est déjà *là*; mieux: reconduire l'être-là au concept dont il est la présence temporelle et historique ou, circulairement, introduire le concept en son être-là. Un certain espacement entre le concept et l'être-là, entre le concept et l'existence, la pensée et le temps, tel serait le logement assez inqualifiable de la préface.[75]

Astræa Redux pauses on the threshold of the new reign; or, rather, on the threshold of the full realization of a reign which had nominally begun more than a decade earlier.[76] As a preface, it teaches us how to join the time up with itself, introducing us to what is already there, to what, at least, its rhetoric wishes us to see as an already existing state now newly presented to our understanding, rather than just another innovation. The detour through which the reader enters the present, recognizes the time as present, and reads the ordinary as significant, is a temporary exile, a preparatory correction of an over-hasty rush to cast the present into signs.

Such an untimely confidence is rebuked in *Astræa Redux*. Here the turn to Latin makes a detour around—so bracketing rather than directly engaging with—the language of the 1650s, including its classical republican idiom. What is being restored is not the government of the Stuart kings, but a mythologized *Pax Romana*, and so Dryden's turn accomplishes a movement out of time, into

---

[75] Jacques Derrida, *La Dissémination* (Paris, 1972), p. 19: 'But since *our time* is not exactly, not simply propitious for such an elevation, since it is not yet quite the right time, since the time, at any rate, is not equal to itself, it is still necessary to prepare it and make it join up with itself by didactic means; and if one judges that the time *has* come, one must make others aware of it and introduce them to what is already *there*; better yet: one must bring the being-there back to the concept of which it is the temporal, historical presence or, in a circular fashion, introduce the concept into its own being-there. A certain spacing between concept and being-there, between concept and existence, between thought and time, would thus constitute the rather unqualifiable lodging of the preface' (trans. Barbara Johnson, p. 12). I omit some parenthetical quotations of German terms.

[76] Charles II punctiliously dated his regnal years from 30 January 1649.

a version of classical culture and back into a recreated present. Though the citation of Astræa and the Golden Age does invite readers to recollect the Tudor and early Stuart applications of this myth, the poem remains unspecific as to when, in English history, this Golden Age might originally have been located. Too precise an encounter with history is evaded as Dryden concentrates on displacing the present into a malleable milieu in and out of time. He draws upon material from the *Aeneid* in calling for a sacrifice to Portunus and the Tempests,[77] but does not actually cast Charles in the role of Aeneas. Thomas Higgons, by contrast, had seen no difficulty in inserting Charles into the very text of the *Aeneid*, replacing *Hector* with CAROLE in lines which he placed on the title page of his poem of welcome:

> Quae tantae tenuere morae? queis CAROLE ab oris
> Expectate venis? ut te, post multa tuorum
> Funera, post varios hominumque urbisque labores
> Defessi aspicimus![78]

Those are the lines in which Aeneas addresses Hector, returning to his city after a long delay, but now as a ghost. Higgons's variation on Virgil perhaps wishes to effect a substitution of the real champion for the ghostly one, but it is symptomatic of the problems inherent in typological readings of history that when we contemplate the actual presence of the hero we are more aware of difference than of similarity. The two periods seem closer in their experience of destruction, and the delayed return of the hero, than in the return itself.

Dryden's poem is more attentive to the awkwardness of mythologizing. It figures Charles's assumption of power in these terms:

> The British *Amphitryte* smooth and clear
> In richer Azure never did appear;
> Proud her returning Prince to entertain
> With the submitted Fasces of the Main.[79]

---

[77] *Astræa Redux*, ll. 121–2; drawing on Virgil, *Aeneid*, v. 241–3, 772.

[78] Thomas Higgons, *A Panegyrick to the King* (1660), title-page; adapting Virgil, *Aeneid*, ii. 282–5: 'What great delay has detained you? From what regions have you come, longed-for Charles [originally 'Hector']? Weary we see you, after the deaths of many of your kin, after various troubles for the people and the city.'

[79] *Astræa Redux*, ll. 246–9.

Dryden's use of the unnaturalized Latin word *fasces* to represent power over the sea advertises the foreignness of the image. The phrase 'submitted Fasces' is virtually a quotation from Livy: when the consul Publius Valerius appeared before the people to answer charges of ambition his lictors walked before him with lowered fasces (*submissis fascibus*) as a sign of the people's superior authority.[80] The Latinity of Dryden's phrasing triggers our recollection of the Roman scene more insistently than an allusion would ordinarily do. What had originally been an anecdote which confessed the sovereignty of the people becomes, in this rewriting, a gesture in which the republican claims of the Commonwealth period are surrendered: both the Roman rhetoric of the *Heroique Stanza's* and the idea that the people are sovereign are made to submit. Through its turn to Rome, the image blots out our memory that the actual transition from republic to monarchy was messy, and that there were many who would not willingly have surrendered the *fasces* to Charles II. Indeed, there were some who would have preferred other ways of using an axe to greet a returning Stuart.

The poem ends with lines which invite readers to hear behind them the speech of Anchises prophesying the return of the Golden Age with Augustus:[81]

> Oh Happy Age! Oh times like those alone
> By Fate reserv'd for Great *Augustus* Throne!
> When the joint growth of Armes and Arts foreshew
> The World a Monarch, and that Monarch *You*.[82]

> Hic vir, hic est, tibi quem promitti saepius audis,
> Augustus Caesar, Divum genus; aurea condet
> Saecula qui rursus Latio, regnata per arva
> Saturno quondam.[83]

---

[80] Livy, *Ab Urbe Condita*, ii. 7.

[81] For discussions of the deployment of Augustan mythology see Howard Erskine-Hill, *The Augustan Idea in English Literature* (London, 1983); and H. T. Swedenberg, '*Astræa Redux* in its Setting', *Studies in Philology*, 50 (1953) 30–44.

[82] *Astræa Redux*, ll. 320–3.

[83] Virgil, *Aeneid*, vi. 791–4: 'This man, this is he whom you have often heard promised to you, Augustus Caesar, of a divine race, he shall restore again the Golden Age which once in the reign of Saturn flourished in Latium.'

Through his turn to Latin, and by insisting on his detour, Dryden has translated the moment of the Restoration not into a ready-made mythology but into a present which we see being made. And in this conclusion the time is at last aligned with the time of Augustus, the god who was present among men.[84] The poem comes to rest in singleness: there is one precedent 'alone' for this age, and there is only one monarch for the world.

THE COLLOCATION OF LONDON, ROME, AND TROY IN *ANNUS MIRABILIS*

Like *Astræa Redux*, *Annus Mirabilis* (1667) has a Latin title.[85] In this case Dryden chooses a phrase which had been deployed principally by the Nonconformist opposition to the court, who were using the term *annus mirabilis* as part of their vocabulary of prophecy and apocalypse.[86] For them the times were full of wonders which could only be read as signs of God's judgement upon the sins of the nation. The phrase thus subjects the present to interpretation, to a single and apparently incontestable interpretation which sees the historical moment opening towards the apocalyptic end of time: *chronos* is seen exclusively as *kairos*, the human present as the time in which God intervenes.[87] In appropriating their phrase and redefining its application, Dryden is asserting control simultaneously over the use of Latin and over the apprehension of time: Latin will now be used with his field of connotations, the wonders of the present will be expounded in his way. The poem's full title is worth citing:[88]

---

[84] One of the phrases associated with Augustus was *praesens divus*, 'the god who is present' (Horace, *Carmina*, III. v. 2), by contrast with the distant Olympian gods (Galinsky, *Augustan Culture*, p. 314).

[85] The following discussion of *Annus Mirabilis* adapts some material from my more detailed account of the poem's use of classical sources in 'John Dryden: The Classicist as Sceptic', *The Seventeenth Century*, 4 (1989) 165–87.

[86] *Poems*, ed. Hammond, i. 106–7; see also Michael McKeon, *Poetry and Politics in Restoration England* (Cambridge, Mass., 1975).

[87] In classical Greek, *chronos* is the ordinary word for time, while *kairos* is the right time, the critical moment; in Christian theology *kairos* is human time apprehended as witnessing to divine purpose, inflected via a sense of *archē* and *telos*.

[88] For the importance of this and other title pages in inducting the reader into Dryden's poems, see John Barnard, 'Dryden: History and "The Mighty Government of the Nine"', *University of Leeds Review*, 84 (1981) 13–42.

ANNUS MIRABILIS:
The Year of
WONDERS,
1666.
AN HISTORICAL
POEM:
CONTAINING
The Progress and various Successes of our Naval War with *Holland*,
under the Conduct of His Highness Prince RUPERT, and His Grace the
Duke of ALBEMARL.
And describing
THE FIRE
OF
LONDON.

This focuses our attention on a particular year, stressing one kind
of time, effecting a form of translation between the lapidary Latin
title and the descriptive English text, so advertising the historicity
of the poem more than its mythographic purpose. This poem
about a specific city and a specific year enacts a displacement of
London into an imagined, semi-classical space. Dryden's poem
brings into play a Latin hinterland of his own definition (his own
tellus), and in particular summons up the Roman values encapsu-
lated in the term *pietas*.[89] The word 'pious' echoes through *Annus
Mirabilis*, playing against Puritan definitions of the word by evoking the values denoted by its etymological Latin root in *pius*: reverence for the gods, the nation, and the family.[90] In this way Dryden
is effecting an internal translation within English, moving us from
one part of the word's semantic field to another. The English stanzas are accompanied by occasional Latin quotations which remind
us of the corpus of Roman texts from which Dryden is drawing.
By weaving fragments of Latin around the English poetry, making
these words part of the fabric of his poem, Dryden is once again
staking out the ground of reading: instead of the Latin texts being

---

[89] For this idea see James D. Garrison, *'Pietas' from Vergil to Dryden* (University Park,
Pa., 1992).

[90] The commanders who shield Albemarle from his enemies stretch out 'their pious
wings' (l. 255); Rupert seeks to aid his comrades with the 'pious care' of an eagle for its
young (l. 425); the City of London makes a present of a ship to the King, a gesture which
is 'piously design'd' (l. 613); and Charles himself sheds 'pious tears' for the plight of his
people (l. 958).

confined to the writer's memory, forming only the secret scene of writing, they are selectively laid out for us to see. Thus they begin to define the ground of interpretation. But these citations by no means exhaust the poem's Latin connections, as Dryden makes clear in his preface when he says that he has not noted all his borrowings.[91] So the marginalia open out the field of reference, prompting the reader to make his own exploration of the poem's classical hinterland.

This ground of interpretation contrasts with Puritan epistemology by insisting on plurality and on the difficulty of attaining secure knowledge. Richard Kroll has argued that oppositional groups often held a dogmatic view of knowledge, whereas discourse which was more closely linked to the established political structures (such as that of the Royal Society) tended to deploy a more contingent epistemology. Moreover, says Kroll,

if knowledge is merely contingent, then various ethical or political positions can be made known or realized only by juxtaposing a series of figures in the political landscape. This has two consequences: no individual can claim to map the entire political territory: such a claim itself implies a false epistemology. And because on this view political claims can be established only by marking a position within that territory, those claims that pretend to some traffic with noumenal (so private or gnostic) grounds of knowledge become impotent, because their premises cannot be opened to public trade.[92]

And Kroll also suggests that sceptical philosophy in the Restoration characteristically envisages an epistemological scene or space:

If we can thus imagine scepticism creating the conditions for certain narrative possibilities, it also encouraged the Restoration to speak of knowledge as inhabiting a *scene* . . . knowledge-as-we-have-it is frequently represented as occupying or creating a space, an architectonic fabric composed of discrete, atomic components . . . this model . . . imagines the possibility of anatomizing and analyzing the constituent elements of knowledge, prior to reassembling them either logically or temporally into some desired edifice.[93]

---

[91] *Poems*, p. 48.
[92] Richard W. F. Kroll, *The Material Word: Literate Culture in the Restoration and Early Eighteenth Century* (Baltimore, 1991), pp. 16–17.   [93] Kroll, p. 56.

Annus Mirabilis is just such a sceptical text. Dryden said that he was 'naturally inclin'd to Scepticism in Philosophy' in the Preface to *Religio Laici*.[94] As Phillip Harth has explained,[95] 'Scepticism' here refers to modesty and diffidence in inquiry, as advocated by the Royal Society and others, rather than to the sceptical approach to epistemology which derives from Greek philosophy and is exemplified by Montaigne. The opposite to 'scepticism' in this sense would be dogmatism. Dryden defines the mode of argument of his essay *Of Dramatick Poesie* as

Sceptical, according to that way of reasoning which was used by *Socrates*, *Plato*, and all the Academiques of old, which *Tully* and the best of the Ancients followed, and which is imitated by the modest Inquisitions of the Royal Society . . . it is a Dialogue sustain'd by persons of several opinions, all of them left doubtful, to be determined by the Readers.[96]

In *Annus Mirabilis* (which is roughly contemporaneous with the essay) the dialogic play of voices is replaced by a play of allusion: it juxtaposes figures from contemporary England and ancient Rome, complicating the way we try to read the one against the other by making that Rome multiple, an intermittent presence brought into the text through citations of different, discontinuous parts of its history, alongside quotations from Virgil's mythologized narrative of Roman origins in the *Aeneid*. The scene which Dryden lays out in this poem is a scene of knowledge—or perhaps more accurately, a scene of epistemological interrogation and experiment. The scene is constituted partly through this association of England and Rome, an association which is at once multiple and deficient, where we become aware of gaps as much as connections, of unlikeness as much as likeness, of tensions in the metaphorical fit. As Kroll remarks,

unlike an a priori figure of identity (a form of determinism), the neoclassical example achieves only a modified authority or power, because analogy is as much *unlike* as *like* what the perceiver already knows, so his or her movement across the gap this difference creates respects the reader's individual integrity because it can only be made willingly.[97]

---

[94] *Poems*, p. 302.
[95] Phillip Harth, *Contexts of Dryden's Thought* (Chicago, 1968), pp. 1–31; see also *Poems*, ed. Hammond, ii. 86–7. [96] *Works*, ix. 15.
[97] Kroll, *The Material Word*, p. 77.

The poem is sceptical about claims for any grasp of the noumenal as a ground for understanding the contingencies of the present, and sets Christian providential vocabulary alongside a classical language of Fortune and Fate. The individual, discrete elements of the poem's narrative and of its philosophical vision work against any systematizing epistemology, handing over to the reader the responsibility for working through this collection of disparate possibilities, and for building his own epistemological structure. However, the local and cumulative effect of *Annus Mirabilis* is to solicit the structures of explanation as they emerge. The multiple differences of time and culture, the evident awkwardness of the fit between the constituent elements of any metaphor or simile, reveal the work of *différance*, which moves against the ostensible solidity of structure.

Rome appears in this poem as a plural site, both historical and mythological. The double epigraphs initiate the reader simultaneously into the poem and into its complex epistemological space through their collocation of the historical and the mythologized. First we have a quotation from the Emperor Trajan writing to Pliny: *Multum interest res poscat, an homines latius imperare velint.*[98] This asks us to make a moral distinction between actions which are necessary responses to the demands of the moment, and those which are motivated by a desire to extend one's power: it is therefore an invitation to read public actions in order to evaluate their moral character, and to avoid approving military exploits which are designed purely for personal or national aggrandizement. It is a caution against imperial ambitions. The second epigraph is drawn from a contrasting, even competing, discourse: *Urbs antiqua ruit, multos dominata per annos.*[99] This begins the work of myth by aligning London and Troy, but the parallel is inexact: the city of Troy was burnt during, and as a result of, a humiliating war; the city of London was burnt during, but *not* as a result of, a humiliating war. War and fire are causally linked in Virgil's poem, whereas in Dryden's they are only chronologically linked, even if

[98] '[The validity of a course of action] depends very much upon whether the occasion demands it, or men are [just] eager to extend their power more widely' (Pliny, *Epistulae*, x. 22).

[99] 'The ancient city falls, having dominated for many years' (Virgil, *Aeneid*, ii. 363).

the implication that trial by water is followed by trial by fire gives the narrative a broad symbolic pattern. (A classic romance pattern would require a third, decisive, trial, but this is unavailable; the structure remains incomplete.[100]) So the Virgilian quotation sits awkwardly in the contemporary text, or at least the range of its application is limited. And reading the two epigraphs together, we begin to see that the plurality of Latin citations makes a coherent mythologizing impossible. The collocation of London and Troy in that word *Urbs* is only temporary.

No one period of Roman history provides a pre-text for *Annus Mirabilis*. The first classical parallel within the poem itself is with republican Rome and its wars with Carthage:

> Thus mighty in her Ships, stood *Carthage* long,
> And swept the riches of the world from far;
> Yet stoop'd to *Rome*, less wealthy, but more strong:
> And this may prove our second Punick War.[101]

The phrasing is anticipatory but tentative: 'this may prove' is not the grammar of prophecy. And against this brief hope that the emplotment of the present may turn out to replicate the emplotment of the Punic Wars, there are several citations of Roman history which emphasize the Romans' endurance of defeat. The marginal quotations invite us to interpret the reverses suffered by the navy not as instances of God's judgement but as occasions for the display of Roman virtues, when the English commanders matched their Roman predecessors in their courageous response to adversity. Albemarle's calm defiance of the Dutch who are encircling him compels in them an admiration comparable to the wonder of the Gauls who entered Rome to find the elders sitting motionless in their chairs:

> At this excess of courage, all amaz'd,
> The foremost of his foes a while withdraw.
> With such respect in enter'd *Rome* they gaz'd,
> Who on high Chairs the God-like Fathers saw.[102]

---

[100] Ironically, the burning by the Dutch of the English fleet in the Medway in 1667, just months after the publication of *Annus Mirabilis*, would have provided Dryden with a third trial by water and fire together. Instead it provided material for the opposition poets like Marvell in *Last Instructions to a Painter*.

[101] *Annus Mirabilis*, ll. 17–20.   [102] Ibid., ll. 249–52.

At this moment, when he needs to describe the innermost space of
Rome being invaded, Dryden moves his English close to Latin. His
phrase 'entered Rome' is a participial construction imitated from
Latin; 'godlike' translates Livy's description of the elders sitting like
gods (*simillimos diis*), while 'fathers' translates *patres*, the Roman
honorific for senators.[103] Reading the Latin historians in his school-
days would have accustomed Dryden to the idea that Rome
achieved greatness by knowing how to bring victory out of defeat;
the epitome of Roman history by Lucius Florus, for example,
emplots the narrative of military triumphs and disasters to emphasize this lesson: *Tot in laboribus periculisque tactatus est, ut ad constituen-
dum eius imperium contendisse Virtus et Fortuna videantur.*[104] Dryden
underlines this view by quoting the tribute to the Romans which
Horace makes Hannibal speak in *Carmina*, IV. iv: the Dutch retire,

> Proud to have so got off with equal stakes,
> *Where 'twas a triumph not to be o'r-come.

★ *From* Horace: Quos opimus fallere & effugere est triumphus.[105]

Horace's poem is a tribute to Drusus, the stepson of Augustus, on
his Alpine victories, and recalls the defeat which his ancestor had
inflicted on Hasdrubal. The Romans' victory that day on the
banks of the river Metaurus was a turning point in their history:

> Post hoc secundis vsque laboribus
> Romana pubes crevit & impio
>   Vastata Poenorum tumultu
>   Fana Deos habuere rectos:
> Dixitque tandem profidus Annibal,
> Cerui luporum praeda rapacium
>   Sectamur vltro quos opimus
>   Fallere, & effugere est triumphus.[106]

---

[103] Livy, *Ab Urbe Condita*, v. 41; *Poems*, ed. Hammond, ii. 147.

[104] 'By so many toils and dangers have they been buffeted that Valour and Fortune
seem to have competed to establish the Roman empire' (Lucius Florus, *Epitome Bellorum
Omnium Annorum DCC*, i, Intro. 2).

[105] '[The wolves] which it is the richest triumph for us to deceive and escape' (Horace,
Carmina, IV. iv. 51–2); *Annus Mirabilis*, ll. 535–6.

[106] 'From that day the Roman manhood plucked momentum and marched from
strength to strength. The shrines that Carthage barbarously laid waste, refurbished saw the
gods stand upright again; till the perfidious Hannibal in despair cried, "We are like deer,
predestined prey, who yet would run after ravening wolves. Triumph for us lies in retreat
and stealth"' (Horace, *Carmina*, IV. iv. 45–52).

This is a defining moment: after it (*post hoc . . .*) Roman history takes a different course, and the shrines of the gods, the symbolic heart of Rome once devastated by her enemies, are restored. The alignment of this pre-text with the present described by the English lines of Dryden's poem is in one respect clear enough: as Hannibal acknowledges the superior strength and tenacity of the Romans, so the Dutch are made to confess the same of the English by their tactical withdrawal. But the poem cannot do more than hint that the parallel may extend further, that the devastated shrines will be restored, and that time will begin anew from this point. The suggested emplotment is inevitably tentative, and cannot be sustained.

Annus Mirabilis draws into the texture of the poem a number of citations from Virgil. Some of these come from the *Aeneid*, and reach back to the loss of the originary home. Sir William Berkeley loses his way like Creüsa;[107] Albemarle, like Aeneas, attempts to look hopeful while inwardly grieving at the fate of his men;[108] Prince Rupert, again like Aeneas, is alarmed by every little noise because of his fears for his comrades' safety.[109] This is far from being an heroic inflation of the present, and is rather a sober appraisal of what heroism means, what responsibility entails. This is not to say that Dryden's comments on the commanders were necessarily justified by the individuals' actual conduct, which in some cases was less than exemplary, but because the poem multiplies the points of comparison it avoids glorifying a single figure. Rupert is like Aeneas in his alarm, but on his disabled ship he is also like Ovid's exhausted hare unable to escape from the equally exhausted dog which is pursuing her.[110] Albemarle is like Turnus, stubbornly refusing to yield, as a lion refuses to give ground to his hunters; he is like Achilles in one of Horace's odes; but on his disabled ship he makes only painful headway like the wounded snake which Virgil describes in the *Georgics*.[111] Virgil is also used

---

[107] *Annus Mirabilis*, ll. 267–8; cp. Virgil, *Aeneid*, ii. 735–95.
[108] *Annus Mirabilis*, l. 292. Dryden's marginal note here cites Virgil: the reference is to *Aeneid*, i. 209. [109] *Annus Mirabilis*, ll. 435–6; cp. Virgil, *Aeneid*, ii. 726–9.
[110] *Annus Mirabilis*, ll. 521–8, drawing on Ovid, *Metamorphoses*, i. 533–42.
[111] Like Turnus and like a lion: *Annus Mirabilis*, ll. 381–4, drawing on Virgil, *Aeneid*, ix. 791–8. Like Achilles: *Annus Mirabilis*, l. 384, drawing on Horace, *Carmina*, I. vi. 6. Like a wounded snake: *Annus Mirabilis*, ll. 491–2, drawing on Virgil, *Georgics*, iii. 423–4.

to bring the ordinary sailors into the sphere of this steady, painful heroism, as they

> Rouze conscious vertue up in every heart,
>   *And seeming to be stronger makes them so.

  * Possunt quia posse videntur. *Virg.*[112]

The phrase 'conscious vertue' not only employs Latinate vocabulary, it is a virtual quotation of Virgil's *conscia virtus*. And the very difficulty of operating in the conditions of war is imaged with a borrowing from Virgil when Dryden says that the sailors are frustrated by 'doubtful Moon-light', Virgil's *per incertam lunam*.[113]

As the tragedies of individual lives are related to classical pretexts, the present is seen to be shaped by forces beyond man's control. Lines adapted from the *Satyricon* speak of the pain suffered by the captured sailor and those who longed for his return, and see this predicament as part of a general human condition:

> Such are the proud designs of human kind,
>   And so we suffer Shipwrack every where!
> Alas, what Port can such a Pilot find,
>   Who in the night of Fate must blindly steer!
>
> The undistinguish'd seeds of good and ill
>   Heav'n, in his bosom, from our knowledge hides;
> And draws them in contempt of human skill,
>   Which oft, for friends, mistaken foes provides.[114]

The tone and import of this stanza are repeated later:

> In fortunes Empire blindly thus we go,
>   And wander after pathless destiny:
> Whose dark resorts since prudence cannot know
>   In vain it would provide for what shall be.[115]

However hard man may try to establish his own empires by trade or war, and seek to map his territory through scientific inquiry,[116] he remains a blind wanderer in the pathless empire of Fortune.

---

[112] *Annus Mirabilis*, ll. 759–60, drawing on Virgil, *Aeneid*, v. 455 and v. 231.

[113] *Annus Mirabilis*, l. 272, drawing on Virgil, *Aeneid*, vi. 270.

[114] *Annus Mirabilis*, ll. 137–44. Dryden's marginal note to line 137 cites Petronius: the reference is to *Satyricon*, 115.   [115] *Annus Mirabilis*, ll. 797–800.

[116] See the 'Apostrophe to the Royal Society', *Annus Mirabilis*, ll. 657–64.

Dryden thus uses a classical philosophical vocabulary to recall the limitations of human knowledge and insight, and the poem repeatedly reminds us of the importance of what may be happening beyond the reach of our vision. There may be sand flats just below the surface of apparently deep water; fate is 'unseen'; the Fire of London was 'obscurely bred'.[117] The flames eventually emerge from unknowable depths:

> In this deep quiet, from what source unknown,
>   Those seeds of fire their fatal birth disclose:[118]

By contrast, the Royal Society is said to 'behold the Law, | And rule of beings in your Makers mind',[119] and the poem itself seems to know the actions of God when, in a notorious image, it presents him extinguishing the Fire of London with a celestial candle-snuffer.[120] Can such metaphysical wit be accepted, in 1667, as a mode of knowledge, as it might have been by Donne? And how secure do such knowledges seem when they are read not as isolated claims but as part of the fabric of the poem? The epistemological scene which Dryden lays out for us shifts us between Christian and classical vocabularies, between confident knowledge and confessed blunders. The whole is a structure without structurality.

Structure is on occasion imagined in *Annus Mirabilis* with help from Ovid, and for the poem to figure structure via the *Metamorphoses* is to confess its provisionality, its openness to transformation. The phrase 'seeds of fire' is translated from Ovid's *semina flammae*[121] in a passage describing the changeability of the earth herself. Then Dryden links the fire which ravaged London with the apocalyptic fire which will one day destroy the whole earth, citing as his source the passage in the *Metamorphoses* where Jove remembers that the fates have decreed that heaven, earth, and sea will one day be consumed by fire.[122] The Latin citation helps to remind readers that this evocation of apocalypse is a poetic conceit, a pleasing fabrication, not a sour Puritan denunciation. Other lines on the growth of the fire echo Ovid on the growth of

---

[117] *Annus Mirabilis*, ll. 450–2; 839; 858.   [118] Ibid., ll. 865–6.
[119] Ibid., ll. 661–2.   [120] *Annus Mirabilis*, ll. 1117–24.
[121] Ovid, *Metamorphoses*, xv. 347.
[122] *Annus Mirabilis*, ll. 847–8; alluding to Ovid, *Metamorphoses*, i. 257–8.

the child.[123] This poem about metamorphosis needs to draw upon
Ovid's vision of how structures change.

Played against this vision are quotations woven together from
Virgil which speak of the building of structures:

> All hands employ'd, ★the Royal work grows warm,
>   Like labouring Bees on a long Summers day,
> Some sound the Trumpet for the rest to swarm,
>   And some on bells of tasted Lillies play:

★ Fervet opus: *the same similitude in* Virgil.

> With glewy wax some new foundation lay
>   Of Virgin combs, which from the roof are hung:
> Some arm'd within doors, upon duty stay,
>   Or tend the sick, or educate the young.[124]

Dryden's own note here refers us back to Virgil's simile in the
Aeneid, where the Carthaginians building the walls of their city are
compared to bees, and besides this overt allusion Dryden's lines
also draw material from two other passages where Virgil is describing the work of bees.[125] So alongside an evocation of the fragility
of our political and conceptual structures, Dryden builds out of his
classical pre-texts some tentative new forms.

Through the work of citation, the nation's history and the
nation's present are both redefined, but neither redefinition
happens in a way which allows an easy apprehension of history or
presence. Dryden uses his Latin references to shape a discontinuous territory, an imagined world of his own creation in which
London and Rome, Charles II and Scipio, Fortune and divine
Providence can be placed side by side. Yet this collocation is not
the weaving of a new fabric, for it makes the fabric of the text an
irregular reticulation of past and present. The texture of the poem,
with the Latin jostling the English, sets *différance* in play.

A poem which has offered a complex, discontinuous epistemological space cannot conclude simply, and the ending of *Annus
Mirabilis* offers a version of the present which is both temporally
and culturally diverse. The poet speaks *in propria persona* as he
delivers a vision of the new city:

---

[123] *Annus Mirabilis*, ll. 869–72 draws upon *Metamorphoses*, xv. 218–24.
[124] *Annus Mirabilis*, ll. 573–80; drawing upon *Aeneid*, i. 430–6.
[125] Virgil, *Aeneid*, vi. 707–9; *Georgics*, iv. 160–3.

Me-thinks already, from this Chymick flame,
   I see a City of more precious mold:
Rich as the Town which gives the *Indies name,
   With Silver pav'd, and all divine with Gold.

* *Mexico.*

Already, Labouring with a mighty fate,
   She shakes the rubbish from her mounting brow,
And seems to have renew'd her Charters date,
   Which Heav'n will to the death of time allow.

More great then humane, now, and more *August*,
   New deifi'd she from her fires does rise:[126]

* Augusta, *the old name of* London.

This is the poet's prophetic vision, of a proud city renewed by fire, a contrast with Puritan visions of a sinful city destroyed by fire (if not brimstone), and Dryden's imagery even suggests that this is a secular version of the new Jerusalem.[127] Time itself is renewed, first through an astrological change as the positions of the planets become more auspicious,[128] then through the renewal of a charter which transcends the charter of the city's privileges granted by the King, and is now guaranteed by heaven itself until the end of time. And yet the present tense which Dryden employs in these stanzas is a present held in suspense as it is contained within the syntax of poetic vision: 'Methinks I see' is the phrase which governs all the temporal perception which follows, making that present in which the city is renewed a special kind of time, an optative moment which can only exist (or even be imagined) within a poetic structure. It is within this implicit (but concealed) optative mood that the city is renamed, made 'more *August*', recovering an ancient name which signals a link to the Rome of Augustus. And another form of mythologized history is brought into play as London is also likened to a 'Maiden Queen', with the further implication that the time which is now beginning is the renewal of an Elizabethan Golden Age of imperial and mercantile glory. At this point Dryden's language takes on an Elizabethan colouration, with its evocations of a shepherdess bathing by a river's side, and of the

---

[126] *Annus Mirabilis*, ll. 1169–78.
[127] 'And the street of the city was pure gold' (Revelation 21: 21).
[128] *Annus Mirabilis*, ll. 1165–8.

silver Thames courting its mistress.[129] The final stanzas remind us that our human time, the time of our national project, is incomplete even as the poem ends: 'Already we have conquer'd half the War, | And the less dang'rous part is left behind'.[130] This is itself a rendering of Virgil: *Hinc adeo media est nobis via*.[131] So the inevitable incompleteness of the poem is signalled by means of a momentary return to Virgil.

But the poem includes another, more serious return to Virgil, to a more tragic incompletion. This is the first poem in the Dryden canon to touch those threads which lead back towards the site of greatest loss, the originary dispossession. When Dryden approaches the sacred symbols of the home, he turns to Latin. In their ruined houses the dispossessed citizens of London forlornly 'watch the Vestal fire' and, as the flames retire, the 'little Lares creep' out from the desolate hearths.[132] The unnaturalized Latin brings a note of strangeness into this evocation of the domestic, particularly 'Lares', for which one has to use the right Latin pronunciation if the English line is to work metrically. When the Londoners seek again their destroyed homes, Dryden makes them the subjects of the Latinate verbs 'require' (meaning 'search for') and 'repeat' (meaning 'seek again'),[133] both of which are unusual. This vocabulary asks us to look elsewhere for the significance of the present, to seek it, in fact, in the burning ruins of Troy: 'repeat' is not merely a Latinate usage, it is an echo of Aeneas' words as he relates the destruction of his home: *urbem repeto*, 'I seek the city again'.[134] Understanding the significance of the destroyed home entails seeking again that first destroyed home, the city of Troy.

This citation of Latin origins brings them into the text without making them recoverable and placing them within our grasp: one cannot move back across the threshold to the sacred source. Even if we limit our discussion of such loss and estrangement to that form of it which is intrinsic to writing, one cannot undo the

---

[129] *Annus Mirabilis*, ll. 1181–92. [130] Ibid., ll. 1209–10.
[131] 'Here we have half our way' (Virgil, *Ecloga*, ix. 59).
[132] *Annus Mirabilis*, ll. 1025, 1127–8. The Lares (the word is disyllabic) were the Roman tutelary gods of the hearth or home, and were also the guardians of crossroads, travellers, and the state itself. [133] Ibid., ll. 1022, 1128.
[134] Virgil, *Aeneid*, ii. 749.

history that inheres in language, a series of traces of lost works, broken forms: one cannot tear Latin out of the fabric of English, nor remove Virgil from the pre-texts which make English poetry possible. Filial piety forbids it. Nor, conversely, can one move out of English entirely into Latin: the time for that has passed. Within our native language there will always be filaments which lead back towards another unattainable home, a site which is at once most familiar and most strange, simultaneously *heimlich* and *unheimlich*. We ourselves speak a language that is foreign.

LATIN PRECEDENTS FOR CONTEMPORARY POLITICS IN *ABSALOM AND ACHITOPHEL*

Absalom and Achitophel (1681) begins with an epigraph from Horace which invites the reader to make a close perusal of the poem:

> —Si Propius stes
> Te Capiet Magis—[135]

That a close reading of *Absalom and Achitophel* would have included an acknowledgement of its Latin pre-texts is evident from the two contemporary Latin translations of the poem, both of which recognize some of Dryden's Latin sources and work them into their own versions.[136] A further example of a contemporary reading which was sympathetically attentive to the poem's Latinity is provided by Nahum Tate in his commendatory verses for the third edition of *Absalom and Achitophel*, published in 1682. Noting Dryden's struggle with the English language, his difficulty in finding or fashioning an appropriate idiom, Tate remarks that Dryden solved this problem by turning to Virgil:

> Our Language fail'd beneath his rising Thought:
> This checks not his Attempt, for *Maro*'s Mines,
> He dreins of all their Gold t' adorn his Lines;
> Through each of which the *Mantuan Genius* shines . . .

---

[135] 'If you stand nearer it will please you more' (Horace, *Ars Poetica*, ll. 361–2).

[136] *Absalon et Achitophel. Carmine Latino Heroico* [trans. William Coward] (Oxford, 1682); *Absalon et Achitophel. Poema Latino Carmine Donatum* [trans. Francis Atterbury] (Oxford, 1682). Details of the translators' recognition of Dryden's sources are given in subsequent notes.

> Thus on our stubborn Language he prevails,
> And makes the *Helicon* in which he sails.
> The Dialect, as well as Sense, invents,
> And, with his Poem, a new Speech presents.[137]

Even allowing for the polemical inflation of Tate's phrasing, the recognition that Virgil shines through Dryden's lines is important. Tate was right to see that Dryden has fashioned a new poetic language in *Absalom and Achitophel*, and however significant the biblical and Miltonic vocabularies may be in this new language (and Tate also recognized the Miltonic element in the poem[138]) Dryden is repeatedly asking us, his classically-trained readers, to hear Latin behind his English, thus distancing his work from the biblically-informed political discourse as defined by Milton and his Whig heirs. Biblical allegory is reappropriated, and at the same time transformed into a subtly different genre as it is mixed with a recurrent thread of classical pre-texts. The authority of the Nonconformist exegetes is contested by an appeal to a wider frame of reference, a more intelligent and cultivated hermeneutics. Thus the potential or ideal readership is quite narrowly defined, since although most contemporaries would have been able to appreciate the broad application of the biblical allegory, the interweaving of this with Latin allusions supposes a sophisticated readership capable first of understanding and then of practising that Horatian invitation to read closely. Readers are expected to identify Latin pre-texts and to ponder their significance. In the opening passage there are examples of Latinate vocabulary which subtly alert the reader to this thread: 'pious', 'ungratefull', 'Conscious'.[139] And

---

[137] *Works*, ii. 471. Dr David Hopkins points out to me that Tate is echoing Thomas Carew's 'An Elegie upon the death of the Deane of Pauls, D^r. Iohn Donne': 'to the awe of thy imperious wit | Our stubborne language bends' (ll. 49–50).

[138] Tate's opening phrase, 'Hail Heav'n-born Muse!' has a Miltonic ring, while the reference to the fanatics' idol Dagon lying shattered as a result of the impact of Dryden's lines suggests an allusion to *Samson Agonistes* which appropriates and reverses Milton's typology. Nathaniel Lee in his commendatory poem makes the comparison explicit: 'As if a *Milton* from the dead arose, | Fil'd off his Rust, and the right Party chose' (*Works*, ii. 469–70).

[139] *Absalom and Achitophel*, ll. 1, 12, 21. Dryden uses 'ungrateful' in the Latin sense 'not responding to cultivation' previously unrecorded in English by the *OED*, and 'conscious' in the Latinate sense 'self-aware'. The latter meaning is not unusual in this period, but Dryden is closely following Latin usage, e.g. Virgil's *conscia virtus*, 'conscious [i.e. self-aware,

there are also phrases which acquire an additional significance if we trace them back to their source. When Dryden speaks in the Preface of the prospect that the body politic may need surgery, his phrase *ense rescindendum* ('must be cut away with the knife') is more than a common tag, it is a quotation from Jove's speech in Ovid[140] about the measures which have become necessary after the rebellion of the giants and the rejection of piety and justice by men. The context of that quotation provides a further placing of the Whig opposition.

In bringing these classical Roman references into his textual world, Dryden is also contesting the way in which Roman history (particularly the degenerate days of the Roman empire) had been invoked by opposition satirists to characterize Charles II.[141] Dryden's use of classical examples and vocabulary challenges not only the analogies themselves (Charles as Nero, Commodus, Domitian, Sardanapalus) but the actual mode of constructing analogies with the simple implication that one example can be read off against another, one foreshadow or repeat another. In place of these forceful but unsubtle parallels, Dryden constructs his own imagined world, multiple and discontinuous, in which the nation and its time are redefined, transposed into a milieu which he has fashioned, where Restoration England, biblical Israel, classical Rome, and the Miltonic universe are mixed. No longer will the opposition's vocabulary be the medium in which the nation is imagined, nor will their hermeneutics or historiography pass unchallenged. The time of the nation has been reimagined.

The opening lines of the poem,

> In pious times, e'r Priest-craft did begin,
> Before *Polygamy* was made a sin;[142]

---

deliberate] virtue' (*Aeneid*, v. 455; x. 872; xii. 668); cp. Dryden's use of 'conscious virtue' in *Annus Mirabilis*, l. 759. Coward's translation responds to this vocabulary by using the Latin equivalents: *pias, ingratum*, and *conscia* (pp. 1–2). Atterbury's translation responds similarly in the first two cases (p. 1).

[140] Ovid, *Metamorphoses*, i. 190–1.

[141] For the oppositional use of Roman allusions see Paul Hammond, 'The King's Two Bodies: Representations of Charles II' in *Culture, Politics and Society in Britain, 1660–1800*, ed. Jeremy Black and Jeremy Gregory (Manchester, 1991), pp. 13–46, esp. p. 31.

[142] *Absalom and Achitophel*, ll. 1–2.

introduce us to a time which is outside the time of standard biblical narrative, since the biblical priesthood originated with Aaron long before the period of King David.[143] We enter a fictionalized history in which the temporality of the familiar biblical narrative is suspended, and this facilitates our reception of it as a displaced version of our own present. It is also a version of the state of nature, that mythic pre-cultural time when there was no distinction between *meum* and *tuum*. Another form of the state of nature appears shortly afterwards, as the Interregnum is recalled as a time when men 'led their wild desires to Woods and Caves, | And thought that all but Savages were Slaves'.[144] The link between these two, incompatible, versions of the state of nature is mythological rather than chronological, for the state of nature can hardly be located at a precise point in time: it is, as Hobbes acknowledges in his deployment of the trope, a conceptual rather than an historical stage.[145] In translating English history into this doubled and fractured time, Dryden displaces Whig historiography and prophecy. Moreover, the use of 'pious' in the opening line, with its Roman semantic hinterland, presents an alternative to Whig and extreme Protestant terminology. With its Virgilian overtones (which the poem will bring into play as it progresses) the word signals that the time of this narrative (and the imaginative geography of this poem) will not be exclusively biblical.

The version of the state of nature which represents the Interregnum brings together two passages from Latin poetry:

> These *Adam*-wits, too fortunately free,
> Began to dream they wanted libertie;
> And when no rule, no president was found
> Of men, by Laws less circumscrib'd and bound,
> They led their wild desires to Woods and Caves,
> And thought that all but Savages were Slaves.[146]

First there is an echo of Lucretius' account of primitive man:

---

[143] Barbara K. Lewalski, 'The Scope and Function of Biblical Allusion in *Absalom and Achitophel*', *English Language Notes*, 3 (1965) 29–35, at p. 30.
[144] *Absalom and Achitophel*, ll. 55–6.
[145] Thomas Hobbes, *Leviathan*, ed. Richard Tuck (Cambridge, 1991), pp. 89–90.
[146] *Absalom and Achitophel*, ll. 53–6.

Nemora, atque cavos Monteis, sylvasque colebant

. . . .

Nec commune bonum poterant spectare, nec ullis
Moribus inter se scibant, nec legibus uti.[147]

But Dryden is not imagining the Interregnum rebels simply as
uncivilized, for in another intertextual gesture he recalls the mad
behaviour of the women who burn Aeneas' ships and then take
refuge in woods and caves: *sylvasque, et sicubi concava furtim | Saxa,
petunt.*[148] This latter reference reminds us that the rebels of the
Interregnum were not simply lawless savages existing in a state
before civilization, but were actively destroying the ship of state.
And since the women in Virgil are acting under the influence of
divine possession, the implication is that the Puritans' claims to
direct divine illumination were equally mad, equally destructive. It
is one of a series of references to the *Aeneid* which bring into play
the great foundational pre-text as a 'hypotexte'[149] which Dryden
wishes to remind us of intermittently through this poem.[150]
Various phrases ask us to read our present against Virgil's mythologized past. The 'wounds, dishonest to the sight'[151] which the
Civil War has inflicted echo *inhonesto vulnere* in Virgil, from a
passage where Aeneas on his visit to the underworld sees
Deiphobus, the son of King Priam, but has difficulty recognizing
him because his body has been so appallingly mutilated. So this
trace leads us to the horrified recognition of the dismemberment
of the body, and symbolically of the body politic. (That it is also
the body of a young man who met an untimely death is not irrelevant: that topos will recur shortly.) Another echo links the
crowds which greeted Charles II on his return to England with the

---

[147] 'They dwelt in the woods and forests and mountain caves . . . they could not look
to the common good, they did not know how to govern their intercourse by custom and
law' (Lucretius, *De Rerum Natura*, v. 953–7).

[148] 'Stealthily they seek woods and rocky caves' (Virgil, *Aeneid*, v. 677–8).

[149] For the term see Gérard Genette, *Palimpsestes: La littérature au second degré* (Paris,
1982), p. 13.

[150] Richard Duke responded to this recurrent intertextual thread by imagining that the
anonymous author of *Absalom and Achitophel*, hearing people praise his poem, would be like
Aeneas, wrapped in the cloud which makes him invisible, hearing the Carthaginians speaking of Troy (*Works*, ii. 470).

[151] *Absalom and Achitophel*, l. 72; drawing on Virgil, *Aeneid*, vi. 497. Atterbury recognizes this, and uses the phrase *inhonesto vulnere* (p. 3). Dryden uses the word 'Dishonest' in
his translation of this passage in Virgil (*Aeneis*, vi. 668).

soldiers of Aeneas on the strand before Carthage.[152] And the end
of the poem, where time is renewed, evokes the renewal of time
in Virgil's fourth *Eclogue*:

> Henceforth a Series of new time began,
> The mighty Years in long Procession ran:
>
> Magnus ab integro saeclorum nascitur ordo.[153]

Time which was renewed in this way once before in *Astræa Redux*
has now to be renewed again. The tense of this ending shifts the
poem out of the fictional present and into a retrospective vision in
which the inauguration of a new period can be recorded as an
accomplished event.

As well as this thread of Virgilian allusions, there are moments
where the poem invites us to register a closely reticulated set of
classical pre-texts. One such moment occurs when Absalom is
addressed thus by Achitophel:

> Auspicious Prince! at whose Nativity
> Some Royal Planet rul'd the Southern sky;
> Thy longing Countries Darling and Desire;
> Their cloudy Pillar, and their guardian Fire:
> Their second *Moses*, whose extended Wand
> Divides the Seas, and shews the promis'd Land:
> Whose dawning Day, in every distant age,
> Has exercis'd the Sacred Prophets rage:
> The Peoples Prayer, the glad Deviners Theam,
> The Young-mens Vision, and the Old mens Dream![154]

Achitophel confidently asserts his reading of time, and yet the
terms which he uses deconstruct his own discourse. As James
Garrison has observed,[155] the term 'auspicious' has specific connotations which link it to Latin panegyric, as seen for example in

---

[152] *Absalom and Achitophel*, ll. 270–2; drawing upon Virgil, *Aeneid*, iv. 401–4; noted by
R. M. Ogilvie, 'Two Notes on Dryden's *Absalom and Achitophel*', *Notes and Queries*, 215
(1970) 415–16.

[153] *Absalom and Achitophel*, ll. 1028–9; 'the great order of the centuries starts again from
the beginning' (Virgil, *Ecloga*, iv. 5), noted by Reuben A. Brower, 'Dryden's Epic Manner
and Virgil', *PMLA*, 55 (1940) 119–38, at p. 132. Atterbury recognizes this, and uses Virgil's
phrase (p. 39).

[154] *Absalom and Achitophel*, ll. 230–9.

[155] James D. Garrison, *Dryden and the Tradition of Panegyric* (Berkeley, 1975), p. 230.

Claudian: *auspiciis iterum sese regalibus annus | induit et nota fruitur iactantior aula.*[156] The auspicious moment is one which inaugurates a new kind of time, the auspicious ruler one whose reign confers the blessings of a purged, renovated time on his people.[157] In a poem which is so conscious of time—of its typological return and its necessary renewal—this is an important sign, for it marks the distance between the true and false heirs, between the time of Monmouth and the time of the King. One might expect a prophecy based upon an astrological interpretation of the heavens to be precise in its terminology (Dryden, as an amateur astrologer himself, would have understood the need for precision) yet Achitophel's reference to '*Some* royal planet' is surprisingly casual, and therefore bogus. The biblical typology which associates Monmouth and Moses is hyperbolic, as is the claim that the dawning day of Absalom has been prophesied in '*every* distant age'. And the supposedly providential time of Monmouth is shown to be merely a Machiavellian moment when opportunity needs to be seized:

> Heav'n, has to all allotted, soon or late,
> Some lucky Revolution of their Fate:
> Whose Motions, if we watch and guide with Skill,
> (For humane Good depends on humane Will,)
> Our Fortune rolls, as from a smooth Descent,
> And, from the first Impression, takes the Bent:
> But, if unseiz'd, she glides away like wind;
> And leaves repenting Folly far behind.
> Now, now she meets you, with a glorious prize,
> And spreads her Locks before you as she flies.
> Had thus Old *David*, from whose Loyns you spring,
> Not dar'd, when Fortune call'd him, to be King,
> At *Gath* an Exile he might still remain,
> And heavens Anointing Oyle had been in vain.[158]

---

[156] 'Once more the year opens under royal auspices and enjoys in fuller pride its famous prince' (Claudian, *Panegyricus De Quarto Consulatu Honorii Augusti*, ll. 1–2). Coward's translation makes the point differently, but equally neatly, by having Achitophel address Absalom as '*Augustissime Princeps*' (p. 9).

[157] For the significance of 'auspicious' in Dryden's early poems see Paul Hammond, 'Dryden's Philosophy of Fortune', *Modern Language Review*, 80 (1985) 769–85, esp. p. 772.

[158] *Absalom and Achitophel*, ll. 252–65. The following discussion of Achitophel's speech draws on my article 'Dryden's Philosophy of Fortune', esp. on p. 773.

Achitophel has previously been described as one who 'Fortunes Ice prefers to Vertues Land',[159] and here in his advice to Absalom he is shown to be an opportunist who prefers Fortune to Providence. Fortune, in an iconography developed in the Middle Ages and the Renaissance from classical roots,[160] is the capricious power who offers men apparently golden opportunities, but whose gifts can be snatched away without warning and without reason. Achitophel assumes that heaven has allotted some merely 'lucky' turn of 'Fate' to all, and David's call to be King over Israel is attributed not to God but to Fortune. He also suggests that the divine anointing of David would have been ineffectual if David had not been sufficiently daring to respond to Fortune's call. Achitophel sees Fortune as Occasio, who has to be seized while she is still within reach, and his narrative emplots recent history as a sequence of momentary opportunities rather than the unfolding of heavenly Providence. His urgent 'Now, now she meets you' ironically repeats Virgil's equally urgent *Jam . . . Jam* in his fourth *Eclogue*,[161] but with a radically different political and moral purpose. Achitophel shares Adam's sin by trying to seize control of his destiny, and so he and his party resemble the '*Adam*-wits' of the Interregnum who were 'too fortunately free'[162]—enthralled by a version of freedom which actually made them slaves to Fortune. Absalom is accused of 'detaining' the general joy by his refusal to seize his chance, but we realize how untimely an intervention that would actually be. And Absalom himself is made to acknowledge both the proper course of time, and (inadvertently) the truly Augustan status of Charles, in referring to the time when his father shall 'late Augment the Number of the Blest', echoing Horace's words to Augustus, *serus in caelum redeas.*[163]

To contrast with this spurious heir who is poised to displace the true heir and to rebel against his father, Dryden inserts a lament for the young Earl of Ossory, son and heir of the Duke of Ormonde,

---

[159]   *Absalom and Achitophel*, l. 199.

[160]   See Frederick Kiefer, 'The Conflation of Fortuna and Occasio in Renaissance Thought and Iconography', *Journal of Medieval and Renaissance Studies*, 9 (1979) 1–27; Howard R. Patch, *The Goddess Fortuna in Medieval Literature* (Cambridge, Mass., 1927); and for Dryden's uses of Fortune, G. E. Wilson, 'Dryden and the Emblem of *Fortuna-Occasio*', *Papers in Language and Literature*, 11 (1975) 199–203.

[161]   Virgil, *Ecloga*, iv. 6–7.   [162]   *Absalom and Achitophel*, l. 51.

[163]   Ibid., l. 350; Horace, *Carmina*, I. ii. 45: 'late may you return to heaven'.

a passage which disturbs the predominantly satirical mode of the poem and moves it into a darker tone.[164] The passage weaves together several pre-texts from Virgil. The first effects Dryden's own narratorial entry into the text, a rare use of the first person singular in *Absalom and Achitophel* which—as we follow the traces—becomes troubled and complex:

> By me (so Heav'n will have it) always Mourn'd,
> And always honour'd, snatcht in Manhoods prime
> By' unequal Fates, and Providences crime:
>
> Jamque dies, ni fallor, adest; quem semper acerbum,
> Semper honoratum (sic Dii voluistis,) habebo.[165]

The link between the two passages is slender but strong: simply the parenthetical reference to the will of heaven, and the phrase 'always Mourn'd, | . . . always honour'd', *semper acerbum,* | *Semper honoratum*. But subtle changes have occurred in the translation, the carrying over from Virgil. The original context is the passage where Aeneas marks the anniversary of his father's death, so the parallel between the two speakers links Aeneas and Dryden (not, for example, Aeneas and the bereaved Ormonde). In Virgil, son mourns father; in Dryden, the poet (so made a father-figure?) mourns the son. In Virgil it is the day which is honoured, in Dryden the man. And the reference to the will of heaven, which in Virgil applies to heaven's choice of this particular day, is applied instead to heaven's choice of Dryden as the one who honours and mourns Ossory. Our attention is directed no longer to the time of mourning, but to the poet as mourner.

Whatever the biographical reasons for Dryden to mourn Ossory (and we know nothing of these) there are perceptible symbolic motives for the depth of Dryden's engagement here. The untimely death of Ossory (he was 26) cannot be accommodated within the usual consolations, and is signed as a fissure in the expected text of life through the metrically awkward phrase 'By' unequal Fates', where the verse stutters, and where we once again hear Virgil

---

[164] *Absalom and Achitophel*, ll. 831–53.

[165] Ibid., ll. 832–4; 'already, if I am not mistaken, the day is at hand which I shall keep always as a day of grief, always as one of honour (such, O gods, was your will)' (Virgil, *Aeneid*, v. 49–50). Atterbury recognizes the borrowing, and incorporates Virgil's wording (p. 32).

behind Dryden's English, in this case his *fatis iniquis*.[166] Two languages of philosophical explanation—the classical Fates and Christian Providence—are jaggedly juxtaposed in the same line, with Providence angrily accused of a 'crime'. The passage becomes an instance of that topos of the death of the promising heir to which he will return in 1684 in 'Mezentius and Lausus' and 'To the Memory of Mr. Oldham'. The image of the race and the goal in this triplet:

> Yet not before the Goal of Honour won,
> All parts fulfill'd of Subject and of Son;
> Swift was the Race, but short the Time to run.[167]

anticipates the similar image in 'To the Memory of Mr. Oldham',[168] while Dryden draws into this lament for Ossory a translation from the lament for Marcellus, the lost heir of Augustus, who will also figure again in the poem for Oldham:

> Oh Ancient Honour, Oh Unconquer'd Hand,
> Whom Foes unpunish'd never coud withstand!
>
> Heu pietas! heu prisca fides! invictaque bello
> Dextera! non illi quisquam se impune tulisset
> Obvius armato.[169]

Ossory perfectly fulfils the roles of subject and son allotted to him, unlike Monmouth. A further reflection on the brevity of Ossory's life recalls Martial's remark on the short span allotted to those who are specially gifted:

> Short is the date of all Immoderate Fame.
>
> immodicis brevis est aetas, et rara senectus.[170]

---

[166] 'unequal [*or* unfair] fates' (Virgil, *Aeneid*, ii. 257 (the gods permitting Sinon to release the Greek soldiers from inside the Trojan horse); x. 380). Atterbury has *iniqui crimine fati* (p. 32).   [167] *Absalom and Achitophel*, ll. 835–7.

[168] 'To the Memory of Mr. Oldham', ll. 7–10.

[169] *Absalom and Achitophel*, ll. 844–5; drawing on Virgil, *Aeneid*, vi. 878–80: 'Alas piety, alas ancient fidelity and a right hand unconquered in war! No enemy opposed him in arms unscathed.' The echo is noted by Brower, 'Dryden's Epic Manner and Virgil', p. 133. Atterbury uses these lines from Virgil verbatim in his translation of this passage (p. 32).

[170] *Absalom and Achitophel*, l. 847; 'short is the life of those who are uncommonly endowed, and they rarely reach old age' (Martial, VI. xxix. 7). Both Atterbury (p. 32) and Coward (p. 29) recognize the allusion, using Martial's line verbatim in their own texts. Coward also cites the source in a marginal note.

We hear *immodicis* behind 'immoderate', but Dryden has also brought into his line other words which have Latin roots and a Roman semantic field: 'date', ultimately from *datum* ('given') and 'fame' from *fama*. The classical shape of the thought—so characteristic of the ancient world but so antithetical to Christian teaching—is being delicately highlighted.

A final turn to Virgil, though this time to *Eclogue* V, effects the apotheosis of Ossory:

> Now, free from Earth, thy disencumbered Soul
> Mounts up, and leaves behind the Clouds and Starry Pole:
>
> Candidus insuetum miratur limen Olympi,
> Sub pedibusque videt nubes et sidera Daphnis.[171]

Following the traces here, we find that Daphnis was thought to represent Julius Caesar,[172] and so Ossory is aligned with another great Roman whose life and career were cut short. But the trace also delivers a self-placing, self-consoling gesture: the eclogue features two poets, Mopsus and Menalcas, who make verses in memory of Daphnis, and Menalcas praises Mopsus' elegy by saying that it has established him in second place to Daphnis himself:

> Fortunate puer, tu nunc eris alter ab illo.
>
> O fortunate young Man, at least your Lays
> Are next to his, and claim the second Praise.[173]

The trace consoles Dryden not only for the death of Ossory, but for the condition of being second.

With such Latin pre-texts audible behind his lines, there are times when Dryden's own contemporaries become supplements, present only to fulfil, to give body to, pre-existing Latin phrases. In the case of Ossory, this fulfilment is poignantly complete and completing, serving to consolidate the figure of the lost youth. In the case of the opposition leaders like the Earl of Shaftesbury, the Duke of Buckingham, and Titus Oates, reading them against Latin

---

[171] *Absalom and Achitophel*, ll. 850–1; 'Daphnis in radiant beauty marvels at Heaven's unfamiliar threshold, and beneath his feet beholds the clouds and the stars' (Virgil, *Ecloga*, v. 56–7); noted by Brower, 'Dryden's Epic Manner and Virgil', p. 133. Atterbury recognizes the source and incorporates Virgil's wording (p. 32).

[172] Dryden's headnote to his translation: *Poems*, p. 889.

[173] Virgil, *Ecloga*, v. 49; 'The Fifth Pastoral. Or, Daphnis', ll. 77–8.

pre-texts confines and contains them through such definition. When we are told of Achitophel that 'Great Wits are sure to Madness near ally'd', we recognize behind the aphorism the Senecan formulation *nullum magnum ingenium sine mixtura dementiae fuit*;[174] when we read the catalogue of Zimri's frenzied activities, we recognize it as an imitation of Juvenal, and see the Duke of Buckingham judged in advance by the Roman satirist, who knew his type;[175] when we are told in the passage on Corah that *'witness* is a Common Name to all', we remember the schoolbook maxim '*Homo*, is a commune name to all men',[176] and understand that Oates has made the generic man into a generic witness, dividing and renaming the common heritage. In each case the Latin words which shadow these lines make the characters temporary embodiments of a timeless formula. The poetry insists that these bodies are themselves defective—Shaftesbury diseased, Oates grotesque, Buckingham not one coherent self but a multiplicity of evanescent roles—not substantial presences but distorted supplementary *exempla* which fulfil the formulae of the Latin writers who have scripted them in advance, but without themselves being full; indeed, they are thereby emptied of presence and reduced to being pieces of text. For characters like Oates who corrupted the public sphere through their lying words, this is an apt fate. Individuals also have been doubled into macaronic identities (Shaftesbury–Achitophel, Buckingham–Zimri, Oates–Corah), and there are some indeterminable cases where the single biblical name slides between different possible modern referents (Caleb may be Capel or Grey). By hearing the Latin pre-texts the reader becomes co-author of a macaronic text which it is beyond the capacity of a Titus Oates to manipulate. The nation is translated out of time, out of the tyranny of contemporary contingency, by the shaping of an Anglo-Latin text, and this text is scripted not simply by Dryden (the poem was, after all, anonymous) but also by an imagined community of classical writers, and by the actual community of Restoration readers as they recognize these Latin allusions and weave them into the poem's semantic field.

[174] *Absalom and Achitophel*, l. 163; 'there was no great wit without an element of madness' (Seneca, *De Tranquillitate Animi*, xvii. 10).

[175] *Absalom and Achitophel*, ll. 545–52; Juvenal, *Satyra*, iii. 75–8.

[176] *Absalom and Achitophel*, l. 681; this example from Lily and Colet's grammar was a familiar 17th-cent. tag: *Poems*, ed. Hammond, i. 510.

ROME AND THE RENEWAL OF TIME IN
BRITANNIA REDIVIVA

How often can time be renewed? Why does time need to be repeatedly purged and purified? At what moments does Dryden need—and need the nation—to start time again, to mark a break in the historical continuum and to recompose the past into a new mythological pattern? After announcing the renewal of time in *Astræa Redux* and again at the end of *Absalom and Achitophel*, Dryden repeats the gesture in order to contain and translate a third crisis over the succession in *Britannia Rediviva* (1688), though here he imagines time and space in a distinctly different way, and turns to different Latin pre-texts to shape these fields.

For Roman Catholics the reign of James II had already altered their experience of time. Time was transfigured daily in the Mass, which could now be openly celebrated. *The Catholic Almanack for the Year 1687*—published by the King's printer[177]—provided adherents with a liturgical calendar, and an explanation of the principal holy days of the church's year. It also gave a list of the popes from St Peter to the present incumbent Innocent XI, and lists of the kings of England and archbishops of Canterbury—but these only up to the Reformation: thereafter kings and primates fell into the black hole of heresy, and deserved no record. Thus past and present were given a new configuration. As for the future of this new Catholic order, only time would tell.

Dryden's poem commemorates the birth of a son and heir to James II on 10 June 1688. The birth was timely, in that having lost several children in infancy, and approaching the limit of child-bearing age, Queen Mary had been thought unlikely to provide the son who would secure a Catholic succession and displace the Protestant heir presumptive, James's eldest daughter Princess Mary. This birth reconfigured the future. Dryden's poem presents the birth of the Prince as inaugurating a new historical period; and so indeed it did, though not in the way that Dryden had envisaged. Before the month was out, a group of peers, alarmed at what

---

[177] *The Catholic Almanack for the Year 1687* (London, 1687) was printed by Henry Hills 'Printer to the King's Most Excellent Majesty, for his Houshold and Chappel'. The copy in the Bodleian Library (Douce A 584) is bound in red morocco, and decorated in gold with the royal cypher.

the future now seemed to hold, issued an invitation to William of
Orange to take the throne by force of arms.

The renewal of time and nation is effected by a turn to Latin,
announced in the poem's title.[178] '*Britannia Rediviva*' asserts that
Britain herself has been reborn with this birth, but the title has
other implications since in classical Latin *redivivus* is applied to
building materials which are reused in another structure, so the
metaphor also imagines Britain being reconstructed, a new fabric
being built by the reconfiguration of elements from the old structure. On the title page Dryden places a quotation from the
Georgics:

> *Dii Patrii Indigetes, & Romule, Vestaque Mater,*
> *Quae Tuscum Tiberim, & Romana Palatia servas,*
> *Hunc saltem everso* Puerum *succurrere saeclo*
> *Ne prohibite: satis jampridem sanguine nostro*
> *Laomedonteae luimus* Perjuria *Trojae*.[179]

This prayer occurs towards the end of the first book of Virgil's
poem, after he has written about the best way of cultivating the
earth and managing the seasonal changes, uncertain weather, and
unexpected natural disasters which affect the farmer. Virgil's turn
to considering a man-made disaster, civil war, requires a special
moment within the poem, a direct address to the tutelary deities
of Rome. The prayer expresses the hope that the sufferings of his
generation have now expiated the crime of Laomedon
(legendary King of Troy and father of Priam), whose perfidy in
cheating Apollo and Poseidon out of their payment for building
the walls of his city brought down the wrath of those gods on
the whole people, in the form of a plague and a sea-monster.
And so the monstrous plague of civil war is traced back to the
founding father of the originary city, whose attempt to give his
people security, to define and consolidate their boundaries, was
marred by sacrilege. There is, it seems, a scandal at the very

---

[178] *Britannia Rediviva* had already been used as the title for the commemorative volume
issued by the University of Oxford on the Restoration in 1660.

[179] 'Gods of the homeland, patron deities [*or* demi-gods, deified heroes], and Romulus,
and mother Vesta, who guard Etruscan Tiber and the Roman palaces, at least do not
prevent this boy from aiding the ruined race [*or* generation, *or* time]: already we have sufficiently expiated with our blood the treachery of the Trojan Laomedon' (Virgil, *Georgics*, i.
498–502).

origins of Rome, a breach between men and gods which wreaks an alienation within the field of the *heimlich*. Virgil's prayer hopes that the young Octavian (not yet 'Augustus', if we date the *Georgics* to 29 BCE: that title would be conferred in 27, when he declined the alternative name of 'Romulus') will be allowed by the gods to renew and restore Rome, ending both its current civil war and a long stretch of time contaminated by an originary crime.

Several questions are raised, several distinct movements along the web of traces are put into play, by this epigraph. As Scott observed,[180] two words in the Virgilian quotation are emphasized by being printed in roman in the middle of lines set in italics: *Puerum* and *Perjuria*. The first is Dryden's substitution for the original *juvenum*, boy for youth, the infant Prince for the youthful Octavian; the second, which is part of Virgil's authentic text, is highlighted, as Scott suggests, to imply a reference to the sufferings of Catholics as a result of the perjured evidence given against them during the Popish Plot trials. The roman type does not perform quite the same function in the two cases. The emphasizing of *Puerum* identifies Dryden's intervention in the Virgilian text, and by highlighting the verbal substitution advertises the ease with which the new-born child can take his place in this prayer for national salvation. But to highlight *Perjuria* is to call attention to the uncanny way in which Virgil's own words seem to reach forward and fit the experience of Restoration Catholics. One typographical signifier initiates two quite different modes of reading. Finally, the two words, linked by alliteration as well as typography, are joined in order to point a contrast between the *Perjuria* of the British people and the *Puer* who will redeem it.

Title and epigraph together redefine the nation, first by asserting that Britain can be reborn or rebuilt through the birth of this Catholic heir, then by appealing to tutelary deities who are—as the poem soon makes clear—Catholic guardian angels and saints. After a gap which allows the reader to ponder the implications of the epigraph, Dryden offers his own application (and quasi-translation) of it:

---

[180] *Works*, ed. Scott, x. 288.

> (*n*) Great *Michael*, Prince of all th' Ætherial Hosts,
> And what e're In-born Saints our *Britain* boasts;
> And thou, th' (*o*)adopted Patron of our Isle,
> With chearful Aspects on this Infant smile:
> The Pledge of Heav'n, which dropping from above,
> Secures our Bliss, and reconciles his Love.

(*n*) *The Motto of the Poem explain'd.*
(*o*) *St. George.*[181]

The invocation of saints is, of course, a Catholic practice which Dryden's Protestant readers would have found uncomfortable if not offensive, and his entrusting of the nation to the care of those saints is a tendentious move. Even more provocative is the inclusion in this prayer of 'what e're In-born Saints our *Britain* boasts' ('In-born' means 'native'), implicitly the Catholic martyrs from Thomas More to the victims of the Popish Plot, not the self-styled 'saints' of Protestant Nonconformity. Virgil's deities are *Indigetes* ('home-born' as Dryden was later to translate the word[182]) but whereas these are the communally reverenced founder and guardian of the nation (Romulus and Vesta) the saints invoked in Dryden's lines are representatives only of one part of the nation. Can the part speak for the whole? The synecdoche is overtly polemical. Dryden's application of the Virgilian quotation asserts the Catholics' right to belong in time and space, not to be dispossessed; but, more than this, their right to stand for and be synonymous with the nation.[183] The suffering of the Catholics at the hands of Protestant liars is made analogous to the suffering which Virgil traces back to the sacrilege of Laomedon; and as Roman history is time contaminated by Laomedon's impiety, so British history is time stained by Protestant godlessness. The analogy is imperfect, but even so Catholics are being written deeply into the myth of origins, displacing Protestants from their ownership of the nation and its history. As classical and Catholic Rome coalesce, this movement deprives Dryden's Protestant opponents of their home ground.

---

[181] *Britannia Rediviva*, ll. 146–51, with Dryden's marginal notes.

[182] 'The First Book of the *Georgics*', l. 668.

[183] Cp. his earlier statement in *Absalom and Achitophel* (l. 87) that the Roman Catholics had a 'Native right' to the country, a remarkable concession at this date, and one which is emphasized by the words concluding a hemistich.

In the epigraph the phrase through which Virgil defines the damaged present, *saeclo everso*, is capable of multiple translations, a suggestive indeterminacy which suits Dryden's deployment of the lines. The word *saeclum* means a race or breed (*OLD* 2), so when applied by Dryden's readers it could signify either the British race in general, or specifically the Catholics. But it also means a particular generation (*OLD* 1), and hence also the times themselves, a specific period which has a distinctive character (*OLD* 3).[184] (The phrase through which Dryden himself would subsequently translate the term, 'the Age',[185] has exactly this last sense.) In this case, then, the word would signify the people and the political traumas of the 1680s. Within the semantic field of *saeclum* there is a shift of definition between time and people, and between the people of the present generation and the race as a whole. Where are contemporary Catholics to be placed within this field, where is the nation to be placed, and how do the two relate to each other? The verb *evertere* also has a significant movement within its range of meaning: to reverse, overthrow, ruin, or destroy something (*OLD* 1–5), but also to expel a man from that which he possesses (*OLD* 6). So a translation of *saeclo everso* into contemporary terms might indicate that the nation, particularly in the present generation, has been ruined, its structures overthrown, and the prayer would therefore be for the political fabric to be restored by this new Prince. Alternatively, time itself, the present, had been exiled, displaced from possession of its native ground. The lines then become a prayer for the reintegration of time with itself, the restoration of self-presence. Or, to select other meanings, the Catholics have been dispossessed, and the prayer is for their restoration. The oscillations in interpretation which the phrase permits leave the relation between time and nation, and between nation and confessional group, open for explication and definition. This will be the work of the poem.

The time which Virgil's lines inhabit is held in parentheses within the *Georgics*. After expounding that form of the present in which the general principles of agriculture apply, as man lives in

---

[184] After the death of Augustus there was a proposal to designate his lifetime as *saeculum Augustum* (Suetonius, *Augustus*, C. 3; Galinsky, p. 10, and see also pp. 100–101).

[185] 'The First Book of the *Georgics*', l. 673.

accordance with the laws of nature, Virgil moves out of this kind of time into a form of the present which is held between painful memories of recent war and perhaps hyperbolic hopes for the future. This present seems to have no character of its own except its memory and its hope, its state of apprehension, its status as interval. Having described how the farmer needs to be able to read the signs which foretell bad weather, Virgil recounts the meteorological signs which presaged the death of Julius Caesar; then he tells of the carnage which resulted from that assassination, and imagines how in the future labourers will turn up rusty weapons and empty helmets as they plough over the battlefield—a grim, unnatural crop from a ground which has been unnaturally sown and fertilized:

> Nec fuit indignum superis, bis sanguine nostro
> Emathiam et latos Haemi pinguescere campos.[186]

Or, as Dryden would translate the lines:

> For this, th' *Emathian* Plains once more were strow'd
> With *Roman* Bodies, and just Heav'n thought good
> To fatten twice those Fields with *Roman* Blood.[187]

This is one way of imagining the future, as the work of raking over the traces of the past; another way is to pray for a saviour.

Britannia Rediviva marks the time of the saviour. Its opening lines are a reprise of that motif of untimely speech which marked the beginning of the *Heroique Stanza's* and *Threnodia Augustalis*:

> Our Vows are heard betimes! and Heaven takes care
> To grant, before we can conclude the Pray'r:
> Preventing Angels met it half the way,
> And sent us back to Praise, who came to Pray.[188]

But on this occasion the poet's words are also (albeit polemically) the words of the community ('*Our* Vows . . .'), and they are interrupted and made incomplete by an unexpectedly swift fulfilment. The Prince is born at a liminal moment, on the longest day at the

---

[186] 'Nor did the gods think it wrong that twice Emathia and the wide fields of Haemus should be fattened with our blood' (Virgil, *Georgics*, i. 491–2).

[187] 'The First Book of the *Georgics*', ll. 659–61.

[188] *Britannia Rediviva*, ll. 1–4.

utmost limit of the sun's northern progress, and the sun even
stretches beyond his natural limits to greet the child.[189] The boy
arrives on the threshold between spring and summer:

> Departing Spring cou'd only stay to shed
> Her bloomy beauties on the Genial Bed,
> But left the manly Summer in her sted,
> With timely Fruit the longing Land to chear,
> And to fulfill the promise of the year.
> Betwixt two Seasons comes th' Auspicious Heir,
> This Age to blossom, and the next to bear.[190]

There is an unobtrusive echo here of the lines in which Dryden
had written of himself as 'betwixt two Ages cast, | The first of this,
and hindmost of the last'.[191] The poet who repeatedly figures
himself as displaced in time is now greeting the moment when an
unexpected turn of events brings the fulfilment of promises, timely
fruit, an auspicious heir. The temporal pattern into which the
Prince is born is the Catholic liturgical year, as Whitsun gives way
to Trinity Sunday, and the descent of the Holy Spirit accompanies
the birth of the child. Inasmuch as the child is the work of the
Holy Spirit he is Christlike; inasmuch as he is a second Adam,[192]
he is also Christlike. Redeeming the time, the Prince's birth makes
the month of June sacred, and the month cleanses the year:

> Five Months to Discord and Debate were giv'n:
> He sanctifies the yet remaining Sev'n.
> Sabbath of Months! henceforth in Him be blest,
> And prelude to the Realms perpetual Rest![193]

In this strained conceit Dryden imagines June beginning a new
seven-month sector of the year like a sabbath at the beginning of
the week, and this sabbath, as a period of rest, is also the prelude
to the country's perpetual rest. Dryden's excitement gets the better
of his clarity here, but it is the excitement of one who suddenly
sees that the future could be wholly different.

As well as taking possession of past and present through Catholic
language, Dryden is also turning back to classical Rome. James II is

---

[189] Ibid., ll. 5–9. [190] Ibid., ll. 12–18.
[191] 'Prologue to *Aureng-Zebe*', ll. 21–2. [192] *Britannia Rediviva*, ll. 25–6.
[193] Ibid., ll. 184–7.

a second Constantine, the first Christian emperor of Rome.[194] The name of the child is as yet unknown, and this recalls the legend that the true name of Rome was kept secret to avoid it being used by her enemies in spells.[195] The child himself is revealed as Aeneas was revealed when the cloud surrounding him disappeared.[196] But there is a more sustained engagement with a poem which, like the first book of the *Georgics*, addresses the turning point in Roman history which came with the triumph of Octavian. This is Horace's *Carmina* I. ii, which has close thematic links with Virgil's poem, particularly with the concluding prayer which Dryden used as an epigraph.[197] Horace supplied Dryden with several motifs, including the flood and the need for atonement,[198] but there is one striking thought which all three poets share. Both Latin poets say that already enough time has been consumed and enough blood spilt in war:

> Satis jampridem sanguine nostro
> Laomedonteae luimus perjuria Trojae.

says Virgil, and Horace's ode opens with an echo of those words:

> Iam satis terris niuis, atque dirae
> Grandinis misit pater, & rubente
> Dextera sacras iaculatus arceis,
> Terruit vrbem:[199]

The refrain is *satis jampridem . . . iam satis*, 'enough already', and Dryden takes up the theme:

> Enough of Ills our dire Rebellion wrought,
> When, to the Dregs, we drank the bitter draught;
> .   .   .   .
> Enough of Early Saints one Womb has giv'n;
> Enough encreas'd the Family of Heav'n:
> .   .   .   .
> Enough already has the Year foreslow'd
> His wonted Course, the Seas have overflow'd . . .[200]

---

[194] *Britannia Rediviva*, ll. 88–9.   [195] Ibid., ll. 199–201.

[196] Ibid., ll. 128–33.

[197] R. G. M. Nisbet and Margaret Hubbard, *A Commentary on Horace, 'Odes', Book 1* (Oxford, 1970), pp. 16–21.   [198] Noted by *Works*, iii. 472.

[199] 'Already Father [Jupiter] has sent enough snow and dire hail to earth, and struck with his red right hand the sacred citadels and brought terror to the city' (Horace, *Carmina*, I. ii. 1–4).   [200] *Britannia Rediviva*, ll. 152–3, 165–6, 169–70.

Such weariness feeds the longing for a renewal of time. And there is another trace of Horace's poem when Dryden apostrophizes the Prince:

> Hail Son of Pray'rs! by holy Violence
> Drawn down from Heav'n; but long be banish'd thence,
> And late to thy Paternal Skyes retire:
> To mend our Crimes whole Ages wou'd require:[201]

which recalls Horace's address to Octavian at the end of the ode:

> Serus in caelum redeas, diuque
> Laetus intersis populo Quirini:
> Neve te nostris vitiis iniquum
>   Ocyor aura
> Tollat:[202]

This makes the sojourn of the Prince among his people only an interval. The verb which Horace uses of Octavian's stay among the Romans, *intersis*, means both 'to be present, to take part in, to be among' (*OLD* 3–5), and also 'to differ from' (*OLD* 6–7). Difference and deferral trouble this moment of indwelling, but only lightly: the chief anxiety is that this loan from the gods, whether Prince or Princeps, should put an end to the suffering.

Neither Dryden nor Horace seems abashed by their somewhat surreal hyperboles, and the conceptual space of *Britannia Rediviva* has a baroque elaboration, busily assigning angels to their duties and marshalling the three persons of the Trinity to stand guard over the three kingdoms. But another form of symbolic space is also being deployed here, a georgic plane. It may be that 'Poets are not Prophets, to foreknow | What Plants will take the Blite, and what will grow',[203] but the poem nevertheless conceives of historical change in terms of natural growth. Sudden disaster need not ruin the harvest altogether, as Dryden suggests in a passage which might have come from a translation of the *Georgics*:

---

[201] *Britannia Rediviva*, ll. 35–7.
[202] 'Return late to the sky, and for a long time be pleased to stay with the people of Romulus, and may no breeze take you up too soon, angered by our sins' (Horace, *Carmina*, I. ii. 45–9).   [203] *Britannia Rediviva*, ll. 71–2.

> As when a sudden Storm of Hail and Rain
> Beats to the ground the yet unbearded Grain,
> Think not the hopes of Harvest are destroy'd
> On the flat Field, and on the naked void;
> The light, unloaded stem, from tempest free'd,
> Will raise the youthful honours of his head;
> And, soon restor'd by native vigour, bear
> The timely product of the bounteous Year.[204]

But Dryden's vision of recent history also acknowledges a tragic georgic:

> Here stop the Current of the sanguine flood,
> Require not, Gracious God, thy Martyrs Blood;
> But let their dying pangs, their living toyl,
> Spread a Rich Harvest through their Native Soil:
> A Harvest ripening for another Reign,
> Of which this Royal Babe may reap the Grain.[205]

This elaborates the saying that the blood of the martyrs is the seed of the church,[206] but also reworks Virgil's lines which speak of the blood of Romans fertilizing the ground. For all the effort and ingenuity which this poem expends on controlling time and space, the significance of the Prince's birth was to be quite other than Dryden hoped. This was to be his last poem before the Revolution.

JOINING CLASSICAL AND CATHOLIC ROME IN *THE HIND AND THE PANTHER*

Was Dryden's conversion to Rome partly an attempt to arrest the continual slippage of meaning that we call *différance*? Was he longing for an end to the debate over words, and authority, and authoritative interpretation? It was another turn to Latin, to the ecclesiastical Latin of the Mass and of Catholic theology, though it is a striking (but habitually ignored) fact that Dryden's conversion coincides with the beginning of his sustained attention to classical

---

[204] *Britannia Rediviva*, ll. 259–66. In fact, the first two lines are quite close to a couplet in Dryden's subsequent translation of Book I: 'Or when the low'ring Spring, with lavish Rain, | Beats down the slender Stem and bearded Grain': 'The First Book of the *Georgics*', ll. 423–4.

[205] *Britannia Rediviva*, ll. 159–64.

[206] Cp. *The Hind and the Panther*, i. 17–18.

translation: the Latin of Virgil and his contemporaries becomes more important to Dryden's poetic work at the time of his conversion to Rome.[207] This was a turn to the eternal city which was, both literally and symbolically, built upon the ruins of ancient Rome. It was a turn from a faith grounded in the scripture to one which located authority in the oral tradition, and so in that respect a flight from writing to speech. *The Hind and the Panther* (1687), Dryden's *apologia* for his conversion, is largely a dialogue[208] between the Hind (representing the Church of Rome) and the Panther (the Church of England), and through this dialogic form Dryden seeks to differentiate true from false speech, and lead the reader to hear divine authority in the voice of the Roman Catholic Church. At the end of *Absalom and Achitophel* Dryden had imagined the English people listening to the words of Charles II 'with awfull fear' as they 'their Maker in their Master hear'.[209] It was an improbable thought then, coming at the end of a poem which had joked about Charles's sexual exploits, and it proves no less difficult to press home the analogous thesis in *The Hind and the Panther* as we are invited to hear divinely inspired speech coming from a deer. In both cases Dryden's relish for the contingent, the earthy, the baroque, plays against his longing for eternal stability. If the turn to Rome could be seen as a turn from a contingent to a noumenal epistemology, it is imperfectly realized because of the strong claim which contingency—and the comedy of contingency—always had on Dryden's imagination. Much as *The Hind and the Panther* may proffer a noumenal epistemology and an unerring guide, it has some difficulty in consolidating that position textually. The poem seeks a transcendent guarantee for the meaning of signs, but becomes all the more enmeshed in a network of traces.

The poem carries a Latin epigraph on its title page. This comes not from the Vulgate, but from Virgil:

---

[207] The date of Dryden's conversion is not known with certainty, but it was probably 1685, the same year in which he published his first major translations in *Sylvæ*. Tom Brown dated the conversion to 1685 (*The Reasons of Mr Bays Changing his Religion* (London, 1688), p. 21), while Evelyn recorded in his *Diary* for 19 January 1686 that Dryden and his sons were reported to go to Mass.

[208] For Dryden's handling of the dialogue see George Myerson, *The Argumentative Imagination: Wordsworth, Dryden, Religious Dialogues* (Manchester, 1992).

[209] *Absalom and Achitophel*, ll. 937–8.

—Antiquam exquirite matrem.
Et vera, incessu, patuit Dea.—

Actually, this epigraph runs together two lines from different books of the *Aeneid*. The first, meaning 'seek your ancient mother', comes from the episode in Book III where Aeneas asks the oracle of Apollo for guidance.[210] In Dryden's version the lines run thus:

> Prostrate we fell; confess'd the present God,
> Who gave this Answer from his dark Abode.
> Undaunted Youths, go seek that Mother Earth
> From which your Ancestors derive their Birth.[211]

As this translation makes clear, the mother to which the oracle refers is the originary homeland of the Trojan race. However, in trying to implement the god's words Aeneas misrecognizes the identity of this homeland: following his father's recollection that the race had come originally from Crete, he makes for that island, and it is only when his own household gods tell him that they had come from Italy, and must return there, that his goal becomes clear. The context of the first line of this epigraph is therefore one in which the words of the god are misunderstood, the words of the father are misleading, and Aeneas' own household gods have to speak in order for him to understand simultaneously his origin and his goal. Though momentarily an encounter with divine presence (and Dryden emphasizes this in his phrase 'confessed the present God', which has no equivalent in the Latin) it soon lapses into that misconstruction of *archē* and *telos* which is the work of *différance*. The simplicity of the injunction, *Antiquam exquirite matrem*, is undone as we trace it to its source. The second part of the epigraph also becomes unsettling as we ponder it: *Et vera, incessu, patuit Dea*. Meaning 'and the true goddess appeared by her gait', and inviting us to recognize our true mother in the Roman Catholic Church, the phrase comes from Book I where Aeneas recognizes his mother Venus only as she turns away from him and departs.[212] It is not, in context, an encouraging precedent for the seeker after truth.

---

[210] Virgil, *Aeneid*, iii. 96. [211] *Aeneis*, iii. 125–8.
[212] Virgil, *Aeneid*, i. 405.

Dryden is asking us to understand that the mother church figured in the opening line of his poem, 'A milk white *Hind*, immortal and unchang'd',[213] is the perfect realization of the *antiquam matrem* and *vera dea* of this epigraph, so that the two Roman texts, with their different original referents, are made to prefigure and find their fulfilment singly in the Church of Rome. But there is a danger that the relation between epigraph and poem, pre-text and text, may be less stable than Dryden would wish, and that a secondariness, a belatedness, may still haunt the English poem. The danger is brought into play if we attend to the sources from which the epigraph is drawn, and remind ourselves that neither offers an example of perfect recognition: one leads to a misrecognition, the other to a belated recognition. Both promise presence but initiate deferral.

Latin was a specially attractive resource for Dryden at the moments when he was seeking to establish the special status of the Hind. In this passage the Hind's words receive divine authentication by a light from heaven:

> Thus, while with heav'nly charity she spoke,
> A streaming blaze the silent shadows broke:
> Shot from the skyes a chearfull azure light;
> The birds obscene to forests wing'd their flight,
> And gaping graves receiv'd the wandring guilty spright.
>   Such were the pleasing triumphs of the sky
> For *James* his late nocturnal victory;
> The pledge of his Almighty patron's love,
> The fire-works which his angel made above.
> I saw my self the lambent easie light   *Poëta loquitur.*
> Guild the brown horrour and dispell the night;
> The messenger with speed the tidings bore,
> News which three lab'ring nations did restore,
> But heav'ns own *Nuncius* was arriv'd before.[214]

The passage begins with divine light approving the Hind's words, which have been an offer to receive the Panther as a returning

---

[213] *The Hind and the Panther*, i. 1.
[214] *The Hind and the Panther*, ii. 649–62. Edward L. Saslow traces the Virgilian echoes in this passage in 'Angelic "Fire-Works": The Background and Significance of *The Hind and the Panther*, ii, 649–62', *Studies in English Literature 1500–1900*, 20 (1980) 373–84.

prodigal, and then moves to a second heavenly light seen in the skies after the Battle of Sedgemoor. Two kinds of time are linked here, the endlessly repeated time of divine forgiveness which is available to the penitent (implicitly contrasting with a Calvinist theology which makes time for penitence impossible, or at least redundant, in the framework of eternal election), and the historical moment of James's military victory. In both cases, though in different ways, *chronos* is made into *kairos*. But there is also a classical hinterland to the lines. The light recalls the sign sent by Jupiter as Aeneas is hesitating over his escape from Troy,[215] and Latin inflects the vocabulary at several points: 'heav'nly charity' is *caritas*; 'triumphs' recalls the celebrations accorded victorious Roman generals; 'obscene' is used in the Latinate sense of ill-omened or inauspicious;[216] 'horrour', 'lab'ring', and 'lambent' have Latin roots, the latter recalling *Lambere* in the description of flames playing on the head of Ascanius;[217] the marginal note '*Poëta loquitur*' which sources the words to Dryden himself is in Latin, while the messenger of heaven is called a '*Nuncius*', a rare word in English, and virtually unnaturalized Latin. The penetration of English by Latin helps to mark out this passage on the penetration of *chronos* by *kairos*.

The Church of Rome had repeatedly been associated with classical Rome, particularly by its enemies, who wished to represent it as another form of paganism.[218] But in *The Hind and the Panther* Dryden explores this connection in a variety of ways, each of which seems designed to provide Roman Catholicism with secure foundations and an unquestioned possession of the truth, and to represent Anglicanism, by contrast, as a usurping force. The opening lines of the poem establish the Hind as the inhabitant of an unlocalized space, and a time beyond change:

[215] Virgil, *Aeneid*, ii. 692–8.
[216] *OED* 3; Saslow compares Virgil's *obscoenae volucres*, 'ill-omened birds', in *Aeneid*, xii. 876, but the phrase is also used of the Harpies in iii. 262, and since Dryden likens the Anglican clergy to Harpies (*vide infra*) this may be the relevant passage.
[217] *Aeneid*, ii. 684; cp. *Mac Flecknoe*, l. 111.
[218] Recent examples include Thomas De Laune, *Eikon tou theriou, or The Image of the Beast, Shewing, by a Parallel Scheme, what a Conformist the Church of Rome is to the Pagan* (London, 1684); and Joshua Stopford, *Pagano-Papismus: or, An Exact Parallel between Rome-Pagan, and Rome-Christian, in their Doctrines and Ceremonies* (London, 1675).

A milk white *Hind*, immortal and unchang'd,
Fed on the lawns, and in the forest rang'd;
Without unspotted, innocent within,
She fear'd no danger, for she knew no sin.
Yet had she oft been chas'd with horns and hounds,
And Scythian shafts; and many winged wounds
Aim'd at Her heart; was often forc'd to fly,
And doom'd to death, though fated not to dy.
    Not so her young, for their unequal line
Was Heroe's make, half humane, half divine.
Their earthly mold obnoxious was to fate,
Th' immortal part assum'd immortal state.
Of these a slaughtered army lay in bloud,
Extended o'er the *Caledonian* wood,
Their native walk;[219]

The geography is unspecific, a romance world of forests and clearings ('lawns'), a world outside time in which the Hind exists 'immortal and unchang'd'. Time intrudes only in the form of persecution, a history which requires to be glossed as a reference both to the persecutions endured by Christians in the early Roman empire, and to the suffering inflicted on Catholics in sixteenth- and seventeenth-century England. Protestants, implicitly, repeat the barbarism of the late Roman empire; another, much more edifying, relation to Rome is reserved for Roman Catholics. While the Catholic Church is immortal, individual Catholics are not, and these are imagined in classical fashion as heroes, half-human, half-god, like the Hercules of Roman legend. The description of the land as a '*Caledonian* wood' stretches the name beyond Caledonia—literally Scotland—to mean 'ancient British', thus fashioning a symbolic geography and history. The name brings into play the proverbially pathless Caledonian wood, and the Calydon of ancient Greece, which was ravaged by a wild boar.[220] The history and geography in which the Roman Catholic Church is thus embedded are forms of sacred mythography.

    Dryden repeatedly figures the Church of England as a house built upon sand, and the Church of Rome as a house built upon

---

[219] *The Hind and the Panther*, i. 1–15.
[220] Lucius Florus, *Epitome*, i. 12; Ovid, *Metamorphoses*, viii. 270–424.

a rock (*petros* in Greek) which is Peter.[221] But the foundational rock is also the literal rock on which the city of Rome is built, and out of which the early Christians carved their catacombs. At one point the Panther mockingly asks the Hind where her great champion Infallibility may be found:

> I fain wou'd see
> That wond'rous wight infallibility.
> Is he from heav'n this mighty champion come,
> Or lodg'd below in subterranean *Rome*?
> First, seat him somewhere, and derive his race,
> Or else conclude that nothing has no place.[222]

Dryden's poem suggests that the Panther is being obtusely literal-minded in demanding a single location for infallibility, which resides in Pope and Councils, plural in time, place, and person. And the Panther's reference to subterranean Rome contains part of the answer to her own question. Archaeological investigations had revealed traces of the early Christian occupation of Rome, and in his *Roma Sotteranea* (1632) Antonio Bosio had described and illustrated the catacombs in which the early Christians had worshipped and had buried their dead.[223] The engraved title page (Plate 5) emphasizes the way that they inhabited and appropriated Roman spaces. The page itself is designed in Roman architectural style like a monument (complete with weeds growing over the cornice); panels echo the decoration on Roman triumphal arches and sarcophagi; the chi-rho monogram replaces the classical SPQR motif at the centre of a Roman laurel wreath; Christians are shown burying their dead in soberly decorated underground tombs; and the panels at the top of the page record (and celebrate the connection between) martyrdom and triumph. At the side Christians are being burnt or flayed, but in the centre a martial female figure, presumably Roma herself, is receiving the papal tiara from some putti, sitting amid discarded armour, and turning her back on a scene in which other smaller putti play with the wolf who represents pre-Christian Rome and its now discarded origins.

---

[221] *The Hind and the Panther*, i. 493–5, ii. 105, 588–9; drawing upon Matthew 7: 24–7 and 16: 18–19.   [222] *The Hind and the Panther*, ii. 64–9.

[223] I cite the edition revised by Paulus Aringhus as *Roma Subterranea Novissima*, 2 vols. (Paris, 1659).

This is a *translatio imperii* of a special kind, a transformation of Rome herself from war to peace, from Romulus to Christ, from one superseded *archē* to that combined *archē* and *telos* who is Alpha and Omega.

By contrast, the Church of England has only recent and rather disreputable origins. 'A *Lyon* old, obscene, and furious made | By lust' (Henry VIII) is said to have wed the Panther's mother 'by a left-hand marr'age', so 'Cov'ring adult'ry with a specious name'.[224] The latter phrase recalls Virgil, writing of the union of Dido and Aeneas: *Conjugium vocat, hoc praetexit nomine culpam.*[225] This allusion suggests that the Church of England is the product of a diversion from the true course of Roman history, and to follow her would be to neglect one's divine calling.

This is one of several uses of the *Aeneid* in *The Hind and the Panther*, which tend to cluster around the motif of taking possession of the promised homeland. One passage likens the Church of England clergy to Harpies who snatch food intended for others, and 'lodge in Habitations not their own'.[226] Another rejoices that the Catholic lands of Italy and Spain have no indigenous Protestant sects:

> Where birth has plac'd 'em let 'em safely share
> The common benefit of vital air.[227]

This recalls Virgil:

> Diis sedem exiguam patriis litusque rogamus
> Innocuum, et cunctis undamque auramque patentem.[228]

---

[224] *The Hind and the Panther*, i. 351–4.

[225] Virgil, *Aeneid*, iv. 172: 'she calls it marriage, and under that name conceals the guilt'. Dryden later translated the line as: 'But call'd it Marriage, by that specious Name, | To veil the Crime and sanctifie the Shame' (*Aeneis*, iv. 249–50), apparently recalling this passage in *The Hind and the Panther*. As George Loane noted ('Notes on the Globe "Dryden" ', *Notes and Queries*, 185 (1943) 272–81, at p. 276) Dryden's phrase 'specious name' probably derives from Ovid: *Conjugiumne vocas, speciosaque nomina culpae | Imponis, Medea, tuae?* ('do you think it to be marriage, Medea, and do you attach specious names to your crime?' (*Metamorphoses*, vii. 69–70)).

[226] *The Hind and the Panther*, iii. 958–60. For the Harpies in Virgil see *Aeneid*, iii. 209–62.

[227] *The Hind and the Panther*, i. 297–8.

[228] Virgil, *Aeneid*, vii. 229–30: 'we ask a safe landing place, and a narrow space for our household gods, and water and air which are common to all.' Dryden translates the last phrase as 'The common Water and the common Air' in *Aeneis*, vii. 314.

This recollection (perhaps a private one, Dryden talking to himself *via* the *Aeneid*, rather than sharing the place with his readers) makes a connection with Aeneas' request on landing in Latium that he and his followers be granted the basic means of survival, and a narrow space, *sedem exiguam*, for their gods. Dryden imagines such an enclave for Protestantism. But the space which the Hind commands is much more than such a precarious foothold. Later in the poem, Dryden revisits this same passage in Book VII, and develops an explicit comparison between the exiled Trojans and the Roman Catholics. The Panther is speaking:

> Methinks such terms of proferr'd peace you bring
> As once *Æneas* to th' *Italian* King:
> By long possession all the land is mine,
> You strangers come with your intruding line,
> To share my sceptre, which you call to join.
> You plead like him an ancient Pedigree,
> And claim a peacefull seat by fates decree.
> In ready pomp your Sacrificer stands,
> T' unite the *Trojan* and the *Latin* bands,
> And that the League more firmly may be ty'd,
> Demand the fair *Lavinia* for your bride.
> Thus plausibly you veil th' intended wrong,
> But still you bring your exil'd gods along;
> And will endeavour in succeeding space,
> Those houshold Poppits on our hearths to place.[229]

In Virgil, Aeneas' ambassador Ilioneus tells King Latinus that the Trojan exiles have arrived in Italy by the will of Jupiter, and that they wish Latinus to give them land for themselves and their household gods. Latinus agrees, and offers Aeneas his daughter Lavinia in marriage. The Virgilian allusions create a parallel between the exiled Trojans, who will be the founders of Rome, and the Roman Catholics, some now in exile or returning from exile and hoping for a stake in the kingdom. The Panther presents

---

[229] *The Hind and the Panther*, iii. 766–80, alluding to Virgil, *Aeneid*, vii. 213–48, trans. Dryden in *Aeneis*, vii. 290–340. The passage includes two other references to *Aeneid* vii: line 768 draws on *Rex arva Latinus et urbes* | *Jam senior longa placidas in pace regebat* (*Aeneid*, vii. 45–6: 'Latinus old and mild, had long possess'd | The *Latian* Scepter, and his People bless'd' (*Aeneis*, vii. 68–9)); and lines 771–2 refer to Aeneas' claim in *Aeneid*, vii. 219–21 that he is of divine descent and comes at Jove's command.

both groups as intruders, but the Trojans and their household gods
are actually returning by divine command to their original homeland, the country which Dardanus had left to found Troy. The
Panther's parallel therefore works ultimately to the Hind's advantage. The Panther's claim to long possession, and her insistence
that these hearths are hers, are implicitly shown to depend on a
tendentious reading of time. The Hind will indeed 'endeavour in
succeeding space' to establish the rites of her religion, but by this
point the poem has argued that she also exists in a different, sacred,
form of time and space.

   At the end of the second part of the poem, the Hind offers the
Panther shelter from the approaching night and inclement
weather. The Panther cautiously accepts, and follows her hostess:

> Who ent'ring first her lowly roof, (a shed
> With hoary moss and winding Ivy spread,
> Honest enough to hide an humble Hermit's head,)
> Thus graciously bespoke her welcome guest:
> So might these walls, with your fair presence blest
> Become your dwelling-place of everlasting rest,
> Not for a night, or quick revolving year,
> Welcome an owner, not a sojourner.
> This peacefull Seat my poverty secures,
> War seldom enters but where wealth allures;
> Nor yet despise it, for this poor aboad
> Has oft receiv'd, and yet receives a god;
> A god victorious of the Stygian race
> Here laid his sacred limbs, and sanctified the place.
> This mean retreat did mighty *Pan* contain;
> Be emulous of him, and pomp disdain,
> And dare not to debase your soul to gain.[230]

The Hind's 'dwelling-place' (a familiar biblical phrase) is 'honest',
which is to say both 'respectable, decent' (*OED* 2b) and 'not
seeming other than it is, genuine' (*OED* 4c). Outward plainness
and simplicity are secure signs of theological truth. (This is perhaps
Dryden's riposte to the locations of Protestant holiness and
Catholic duplicity in Book I of Spenser's *The Faerie Queene*.) This
could be the place for the Panther to dwell in too, not simply to

---

[230] *The Hind and the Panther*, ii. 697–713.

visit. If the Panther were to accept the Hind's invitation, the configurations of time, space, and text would all change, and the poem would finish at this point, as there would be no need for Part III with its rival allegories of recent history and the near future. As a place of exceptional significance, the Hind's cell is conceptualized in exceptional ways. It is significant not because the Hind inhabits it, but because a god is received there: this is the site of a theoxeny. Primarily, of course, God is received here through the Mass, but to grasp the meaning of this we have to make a detour.

The passage echoes the episode in *Aeneid* VIII where King Evander is addressing Aeneas as they approach his modest home:

> Ut uentum ad sedes: 'Haec, inquit, limina victor
> 'Alcides subiit; haec illum regia cepit.
> 'Aude, hospes, contemnere opes, et te quoque dignum
> 'Finge Deo, rebusque veni non asper egenis.'[231]

In his *Aeneis* Dryden would translate the lines thus:

> Mean as it is, this Palace, and this Door,
> Receiv'd *Alcides*, then a Conquerour.
> Dare to be poor: accept our homely Food
> Which feasted him; and emulate a God.[232]

This was one of the moments in the *Aeneid* which most impressed Dryden, and in the 'Dedication of the *Aeneis*' he said of the sentiment *Aude, hospes, contemnere opes, et te quoque dignum | Finge Deo*, 'For my part I am lost in the admiration of it: I contemn the World, when I think on it, and my self when I Translate it'.[233] The 'god victorious of [i.e. 'over'] the Stygian race' is Hercules, who overcame the dog Cerberus in the underworld, paralleled here with Christ who harrowed hell. Dryden does not often use typology in order to make religious points, and it may be a sign of awkwardness with the mode that Hercules is not named, but Dryden is drawing upon well-established typological interpretations of classical legend.

---

[231] *Aeneid*, viii. 362–5: 'When they came to the house, [Evander] said, "The victorious Hercules passed across this threshold, and this palace received him. Guest, dare to despise wealth and make yourself also worthy of the god; come, and do not disdain poverty." '

[232] *Aeneis*, viii. 477–80.

[233] *Poems*, p. 1059. Cowley also admired these lines, quoting them in his essay 'Of Agriculture' (*Essays*, pp. 407–8).

As Hercules conquered various beasts, he may be interpreted to represent 'spiritual fortitude' which gains a reward 'above the starry heaven'; he also stands for 'every good Christian, *who must be a valiant Champion, to encounter against the Snakes of malice and envy, the Lion of anger, the Boar of Wantonness . . . and the Devil that great Dragon*'; and also for 'a good King, who ought to subdue all monsters, cruelty, disorder, and oppression in his Kingdom, who should support the Heaven of the Church with the Shoulders of Authority' and console himself with the reflection that '*Hercules* was persecuted and maligned'. Finally, 'Our blessed Saviour is the true *Hercules* . . . who was persecuted out of malice, and exposed to all dangers . . . he subdued the roaring Lion . . . that tyrant and devourer of mankinde, the devil'.[234] But the typology is duplicated as Christ is additionally represented here as Pan.[235] In this passage Dryden is, unusually, presenting Christianity as the rectification and fulfilment of classical mythology. This is a place in and out of time, where the temporal receives the eternal. Difference is elided as several classical stories coincide to sign the site where the true church receives the true god.

Yet ironically *différance* plays most awkwardly around the moment when the Hind claims her status as the true church by speaking words which should be exempt from supplementarity:

> The Dame, who saw her fainting foe retir'd,
> With force renew'd, to victory aspir'd;
> (And looking upward to her kindred sky,
> As once our Saviour own'd his Deity,
> Pronounc'd his words—*she whom ye seek am I*.)
> Nor less amaz'd this voice the *Panther* heard,
> Than were those *Jews* to hear a god declar'd.[236]

This should be the moment when the play of *différance* is halted by the making present of the transcendental signified through the speech of the Church of Rome. But the text stumbles. Even leaving aside the awkwardness of the allegory which requires the

---

[234] Alexander Ross, *Mystagogus Poeticus, or The Muses Interpreter*, 5th edn. (London, 1672), pp. 168–71.
[235] For Pan as Christ see 'E. K.' in Spenser's *The Shepheardes Calender* (gloss to 'Maye', l. 54); Milton, 'On the Morning of Christ's Nativity', ll. 79–90.
[236] *The Hind and the Panther*, ii. 394–400.

words of Jesus to be spoken by a deer, there are changes to the sacred text. In the King James Bible Jesus asks 'Whom seek ye?', and when the Jews reply 'Jesus of Nazareth' he says, 'I am he'.[237] Jesus here is not simply identifying himself by name: he is, as the Hind says, claiming divinity, because according to the Greek text of the New Testament he says *ego eimi*, literally 'I I-am', which echoes God's description of himself to Moses, 'I AM THAT I AM'.[238] Jesus certainly does not say '*she whom ye seek am I*'. It is a blatant misquotation. The Hind's words conflate the two utterances of Jesus, rephrasing his words partly in order to fulfil the poem's Virgilian epigraph, *Antiquam exquirite matrem*. And the text has other awkwardnesses: the 'as' invites a realization of separation as well as likeness, since this is a simile not a repetition; what the Jews heard declared in the phrase 'I am' was God, rather than 'a god'; and even typographically the passage has been unlucky, since the triplet which should be emphatic is awkwardly tucked by the compositor into a parenthesis. The instability extends further if we turn to Dryden's translation of *Aeneid* Book I, where there is a moment of epiphany as the cloud surrounding Aeneas dissolves, the prince stands revealed in radiant beauty, and he says to Dido, 'He whom you seek am I'.[239] So the Hind's words, far from being privileged, are caught in a chain of misquotation, easily transferred, it would seem, back into the primal Roman story. How uncanny that the representatives of these two homelands should speak the same language.

THE POET AND HIS *PENATES*

When escaping from Troy, Aeneas asks his father to carry the household gods, the *Penates*, because his own hands are tainted with blood:

> 'Tu, genitor, cape sacra manu, patriosque Penates.
> 'Me, bello e tanto digressum et caede recenti,
> 'Attrectare nefas; donec me flumine vivo
> 'Abluero.[240]

---

[237] John 18: 4–5.   [238] Exodus 3: 14.   [239] *Aeneis*, i. 834.
[240] 'You, father, take in your hand the sacred things and the household gods of our country. For me, coming from such a war and recent slaughter, it would be a sin to touch them, until I cleanse myself in a living stream' (Virgil, *Aeneid*, ii. 717–20).

Did Dryden too think that his hands were somehow stained, and that he had to leave the household gods in his father's hands? His translation inserts a supplement into Virgil's text, as if completing the hemistich:

> 'Till in some living Stream I cleanse the Guilt
> Of dire Debate, and Blood in Battel spilt.[241]

'Debate' could mean 'battle', but this was not a normal usage in contemporary English; Dryden has chosen a word which also evokes the controversies in which he had become embroiled, and which had all too often confined him to an impoverished kind of present when he might have been moving freely in that imaginary present where he could commune with those who had written in a language that was foreign. His household gods were, indeed, *Penates*—a word which cannot be properly naturalized in the English tongue, nor translated without periphrasis. In classical Rome they were the tutelary gods of the household and of the state, and the state's *Penates* were said to be those which Anchises had carried from Troy. Perhaps Dryden's *Penates*, too, were of foreign origin.

Though this uncanny homeland troubled Dryden, it did not render him powerless; on the contrary. It is to encounter and thereby to master his loss and his anxiety that Dryden turns away from English when he approaches the topics of the home, of his self, of his own writing. The turn to Latin is motivated not by the desire to fashion a quasi-Augustan assurance, but by the resources which it provided for contemplating the dissolution of stable identities, a recurring motif in Dryden's translations. Virgil writes of the originary city in ruins, always already lost at the opening of the *Aeneid*, its destruction translated into art on the walls of Dido's temple even before we hear the narrative of its fall. He longs for secure structures, but knows that the human world is fraught with incoherence and tragedy.[242] Ovid invites us to imagine the dissolution of the boundaries between the human and the non-human. Horace takes possession of the present moment in the face of those

---

[241] *Aeneis*, ii. 978–9.
[242] This is the thesis of the classic essay by Adam Parry, 'The Two Voices of Virgil's *Aeneid*', *Arion*, 2:4 (1963) 66–80.

powers which might snatch away our goods and our lives. Lucretius asks us not to fear the loss of our corporeal selves and the idea of individuality which we predicate upon physical continuity, for

> When once an interrupting pause is made,
> That individual Being is decay'd.[243]

(That last line is Dryden's addition, and in 'individual' he turns to an English word with Latin roots in order to express singleness.) As Lucretius explains, it is precisely the interrupting pause which makes new configurations of life possible.

Dryden expects us to hear Latin as a repeated presence in his English texts—but it is never exactly repeated, rather remade; never exactly present, but a signifier of spiritual and cultural possibilities which are always already lost, and yet thereby, through that very loss, always ready at hand. Happily, to obtain possession of this golden bough, Dryden did not have to kill his predecessors: he had only to misquote them.

---

[243] 'Translation of the Latter Part of the Third Book of Lucretius: Against the Fear of Death', ll. 25–6.

PART II

TRANSLATION

3

MUTABILITY AND
METAMORPHOSIS

DRYDEN'S THEORY AND PRACTICE OF TRANSLATION[1]

In his Preface to *Ovid's Epistles* (1680), the volume which includes his first published versions of the classics, Dryden offers his famous tripartite analysis of translation:

All Translation I suppose may be reduced to these three heads.

First, that of Metaphrase, or turning an Authour word by word, and Line by Line, from one Language into another. Thus, or near this manner, was *Horace* his Art of Poetry translated by *Ben. Johnson*. The second way is that of Paraphrase, or translation with Latitude, where the Authour is kept in view by the Translator, so as never to be lost, but his words are not so strictly follow'd as his sense, and that too is admitted to

---

[1] Until recently, Dryden's translations have been comparatively neglected by critics. An early attempt to signal their importance was William Frost's *Dryden and the Art of Translation* (New Haven, 1955); later work includes Judith Sloman's uneven *Dryden: The Poetics of Translation* (Toronto, 1985), and Cedric D. Reverand II's perceptive *Dryden's Final Poetic Mode: The Fables* (Philadelphia, 1988), along with chapters in David Hopkins's *John Dryden* (Cambridge, 1986), and my own *John Dryden: A Literary Life* (Basingstoke, 1991). Worthwhile studies of individual translations from Latin are cited below at the appropriate points, but one essay on Dryden's Homer deserves special mention for the light which it casts on Dryden's thinking about the classics, the heroic, and power: Robin Sowerby, 'The Freedom of Dryden's Homer', *Translation and Literature*, 5 (1996) 26–50. Dryden's association with his publisher Jacob Tonson was crucial to his career as a translator, since together they pioneered both miscellanies and complete translations: for this see James Anderson Winn, *John Dryden and his World* (New Haven, 1987), *passim*; Stuart Gillespie, 'The Early Years of the Dryden–Tonson Partnership: The Background to their Composite Translations and Miscellanies of the 1680s', *Restoration*, 12 (1988) 10–19; and Paul Hammond, 'The Circulation of Dryden's Poetry', *Papers of the Bibliographical Society of America*, 86 (1992) 379–409. A useful context for Dryden's work is provided by Stuart Gillespie's 'A Checklist of Restoration English Translations and Adaptations of Classical Greek and Latin Poetry, 1660–1700', *Translation and Literature*, 1 (1991) 52–67.

be amplyfied, but not alter'd. Such is Mr. *Wallers* Translation of *Virgils* Fourth *Æneid*. The Third way is that of Imitation, where the Translator (if now he has not lost that Name) assumes the liberty not only to vary from the words and sence, but to forsake them both as he sees occasion: and taking only some general hints from the Original, to run division on the ground-work, as he pleases. Such is Mr. *Cowleys* practice in turning two odes of *Pindar*, and one of *Horace* into *English*.[2]

Dryden's own way of translating is, he says, the middle way between the two extremes of literal rendering and free imitation. This method preserves the author's sense without 'innovation of thoughts', but respects the distinctive temper of the translator's language, not holding it 'necessary that Words and Lines should be confin'd to the measure of their Original'. If the translator's English were to be cramped and made almost unintelligible by too close an adherence to the syntax and word-order of the Latin, such attempted faithfulness would actually betray the original by words 'so ill chosen as to make it appear in an unhandsome dress, and rob it of its native Lustre'. But by the middle way, says Dryden, 'the Spirit of an Authour may be transfus'd, and yet not lost'.[3] The encounter between author and translator is, in Dryden's terms, an act of double recognition. Beyond his technical mastery of the two languages, the translator must understand his author's 'particular turn of Thoughts, and of Expression, which are the Characters that distinguish, and as it were individuate him from all other writers. When we are come thus far, 'tis time to look into our selves, to conform our Genius to his'.[4] So the translator must, on the one hand, appreciate his author's distinctive habits of thought, that which 'individuates' him; and, on the other, he must through introspection understand his own characteristics, and then seek to 'conform' his genius to the genius of his author, adopting a language and a manner which are consonant with the original. Translation is, in part, a mode of self-knowledge.

Dryden returns to this subject in the Preface to *Sylvæ* (1685), where he explains that it is not enough for the translator

to give his Authors sence, in good *English*, in Poetical expressions, and in Musical numbers: For, though all these are exceeding difficult to perform, there yet remains an harder task . . . that is, the maintaining the

---

[2] *Poems*, p. 182.   [3] *Poems*, p. 185.   [4] Ibid.

Character of an Author, which distinguishes him from all others, and makes him appear that individual Poet whom you wou'd interpret. For example, not only the thoughts, but the Style and Versification of *Virgil* and *Ovid*, are very different: Yet I see, even in our best Poets, who have Translated some parts of them, that they have confounded their several Talents; and by endeavouring only at the sweetness and harmony of Numbers, have made them both so much alike, that if I did not know the Originals, I shou'd never be able to Judge by the Copies, which was *Virgil*, and which was *Ovid*.[5]

What Dryden wants us to hear is the distinctive voice of each Latin poet: as he puts it in his Dedication to the *Aeneis*, 'I have endeavour'd to make *Virgil* speak such *English*, as he wou'd himself have spoken, if he had been born in *England*, and in this present Age.'[6] And when translating Lucretius, he says, 'I lay'd by my natural Diffidence and Scepticism for a while, to take up that Dogmatical way of his, which as I said, is so much his Character, as to make him that individual Poet.'[7]

In these encounters with classical writers, Dryden is seeking to modulate his own poetic voice into an equivalent for that of Ovid or Virgil or Lucretius; he discovers a new voice through the disciplines of translation, disciplines which offer new forms of freedom and opportunity. The single voice rarely interested Dryden: his *œuvre* is dominated by plays (which are often dramas of debate); translations (in which the voice of the poet is half-submerged in a form of dialogue with the original author); critical essays which move between different viewpoints (whether the formal dialogue of the essay *Of Dramatick Poesie* or the extended citation of previous critics in the 'Discourse Concerning Satire'); and poems of argument, dialogue, and ventriloquism exploring positions and staging arguments with which the poet himself did not agree (*Absalom and Achitophel*, *Religio Laici*, *The Hind and the Panther*). Translation provided Dryden with the medium through which he could experiment with different poetic voices, different degrees of proximity to and distance from his own text, less direct authorial responsibility for the ideas and viewpoints with which he was playing. At the end of his version of Virgil's *Eclogue* IX, a poem lamenting the poet's ill fortune and lack of rewards, Moeris says

---

[5] *Poems*, p. 392.   [6] *Poems*, p. 1055.   [7] *Poems*, p. 395.

'I'le find a voice'.[8] The 'I' here is neither Virgil nor Moeris nor Dryden, but a signifier which moves between the three. 'I'le find a voice' translates Virgil's *canemus* ('we shall sing'), moving it from plural to singular, but this newly created 'I' (ironically but deliberately) signifies not a singular poet but an indeterminate plural which contrasts with the comradely plural (Moeris and Lycidas) of Virgil's *canemus*, and highlights the poet's isolation.

Whatever he may have announced in the Preface to *Ovid's Epistles* at the outset of his career as a translator, in practice Dryden would combine all three methods of translation—metaphrase, paraphrase, and imitation—allowing into his versions some literal renderings which remind us immediately of the Latin which they are shadowing, and some additional ideas which may be in the spirit of what he takes his original to be, but cannot be immediately authorized by the Latin or its accompanying glosses. Dryden cautions against adding to the originals, for to supplement the sense of the text is to betray something which is 'Sacred and inviolable';[9] and yet he also quotes with approval Sir John Denham's dictum that the text to which the translator does not bring his own spirit is merely a dead residue, a *caput mortuum*.[10] Indeed, he admits his use of such amplification:

I must acknowledge, that I have many times exceeded my Commission; for I have both added and omitted, and even sometimes very boldly made such expositions of my Authors, as no *Dutch* Commentator will forgive me . . . where I have enlarg'd them, I desire the false Criticks wou'd not always think that those thoughts are wholly mine, but that either they are secretly in the Poet, or may be fairly deduc'd from him: or at least, if both those considerations should fail, that my own is of a piece with his, and that if he were living, and an *Englishman*, they are such, as he wou'd probably have written.[11]

What Dryden creates, in effect, is a translation which is a double-faced but not duplicitous commentary, a text folded at once towards its Latin original and towards its origin in Restoration culture. On the one side, Dryden's text explains obscurities and specific historical details in the Latin by including brief glosses within the text of the

---

[8] 'The Ninth Eclogue', l. 94, in *Miscellany Poems* (London, 1684).

[9] *Poems*, p. 185.

[10] *Poems*, pp. 185–6. Denham's phrase comes from his Preface to *The Destruction of Troy* (1656), his translation of *Aeneid* II.   [11] *Poems*, pp. 390–1.

translation rather than in notes; and on the other side, in its second fold, it turns the original poems towards late seventeenth-century England as a mirror for the times, a commentary on the needs and follies of the age. What makes the single movement of translation possible is the assumption that thoughts are clothed in words, and so can be changed from a Latin into an English dress. But what makes its double movement both possible and valuable is the assumption that human nature is sufficiently stable across time and across cultures for translation to be an enlightening mutual commentary.

All translation entails the management of loss. The original text is no longer present on the page, but lurks behind the translation, temporarily displaced by it, teasingly inaccessible to those who do not have access to the original language, haunting the page like a ghostly presence for those who do. But the original text has already been displaced and repositioned several times through the activities of Renaissance editors. In that respect there is no single 'original', only a series of ostensible originals. Classical scrolls and medieval codices give way to the printed *editio princeps*, and then that newly legible and accessible text accrues an incrustation of glosses and editorial commentary. Dryden worked from as many different editions as he could buy or borrow, and so his sense of the Latin poems was coloured by the work of previous commentators, and by the translations and imitations which various skilled hands had produced: he was working in a field which had been defined not only by Horace and Virgil, but by their learned interpreters. Among those editions which Dryden favoured,[12] some

---

[12] For the editions used by Dryden see J. McG. Bottkol, 'Dryden's Latin Scholarship', *Modern Philology*, 40 (1943) 241–54; and Paul Hammond, 'Figures of Horace in Dryden's Literary Criticism', in *Horace Made New: Horatian Influences on British Writing from the Renaissance to the Twentieth Century*, ed. Charles Martindale and David Hopkins (Cambridge, 1993), pp. 127–47, 294–7, at p. 294. In the 'Postscript to the Reader' after his *Aeneis* (*Poems*, p. 1425) Dryden records his gratitude to Gilbert Dolben for supplying him with various editions of Virgil. Few books from Dryden's library have been identified, but among them is a pocket Virgil (see Paul Hammond, 'Dryden's Library', *Notes and Queries*, 229 (1984) 344–5). Locke and Congreve collected annotated editions of the classics, including parallel texts in Latin and French, and their libraries give some clues as to the kinds of edition which Dryden would have owned. Locke owned twenty editions of Horace and four of Juvenal; Congreve owned multiple editions of Horace, various editions and translations of Ovid, and a 1682 copy of the Ruaeus Virgil, the edition from which Dryden chiefly worked (see John Harrison and Peter Laslett, *The Library of John Locke*, second edition (Oxford, 1971); John C. Hodges, *The Library of William Congreve* (New York, 1955)).

present an elegantly designed page which clearly differentiates text and notes, as in the case of the Schrevelius Juvenal or the Cnipping Ovid; others, like Ruaeus' Virgil, surround the text with a Latin prose *interpretatio* and add explanatory notes at the foot of the page (Plate 6); while in editions like Lambinus' Horace the text fights for visibility in a densely printed page of annotations.[13] Readers were presented with several different kinds of material out of which to construct 'Horace' or 'Virgil', so that the familiar distinction between text and margin begins to be blurred: the marginal glosses become part of the text which the reader fashions for himself when interpreting the poetry, while parts of the commentary may slip into or displace portions of the poem in the reader's memory. So when Dryden read what Horace had to say about the ideal length for a play:

Neve minor, neu sit quinto productior actu[14]

he evidently noted the editorial gloss *brevior* for *minor* in Lubinus, for it was this combination of text and commentary which lodged in his mind and generated this ostensible quotation from Horace in the essay *Of Dramatick Poesie*:

Neu brevior quinto, neu sit productior actu:[15]

This is not what Horace wrote, nor what any Renaissance edition ever printed as the text of the *Ars Poetica*: it is Dryden's fusion of text and margin into a new line of Latin verse. As one would expect of Dryden, the new line, with its different vocabulary and word order, still scans.

Dryden was also aware that he was matching himself against distinguished predecessors among the English poets. Some previous translations of Latin poets had been crabbed or bland, but Jonson, Milton, Denham, and Cowley were among those whose versions of Horace and Virgil challenged Dryden to compete, and helped him to rethink the significance of the originals.[16] In scouring those

---

[13] The remainder of this paragraph is adapted from my 'Figures of Horace', p. 128.

[14] 'Let no play be either shorter or longer than five acts': Horace, *Ars Poetica*, l. 189.

[15] *Works*, xvii. 23.

[16] In the Preface to *Sylvæ* Dryden commends Creech's translation of Lucretius, and in the Dedication to the *Aeneis* he praises the translations from Virgil by Roscommon, Denham, Waller, and Cowley (*Poems*, pp. 398, 1051).

translations for the best turns of phrase and the happiest vocabulary, he was making his own poem in part a distillation of earlier versions: a rendering which registered the form and pressure of his own age, while directing the reader to other ways of thinking.

The textual field which Dryden fashions in his translations is a complex, macaronic text where the Latin continually shadows the English: occasional Latin idioms or Roman references remind us of the missing original—that original which some readers may be holding in their minds as they read, thus permitting a dialogue between the Latin and the English.[17] The time and space of the translation are a third field, a synthesis of Roman and English worlds, a new kind of time in which readers find both alterity and resemblance, encountering the origins of their own culture while finding that modern culture subjected to an intermittent oblique commentary. Within such a textual field those much-discussed political allusions in the translations which were published after 1688 are not jagged shards on an otherwise smooth path: rather they are part of a continuum, an extended meditation on likeness and difference which is sustained by a fundamental fascination with the management of change. For as Dryden said in the Preface to *Fables Ancient and Modern* (1700): 'Mankind is ever the same, and nothing lost out of Nature, though every thing is alter'd.'[18]

Through translation Dryden confronted the mystery of how a sense of selfhood and identity persists in spite of change. The characteristics of a writer should be recognizable even when he has been translated into another language: we should recognize what it is which individuates him. On the other hand, the translator seeks to conform his own genius to that of his original, losing himself to some degree. Moreover, Dryden repeatedly selected for translation poems or passages which dramatize the precariousness of selfhood and individuation: from Virgil and Lucretius he took accounts of man facing extinction in death, or striving to merge himself with his partner in sexual union, or deliberately joining

---

[17] Tonson seems to have been aware that some readers would wish to compare translations closely with the originals, for he supplies the Latin text on facing pages for Rochester's translations from Lucretius (in *Poems, etc. On Several Occasions: With Valentinian; A Tragedy. Written by the Right Honourable John Late Earl of Rochester* (London, 1691)), and for Roscommon's translations from Horace (*Poems by the Earl of Roscomon* (London, 1717)).

[18] *Poems*, p. 1455.

that partner in death; from Lucretius too, evocations of those
changes which come by the random movement of atoms; from
Ovid and Virgil, accounts of change which follow the rhythms of
the seasons and the laws of nature; also from Ovid, other mythical
metamorphoses across the boundaries between the human and the
non-human; and in Horace he found ways of living untroubled by
those apparently arbitrary changes which men attribute to
Fortune. Translation was for Dryden the inescapable condition of
the world, the shifting ground on which forms of singleness and
stability could be fashioned.

FROM THE *AENEID*: MOURNING THE DEATHS OF
YOUNG MEN

Sylvæ: or, The Second Part of Poetical Miscellanies (1685) includes a
series of translations from the Latin poets which constitute
Dryden's first use of the form as a way of exploring philosophical
questions.[19] It begins with several selections from the *Aeneid*:[20] the
two episodes featuring Nisus and Euryalus, the first from Book V,
telling of the race in which they take part, and the second from
Book IX, relating their deaths; the story of the deaths of Mezentius
and his son Lausus from Book X; and from Book VIII the request
of Venus to Vulcan that he should forge a shield for her son
Aeneas. Selections follow from Lucretius; then three idylls from
Theocritus; and finally three odes from Horace, together with his
second Epode. Themes which link these texts are the confrontation of death, particularly the death of young men; the power of
sexual desire; and the need to take hold of one's life in the present
in order to avoid being a slave to Fortune.

   The story of Nisus and Euryalus was in Dryden's mind as he
composed his memorial poem for John Oldham (written in the
same year as the episodes in *Sylvæ*) and it provides one of that
poem's two dominant classical references, the other being to

---

[19]   For a discussion of *Sylvæ* see Stuart Gillespie, 'Dryden's *Sylvæ*: A Study of Dryden's
Translations from the Latin in the Second Tonson Miscellany, 1685', unpublished PhD
thesis, University of Cambridge, 1987.

[20]   These episodes were revised for inclusion in the complete Virgil of 1697. Since they
are not included in *Poems*, ed. Kinsley, they are quoted from *Sylvæ*, with line numbers
added from the modernized text in *Poems*, ed. Hammond.

Marcellus, the lost heir of Augustus. Verbal echoes link the memorial poem and the translation.[21] In 'To the Memory of Mr. Oldham', Dryden had given the allusion a double purchase, suggesting that the fallen Nisus might stand either for Oldham or for himself. In *Sylvæ* he extends this anguished contemplation of the extinction of youthful promise by translating the whole episode which tells how Nisus and Euryalus set out through enemy lines in order to reach Aeneas, only to be intercepted and killed. It was one of the most famous episodes in the *Aeneid*, speaking of homosexual love and comradeship, a bond so strong that one of the pair risks death in a reckless attempt first to protect and then to avenge his lover. It speaks also of the perilous transition from boyhood to manhood as the young men seek to prove their masculinity in a hazardous exploit; of restlessness, and the danger of overstepping boundaries, in that they court disaster by a heedless pursuit of spoil rather than a circumspect attention to the task in hand; and throughout it brings before us the precariousness of our knowledge and security.[22]

Prominent in these two extracts is the unsettling presence of Fortune, which is a recurring theme in *Sylvæ* and beyond. Dryden frequently turned to this personification as a way of thinking through the casual and irrational element in life: it is Fortune which gives worldly goods and satisfactions, but is liable to snatch them away without warning, and apparently without reason. Fortune, therefore, cannot be trusted, and nothing which one cares about should be within her gift. In Dryden's thinking, Fortune's power to hurt may be rendered ineffectual by refusing to accord her the power to enrich. Fortune as 'Occasion' offers opportunities which have to be seized before they are snatched away, as Machiavelli classically expounded in *Il Principe*, but the control which she thus has over us and our time is to be resisted, since it undermines a man's self-presence, his capacity to be

---

[21] See *Poems*, ed. Hammond, ii. 273; and see ii. 293 for parallels between 'Mezentius and Lausus' and 'To the Memory of Mr. Oldham.'

[22] For these motifs see *Virgil: Aeneid Book IX*, ed. Philip Hardie (Cambridge, 1994), pp. 14–34. Joseph Farrell notes verbal echoes of Lucretius in Virgil which connect this episode with Lucretius' analysis of man's lack of tranquillity: see 'The Virgilian intertext', in *The Cambridge Companion to Virgil*, ed. Charles Martindale (Cambridge, 1997), pp. 222–38, at p. 235. See also the discussion of the episode by Nicholas Horsfall in *A Companion to the Study of Virgil*, ed. Nicholas Horsfall, Mnemosyne Supplementum 151 (Leiden, 1995), pp. 170–8.

himself in his own time. It is in opposition to such decomposition, against life's lability, that Dryden's translations shape modes of coherence in their own particular form of temporality.

In his translation from Book V of the *Aeneid*, recounting the foot-race which is part of the funeral games for Anchises, Dryden inflects the episode with references to Fortune. He describes the fall of two runners as 'two misfortunes', and makes Aeneas award the prize 'Where Fortune plac'd it' while nevertheless seeking 'her Errours to amend'; these allusions to Fortune are not present in Virgil. When Nisus exclaims,

> In falling, both did equal fortune try,
> Wou'd fortune make me fall as happily.

the emphatic repetition is Dryden's, for Virgil just has the single reference to fortune.[23] These touches remind us that the story of the race, in which the effort of the runners is thwarted both by accident and by foul play, is emblematic of the vulnerability of human life (conventionally imaged as a race) to the intervention of chance.

When in the extract from Book IX Nisus and Euryalus come across the enemy asleep, Dryden has Nisus say that 'Occasion calls the Sword to be prepar'd', where Virgil writes *ipsa vocat res*.[24] Dryden sees the friends as responding to the call of Fortuna-Occasio, and entering her dangerous territory. Nisus tells his comrade to guard his back 'while I securely go',[25] but that word 'securely' should trouble us. It is Dryden's addition here, and is one of a series of uses which echo through this passage. Nisus had noticed that the enemy were 'secure', but they are 'secure' only in the sense of being 'free from apprehension, over-confident' (*OED* 1), not in the sense 'safe, not exposed to danger' (*OED* 3). Theirs is a false, deluding sense of security:

> Thou seest the Foe secure . . .
> . . . the most in Sleep supine;
> Dissolv'd in Ease, and drunk with Victory.
>
> .   .   .   .   .   .
>
> The Foes securely drench'd in Sleep and wine
> Their Watch neglect.[26]

---

[23] 'Nisus and Euryalus', ll. 70, 82–3, 93–4; Virgil, *Aeneid*, v. 356.
[24] 'Nisus and Euryalus', l. 315; *Aeneid*, ix. 320: 'the thing itself calls'.
[25] 'Nisus and Euryalus', l. 317.   [26] Ibid., ll. 123–5, 195–6.

Men may mistake being secure for being secure. The whole episode exemplifies the precariousness of our security and the doubtfulness of our perception, as Virgil contrasts 'the partial and impassioned perceptions of the actors' with 'a detailed and lingering particularity in the narrator's descriptions, above all of wounds and death'.[27]

Dryden's translation emphasizes the passionate human bonds which are about to be destroyed. First, the love between Nisus and Euryalus is underscored by a cluster of additions, phrases such as 'ever Faithful', 'their desire was one', 'pious Friends', 'whom living he ador'd', 'on his dear Breast', and several occurrences of the word 'lover'.[28] Lines are added strengthening the devotion of Euryalus' mother.[29] And the speech which Ascanius makes to Euryalus before sending the pair off on their venture is heavy with emotion:

> But thou, whose years are more to mine ally'd,
> No fate my vow'd affection shall divide
> From thee O wondrous Youth: be ever mine,
> Take full possession, all my Soul is thine:
> My lifes Companion, and my bosom Friend;
> One faith, one fame, one fate shall both attend.[30]

> Te vero, mea quem spatiis proprioribus aetas
> Insequitur, venerande puer, jam pectore toto
> Accipio, et comitem casus complector in omnes,
> Nulla meis sine te quaeretur gloria rebus.[31]

Several elements in the vocabulary here link this passage to the elegy for Oldham,[32] the tone is more impassioned than in Virgil, and there are some striking expansions of the Latin. Virgil's Ascanius receives Euryalus with his whole heart, whereas Dryden's asks Euryalus to take full possession of him.

Dryden similarly heightens the despair which the older man, Nisus, feels when he loses the young Euryalus in the wood as they attempt to escape. He effectively introduces a quasi-Virgilian

---

[27] *Aeneid IX*, ed. Hardie, p. 150. [28] *Poems*, ed. Hammond, ii. 265.
[29] Ibid., ii. 268. [30] 'Nisus and Euryalus', ll. 249–54.
[31] *Aeneid*, ix. 275–8: 'You, indeed, who approach my age more closely, revered youth, I now receive with my whole heart, and embrace you as my companion in all that may chance. I shall never seek any glory without you.'
[32] *Poems*, ed. Hammond, ii. 273.

hemistich, matching by different means Virgil's poignant word order which eventually delivers the absent *amicum*:

> Ut stetit, et frustra absentem respexit amicum.[33]
>
> Till turning at the length he stood his ground,
> And vainly cast his longing eyes around
> For his lost friend![34]

Dryden realizes that Nisus' glance will be more than anxious; as it seeks his lover, it will be 'longing'. The friend who in Virgil is only absent, is here already 'lost'. Soon Nisus sees Volscens rush at Euryalus with his sword, but 'That fatal sight the lover could not bear', and he cries out, demanding to suffer instead of his friend. Virgil says that Nisus is *exterritus, amens* ('terrified, frantic'), but Dryden is concentrating on the predicament of Nisus primarily *qua* lover, perhaps inspired to misread *amens* as *amans* ('loving'). But Nisus' intervention is unavailing:

> Too late alas, he speaks;
> The Sword, which unrelenting fury guides
> Driv'n with full force had pierc'd his tender sides;
> Down fell the beauteous Youth, the gaping wound
> Gush'd out a Crimson stream and stain'd the ground:
> His nodding neck reclines on his white breast,
> Like a fair Flow'r, in furrow'd Fields opprest,
> By the keen Share: or Poppy on the plain,
> Whose heavy head is overcharg'd with rain.[35]

Again Dryden uses a hemistich to register emotion, inaugurating a passage in which the rhythm contributes powerfully to the feeling, first with heavy beats to narrate the killing, then enjambement to suggest the unstoppable flow of the boy's blood, and finally a solemn movement of mourning. Just as Virgil places his strong verbs at the beginning of his lines (*Transadigit . . .* | *Volvitur.* '[the sword] thrusts through . . . | [Euryalus] rolls over'), so Dryden opens his lines with the sequence 'Driven . . . | Down fell . . . | Gushed out . . .'. Virgil focuses our gaze on the terrible wound which the sword inflicts on the youth: *Transadigit costas, et*

---

[33]   *Aeneid*, ix. 389: 'then he stopped, and in vain looked back for his absent friend.'

[34]   'Nisus and Euryalus', ll. 412–14. In the revised 1697 text Dryden had second thoughts about this striking effect, and compressed the lines into a regular couplet.

[35]   'Nisus and Euryalus', ll. 464–71; *Aeneid*, ix. 431–7. Dryden's hemistich is once again removed in 1697.

candida pectora rumpit ('it thrusts through the ribs, and bursts open the white chest'). Virgil's choice of *candida* is richly, poignantly, resonant: 'white' (*OLD* 2), so that we see the gleam of the boy's bare chest in the darkness; also 'fair skinned' (*OLD* 5), which was a sign of beauty in the ancient world, reminding us of the lad's erotic appeal. But *candida* also meant 'innocent, pure' (*OLD* 8b), and 'unripe' (*OLD* 3b), and, ironically, 'lucky, fortunate' (*OLD* 7). To ponder the polysemic field of *candida* is to bring into one's mind all that makes the loss of Euryalus so terrible. Dryden's response to this can be seen in his sequence 'tender', 'beauteous Youth' and 'white breast', which together keep many of the implications of Virgil's dense term.[36] The whole passage is narrated in the present tense by Virgil, so that the events unfold before our eyes as they do before the horrified gaze of Nisus. Dryden, however, varies his tenses: the first sentence moves from the present ('speaks . . . guides') into a past ('had pierced') in which the deed is already irrecoverable. Then we move from the completed action of the killing ('fell . . . gushed . . . stained') to a present in which the boy is transformed into the tragic object of the onlooker's contemplation ('His nodding neck reclines . . .') as we reach the simile of the nodding poppy.

Nisus in despair rushes at Volscens, and dies in the act of taking his revenge:

> Dying he slew: and stagg'ring on the plain,
> Sought for the Body of his Lover slain:
> Then quietly on his dear Breast he fell;
> Content in death to be reveng'd so well.
> O happy pair! for if my verse can give
> Eternity; your fame shall ever live:

>   moriens animam abstulit hosti.
> Tum super exanimem sese projecit amicum
> Confossus, placidaque ibi demum morte quievit.
> Fortunati ambo! si quid mea carmina possunt,
> Nulla dies unquam memori vos eximet aevo.[37]

---

[36] In his 1697 revision Dryden returned to *candida* and drew out further implications, calling the boy's neck 'snowy' and likening him to a 'white poppy'.

[37] 'Nisus and Euryalus', ll. 481–6; *Aeneid*, ix. 443–7: 'Dying he took the life from his enemy. Then, pierced, he threw himself forward over his lifeless friend, and there at length found rest in peaceful death. Fortunate pair! If my verse can achieve anything, no day will ever steal you from the memory of time.'

Dryden has Nisus seek out 'the Body of his Lover', and fall 'on his dear Breast', details which bring to the fore the physical and emotional bond between the two men. The note on which Virgil ends this episode contrasts with the protagonists' earlier restlessness, and Dryden responds to this with his 'quietly' and 'content'. When translating Virgil's *makarismos* (beginning *Fortunati ambo!*), Dryden avoids rendering *Fortunati* with the ostensibly obvious equivalent 'fortunate', because for him Fortune has acquired too destructive a connotation. Instead his final gesture translates the pair out of Fortune's domain into very different philosophical territory. Like 'quietly', and 'content', the word 'happy' belongs to the lexis of seventeenth-century definitions of 'The Happy Man', and places Nisus and Euryalus in the company of the Horatian husbandman among those who find peace away from the chances and changes of the world.[38]

FROM LUCRETIUS: IMAGINING A SELF IN A UNIVERSE OF RANDOM MOTION

The writer whom Dryden represents as having the most distinctive voice, the most clearly individuated, is Lucretius.[39] But this is an individuality which is not comfortably congruent with Dryden's own manner and viewpoint: the two voices make neither unison nor harmony. Dryden tells his readers that in translating extracts

[38] See Maren-Sofie Røstvig, *The Happy Man: Studies in the Metamorphoses of a Classical Ideal, 1600–1700*, 2nd edn. (Oslo, 1962); and Bernard Beugnot, *Le Discours de la retraite au XVIIᵉ siècle* (Paris, 1996).

[39] Some portions of the following discussion derive from my essay 'The Integrity of Dryden's Lucretius', *Modern Language Review*, 78 (1983) 1–23, *q.v.* for a fuller account of Dryden's previous uses of Lucretius, and contemporary attitudes to him. See also the headnote and annotations to the Lucretian translations in *Poems*, ed. Hammond. Valuable recent work on Epicureanism in 17th-cent. England includes *Atoms, 'Pneuma', and Tranquillity: Epicurean and Stoic Themes in European Thought*, ed. Margaret J. Osler (Cambridge, 1991), and Charles Kay Smith, 'French Philosophy and English Politics in Interregnum Poetry', in *The Stuart Court and Europe: Essays in Politics and Political Culture*, ed. R. Malcolm Smuts (Cambridge, 1996), pp. 177–209. Dryden's principal English predecessors in translating Lucretius were Lucy Hutchinson in the 1650s (British Library MS Add 19333, first printed as *Lucy Hutchinson's Translation of Lucretius: 'De Rerum Natura'*, ed. Hugh de Quehen (London, 1996)); an anonymous prose translation (Bodleian Library MS Rawl. D. 314); John Evelyn's translation of Book I (printed 1656), and of Books III–VI (in MS in the British Library, presently uncatalogued); and Thomas Creech, *T. Lucretius Carus The Epicurean Philosopher, His Six Books De Natura Rerum Done into English Verse* (Oxford, 1682).

from *De Rerum Natura* he has 'lay'd by my natural Diffidence and Scepticism for a while, to take up that Dogmatical way of his, which as I said, is so much his Character, as to make him that individual Poet'.[40] The diffidence and scepticism which Dryden regards as characteristic of his own nature are qualities which refuse to insist upon the individual's own viewpoint, for 'Scepticism' here means the ability to see both sides of a question and to keep different possibilities in play, rather than a distrust of epistemology: its opposite is dogmatism.[41] What Dryden has to surrender in order to be a faithful translator of Lucretius is his characteristic lack of self-assertion. (In this he may have been influenced by Montaigne, who frequently cites Lucretius, including the passages which Dryden selected for translation.) And yet Dryden's own voice, and his own philosophical interests, do impart a distinctive inflection to these translations. Both through the initial selection and in the local vocabulary they place before us the predicament of man in prey to anxiety and desire, to those passions which disturb his equanimity and rob him of a tranquil, collected self-presence. 'Lucretius: Against the Fear of Death' and 'Lucretius: Concerning the Nature of Love' explore two of the principal passions to which man may be enslaved. And both extracts also highlight the strange relationship of human beings to the physical world of which they are—rather awkwardly—a part. The passage from Book III shows us man as a chance assembly of atoms which death will disassemble, and which the random motion of the universe will then toss around and turn into new combinations. And the account of sexual desire from Book IV emphasizes the comic predicament of the lover who desires physical satisfaction but is actually prevented by his very physicality from attaining that union which he seeks, the extinction of self through fusion with his beloved.[42]

Individuation is in question throughout these versions from Lucretius, since the Epicurean philosophy—with its doctrine of a material universe consisting of atoms in random motion—presents a vision of the world, and of man, and of the connection between

---

[40] *Poems*, p. 395.
[41] Thus Phillip Harth, *Contexts of Dryden's Thought* (Chicago, 1968), pp. 5–8.
[42] 'Lucretius: Concerning the Nature of Love', ll. 56–62, 89–90; see *Poems*, ed. Hammond, ii. 332–44 for a commentary on this.

the two, which makes our usual fictions of selfhood seem precarious, and is radically at odds with Christian teaching. How could one maintain a sense of selfhood (let alone a moral self) within such a world view?

In the Preface to *Sylvæ* Dryden distances himself from certain aspects of Lucretius' philosophy, particularly his ideas about the mortality of the soul, for 'they are so absurd, that I cannot if I wou'd believe them'.[43] And yet, he continues,

there are other Arguments in this Poem ... not belonging to the Mortality of the Soul, which are strong enough to a reasonable Man, to make him less in love with Life, and consequently in less apprehensions of Death. Such as are the natural Satiety, proceeding from a perpetual enjoyment of the same things; the inconveniencies of old age, which make him uncapable of corporeal pleasures; the decay of understanding and memory, which render him contemptible and useless to others; these and many other reasons so pathetically urg'd, so beautifully express'd, so adorn'd with examples, and so admirably rais'd by the *Prosopopeia* of Nature, who is brought in speaking to her Children, with so much authority and vigour, deserve the pains I have taken with them.[44]

Then, turning to the passage from Book IV concerning the nature of love, he says: 'I am not yet so secure from that passion, but that I want my Authors Antidotes against it. He has given the truest and most Philosophical account both of the Disease and Remedy, which I ever found in any Author.'[45]

In rejecting those aspects of Lucretius' philosophy which run counter to Christian teaching, while seeing in his poem great beauties and powerful moral arguments, Dryden is following the approach exemplified by the principal Renaissance editor of Lucretius, Dionysius Lambinus, who urged that Lucretius should not be dismissed simply because some parts of his poem were theologically unacceptable:

Quamobrem sic agamus potius. id, quod adest, laudemus, eoque fruamur: eo, quod abest, aequo animo, patienterque careamus: hoc est, huius poematis elegantiam, venustatem, pulchritudinem amemus, atque amplectamur: argumenti melioris sortem in eo desideremus. Quid enim? eos poetas, ex quibus solam curarum nostrarum obliuionem, solamque oblectationem quaerimus, cupidissime legere solemus: poetam non modo

[43] *Poems*, p. 395.   [44] *Poems*, p. 396.   [45] *Poems*, pp. 396–7.

nostros animos delectantem, verum etiam obscurissimas de rerum natura quaestiones pulcherrimis versibus explicantem, negligemus? Homerum, propterea quod in quibusdam fabularum partim turpium, partim absurdarum inuolucris omnium rerum naturalium, atque humanarum cognitionem inclusam continere existimatur, non solum legimus, verum etiam ediscimus: Lucretium, sine fabularum, taliumque nugarum integumentis, de principiis & causis rerum, de mundo, de mundi partibus, de vita beata, de rebus caelestibus ac terrenis, non vere illum quidem, neque pie, sed tamen simpliciter, & aperte, &, vt Epicureum, ingeniose, & acute, & erudite, & purissimo sermone loquentem non audiemus? Non enim, si multis locis a Platone dissidet: non si multa cum religione nostra pugnantia dicit, iccirco ea etiam, quae cum illorum, & Christianorum sententia congruunt, spernere debemus. Quam praeclare de coercendis cupiditatibus, de sedandis animorum motibus, de mentis tranquillitate comparanda disputat?[46]

Lambinus values Lucretius particularly for the arguments which he presents tending to 'quiet of mind', helping the reader to counteract the ways in which man is disturbed by anxiety and fear and desire. The aim is Epicurean *ataraxia*, calmness, equanimity. Etymologically *ataraxia* is the opposite of *tarachē*, confusion and disorder, so the Epicurean philosophy seeks to achieve in the human mind a calm and tranquillity which contrasts with the random motion of the universe.

Many contemporaries of Lambinus, and of Dryden, would have been surprised at this reading of Epicureanism, for this philosophy was often crudely represented as pure hedonistic self-indulgence.

---

[46] *T. Lucretii Cari De Rerum Natura Libri VI*, ed. Dionysius Lambinus (Paris, 1570), sig. b2ʳ⁻ᵛ: 'So let our course of action be to praise and enjoy what we do have, and to accept with calm patience the absence of that which we do not have. So let us relish and take delight in the elegance, sweetness, and beauty of this poem. Doubtless we wish that it had a better thesis. But we are accustomed to devour those poets from whom we seek only oblivion from our cares, and sheer delight: shall we then pass over this poet, who not only delights the soul but also expounds in the most beautiful verse the profoundest questions about the nature of things? Although Homer wraps up his meaning in stories which are sometimes absurd and sometimes immoral, we nevertheless consider him to have a comprehensive knowledge of man and nature: so we not only read him, we learn him. Lucretius, without these fables and obscure wrappings, speaks of the origins and causes of things, of the world and its parts, of the happy life, of the ways of the heavens and the earth—not always accurately, indeed, or piously, but with simplicity and clarity; and, following Epicurus himself, cleverly, sharply, learnedly, and in the purest language: and shall we not hear him? If in many places he dissents from Plato, and says much which is contrary to our religion, we should not therefore reject that which is consonant with those principles. How wonderfully he writes about the compulsion of desire, about calming the turbulence of the spirit, about attaining quiet of mind!'

Here one may stand for many: Nathaniel Ingelo writes of Epicurus that 'his Opinion concerning *Pleasure* was declar'd in the time of his Life by his most intimate Companions to be this; *That our Happiness doth consist in brutish Voluptuousness*'.[47] But here is Epicurus himself, in his epistle to Menoeceus, as translated by his seventeenth-century apologist Walter Charleton, who was one of Dryden's friends:

when we say; that Pleasure in the Generall is the end of a happy life, or the Chiefest Good; we are very far from understanding those Pleasures, which are so much admired, courted and pursued by men wallowing in Luxury, or any other pleasures that are placed in the meer motion or action of Fruition,[48] wereby, the sense is pleasantly tickled; as some, either out of Ignorance of the right, or dissent of opinion, or praejudice and Evill will against us, have wrongfully expounded our words: but onely this (the importance of the matter will excuse our repetition of it). Not to be pained in Body, nor perturbed in Mind.

For, it is not perpetuall Feastings and Drinkings; it is not the love of, and Familiarity with beautifull boyes and women; it is not the Delicacies of rare Fishes, sweet meats, rich Wines, nor any other Dainties of the Table, that can make a Happy life: But, it is Reason, with Sobriety, and consequently a serene Mind; investigating the Causes, why this Object is to be Elected, and that to be Rejected; and chasing away those vain, superstitious and deluding opinions, which would occasion very great disquiet in the mind.[49]

Dryden's selections from *De Rerum Natura* are chosen partly to show this understanding of pleasure—pleasure as quiet of mind— and to suggest how one may overcome the restlessness and self-alienation which disturb our tranquillity.

The passage which Dryden translates from the beginning of Book II seeks to define a state of true philosophical detachment from the cares of this world. It had already become a *topos* of humanist discussion,[50] and had previously been adapted by Dryden

---

[47] Nathaniel Ingelo, *Bentivolio and Urania: The Second Part*, 4th edn. (London, 1682), sig. A5ᵛ.

[48] i.e. sexual intercourse.

[49] [Walter Charleton], *Epicurus's Morals* (London, 1656), p. 23.

[50] Trans. Jacques Amyot in *Les Vies des hommes illustres*, 6 vols. (Paris, 1568), sig. **iiijʳ; and as 'The felicitie of a mind imbracing vertue, that beholdeth the wretched desyres of the worlde' in *Songes and Sonettes* ['Tottel's Miscellany'] (London, 1557), sig. T iiiiᵛ–Uiʳ; and by Sir Francis Bacon, 'Of Truth', in *The Essayes or Counsels, Civill and Morall*, ed. Michael Kiernan (Oxford, 1985), p. 8.

for a speech by St Catharine in *Tyrannick Love* (1670).[51] We are
offered a secure viewpoint upon the chances and changes of the
world:

> 'Tis pleasant, safely to behold from shore
> The rowling Ship; and hear the Tempest roar:
> Not that anothers pain is our delight;
> But pains unfelt produce the pleasing sight.
> 'Tis pleasant also to behold from far
> The moving Legions mingled in the War:
> But much more sweet thy lab'ring steps to guide,
> To Vertues heights, with wisdom well supply'd,
> And all the *Magazins* of Learning fortify'd:[52]

From his standpoint on 'Vertues heights' the happy man can
survey 'humane kind, | Bewilder'd in the Maze of Life, and
blind'. What exactly this secure vantage-point is varies for differ-
ent translators. Lucretius says *munita tenere | Edita doctrina sapientum
templa serena* ('to possess the lofty temples serene, fortified by the
teachings of the wise'), where *templa* is perhaps Lucretius' mischiev-
ous appropriation of sacred ground for his own purposes, since the
Epicurean philosophy displaced the gods from their temples. To
the sixteenth-century translator in Tottel's Miscellany this is 'the
temple hye, where wisdom troned is', while for Bacon it is 'the
vantage ground of truth'. Creech thinks of it as 'The top of high
Philosophy', while Hutchinson has 'that high tower which wise
mens learning builds'. Dryden, however, focuses not on the
possession of these heights but on the process of attaining them,
which he emphasizes by adding the words 'thy labouring steps to
guide'. And his attention is on virtue rather than truth: what is at
issue for him is the attainment of a moral outlook on life, and a
serene detachment from its busy follies. Truth (he would say at this
date) is found by other means, by following the unerring guide;
for these translations are being written around the time of his
conversion to Rome.

---

[51] *Tyrannick Love*, III. i. 46–53. Dryden's use of Lucretius there was noted in John
Digby's edition of Creech's translation, *T. Lucretius Carus, Of the Nature of Things*, 2 vols.
(London, 1714), i. 98.
[52] 'Lucretius: The Beginning of the Second Book', ll. 1–9. The tone of Lucretius here
was sometimes thought uncharitable, e.g. by Dryden himself in the Dedication to *Aureng-
Zebe*.

What is it, then, that makes man's life unhappy?

> O wretched man! in what a mist of Life,
> Inclos'd with dangers and with noisie strife,
> He spends his little Span: And overfeeds
> His cramm'd desires, with more than nature needs:
> For Nature wisely stints our appetite,
> And craves no more than undisturb'd delight;
> Which minds unmix'd with cares, and fears, obtain;
> A Soul serene, a body void of pain.
> So little this corporeal frame requires;
> So bounded are our natural desires,
> That wanting all, and setting pain aside,
> With bare privation, sence is satisfi'd.[53]

> O miseras hominum menteis, o pectora caeca:
> Qualibus in tenebris vitae, quantisque periclis
> Degitur hoc aeui, quodcunque est! nonne videre,
> Nil aliud sibi naturam latrare, nisi vt, cum
> Corpore seiunctus dolor absit, mente fruatur
> Iucundo sensu, cura semota, metuque?
> Ergo corpoream ad naturam pauca videmus
> Esse opus omnino, quae demant quemque dolorem.
> Delicias quoque vti nullas substernere possint:
> Gratius interdum neque natura ipsa requirit.[54]

The substantial addition which Dryden makes to Lucretius ('And overfeeds | His cramm'd desires, with more than nature needs: | For Nature wisely stints our appetite') is consonant with the ideas of Epicurus exemplified in the passage quoted earlier from his epistle to Menoeceus, and acts as a rejoinder to the distorted presentations of the Epicurean philosophy of pleasure promoted by Ingelo and his kind. In his handling of the subsequent textual crux, Dryden is following the same understanding of Epicureanism. Modern editors of Lucretius print *multas* in line 22, and therefore

---

[53] 'Lucretius: The Beginning of the Second Book', ll. 16–27.

[54] *De Rerum Natura*, ii. 14–23: 'O miserable minds of men, O blind hearts! In what darkness of life, in what great dangers you spend this little span of time! Do you not see that nature cries aloud for nothing else but that pain may be kept far away from the body, and that, withdrawn from care and fear, she may enjoy in the mind the sense of pleasure? And so we see that for the body's nature only a few things at all are needful, even such as can take away pain, and can supply no delights besides; nor does nature herself ever require anything more pleasing.'

translate thus: 'and can also provide for our use many delights'. Lambinus reads *nullas*, and his note reminds us of the true Epicurean definition of pleasure:

iisdem placuisse nihil esse medium inter dolorem, & voluptatem: eumque, qui dolore careat, summa voluptate perfrui: denique omnis doloris priuatione summam voluptatem terminari.[55]

In using the term 'privation' (which he has adapted from Lambinus' note here), Dryden is making Lucretius advocate not masochistic self-deprivation but the calmly-accepted absence both of benefits and of pain. True pleasure consists in that equanimity of spirit which is achieved when one is exempt equally from slavery to pain or to sensual delight, the condition of *ataraxia*.

In using the word 'Soul' where Lucretius has *mente*, Dryden is not attempting to produce a Christianized version of Lucretius, since in context the word refers to a state of mind rather than a metaphysical entity. But at the same time, 'A Soul serene' does gesture towards the seventeenth-century tradition of writing about the happy man, who attains serenity in a contemplative state at a distance from the noise and corruption of the world. Indeed, Dryden has been careful to keep explicitly Christian ideas out of his translation, while using a language which has an appropriate solemnity—and so, for a man in the late seventeenth century, a language with some biblical and liturgical echoes. The phrasing in ''Tis just the same as we had never been' carries traces of 'Who are perished as though they had never been' from Ecclesiasticus 44: 9; while 'Nature gives and takes' adapts 'The Lord giveth, and the Lord taketh away' from Job 1: 21, which is used in the burial service; and 'A life which all our care can never save' recalls Jesus' saying, 'whosoever will save his life shall lose it' from Mark 7: 35.[56] When writing of the fears which possess us he translates *tenebras* ('darkness') as 'inward Hell', a phrase which is consonant with Lucretius' demythologizing of hell, while also being perfectly acceptable to a Christian readership. And the power to dispel those fears, *naturae species, ratioque* ('the appearance and reason of nature')

---

[55] Lucretius, ed. Lambinus, p. 111: 'For Epicureans there is no mean between pain and pleasure, and he who is without pain enjoys the highest pleasure: and so the highest pleasure is defined as the absence of all pain.'

[56] 'Lucretius: Against the Fear of Death', ll. 48, 168, 303.

becomes 'nature and right reason',[57] using the Restoration phrase 'right reason', which means reason properly instructed as a guide to behaviour.[58] Through such a vocabulary, Dryden is fashioning a form of English for Lucretius which is faithful to the Roman's vision, while making illuminating and perhaps unsettling connections with the philosophical language of his own contemporaries.

Once again, Fortune figures in Dryden's rethinking of this text. When he tells us that 'our Bodies are not eas'd the more | By Birth, or Pow'r, or Fortunes wealthy store', the idea that Fortune presides over wealth is Dryden's addition.[59] He also transforms one portion of Lucretius into an argument against the fear of princely power: when Lucretius says that since cares attend even princes, and cannot be driven away by the trappings of worldly power, we should not seek such consolations but rely only upon reason to overcome our worries; Dryden, by contrast, says that since cares attend even princes, we have no cause to fear them— the princes—and their intimidating but empty trappings. Their 'worth but in our want of reason lies'.[60] It is an emphasis repeated later when Dryden writes of the Punic wars when men 'aw'd with dreadful expectation lay, | Sure to be Slaves, uncertain who shou'd sway'.[61] Fear of rulers, and fear of anarchy, alike rob men of their equanimity, but the most powerful source of such disruption is within, as Dryden expounds in 'Lucretius: Against the Fear of Death', extracted from Book III.

Book III of *De Rerum Natura*, which treats of the mortality of the soul, was one of the points at which some of Lucretius' readers deserted him. Lambinus' introduction to Book III says that this question has been settled definitively by Christian revelation,[62] while Walter Charleton, otherwise a promoter of the Epicurean philosophy, devoted a whole treatise to a debate with Lucretius on this very point.[63] Yet some aspects of this text were consistent

---

[57] 'Lucretius: The Beginning of the Second Book,' ll. 64, 66; *De Rerum Natura*, ii. 59, 61.   [58] For the idea see *Poems*, ed. Hammond, ii. 315.

[59] 'Lucretius: The Beginning of the Second Book', ll. 42–3; *De Rerum Natura*, ii. 37.

[60] 'Lucretius: The Beginning of the Second Book', ll. 51–7; *De Rerum Natura*, ii. 48–53.   [61] 'Lucretius: Against the Fear of Death', ll. 7–8.

[62] Lucretius, ed. Lambinus, p. 206.

[63] Walter Charleton, *The Immortality of the Human Soul, Demonstrated by the Light of Nature* (London, 1657), a dialogue between 'Lucretius' and 'Athanasius', the latter representing Charleton.

PLATE 1. Claude Lorrain, *Landscape with Aeneas at Delos* (1672)

PLATE 2. A plan of ancient Rome, from Basil Kennett, *Romae Antiquae Notitia: or, The Antiquities of Rome* (London, 1721), facing p. 29

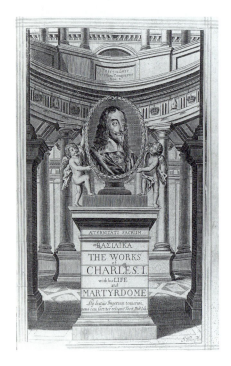

PLATE 3. Frontispiece to *Basilika: The Workes of King Charles the Martyr* (London, 1662)

PLATE 4. The funeral ceremony for a Roman Emperor, from Basil Kennett, *Romae Antiquae Notitia: or The Antiquities of Rome* (London, 1721), facing p. 336

PLATE 5. Title page from Paulus Aringhus, *Roma Subterranea Novissima*, 2 vols. (Paris, 1659)

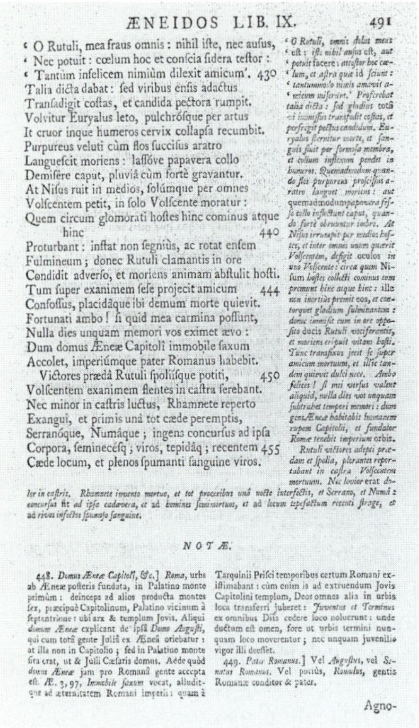

' O Rutuli, mea fraus omnis : nihil iste, nec ausus,
' Nec potuit : cœlum hoc et conscia sidera testor :
' Tantum infelicem nimium dilexit amicum'. 430
Talia dicta dabat : sed viribus ensis adactus
Transadigit costas, et candida pectora rumpit.
Volvitur Euryalus leto, pulchrosque per artus
It cruor inque humeros cervix collapsa recumbit.
Purpureus veluti cùm flos succisus aratro
Languescit moriens : lassòve papavera collo
Demisère caput, pluviâ cùm forte gravantur.
At Nisus ruit in medios, solùmque per omnes
Volscentem petit, in solo Volscente moratur :
Quem circum glomerati hostes hinc cominus atque
hinc   440
Proturbant : instat non segniùs, ac rotat ensem
Fulmineum ; donec Rutuli clamantis in ore
Condidit adverso, et moriens animam abstulit hosti.
Tum super exanimem sese projecit amicum 444
Confossus, placidâque ibi demùm morte quievit.
Fortunati ambo ! si quid mea carmina possunt,
Nulla dies unquam memori vos eximet ævo :
Dum domus Æneæ Capitoli immobile saxum
Accolet, imperiúmque pater Romanus habebit.
Victores prædâ Rutuli spoliísque potiti, 450
Volscentem exanimem flentes in castra ferebant.
Nec minor in castris luctus, Rhamnete reperto
Exangui, et primis una tot cæde peremptis,
Serranóque, Numâque ; ingens concursus ad ipsa
Corpora, seminecésq ; viros, tepidâq ; recentem 455
Cæde locum, et plenos spumanti sanguine viros.

In castris. Rhamnes inventus mortuus, et tot proceribus unà naste interfectis, et Serrano, et Numâ : concursus sit ad ipsa cadavera, et ad homines seminecrtuos, et ad locum tepesactum recenti strage, et ad viros infectos secundo sanguine.

NOTÆ.

448. *Domus Æneæ Capitoli, &c.*] *Roma*, urbs ab Æneæ posteris fundata, in Palatino monte primùm : deinceps ad alios perdocta montes sex, præcipuè Capitolinum, Palatino vicinum à septentrione : ubi arx & templum Jovis. Aliqui *domum Æneæ* explicant de ipsâ *Domo Augusti*, qui cum turri gente Juliâ ex Æneâ oriebatur : at illa non in Capitolio ; sed in Palatino monte sita erat, ut & Julii Cæsaris domus. Adde quòd domus Æneæ jam pro Romanâ gente accepta est. Æ. 1, 97. *Immobile saxum* vocat, alludítque ad æternitatem Romani Imperii : quàm â

Tarquinii Prisci temporibus certum Romani extinabant : cùm enim is ad extruendum Jovis Capitolini templum, Deos omnes alia in urbis loca transferri juberet : *Terminus* et *Terminus* ex omnibus Diis cedere loco noluerunt : unde ductum est omen, fore ut urbis terminis nunquam loco moverentur ; nec unquam juvenilis vigor illi deerset.

449. *Pater Romanus.*] Vel *Augustus*, vel *Senator Romanus*. Vel potiùs, *Romulus*, gentis Romanæ conditor & pater.

Agno-

[right column — Latin gloss]

' O Rutuli, mea culpa mea : est : nihil iste, aut potuit tacere : testor hoc cœlum, et astra quæ iste sciunt : tantummodo nimis amavit amicum miserum.' Proferebat talia dicta : sed gladius totâ vi insensus transsuit costas, et prosciget pectus candidum. Euryalus sternitur morte, et sanguis sluit per formosa membra, et civium insectum pendet in humeros. Quemadmodum quando sos purpureus prosciditur aratro languet moriens : aut quemadmodum papavera sessile inslectunt caput, quando sorte degravantur imbre. At Nisus irruit per medios hostes, et inter omnes unum quærit Volscentem, desistit oculos in uno Volscente : circa quem Nisum hostes collecti cominus una premunt hinc atque hinc : ille non irritatus premit eos, et contorquet gladium sulminantem : donec immersit eum in ore opposita ducti Rutuli vociserantis, et moriens eripuit volsum hosti. Tunc transsunus jecit se super amicum mortuum, et ille tandem quievit dulci nece. Ambo selices ! si mei versus valent aliquid, nulla dies vos unquam subtrahet tempori memori : dum gens Æneæ habitabit immotam rupem Capitolii, et sundator Romæ tenebit imperium orbis.

Rutuli victores adepti prædam et spolia, plorantes reportabant in castra Volscentem mortuum. Nec levior erat in castris luctus, Rhamnete reperto exangui, et tot proceribus simul occisis primâ cæde, et Serrano Numâque : ingens concursus sit ad ipsa corpora, et ad homines semivivos, et ad locum adhuc calentem recenti strage, et

PLATE 6. The death of Nisus and Euryalus from *P. Virgilii Maronis Opera*, ed. Carolus Ruaeus (London, 1759), p. 491

PLATE 7. Virgil reading the passage *Tu Marcellus eris . . .* to Augustus, from *The Works of Virgil: Containing his Pastorals, Georgics, and Aeneis. Translated into English Verse; By Mr. Dryden* (London, 1697), facing sig. ★★2ᵛ

with the emphasis on interiority promoted by the Cambridge Platonists, and Henry More included in his *Psychozoia* a paraphrase of Lucretius' lines explaining how the mythological inhabitants of hell (Tityos, Sisyphus, the Danaids, Tantalus) represent states of the mind.[64] In 'Lucretius: Against the Fear of Death' Dryden imaginatively embraces the Lucretian vision, neither shying away from its materialist understanding of human life in a world of atoms in random motion, nor attempting to accommodate it to a Christian view of the transience of worldly goods. Many of the editorial interventions which Dryden makes are actually aimed at drawing out the implications of Lucretius' text in order to expound his philosophy for a Restoration readership: an addition such as 'From sense of grief and pain we shall be free' clarifies the Epicurean idea of pleasure as absence of pain, while 'We shou'd not move, we only shou'd be tost' explains the nature of motion in an Epicurean universe.[65]

The corrective movement from an active verb to a passive one in that last quotation is one instance of Dryden highlighting the predicament of the individual in the Epicurean world. The first person pronouns 'we' and 'us' echo through the opening passage of this extract in a way which is not available in Latin, insisting by such repetition that this first person has no existence after death has dissolved us into our constituent elements:

> So, when our mortal frame shall be disjoyn'd,
> The lifeless Lump, uncoupled from the mind,
> From sense of grief and pain we shall be free;
> We shall not feel, because we shall not *Be*.
> Though Earth in Seas, and Seas in Heav'n were lost,
> We shou'd not move, we only shou'd be tost.
> Nay, ev'n suppose when we have suffer'd Fate,
> The Soul cou'd feel in her divided state,
> What's that to us, for we are only we
> While Souls and bodies in one frame agree?[66]

---

[64] Henry More, *Philosophical Poems* (Cambridge, 1647), p. 59. For further examples see *The Cambridge Platonists*, ed. C. A. Patrides (London, 1969), pp. 46, 116, 123; and C. A. Patrides, 'Renaissance and Modern Views on Hell', *Harvard Theological Review*, 57 (1964) 217–36.

[65] 'Lucretius: Against the Fear of Death', ll. 11, 14.

[66] Ibid., ll. 9–18, with underlining added; '*Be*' is italicized in the original. 'Fate' in l. 15 means 'death, destruction' (*OED* 4b, c). Dryden has perhaps taken a hint here from Creech, whose translation also emphasizes the pronouns, though less skilfully.

This play with 'we', proliferating the word until we realize that it has no simple meaning but requires redefinition, is designed to stop us unreasonably proliferating our notions of selfhood and extending them beyond death, positing identity, coherence, and feeling where none of these exists. Then, says Dryden, if the atoms which once constituted us 'shou'd revolve by chance, | And matter leape into the former dance', it would not affect us: 'The new made man wou'd be another thing', since 'That individual Being is decay'd'.[67] All these points are Dryden's additions, made in order to expound Lucretius' philosophy the more clearly and emphatically, and to accentuate the tendentious way in which we construct our ideas of individuality. Yet even here Dryden has not wholly laid by his own imagination, for the image of atoms leaping into a dance is his own, the future author of *A Song for St Cecilia's Day, 1687* introducing a momentary touch of harmonious order into this Epicurean universe of chance.

The figure who dominates this extract, and in Dryden's handling of it acts in some respects as an antithesis to Fortune, is the personification of Nature. In the prosopopeia which Dryden singles out for special praise in his Preface, Nature chides the foolish man who anxiously and selfishly attempts to keep hold of a life which he has never known how to use:

> For if thy life were pleasant heretofore,
> If all the bounteous blessings I cou'd give
> Thou hast enjoy'd, if thou hast known to live,
> And pleasure not leak'd thro' thee like a Seive,
> Why dost thou not give thanks as at a plenteous feast
> Cram'd to the throat with life, and rise and take thy rest?
> But if my blessings thou hast thrown away,
> If indigested joys pass'd thro' and wou'd not stay,
> Why dost thou wish for more to squander still?
> If Life be grown a load, a real ill,
> And I wou'd all thy cares and labours end,
> Lay down thy burden fool, and know thy friend.
> To please thee I have empti'd all my store,
> I can invent, and can supply no more;
> But run the round again, the round I ran before.[68]

---

[67] 'Lucretius: Against the Fear of Death', ll. 19–26.
[68] Ibid., ll. 126–40.

The idea that one has 'known' to live is Dryden's addition, drawing into Lucretius' argument the parallel passage in Horace which is cited at this point by Lambinus: *vivere si recte nescis, decede peritis.*[69] By placing the word 'live' emphatically at the end of the line, Dryden underlines its significance, as he will do later in his translation of Persius, 'Live, while thou liv'st', and in *Fables*, 'Possess our Souls, and while we live, to live'.[70] The reader is challenged to invest the word 'live' with the fullest significance, invited to think about what way of living would give it the most ample definition. The triplet which ends this passage imports a note which is subtly different from that of Lucretius himself:

> Nam tibi praeterea quod machiner, inueniamque
> Quod placeat, nihil est: eadem sunt omnia semper.[71]

Dryden's lines, with the rhyme of 'store' and 'more', echo the question which he was asking (at around the same time) about the young John Oldham:

> O early ripe! to thy abundant store
> What could advancing Age have added more?[72]

By contrast with this truncated, imperfectly fulfilled life, the man who has 'outlived content' can receive no more; there would be only fruitless repetition. The third line of the triplet imagines Nature travelling in a perpetual circle (contrast the stasis of *eadem sunt omnia semper*), another small example of Dryden moving Lucretius' poem towards a vision of some pattern or rhythm in the universe, anticipating the interest in the cycles of change which he would explore later in his translations from Ovid's *Metamorphoses*.

As if to emphasize the sterility of mere repetition, the folly of not recognizing plenitude and apprehending the present, the 'store/more' rhyme returns:

---

[69] Horace, *Epistulae*, II. ii. 213: 'if you do not know how to live, make way for those who do.'

[70] 'The Fifth Satyr of Aulus Persius Flaccus', l. 224; 'Palamon and Arcite', iii. 1114.

[71] *De Rerum Natura*, iii. 944–5: 'for there is nothing else I can devise and invent to please you; everything is always the same.'

[72] 'To the Memory of Mr. Oldham', ll. 11–12.

> Dost thou complain, who hast enjoy'd my store?
> But this is still th' effect of wishing more!
> Unsatisfy'd with all that Nature brings;
> Loathing the present, liking absent things;
> From hence it comes thy vain desires at strife
> Within themselves, have tantaliz'd thy Life.[73]

The idea that this man's desires are at strife within themselves is Dryden's supplement to Lucretius' text, and contributes to a line of thought which appears again in his translation from Book IV: 'anxious thoughts within themselves at strife, | Upbraid the long mispent, luxurious life.'[74] It is the unreflective individual himself who destroys his own coherence and self-presence. Just as these additions are in harmony with Lucretius' basic message, so too 'tantaliz'd' applies the myth of Tantalus to the ever-disappointed individual in a thoroughly Lucretian manner.

Such a man, self-alienated, self-frustrating, has

> No prospect of repose, nor hope of ease;
> The Wretch is ignorant of his disease;
> Which known wou'd all his fruitless trouble spare;
> For he wou'd know the World not worth his care:
> Then wou'd he search more deeply for the cause;
> And study Nature well, and Natures laws:[75]

> Propterea, morbi quia causam non tenet aeger:
> Quam bene si videat: iam, rebus quisque relictis,
> Naturam primum studeat cognoscere rerum,[76]

Two important emphases are imparted by Dryden to this passage: care, and knowledge. In the first case Dryden expands *rebus relictis* (simply 'having abandoned his business') into 'he wou'd know the World not worth his care'. The word 'care' echoes through this part of the translation, and through several of the translations printed in *Sylvæ*.[77] The world, we are told, is not worth the kind of anxious

---

[73] 'Lucretius: Against the Fear of Death', ll. 153–8.

[74] 'Lucretius: Concerning the Nature of Love', ll. 114–15.

[75] 'Lucretius: Against the Fear of Death', ll. 291–6.

[76] *De Rerum Natura*, iii. 1070–72: 'because the sick man does not know the cause of his complaint; which if he could see well, he would put his business aside and first study to learn the nature of things.'

[77] 'Lucretius: Against the Fear of Death', ll. 82, 136, 199, 272, 303; see also 'Lucretius: The Beginning of the Second Book', ll. 22, 35, 51; 'Lucretius: Concerning the Nature of Love', l. 127; 'From Horace, *Epod.* 2d.', ll. 12, 55, 60; 'Horat. Ode 29. Book 3', l. 10.

cares which would disturb our equanimity. This sentiment is not new in Dryden's *œuvre*, for it has already occurred in varying tones in other texts. In *Aureng-Zebe* (1676) the Emperor tells Morat:

> Believe me, Son, and needless trouble spare;
> 'Tis a base World, and is not worth our care.

This is spoken in the context of his decision to retire, and hand over the cares of office to his son:

> To thee that drudgery of Pow'r I give:
> Cares be thy lot: Reign thou, and let me live.

Here too 'live' is a strong verb, defined in this context as something which is the antithesis of rule. But the Emperor's view of freedom from care sounds a hedonistic note and expresses a vulgar form of Epicureanism:

> Few know the use of life before 'tis past.
> Had I once more thy vigour to command,
> I would not let it die upon my hand:
> No hour of pleasure should pass empty by,
> Youth should watch joys, and shoot 'em as they flie.

And when he has opined that the world is not worth his care, he fantasizes:

> Were I a God, the drunken Globe should roul:
> The little Emmets with the humane Soul
> Care for themselves, while at my ease I sat,
> And second Causes did the work of Fate.
> Or, if I would take care, that care should be
> For Wit that scorn'd the World, and liv'd like me.[78]

This passage draws upon Lucretius' vision of gods reposing without a care for the world; in Rochester's translation it runs thus:

> The *Gods*, by right of Nature, must possess
> An Everlasting Age, of perfect Peace:
> Far off, remov'd from us, and our Affairs:
> Neither approach'd by *Dangers*, nor by *Cares*:
> Rich in themselves, to whom we cannot add:
> Not pleas'd by *Good* Deeds; nor provok'd by *Bad*.[79]

[78] *Aureng-Zebe*, III. i. 161–89; cp. *All for Love*, I. i. 123.
[79] *The Poems of John Wilmot, Earl of Rochester*, ed. Keith Walker (Oxford, 1984), p. 51; translating *De Rerum Natura*, i. 44–9.

But the Emperor becomes the victim of an Epicurean argument later in the play, when Morat turns on him with this sarcastic adaptation of Nature's speech from Book III:

> If you have liv'd, take thankfully the past:
> Make, as you can, the sweet remembrance last.
> If you have not enjoy'd what Youth could give,
> But life sunk through you like a leaky Sieve,
> Accuse yourself you liv'd not while you might.[80]

What Dryden is exploring here in *Aureng-Zebe* is a self-indulgent version of Epicureanism, rather than the more morally informed vision which he defines in *Sylvæ*. 'Pleasure' and 'care' are both polysemic, and his imagination seems attracted by the task of exploring and delineating their semantic fields, pointing the difference between self-indulgence and equanimity, and between anxiety and thoughtfulness.

Besides the stress on care, there is also in this passage from Book III a stress on knowledge. It is the study of the nature of things, *rerum natura*, which will free man from care and fear. In Dryden's hands this becomes the need to understand 'Natures laws', using a personification which may be licensed by Lucretius' earlier figure, but also adding the idea of laws which has no precedent in Lucretius (for whom 'laws' would perhaps impute too much regularity to the universe). Prompted no doubt by the verbal echo of *cognoscere rerum*, Dryden moves Lucretius closer to Virgil's account of the happy man who studies Nature's laws:

> Felix, qui potuit rerum cognoscere causas
>
> Happy the Man, who, studying Nature's Laws,
> Thro' known Effects can trace the secret Cause.[81]

Like Virgil, Dryden is an admiring but unconvinced student of Lucretius. His own vision of things includes an acute response to chaos, to the lability of forms and fabrics, but also demands a greater degree of coherence, order, and rhythm than Lucretius can permit.

---

[80] *Aureng-Zebe*, IV. i. 344–8.

[81] *Georgics*, ii. 490: 'happy he who can understand the causes of things'; Dryden, 'The Second Book of the *Georgics*', ll. 698–9.

FROM HORACE: EMBRACING THE PRESENT,
SPURNING FORTUNE

The question of how one takes hold of life in the present without being thereby in thrall to the world is one which Dryden approaches from another angle in his translations from Horace in *Sylvæ*, notably in his versions of *Epode* II and *Carmina* III. xxix. *Epode* II had become the *locus classicus* for the praise of country life, and among Dryden's predecessors Jonson and Cowley had each translated the poem, the latter including it in his essay 'Of Agriculture'. But it is not primarily the rural life as such which attracts Dryden in this poem, although he is alive to the actuality of the countryside, as his choice of vocabulary shows: rather, it is the mode of life which the countryside makes possible, the life of freedom from care and disturbance. And so the terrain which this translation describes is both geographical and moral. Dryden does not consistently preserve Horace's references to the Italian countryside as Jonson had done; neither does he simply transpose it into an English setting, as Oldham had chosen to do with Horace's *Carmina* I. xxxi, which he transferred to the Cotswolds.[82] Instead, he fashions a poetic world in which Roman references can coexist with a plausibly English life, and the resulting complex textual field can the more readily carry a clear moral inflection.

Here is the opening:

> How happy in his low degree,
> How rich in humble Poverty, is he,
>   Who leads a quiet country life!
>   Discharg'd of business, void of strife,
> And from the gripeing Scrivener free.
> (Thus e're the Seeds of Vice were sown,
>   Liv'd men in better Ages born,
> Who Plow'd with Oxen of their own
>   Their small paternal field of Corn.)
> Nor Trumpets summon him to War
>   Nor drums disturb his morning Sleep,
> Nor knows he Merchants gainful care,
>   Nor fears the dangers of the deep.

---

[82] In *Some New Pieces* (London, 1681): see Paul Hammond, *John Oldham and the Renewal of Classical Culture* (Cambridge, 1983), pp. 132–42.

The clamours of contentious Law,
  And Court and state he wisely shuns,
Nor brib'd with hopes nor dar'd with awe
  To servile Salutations runs:[83]

Beatus ille qui procul negotiis,
  Vt prisca gens mortalium.
Paterna rura bubus exercet suis,
  Solutus omnis faenore:
Neque excitatur classico miles truci:
  Neque horret iratum mare:
Forumque vitat, & superba ciuium
  Potentiorum limina.[84]

This is neither metaphrase nor paraphrase nor imitation, but a version which is often close to the Latin while sometimes adding whole lines (ll. 2–3, 7, and 11–12 are additions, while others are substantial expansions of single words or short phrases).[85] As we move on to the account of rural life, the imagined world of the poem seems to belong recognizably to Horace's Italy, where men grow vines and olives, plough with oxen, and observe the cults of Priapus and Sylvanus; but also recognizably to Dryden's England, where men grow pears, eat turbot, and complain of scriveners. (A scrivener was a money-lender, and at the end of the poem we discover that this praise of country life has been spoken by a money-lender called Morecraft—a name which Dryden has taken from the English tradition of satirical comedy.) In lines 14–15 Dryden eliminates the specifically Roman reference in *Forumque vitat* ('and he avoids the Forum'), and by choosing the word 'Court' he allows the reader to see both the lawcourt and the

---

[83] 'From Horace, *Epod.* 2d.', ll. 1–17. The following discussion of this epode adapts some material from my essay 'Classical Texts: Translations and Transformations', in *The Cambridge Companion to English Literature 1650–1740*, ed. Steven N. Zwicker (Cambridge, 1998), pp. 143–61.

[84] Horace, *Epode* ii. 1–8; 'Happy is he who far from business, like the first race of mortals, cultivates his paternal fields with his oxen, free from all debts: and is not roused as a soldier by the harsh trumpet call, nor trembles at the violent sea. He avoids the forum, and the proud thresholds of powerful citizens.'

[85] For details of Dryden's treatment of Horace's original, see *Poems*, ed. Hammond, ii. 378–85. An extensive discussion of Dryden's poem and its sources is provided by H. A. Mason, 'The Dream of Happiness', *The Cambridge Quarterly*, 8 (1978) 11–55 and 9 (1980) 218–71.

King's court as oppressive places. And the landscape itself is made polysemic, folding together England and Italy, classical and contemporary times.

Moreover, without losing the sense that this is a world of hard work, in which men return home not just *lassi* ('tired'), but 'Sweaty and overlabour'd',[86] Dryden gives this landscape something of the character of an earthly paradise by including details which had become part of the poetic vocabulary for paradise in the English tradition. The vine is 'clasping' like the 'clasping ivy' in Milton's Eden; the grapes are 'clustering' like Milton's 'clustering vine'; and the phrase 'fairest fruit' has also been culled from *Paradise Lost*.[87] Dryden's vision of this earthly paradise includes aural pleasures:

> The stream that o're the pebbles flies
> With gentle slumber crowns his Eyes.
> The Wind that Whistles through the sprays
> Maintains the consort of the Song;
> And hidden Birds with native layes
> The golden sleep prolong.[88]

The music of the stream is created as it flies 'o're the pebbles', which is Dryden's addition, showing how carefully he is imagining the scene and the sound. The second, third, and fourth lines of this quotation are wholly Dryden's addition. As H. A. Mason noticed, Dryden's description of the wind taking its part in the consort which produces this song was prompted by a couplet in John Caryll's translation of Virgil's first *Eclogue* which appeared in 1684, at the very moment when Dryden was composing this poem:

> How, with their drowsie tone, the whistling Air
> (Your sleep to tempt) a Consort does prepare![89]

For Dryden, friend of Purcell and devotee of St Cecilia, paradise has to include song, its harmonies soothing us into rest and sleep;

---

[86] *Epode* ii. 44; 'From Horace, *Epod*. 2d.', l. 69.

[87] 'From Horace, *Epod*. 2d.', ll. 18, 31, 32; cp. *Paradise Lost*, ix. 217, vii. 320, iv. 147. These echoes were noted by J. R. Mason in 'To Milton through Dryden and Pope', unpublished PhD thesis, University of Cambridge, 1987.

[88] 'From Horace, *Epod*. 2d.', ll. 39–44.   [89] *Miscellany Poems* (London, 1684), p. 6.

but the way in which the different natural components of the scene come together as a musical consort also implicitly reassures us of the harmonious order and motion of the universe at large.

Epode II had already been made a source of moral commonplace, notably in the volume compiled by Otto van Veen.[90] There the opening lines of *Epode* II are quoted under the heading AGRICULTVRAE BEATITVDO ('The happiness of a farmer's life'), with quotations from Cicero, Virgil, and others extolling the virtue of the rural life: *nihil est agricultura melius, nihil vberius, nihil dulcius, nihil libero homine dignius.*[91] But Dryden resists making the poem into a collection of *sententiae*, and instead works his moral thinking into the field of reference which his text creates, as in his suggestions of a paradisal terrain. Some of the vocabulary is taken from the seventeenth-century tradition of writing about the joys of rural retirement: 'How happy' and 'quiet' and 'business' are part of this hallowed vocabulary, and help to evoke that collection of morally informed meditations on the countryside. Other ideas are prompted by the glosses in the editions which Dryden was using: from the 1605 commentary by Lubinus the phrase *lucri spe* ('hope of gain') seems to have suggested 'Nor knows he Merchants gainful care', which has no equivalent in Horace; 'care' recalls the cares which were the burden (in both senses) of the translations from Lucretius. Other phrases have been shaped by recollections of Spenser's *Faerie Queene*, of Cowley's *Essays*, Virgil's *Eclogues* and *Georgics*, and other poems by Horace.[92] So what Dryden is fashioning here is not only a translation of Horace's *Epode* II, but a concentrated meditation on the poem and the questions which it raises, with its vocabulary bringing into play a tradition of both classical and contemporary thought. Lubinus had crowded his commentary with quotations from other classical authors on similar themes; Dryden distils these and comparable English writers not into a separate commentary but into the text itself, enriching its wide, polysemic range.

The opening lines of Dryden's version give a strong moral

---

[90] *Quinti Horatii Flacci Emblemata . . . Studio Othonis Vaeni* (Antwerp, 1612), p. 88. See also Røstvig, *The Happy Man*, and Beugnot, *Le Discours de la retraite*.

[91] Quoted from Cicero, *De Officiis*: 'nothing is better than the farmer's life, nothing richer, nothing sweeter, nothing more fitting for a free man.'

[92] For details see *Poems*, ed. Hammond, ii. 377–85.

direction to the poem. It is Dryden rather than Horace who stresses the humble social status and the poverty of the happy man, importing into the poem a note which he sounded in his emphasis on *privatio* in his translation from Lucretius. He adds the striking quasi-biblical paradox 'How rich in humble Poverty' in the second line. The word 'quiet' associates the aural peace of the countryside with man's mental, spiritual, and emotional tranquillity, Epicurus' *ataraxia* but also Virgil's *secura quies*.[93] Horace imagines his happy man being *procul negotiis*, 'far from business', but Dryden's 'Discharg'd' carries the sense of 'unburdened', while 'void of strife' is his own addition. To translate *Vt prisca gens mortalium* as 'Thus e're the Seeds of Vice were sown, | Liv'd men in better Ages born', is to insert a brief account of a time before the world grew corrupt, a Golden Age, which is further characterized for us if we recognize that the second of those lines comes not from Horace but from Virgil's *magnanimi heroes nati melioribus annis*, a description of the great Trojan ancestors whom Aeneas sees in the underworld.[94] In the lines

> Nor brib'd with hopes nor dar'd with awe
> To servile Salutations runs:

the emphasis changes from Horace's attention to the proud thresholds of powerful citizens, to Dryden's interest in the state of mind with which such people are approached: their suitors are not only servile, they are 'dar'd with awe'. Like larks who are caught by being 'dared' (dazzled with mirrors), such men are helplessly intimidated by power. It is the frame of mind, the voluntary servitude, which matters. The happy man, by contrast, finds that

> No anxious care invades his health,
> Nor Love his peace of mind destroys.[95]

That emphasis on peace of mind is Dryden's own.

Dryden's version of Horace's *Carmina* III. xxix is similarly focused on fashioning a life free from unnecessary cares.[96] The

---

[93] *Georgics*, ii. 467.   [94] *Aeneid*, vi. 649: 'great heroes born in better times'.

[95] 'From Horace, *Epod.* 2d.', ll. 55–6.

[96] For details of Dryden's treatment of Horace's original, see the notes in *Poems*, ed. Hammond, ii. 369–76. An extensive discussion of Dryden's poem and its sources is provided by H. A. Mason, 'Living in the Present', *Cambridge Quarterly*, 10 (1981) 91–129.

title, 'Horat. Ode 29. Book 3 Paraphras'd in *Pindarique* Verse'
shows that this will be something other than a close translation: as
a paraphrase it introduces ideas (sometimes for several lines at a
time) which are not present in the original, and mixes classical and
contemporary references. The Pindaric form is a significant departure from the tightly disciplined four-line stanzas used by Horace,
allowing Dryden scope to vary the pace and tone; he says to his
reader, 'Come, give thy Soul a loose' (that is, slacken the reins),
and he gives himself the same freedom with his verse form. And
by using stanzas of varying length, Dryden articulates the elements
of the poem in a different way from Horace, who often effects
important transitions in the middle of a line.

As *Epode* II distances its readers from the cares of the city, so
Dryden adds to this ode a recurring emphasis upon the need to
forget—at least temporarily—'thy business and thy care'.[97] This
phrase translates a gloss which Lubinus had supplied (*curis ac
negotijs*), but for Dryden the idea is anything but marginal, and it
generates a whole additional stanza:

II
When the Wine sparkles from a far,
   And the well-natur'd Friend cries, come away;
Make haste, and leave thy business and thy care,
   No mortal int'rest can be worth thy stay.[98]

For Dryden 'business' is not simply 'professional duties' (*OED* 12)
but 'anxiety, care' (*OED* 5).[99] And the business which draws us
away from our selves, undermining our foundations, is likened to
an unpredictable river:

VII
Enjoy the present smiling hour;
   And put it out of Fortunes pow'r:
The tide of bus'ness, like the running stream,
   Is sometimes high, and sometimes low,
A quiet ebb, or a tempestuous flow,
   And alwayes in extream.[100]

---

[97] 'Horat. Ode 29. Book 3', l. 10. See *Poems*, ed. Hammond *ad loc.* for the resonances
of these words in *Sylvæ*.   [98] 'Horat. Ode 29. Book 3', ll. 8–11.

[99] The point is made by Stuart Gillespie, 'Horace's *Ode* 3. 29: Dryden's "Masterpiece
in English" ', in *Horace Made New*, ed. Charles Martindale and David Hopkins (Cambridge,
1993), pp. 148–58, 297–9, at p. 298.   [100] 'Horat. Ode 29. Book 3', ll. 50–5.

> quod adest, memento
> Componere aequus: cetera fluminis
> Ritu feruntur,[101]

Dryden's stanza begins with an injunction which is warmer than Horace's tone: 'Enjoy the present smiling hour', not just 'deal calmly with what is at hand'. Each moment, welcomed and enjoyed properly, is placed beyond the reach of Fortune.[102] Whereas Horace says that 'the rest' is carried along as if by a river, Dryden makes the river a simile for the destructive power of 'business', and (adding here to Horace) of Fortune, going on to create a ruined landscape which contrasts with the harmonious world of *Epode* II.

The care which disturbs us is, in part, the anxiety of one who is too much concerned with public events:

> VI
> Thou, what befits the new Lord May'r,
> And what the City Faction dare,
> And what the *Gallique* Arms will do,
> And what the Quiver bearing Foe,
> Art anxiously inquisitive to know:
> But God has, wisely, hid from humane sight
> The dark decrees of future fate;
> And sown their seeds in depth of night;
> He laughs at all the giddy turns of State;
> When Mortals search too soon, and fear too late.[103]

These are topical equivalents for Horace's references (allusions to London politics, to Louis XIV's aggressive militarism, to the Turks at the gates of Vienna) though phrased in a way which does not make their contemporaneity obtrusive: 'the *Gallique* Arms' includes the possibility of Gaul as a threat to Rome. The latter part of the stanza draws some of its vocabulary from Raphael's speech

---

[101] Horace, *Carmina*, III. xxix, ll. 32–4: 'Remember to deal calmly with what is at hand: the rest is carried along as if by a river.'

[102] This stress on the right use of time had been identified as a distinctive thesis of the poem by Van Veen, who included the lines just quoted under the heading *Tempera te tempori* ('Behave with moderation in your use of time'), and used the following lines to illustrate the maxim *Tempus rite impensum sapiens non revocat* ('The wise man does not call back time which has been well spent'): *Quinti Horatii Flacci Emblemata*, pp. 168, 170.

[103] 'Horat. Ode 29. Book 3', ll. 40–9.

to Adam in *Paradise Lost*, a speech which had itself drawn upon
this ode by Horace:

> To ask or search I blame thee not . . .
>
> .   .   .   .   .   .
>
> the rest
> From Man or Angel the great Architect
> Did wisely to conceal . . .
>
> .   .   .   .
>
> Sollicit not thy thoughts with matters hid,
> Leave them to God above, him serve and feare.[104]

But while Dryden may have turned to Milton for some help in
attaining the seriousness of tone which he wanted here, the overall
result is at some distance from the world which Milton imagined,
for Dryden retains Horace's idea of a god who laughs at mortals'
efforts to seek forbidden knowledge. The particular way in which
Dryden phrases this, however, 'all the giddy turns of State', recalls
the image of Fortune's wheel. Fortune had been introduced by
Dryden into stanza VII, and in stanza IX Dryden expands Horace's
brief description to characterize her as 'various and inconstant still',
an adaptation of Virgil's comment on woman, *varium et mutabile
semper*.[105] She is even called a prostitute. That Dryden's mind
should move from Fortune to Dido is another indication that the
disruptive power of sexual desire is one of the aspects of life which
he places mythologically under the sign of Fortune, that terrain
from which the wise man would seek to keep his distance.

Against the power of Fortune, Dryden says, 'my Soul, I arm',
adding a spiritual note which is alien to Horace. He also makes
important changes to the end of the ode. Horace says that if storms
arise at sea, this is nothing to him (*non est meum*): he will sail along
safely in his little boat, protected by Castor and Pollux. Dryden
makes the stormy sea explicitly Fortune's domain:

> What is't to me
> Who never sail in her unfaithful Sea,
> If Storms arise, and Clouds grow black;

He is safe because he is

---

[104] *Paradise Lost*, viii. 66, 71–3, 167–8; noted by J. R. Mason.
[105] 'Horat. Ode 29. Book 3', l. 77; 'various and changeable always': *Aeneid*, iv. 569.

> secure from Fortunes blows,
> (Secure of what I cannot lose,)

and he will

> With friendly Stars my safety seek
> Within some little winding Creek;
> And see the storm ashore.[106]

At the end of his version, Dryden has removed himself altogether from Fortune's stormy domain, and surveys the scene like the serene observer in Book II of Lucretius. These additions and alterations contribute to the definition of the kind of space which needs to be occupied by the man who values his tranquillity. The repetition of 'secure' (which has no equivalent in Horace) echoes the emphasis which we noted in 'Nisus and Euryalus', and signals the longing with which Dryden has inflected this translation. Nor is this train of thought confined to *Sylvæ*, for in his translation of Persius we find:

> Secure and free from Business of the State;
> And more secure of what the vulgar Prate,
> Here I enjoy my private Thoughts;[107]

But between *Sylvæ* and Persius falls the Revolution of 1688–9, and while the concerns about freedom and servitude are the same, their definitions have changed. The later text now interprets business specifically as political affairs; the freedom which interests the poet is not freedom from inner turmoil but protection from the discourse of the vulgar, and the freedom to enjoy his own thoughts in private, unmolested. And so yet another Latin poem becomes an opportunity to define and assert the English poet's integrity.

FROM JUVENAL: LIVING IN THE POST-REVOLUTIONARY
WORLD

The translation of Juvenal and Persius which Tonson published late in 1692 (dated 1693), was a collaborative work, but the principal voice is Dryden's: he contributed a substantial 'Discourse Concerning the Original and Progress of Satire', five of Juvenal's

---

[106] 'Horat. Ode 29. Book 3', ll. 88–90, 97–8, 102–4; 'ashore' is my emendation of 'a shore'. [107] 'The Sixth Satyr of Aulus Persius Flaccus', ll. 27–9.

satires, and all of Persius.[108] This constitutes the first substantial non-dramatic poetry which Dryden had published since the Revolution. It is not a commentary on the times in any overt way, for Dryden eschews the mode of imitation which Oldham, for example, had used in his versions of Juvenal's third and thirteenth satires, which transposed them to modern London.[109] Indeed, in the years preceding Dryden's translation there had been several appropriations of Juvenal which had enlisted him in contemporary literary squabbles, and some readers of Dryden's Juvenal might have been expecting him to continue this tradition. Thomas Wood's *Juvenalis Redivivus, or The First Satyr of Juvenal taught to speak plain English* (1683) had been outspoken in its esteem for Dryden and its denunciation of some of his literary and political opponents, several times using the rhetoric of *Absalom and Achitophel*. Wood refers to Dryden as 'our admirable Laureat', and 'sharp and noble *Dryden* . . . Lashing full stretch his fiery foaming Muse', as if Dryden himself were Juvenal Redivivus.[110] He even imagines Dryden as a second Jove:

> See our Fam'd *Laureats* frown does fright the Croud,
> All fly the vengeance of an angry God.
> Their Guilt and Shame an Horrour does express,
> Devoutly to Him they their *sins* confess.[111]

Shadwell, by contrast, is pilloried:

> But of all plagues *Mack Fleckno* is the worst,
> With Guts and Poverty severely curst:
> Large is his Corps, his mighty works do swell,
> Both *carefully* fill'd up, and stuff'd from Hell:
> *Eternal* Sot, *all o're* a publick Ass,
> Is cypher'd in the *margin* of his Face.[112]

---

[108] David Hopkins's 'Dryden and the Tenth Satire of Juvenal', *Translation and Literature*, 4 (1995) 31–60, provides an astute reading of that translation, together with a helpful account of Dryden's methods as a translator of Juvenal, and a critical overview of recent interpretations of Dryden's Juvenal. For a classic consideration of Dryden's translation within a wider study of Juvenal see H. A. Mason, 'Is Juvenal a Classic?', in *Critical Essays on Roman Literature: Satire*, ed. J. P. Sullivan (London, 1963), pp. 93–176.

[109] John Oldham, *Poems, and Translations* (London, 1683). For a discussion of Oldham's versions, and of Juvenal in the 17th cent., see Hammond, *John Oldham*, pp. 148–81.

[110] Thomas Wood, *Juvenalis Redivivus, or The First Satyr of Juvenal taught to speak plain English* (London, 1683), sig. A2ᵛ, p. 4. The copy in the Brotherton Collection, Leeds University Library, has MS annotations identifying those writers who are referred to indirectly.

[111] Wood, *Juvenalis Redivivus*, p. 30.   [112] Wood, *Juvenalis Redivivus*, p. 2.

Shadwell himself had used Juvenal in an attempt to reclaim his literary status, dedicating his version of *The Tenth Satyr of Juvenal* (1687)
to Sir Charles Sedley in an implicit riposte to Dryden's evocation of
a classical friendship with Sedley in the Dedication of *The
Assignation*. Here Shadwell protests at the picture of him painted in
Mac Flecknoe, denies the allegation that he knows no Latin or Greek,
and scorns Dryden's own alignment of himself with classical poets:

I will not say as a *Cock Translator* does of *Lucretius* and *Virgil*, that he has
added nothing but what he is confident the Authors would themselves
were they now Living, by which arrogant saying he would insinuate that
his *Genius* is much like theirs, or equal with them.[113]

A rival version of the tenth satire by Henry Higden was published
shortly after Shadwell's,[114] with a commendatory poem by
Dryden. Here Dryden takes the opportunity to distance himself
from the cycle of insult and revenge, and attributes this to the
example of Juvenal, who in Higden's rendering emerges as one
who preferred to smile at the world's follies:

> Oh! were your Author's Principle receiv'd
>
> .   .   .   .
>
> *Revenge* wou'd into *Charity* be chang'd,
> Because it costs too Dear to be *Reveng'd*:
> It costs our *Quiet* and *Content of Mind*;
> And when 'tis compass'd, leaves a Sting behind.
> Suppose I had the better End o' th' Staff,
> Why shou'd I help th' ill-natur'd World to laugh?
> 'Tis all alike to them, who gets the Day;
> They Love the Spight and Mischief of the *Fray*.
> No; I have Cur'd my Self of that *Disease*;
> Nor will I be provok'd, but when I please.[115]

So Dryden disengages himself from literary squabbles, and prepares
the ground for his own less partisan version of Juvenal a few years
later.

---

[113] *The Tenth Satyr of Juvenal, English and Latin, The English by Tho. Shadwell* (London,
1687), sig. A2ᵛ–A3ᵛ.

[114] Hugh Macdonald, *John Dryden: A Bibliography of Early Editions and of Drydeniana*
(Oxford, 1939), p. 43, notes that Shadwell borrowed the MS of Higden's version, and
hastily published his own before Higden's could appear; Higden's displeasure at Shadwell's
action is apparent in his preface.

[115] 'To my Ingenious Friend, Mr. Henry Higden, Esq; On his Translation of the Tenth
Satyr of Juvenal', ll. 22, 25–34.

The world created in Dryden's translations is nominally that of ancient Rome, since the original references are retained. Dryden says that he has translated Juvenal's first satire 'somewhat largely', and omitted most of the proper names 'because I thought they wou'd not much edifie the Reader'.[116] This mode of translation gives him scope to reduce the particularity of the Roman poem and extend its reach. Moreover, in the 'Discourse' Dryden explains that he and his fellow translators have sometimes introduced English equivalents for Roman habits:

We . . . have endeavour'd to make him speak that kind of *English*, which he wou'd have spoken had he liv'd in *England*, and had Written to this Age. If sometimes any of us (and 'tis but seldome) make him express the Customs and Manners of our Native Country, rather than of *Rome*; 'tis, either when there was some kind of Analogy, betwixt their Customes and ours; or when, to make him more easy to Vulgar Understandings, we gave him those Manners which are familiar to us. But I defend not this Innovation, 'tis enough if I can excuse it. For to speak sincerely, the Manners of Nations and Ages, are not to be confounded: We shou'd either make them *English*, or leave them *Roman*.[117]

Despite this apparent preference for a wholly English or wholly Roman semantic field, the city which Dryden imagines in 'The Third Satyr of Juvenal' is in some respects contemporary London as much as it is ancient Rome:

> The scouring Drunkard, if he does not fight
> Before his Bed-time, takes no rest that Night.
> Passing the tedious Hours in greater pain
> Than stern *Achilles*, when his Friend was slain:
> 'Tis so ridic'lous, but so true withall,
> A Bully cannot sleep without a Braul.
> Yet tho his youthful Blood be fir'd with Wine,
> He wants not Wit, the Danger to decline:
> Is cautious to avoid the Coach and Six,
> And on the Lacquies will no Quarrel fix.
> His Train of Flambeaus, and Embroider'd Coat
> May Priviledge my Lord to walk secure on Foot.[118]

---

[116] 'Argument of the First Satyr': *Poems*, p. 671.
[117] *Poems*, pp. 669–70.
[118] 'The Third Satyr of Juvenal', ll. 440–51, translating Juvenal, *Satyra* iii. 278–85.

The reference to Achilles maintains a link to the classical world, but there are no specifically Roman details in this passage, and the vocabulary has several elements which are characteristic of Restoration England. 'Scouring' is a word which Dryden took over from Oldham's version of this satire, where he writes of the 'drunken Scowrers of the Street'.[119] Scourers were the drunken brawlers who frequented the streets of Restoration London, and the term is first recorded by the *OED* in 1672, in Wycherley. 'Bully' is another word from the same idiomatic field: bullies were blustering gallants, and the *OED*'s first citation in this sense comes from Shadwell, writing in 1688.[120] The coach and six fit the streets of London more readily than the streets of Rome. Here and elsewhere much of the vocabulary belongs specifically to English rather than Roman customs: the 'farm'd Excise', the 'Beau', the Lord's 'Rhimes'.[121] Yet because the proper names are Roman, the effect is a description of Rome with repeated connections to the local experiences of the Restoration reader. Dryden cross-cuts between two worlds, sometimes quite startlingly:

> Old *Romulus*, and Father *Mars* look down,
> Your Herdsman Primitive, your homely Clown
> Is turn'd a *Beau* in a loose tawdry Gown.[122]

The incongruity of starting the triplet with Romulus and ending it with a beau reminds us that we, as Restoration Englishmen, have failed to inherit Roman simplicity and virtue, however much we may proclaim our interest in the Roman cultural heritage.

The argument which Dryden prefixed to the first of Juvenal's satires explains that Juvenal himself used names of people from an earlier period in order to criticize more safely the corruptions of his own time:

But our Poet being desirous to reform his own Age, and not daring to attempt it by an Overt act of naming living Persons, inveighs onely against those who were infamous in the times immediately preceding his,

---

[119] Oldham, 'A Satyr, in Imitation of the Third of Juvenal', l. 406.
[120] Dryden had associated 'bullies' and 'scouring' in the 'Prologue to *The Spanish Fryar*' (1680), ll. 39–41.   [121] 'The Third Satyr of Juvenal', ll. 57, 120, 77.
[122] Ibid., ll. 118–20.

whereby he not only gives a fair warning to Great Men, that their
Memory lies at the mercy of future Poets and Historians, but also with a
finer stroke of his Pen, brands ev'n the living, and personates them under
dead mens Names.[123]

This implicitly invites readers to interpret these translations too as
a *texte à clef*. As he says at the end of the first satire,

> Since none the Living-Villains dare implead,
> Arraign them in the Persons of the Dead.[124]

A similar theme runs through the introductory materials on
Persius. He was 'of a free Spirit, and has not forgotten that *Rome*
was once a Commonwealth . . . and boldly Arraigns the false
Judgment of the Age in which he Lives'.[125] Persius' strategy was
'to conceal his Name and Quality. He liv'd in the dangerous
Times of the Tyrant *Nero*; and aims particularly at him, in most of
his Satyrs.'[126] This caution is particularly important in respect of
the fourth satire:

Our Author, living in the time of *Nero*, was Contemporary and Friend
to the Noble Poet *Lucan*; both of them, were sufficiently sensible, with
all Good Men, how Unskilfully he manag'd the Commonwealth: And
perhaps might guess at his future Tyranny, by some Passages, during the
latter part of his first five years.

This note was published five years into the reign of William III.
Dryden continues:

'Tis probable that he . . . discovers some secret Vices of *Nero*, concerning his Lust, his Drunkenness and his Effeminacy, which had not yet
arriv'd to publick Notice. He also reprehends the Flattery of his
Courtiers, who endeavour'd to make all his Vices pass for Virtues.
Covetousness was undoubtedly none of his Faults; but it is here describ'd
as a Veyl cast over the True Meaning of the Poet, which was to Satyrise
his Prodigality, and Voluptuousness; to which he makes a transition. I
find no Instance in History, of that Emperour's being a *Pathique*; tho
Persius seems to brand him with it.

---

[123] *Poems*, p. 671.   [124] 'The First Satyr of Juvenal', ll. 257–8.
[125] 'Argument of the First Satyr': *Poems*, p. 742.
[126] 'Argument of the Prologue to the First Satyr': *Poems*, p. 741.

Stories about William's homosexuality were circulating at this time, probably in the London coffee houses and certainly in manuscript satires.[127] Dryden concludes:

The Commentatours before *Casaubon*, were ignorant of our Author's secret meaning; and thought he had only written against Young Noblemen in General, who were too forward in aspiring to publick Magistracy: But this Excellent Scholiast has unravell'd the whole Mystery: And made it apparent, that the Sting of this Satyr, was particularly aim'd at *Nero*.[128]

This is a lesson in how to read. In dangerous times, writers generalize their case and avoid particulars; they use names from the past as indirect allusions to contemporary figures; they describe one vice as a metaphor for another. Nothing in Dryden's headnote or translation explicitly invites us to read Nero as William: the invitation is more subtle, to ponder the play of similarity and difference.

Admittedly, there are some moments in the translations when Dryden invites us to register such correspondences more explicitly. Commentators have often noted these lines in 'The Third Satyr of Juvenal', which seem to be a direct autobiographical comment on the new régime:

> Since Noble Arts in *Rome* have no support,
> And ragged Virtue not a Friend at Court,
> No Profit rises from th' ungrateful Stage,
> My Poverty encreasing with my Age;
> 'Tis time to give my just Disdain a vent,
> And, Cursing, leave so base a Government.

Later the speaker describes himself as:

> Like a dead Member from the Body rent;
> Maim'd and unuseful to the Government.[129]

---

[127] See Rachel Miller, 'Physic for the Great: Dryden's Satiric Translations of Juvenal, Persius, and Boccaccio', *Philological Quarterly*, 68 (1989) 53–75, at p. 65. For poems on William's homosexuality see *Poems on Affairs of State*, ed. George deF. Lord *et al*, 7 vols. (New Haven, 1963–75), vol. 5; Paul Hammond, 'Titus Oates and "Sodomy" ', in *Culture and Society in Britain 1660–1800*, ed. Jeremy Black (Manchester, 1997), pp. 85–101, at p. 97.

[128] 'Argument of the Fourth Satyr': *Poems*, pp. 765–6.

[129] 'The Third Satyr of Juvenal', ll. 39–44, 87–8; translating Juvenal, *Satyra* iii. 21–3, 47–8.

But we should not rush to associate this first person singular with Dryden, since there are multiple personae in play here. This is Dryden's translation of a poem by Juvenal (who was well known for the rhetorical inflation of his writing); the original is spoken by an anonymous narrator; and it is he who introduces the figure of the discontented Umbritius who is speaking here. Three intervening speakers separate the first person singular from Dryden himself. Nevertheless, Dryden has given this passage some significant colouration. The second line of the quotation is Dryden's addition, and the word 'Court' clearly implies criticism of William's régime. In the third line Dryden is translating *nulla emolumenta laborum* ('there is no reward for labours') with a particular allusion to the stage (which had provided him with some temporary, if not very remunerative, work after the loss of his public offices). The last couplet of the quotation is also Dryden's addition. Anyone who compared Dryden's translation with Juvenal's original would quickly discover which elements in the translation are without a source, and so by reference back to Latin the English text begins to disassemble itself into differently grounded elements: not all the lines in this apparently seamless text have the same status, for in some places the Latin is a pre-text, in others only a pretext.[130]

What Dryden has created is a mobile text which offers readers unusual scope to develop their own inferences. The following couplet from 'The Tenth Satyr of Juvenal' seems an obvious jibe at William III:

> For few Usurpers to the Shades descend
> By a dry Death, or with a quiet End.[131]

But the lines are rounding off a paragraph about Pompey. It is our responsibility if we give it a transhistorical reach and apply it to modern instances, yet such applicability is exactly what the sententious shape of the observation supposes. If we apply the term 'Usurpers' to include William III, that becomes our judgement on him, and not Dryden's responsibility: Dryden (or so he might wryly argue) has actually diplomatically avoided translating

---

[130] And Dryden also switched between translating the text and translating the editorial commentary instead: Hopkins (p. 33) notes that Dryden based ll. 87–8 on a gloss in Prateus' edition.

[131] 'The Tenth Satyr of Juvenal', ll. 178–9; translating Juvenal, *Satyra* x. 112–13.

Juvenal's *reges* ('kings') literally, and has simply adapted Sir Robert Stapylton's translation:[132]

> *To* Ceres *sonne in law but few go down*
> *In Peace that weare, none that usurpe a Crown.*[133]

Actually, that couplet with its '*usurpe a Crown*' and its way of describing Pluto, ruler of the underworld, as Ceres' son-in-law, is liable to be construed as a more pointed reference to the usurping William, son-in-law to James. But it was published in 1647.

In the same satire we find this comment on the relation of men to their environment:

> a Land of Bogs
> With Ditches fenc'd, a Heaven Fat with Fogs,
> May form a Spirit fit to sway the State;
> And make the Neighb'ring Monarchs fear their Fate.[134]

The land of bogs and ditches is inevitably, for most Restoration readers, Holland, whose inhabitants were stereotypically 'Fat'; and the reference to the leader who sways his own republic ('State') and makes neighbouring monarchs fear him reads inescapably like an allusion to William of Orange, the Stadtholder whose military skills checked Louis XIV and chased away James II. But the reference is more complimentary than pejorative, since it refers in context to great men overcoming their unpropitious environment.[135] Yet there is a submerged joke here which drastically undercuts that compliment, for Juvenal describes the country as *Vervecum patria*. Now *vervex* means literally a castrated male sheep (allowing an inference about William's impotence[136]) and figuratively a dull, stupid person, such as the Dutch were proverbially considered to be by Dryden's countrymen.[137] This is one of the points at which Dryden's text becomes intricately polysemic, but

---

[132] As David Hopkins points out ('Dryden and the Tenth Satire of Juvenal', p. 40).

[133] *Juvenal's Sixteen Satyrs, or, A Survey of the Manners and Actions of Mankind*, translated by Sir Robert Stapylton (London, 1647), p. 182.

[134] 'The Tenth Satyr of Juvenal', ll. 75–8; translating Juvenal, *Satyra* x. 49–50. Kinsley follows the first edition in printing 'Heav'n', but *Works* rightly emends to 'Heaven' for the metre.

[135] As David Hopkins points out ('Dryden and the Tenth Satire of Juvenal', p. 41).

[136] For contemporary politically motivated associations of castration with effeminacy and sodomy see Paul Hammond, 'Marvell's Sexuality', *The Seventeenth Century*, 11 (1996) 87–123.   [137] And by Dryden himself in the 'Epilogue to *Amboyna*'.

only for those readers who know the Latin and its resonances as closely as Dryden himself.

The extension of the text to include contemporary England is not limited to covert allusions to the Williamite régime. In translating the passage about the lynching of Sejanus, Dryden recalls the collective hysteria of the Popish Plot and brings this within the compass of his text:

> *Sejanus* with a Rope, is drag'd along;
> The Sport and Laughter of the giddy Throng!
> Good Lord, they Cry, what Ethiop Lips he has,
> How foul a Snout, and what a hanging Face:
> By Heav'n I never cou'd endure his sight;
> But say, how came his Monstrous Crimes to Light?
> What is the Charge, and who the Evidence
> (The Saviour of the Nation and the Prince?)
> Nothing of this; but our Old *Caesar* sent
> A Noisie Letter to his Parliament:
> Nay Sirs, if *Caesar* writ, I ask no more:
> He's Guilty; and the Question's out of Door.
> How goes the Mob, (for that's a Mighty thing.)
> When the King's Trump, the Mob are for the King:
> They follow Fortune, and the Common Cry
> Is still against the Rogue Condemn'd to Dye.[138]

>   Sejanus ducitur unco
> Spectandus: gaudent omnes. quae labra? quis illi
> Vultus erat? nunquam, si quid mihi credis, amavi
> Hunc hominem. sed quo cecidit sub crimine? quisnam
> Delator? quibus indiciis, quo teste probavit?
> Nil horum: verbosa & grandis epistola venit
> A Capreis: bene habet; nil plus interrogo. Sed quid
> Turba Remi? sequitur fortunam, ut semper, & odit
> Damnatos.[139]

The connection of this episode with recent English experience is effected in part by the use of 'King' and 'Parliament' (neither of

---

[138] 'The Tenth Satyr of Juvenal', ll. 100–15.

[139] *Satyra* x. 66–74: 'Sejanus is dragged on a hook to be gazed at. All rejoice. "What lips, what a face he had! Believe me, I never liked the man. But on what charge did he fall? Who denounced him? By what informers, what evidence was this proved?" "There was nothing like that: a wordy and lofty letter came from Capri." "That is enough, I ask no more." But what does the Roman crowd do? It follows fortune, as always, and hates the condemned.'

which translates, or even approximates to, any reference in the Latin), but more strikingly by the use of the phrase 'The Saviour of the Nation', which was the title applied to Titus Oates by his supporters. The uncomfortable contemporary resonance of the passage is accentuated by Dryden's ear for popular idiom ('Good Lord', 'out of Door'[140]), and especially for the savage jokes of a crowd taunting its victim (the racist 'Ethiop Lips'—an addition to Juvenal—'Snout', 'hanging Face'[141]). Then the penultimate couplet about the mob[142] excises Juvenal's specific allusion to Rome, adds the reference to kings, and gives the whole an epigrammatic, sententious shape which implies that this is a universal phenomenon. The mob which kills Sejanus, or lynches Catholics, or—as we shall see in *Aeneid* II—stupidly demands that the wooden horse be brought inside the walls of Troy, is much the same whatever the different historical and cultural conditions.

But this topicality is only one of the inflections which Dryden gives to Juvenal's passage on the fall of Sejanus. This particular *exemplum* arises from lines in which the philosopher Democritus laughs at the errors of men:

> He laughs at all the Vulgar Cares and Fears;
> At their vain Triumphs, and their vainer Tears:
> An equal Temper in his Mind he found,
> When Fortune flatter'd him, and when she frown'd.
> 'Tis plain from hence that what our Vows request,
> Are hurtful things, or Useless at the best.
> 　　Some ask for Envy'd Pow'r; which publick Hate
> Pursues, and hurries headlong to their Fate:
> Down go the Titles; and the Statue Crown'd,
> Is by base Hands in the next River Drown'd.
> The Guiltless Horses, and the Chariot Wheel
> The same Effects of Vulgar Fury feel:
> The Smith prepares his Hammer for the Stroke,
> While the Lung'd Bellows hissing Fire provoke;
> *Sejanus* almost first of *Roman* Names,

---

[140] This means 'irrelevant': *OED* s.v. door 5.

[141] This means both 'gloomy-looking' and 'deserving to be hanged': the pun goes back at least to *Measure for Measure*, IV. ii. 31–2.

[142] This is Dryden's expansion of *quid | Turba Remi* ('what about the Roman crowd'). Juvenal's wording transposes the familiar and formal *Populus Romanus* into a darker key which would certainly have appealed to Dryden.

> The great *Sejanus* crackles in the flames:
> Form'd in the Forge, the Pliant Brass is laid
> On Anvils; and of Head and Limbs are made,
> Pans, Cans, and Pispots, a whole Kitchin Trade.
>   Adorn your Doors with Laurels; and a Bull
> Milk white and large, lead to the Capitol;
> *Sejanus* with a Rope, is drag'd along . . .[143]

A remarkable feature of this passage is the variety of tone. The second line has a rhetorical balance which is entirely Dryden's creation: Juvenal has no effect equivalent to the antithesis (with alliteration) of 'Triumphs' and 'Tears', or the poignant movement from 'vain' to 'vainer'; indeed, this emphasis on the vanity of human wishes is itself Dryden's addition. The third line is also Dryden's addition, and his decision to focus on equanimity in the face of Fortune is in contrast to the rough vigour of Juvenal at this point: *Mandaret laqueum, mediumque ostenderet unguem* (as it were, 'he told her to push off, and stuck two fingers up at her'). The account of Sejanus' statue being melted down uses the vocabulary and rhetoric of epic until we reach that crudely colloquial and jangling final line: 'Pans, Cans, and Pispots, a whole Kitchin Trade'. Immediately, however, there is another tonal shift, back into the milieu of epic and its attention to religious ritual:

> Adorn your Doors with Laurels; and a Bull
> Milk white and large, lead to the Capitol;

But it is Sejanus himself, not the bull, who is being dragged, not led, through the streets; for a moment we may think that Dryden is still talking about the statue, until the horror of the true scene dawns on us. Another shocking change of register inaugurates the passage on the mob's contemptuous treatment of the fallen ruler which was quoted earlier. In moving so adroitly, so disconcertingly, between linguistic and generic registers, Dryden underlines the instability of human life which this passage is describing. No single and coherent language is usable for such a theme, and the occasional contemporary allusions should be seen as one part of the poem's way of setting before us this thoroughly labile world.

Running through the translations from Juvenal, and even more

---

[143] 'The Tenth Satyr of Juvenal', ll. 79–100; translating Juvenal, *Satyra* x. 51–67.

strongly through those from Persius, is the theme that in bad times
the honest man has no business in the public sphere: it will do him
harm, and he can do it no good. In the third satire Umbritius leaves
Rome for the country where 'secure he Lives'; he cannot flatter a
patron, nor 'comply with him, nor with his Times', for 'Who now
is lov'd, but he who loves the Times'.[144] The wise man can only
distance himself from such temporizing. The tone of the tenth
satire is more philosophical, drawing upon Stoic and Epicurean
thinking[145] which evidently appealed to Dryden. In his prose argument he calls it 'this Divine Satyr',[146] and says that its message is:

that since we generally chuse so ill for our selves; we shou'd do better to
leave it to the Gods, to make the choice for us. All we can safely ask of
Heaven, lies within a very small Compass. 'Tis but *Health of Body and
Mind*—And if we have these, 'tis not much matter, what we want[147]
besides: For we have already enough to make us Happy.[148]

The opening lines of the poem carry the stamp of Dryden's own
concern, familiar from *Sylvæ*, for true knowledge of true happiness:

> Look round the Habitable World, how few
> Know their own Good; or knowing it, pursue.
> How void of Reason are our Hopes and Fears![149]

And towards the end of this satire, Dryden emphasizes that one
should entrust oneself to the powers above, who are unerring:

> What then remains? Are we depriv'd of Will?
> Must we not Wish, for fear of wishing Ill?
> Receive my Counsel, and securely move;
> Intrust thy Fortune to the Pow'rs above.
> Leave them to manage for thee, and to grant
> What their unerring Wisdom sees thee want:[150]

.   .   .   .

---

144 'The Third Satyr of Juvenal', ll. 4, 78, 89.

145 *Juvenal: The Satires*, ed. John Ferguson (Basingstoke, 1979), pp. 254–5.

146 The prose arguments are adapted from those supplied in seventeenth-century
editions; where Dryden calls the satire 'Divine', Schrevelius calls it *pulcherrimae* ('most beautiful': p. 315).   147 i.e. lack.

148 'The Argument of the Tenth Satyr', *Poems*, p. 720.

149 'The Tenth Satyr of Juvenal', ll. 1–3; translating Juvenal, *Satyra* x. 1–4.

150 'Want' here again means 'lack, need', rather than 'desire'.

> The Path to Peace is Virtue: What I show,
> Thy Self may freely, on Thy Self bestow:
> Fortune was never Worshipp'd by the Wise;
> But, set aloft by Fools, Usurps the Skies.[151]

> Nil ergo optabunt homines? Si consilium vis,
> Permittes ipsis expendere Numinibus, quid
> Conveniat nobis, rebusque sit utile nostris:

> .   .   .   .

> Monstro, quod ipse tibi possis dare. SEMITA certe
> Tranquillae per virtutem patet unica vitae.
> Nullum Numen habes, si sit prudentia: nos te,
> Nos facimus, Fortuna, Deam, coeloque locamus.[152]

What would enable man to live 'securely'? Dryden advocates
entrusting oneself to 'the Pow'rs above', a phrase which closely
translates *Numinibus* (since *numina*, 'the divine powers', is less
specific than *di*, 'the gods'), and at the same time avoids choosing
either a Roman or a Christian deity. To call the wisdom of these
divine powers 'unerring' is to evoke for the attentive English
reader the unerring guidance of God conveyed through the
Roman Catholic Church, without overtly disturbing the Stoic
temper of Juvenal's poem.

FROM THE *GEORGICS*: KNOWING THE GROUND OF
TRUE HAPPINESS

Dryden never wrote a country house poem.[153] Though he had
patrons and friends with country seats, and often enjoyed their
hospitality to compose in peace, he did not write any work which
imagined the country house and estate as the site of cultural values.
The land of England seems to have held no historical depth for
him, at least in so far as his poetry is concerned: the countryside
and its houses were not for him the bearers of social and moral

---

[151] 'The Tenth Satyr of Juvenal', ll. 533–8, 558–61.

[152] *Satyra* x. 346–8, 363–6: 'So shall men not pray for anything? If you wish for my
advice, you will leave it to the powers above to decide what is fitting for us, and what is
useful for our life . . . I show you what you can provide for yourself. The only true path to
a tranquil life lies through virtue. Fortune has no power over you if you have wisdom: it
is we, we who make you a goddess, Fortune, and place you in the heavens.'

[153] Though 'To my Honour'd Kinsman, John Driden, of Chesterton' is included by
Alastair Fowler in his anthology *The Country House Poem* (Edinburgh, 1994).

meaning by virtue of their historicity and their place in a tradition. This may seem curious in one who had such a strong reverence for tradition, and was Historiographer Royal, but it returns us to the thesis that Dryden invents space rather than place, and that his way of imagining cultural space is grounded in Latin.

The contrast with Ben Jonson (his problematic classical father-figure) is instructive. 'To Penshurst' locates the poet as a welcome guest in an 'ancient' house which is made the epitome of the civilized life. The poem crafts a harmonious relationship between aristocrats, farmers, and servants; between man and the natural world; between past and present. Penshurst has sacred ghosts, for this is ground hallowed by the memory of Sir Philip Sidney; and this is the ground upon which Jonson can (or must show that he can) enter without anxiety into the symbolic order. He never actually names Sidney, the poetic father-figure, only (in a significant displacement) the copse which bears the family name. The fabric of the poem weaves classical references into a present which also accommodates traces of Sidney:

> Thou ioy'st in better markes, of soyle, of ayre,
>   Of wood, of water: therein thou art faire.
> Thou hast thy walkes for health, as well as sport:
>   Thy *Mount*, to which the *Dryads* doe resort,
> Where PAN, and BACCHVS their high feasts haue made,
>   Beneath the broad beech, and the chest-nut shade;
> That taller tree, which of a nut was set,
>   At his great birth, where all the *Muses* met.[154]

The space which these lines fashion begins as a collection of natural elements (soil, air, wood, water) whose simplicity contrasts with the 'enuious show' of the other houses; these 'markes' are signs of Penshurst's moral integrity, unlike the examples of artifice elsewhere which are merely signifiers of expense ('polish'd pillars, or a roofe of gold'). This grounding of Penshurst in nature, and in a linguistic simplicity, prepares us to read the modest artistry of the grounds, and Jonson's own limpid artistry, as a morally responsible art. The grounds of Penshurst (which are themselves the site where morality is grounded) are a meeting place for classical

---

[154] 'To Penshurst', ll. 7–14.

deities. Jonson's shift of tenses between 'doe resort' and 'haue made' makes this classical occupation of the terrain something which does not quite happen in the everyday present, under the ordinary laws of time, and so the present is re-figured as a textual space in which the happy feasts of dryads and gods translate Penshurst into a mythological site. The oak tree planted on the day of Sidney's birth flourishes here in the quotidian present as a tangible sign (a metonymy rather than a metaphor) which establishes a connection back to a time of special presence, the meeting of all the Muses. An event (the birth and the planting) and an allegory (the gathering of the Muses) are placed together in a fusion of the historical and the symbolic, a form of synchronicity which allows the modern writer access to the symbolic order through his access to the oak. The site of Penshurst is imagined as an originary site for English poetry.

But what makes this site legible as *archē* is the textual presence of classical names, and the pre-textual proximity of Roman literature. The oak planted at Sidney's birth recalls the poplar planted at Virgil's birth; Jonson's description of the wood is modelled on Martial's account of a grove planted by Julius Caesar on his estate; the fish are eager to be caught, as they are in another poem by Martial; the fruit offers itself, as it does in Virgil.[155] We recognize these Latin *topoi* as the figures through which the land is made recognizable, and through our recognition its value is established. Penshurst is a fully contemporary site, but one which without apparent stress makes available two ideals: an abundantly satisfying physical life, and participation in the imagined community of classical writing. But what is the point of connection between these two ideals; why should one be necessary in order to make the other available? As Jonson's consumption of food and drink is unrestricted, and not begrudged by the waiter, so his raiding of the classical store is unpatrolled, ungrudged: the store is full, and when Jonson has taken all he can, plenty remains. Here is an estate which has not been ruined, unlike the literary inheritance imagined in Dryden's essay *Of Dramatick Poesie*.

---

[155] Suetonius, *Vita Virgili*, 5; Martial, IX. lxi. 11–16, X. xxx. 21–4; Virgil, *Georgics*, ii. 501–2. I am indebted here to the excellent annotation in *Ben Jonson: Poems*, ed. Ian Donaldson (Oxford, 1975).

When the King and the Prince pass this way, they see that the fires of Penshurst

> Shine bright on euery harth as the desires
> Of thy *Penates* had beene set on flame,
> To entertayne them;[156]

Because Jonson has built this site from Roman pre-texts, his use of '*Penates*' is entirely apt: the hearth, the central living source of this house is indeed classical Rome, for it is the central living source of Jonson's own imagined world. The poem ends with an insistence that Penshurst is more than an architectural, a social, or a poetic structure: other owners may build, but 'thy lord dwells'. The lord is fully present. And yet he is never named; he is, in this crucial respect, absent from a poem which celebrates and defines not a structure but a verb, 'dwells'.[157] The lord of this site, the one who dwells here, is also the poet himself, the guest at Penshurst, the heir to the classical estate, and the artificer of this imagined world.

Dryden stands on different ground. His encounter with the classical poetry of the ideal place maintains the Roman references and does not seek to transform particular English houses (like Jonson's Penshurst, Carew's Saxham, Marvell's Nun Appleton) into sites which the poet can rebuild according to his own ideals, erecting structures to contain his anxieties. In his rendering of the *Georgics* Dryden preserves the details which make this a poem about Italian agriculture, while recognizing that Virgil's poem is more than a versified treatise, since it places man in his proper relationship with the soil, the vegetable and animal worlds, the seasons, and the gods. Here Virgil locates man in time and space, and defines the kind of being-in-the-world which makes man happy. Dryden's translation responds to this vision with its own desires and fears, interpolating a similar but subtly different philosophy into Virgil's poem. This solicitation of Virgil is also Virgil's solicitation of Dryden, at once beckoning him forward on to new ground, and shaking the structure of Dryden's own thought.

Such a solicitation of Dryden by Virgil appears particularly in

---

[156] 'To Penshurst', ll. 78–80.
[157] For the significance of 'dwells' see Judith H. Anderson, *Words that Matter: Linguistic Perception in Renaissance English* (Stanford, 1996), pp. 110–16, who notes that its OE root *dwellan* includes the meanings 'go astray, err' as well as 'tarry, stay'.

the translation of *Georgics* II,[158] where Dryden's engagement with Virgil's praise of the happy farmer leads him into some difficulties and hesitations as he imagines what constitutes the happy life. Happiness in the present is once more imagined by means of the translation of a text from the past; this is, it seems, the only way for contented self-presence to be written.

This line of thought is taken up in the Dedication of the *Georgics* to the Earl of Chesterfield, which Dryden begins with a quotation from Virgil:

> —Quod optandi, Divum promittere Nemo
> Auderet, volvenda Dies, en, attulit ultro.[159]

And Dryden compares himself with Aeneas, wandering for seven years before reaching his promised homeland. The comparison is formulated so as to compliment Chesterfield (Dryden has been waiting seven years for the right opportunity to approach him) but it also introduces the theme which shapes this Dedication, the theme of the poet's time. Poetic powers wax and wane like the rhythm of the seasons. This is an appropriate preface for the *Georgics*, the poem which explains how to cultivate the earth according to the seasons, and locate oneself in harmony with time and the gods. Virgil, says Dryden, wrote the *Georgics* at the height of his powers, whereas in Horace's *Carmina* one can trace the rise and decline of his poetic genius. In both cases, 'though they wrote before with a certain heat of Genius which inspir'd them, yet that heat was not perfectly digested. There is requir'd a continuance of warmth to ripen the best and Noblest Fruits'.[160] Here Dryden is repeating the language which he had used of Oldham, but now with a stronger valuation of the results which maturing time can accomplish. Advancing years may leave the poet with no more than 'the stubble of his own Harvest', but good health may still make this a 'green Old Age'.[161]

By contrast, Dryden looks back on his memories of the politicians who 'from time to time have shot themselves into the World'. Many professed to wish only for retirement and private life:

---

[158] This was first published in *The Works of Virgil* (1697).

[159] *Poems*, p. 912; *Aeneid*, ix. 6–7: 'What none of the gods would dare to promise in answer to your prayer, circling time has brought about on its own.'

[160] *Poems*, p. 913.   [161] *Poems*, pp. 913–14.

But they deferr'd it, and linger'd still at Court, because they thought they had not yet enough to make them happy: They wou'd have more, and laid in to make their Solitude Luxurious. A wretched Philosophy, which *Epicurus* never taught them in his Garden: They lov'd the prospect of this quiet in reversion, but were not willing to have it in possession.[162]

This is one folly, to defer living the happy life; another is not to understand that happiness properly:

Virgil seems to think that the Blessings of a Country Life are not compleat, without an improvement of Knowledge by Contemplation and Reading.

> O Fortunatos nimium, bona si sua norint
> Agricolas!

'Tis but half possession not to understand that happiness which we possess:[163] A foundation of good Sense, and a cultivation of Learning, are requir'd to give a seasoning to Retirement, and make us taste the blessing.[164]

And when Dryden translates the passage in the second book of the *Georgics* from which his quotation comes, he takes to heart the idea that true happiness requires knowledge.

Virgil's *makarismos* begins:

> O fortunatos nimium, sua si bona norint,
> Agricolas! quibus ipsa, procul discordibus armis,
> Fundit humo facilem victum justissima tellus.[165]

> Oh happy, if he knew his happy State!
> The Swain, who free from Business and Debate,
> Receives his easy Food from Nature's Hand,
> And just Returns of cultivated Land![166]

The first change which Dryden has made is to reject *fortunatos* and the associations which for him made Fortune an emblem of the

---

[162] *Poems*, pp. 915–16.

[163] This seems to recall, and reverse, the glib dictum of Rochester: 'His wisdom did his happiness destroy, | Aiming to know that *World* he shou'd enjoy' ('Satyr Against Reason and Mankind', ll. 33–4).   [164] *Poems*, p. 917.

[165] *Georgics*, ii. 458–60: 'O too fortunate farmers, if only they knew their good! For whom, while they are far removed from the discord of war, the most just earth itself pours forth easy provisions on the ground.' These lines are quoted by Van Veen as part of his Horatian emblem AGRICULTVRAE BEATITVDO.

[166] 'The Second Book of the *Georgics*', ll. 639–42.

instability of human goods. So instead 'happy' brings into play the corpus of sevententh-century poems which extolled the life of 'The Happy Man' who retired from the corruptions of public life into a private world where he could contemplate God and nature, and cultivate his own soul. Such self-presence is celebrated in Sir Henry Wootton's poem 'How happy is he born and taught', and throughout the tradition which stems from Horace's *Epode* II, which in Dryden's translation begins, 'How happy . . .': 'happy' not 'fortunate', because Fortune is no foundation but rather the destroyer of stabilities.

Virgil's syntax requires us to wait until the second line to find the noun to which *fortunatos* applies, and *agricolas* ('farmers') is therefore emphatically placed. The movement from Virgil's *agricolas* to Dryden's singular 'Swain' is from a group to an individual. By choosing 'Swain' (a word originally from chivalric writing, which latterly passed into pastoral) for the ordinary word *agricolas*, Dryden locates this happiness not in a realizable countryside but in an idealized pastoral. There may also be a different relationship between the nouns and their relative pronouns: *Agricolas! quibus* explains why farmers as a group are happy; 'The Swain, who' perhaps defines the happy man from among a group of swains, not all of whom necessarily enjoy the conditions which make for happiness. There is also a shadow here cast—ironically—by the words 'happy State'. This apparently innocent phrase is coloured now by the way it has echoed through *Paradise Lost* as Milton's recurring sign of an edenic state which is inevitably lost. The poet asks:

> what cause
> Mov'd our Grand Parents in that *happy State*,
> Favour'd of Heav'n so highly, to fall off
> From thir Creator . . .?

Beelzebub laments:

> all our Glory extinct, and *happy state*
> Here swallow'd up in endless misery.

Raphael warns Adam:

> enjoy
> Your fill what happiness this *happie state*
> Can comprehend, incapable of more.

.   .   .   .   .   .

> My self and all th' Angelic Host that stand
> In sight of God enthron'd, our *happie state*
> Hold, as you yours, while our obedience holds;
> On other surety none;

Adam recalls God's injunction:

> The day thou eat'st thereof, my sole command
> Transgrest, inevitably thou shalt dye;
> From that day mortal, and this *happie State*
> Shalt loose, expell'd from hence into a World
> Of woe and sorrow.

And Eve fatally argues:

> Let us not then suspect our *happie State*
> Left so imperfet by the Maker wise,
> As not secure to single or combin'd.[167]

In each case the phrase is placed emphatically at the end of the line, as it is in Dryden's use. In each case the security of the happy state is threatened, either by imperfect knowledge or by a desire for more than is permitted. And Milton himself recalls Virgil's stress on knowing the happy state in lines which directly echo the *Georgics*:

> a Race of Worshippers
> Holy and just: thrice happie if they know
> Thir happiness, and persevere upright.[168]

The happy state is conditional, if not always already lost. Virgil's *bona* is literally 'good things' (Ruaeus' gloss *felicitatem* would have suggested the abstract nouns 'felicity' or 'happiness'). Dryden's 'state' envisages a condition which is inevitably temporary.[169]

Virgil's farmers are *procul discordibus armis*, 'far from discordant war', whereas Dryden's swain is 'free from Business and Debate'. At issue here is no longer the literal distance from war, but a spiritual freedom from disturbance. Virgil's farmers receive their supplies from the earth (*tellus*), while Dryden replaces this with

---

[167] *Paradise Lost*, i. 28–31; i. 141–2; v. 503–5; v. 535–8; viii. 329–33; ix. 337–9, answered by Adam at ix. 344–8; italics added.

[168] *Paradise Lost*, vii. 630–2.

[169] It also echoes the title of his own adaptation of *Paradise Lost* as *The State of Innocence*.

'Nature's hand', a personification which leads us back to the figure
in his translations from Lucretius who presided over existence, not
just over harvest.

That Dryden is primarily bent upon delineating a moral state
rather than an occupation is clear from this passage:

> But easie Quiet, a secure Retreat,
> A harmless Life that knows not how to cheat,
> With homebred Plenty the rich Owner bless,
> And rural Pleasures crown his Happiness.
> Unvex'd with Quarrels, undisturb'd with Noise,
> The Country King his peaceful Realm enjoys:
> Cool Grots, and living Lakes, the Flow'ry Pride
> Of Meads, and Streams that thro' the Valley glide;
> And shady Groves that easie Sleep invite,
> And after toilsome Days, a soft repose at Night.[170]

> At secura quies, et nescia fallere vita,
> Dives opum variarum; at latis otia fundis,
> Speluncae, vivique lacus; at frigida Tempe,
> Mugitusque boum, mollesque sub arbore somni
> Non absunt.[171]

Dryden imagines his swain as a king, his pleasures crowned with
happiness, enjoying his peaceful realm. Virgil does not make this
farmer's terrain into a kingdom of the mind: his landscape is a rich
and recognizably Italian one, made up of estates, caves, lakes, cool
Tempe, and the lowing of cattle. Dryden has moved it towards an
idealized landscape: there are no place names, for Tempe becomes
generically 'Cool Grots', perhaps prompted by Ruaeus' note that
Virgilius amoena quaelibet loca intelligit;[172] 'Grot' had acquired a
picturesque sense by this date; and 'the Flow'ry Pride | Of Meads'
is an elegant periphrasis. Dryden adds the streams and groves
(plural, for the singular tree, *arbore*), and removes the lowing cattle.
This has become a poetic site, an imaginary generic landscape from
Claude or Poussin, furnished so as to be the scene of some moral
tale.

---

[170] 'The Second Book of the *Georgics*', ll. 655–64.
[171] *Georgics*, ii. 467–71: 'But secure quiet, and a life which does not know how to
deceive, rich with various treasures; but peace in broad fields, caves and living lakes; and
cool Tempe, and the lowing of cattle, and soft sleep under a tree are not absent.'
[172] 'Virgil means any beautiful places'.

In this place, says Virgil, there are *sacra Deum*, 'the sacred things of the gods', glossed by Ruaeus as *ceremoniae Deorum*. Perhaps prompted by this hint Dryden translates this as 'Nor are the Gods ador'd with Rites prophane', allowing the suggestion of a contrast with the English Protestant liturgy. In this place there was justice, until

> From hence *Astrea* took her Flight, and here
> The Prints of her departing Steps appear.[173]

> Extrema per illos
> Justitia excedens terris vestigia fecit.[174]

The tense of Virgil's *fecit* ('made') is perfect, so the action of making the footprints is completed. In Dryden's translation, however, the traces 'appear' in the present tense. What kind of present is this? The place where the prints appear is the terrain fashioned by Dryden's translation, which makes the trace present, accentuating the sense of separation. In these lines Dryden's text makes present the marks of an irreversible absence: the claim made in 1660 that Astræa was being brought back in historical time has been quietly forgotten.

Through this translation Dryden is creating an authorial voice which is neither one of his own identifiable personae nor a version of Virgil speaking English; for much as Dryden said that he tried to make Virgil speak as if he were a contemporary Englishman, that is manifestly an impossible fiction, and the text bears many traces of Dryden's distinctive philosophical interests—traces, indeed, of his solicitation of Virgil. But Virgil solicits Dryden too, both beckoning and unsettling, as we see—significantly—at the point where Virgil asks that the Muses receive him:

> Me vero primum dulces ante omnia Musae,
> Quarum sacra fero ingenti perculsus amore,
> Accipiant;[175]

> Ye Sacred Muses, with whose Beauty fir'd,
> My Soul is ravish'd, and my Brain inspir'd:
> Whose Priest I am, whose holy Fillets wear;
> Wou'd you your Poet's first Petition hear.[176]

---

[173] 'The Second Book of the *Georgics*', ll. 671–2.
[174] *Georgics*, ii. 473–4: 'Among them Justice leaving the earth made her last footprints'.
[175] *Georgics*, ii. 475–7: 'Truly first may the Muses, sweet above all things, whose sacred things I carry, having been struck with great love, accept me.'
[176] 'The Second Book of the *Georgics*', ll. 673–6.

Dryden addresses the Muses directly, turning Virgil's subjunctive
(*accipiant*, 'may they accept') into an invocation in direct speech,
writing of present rapture and inspiration. His claim to be their
priest expands on Virgil's *sacra fero* ('I carry the sacred things') via
Ruaeus' *Poetae Musarum se sacerdotes appellant* ('poets call themselves the priests of the Muses'), but adding the detail that he
wears the 'holy Fillets', a distinctively Roman priestly sign. Who
is this Roman poet-priest? In the first edition of the translation,
in 1697, Dryden wrote: 'Wou'd you your *Virgil's* first Petition
hear', but when revising it for the second edition in 1698 he
changed 'your *Virgil*' to 'your Poet'. Committed to using the first
person singular in a passage which so crucially articulates the
poet's role, his sense of the sacredness of his duty, and his need
for inspiration, Dryden hesitates before supplanting Virgil in this
text, and even then he only does it anonymously as 'your Poet'.
It is a much more diffident casting of himself in a Virgilian role
than Milton's adaptation of the same passage, when in the invocation to light he says that he is 'Smit with the love of sacred
Song'.[177] The whole line is, moreover, Dryden's addition. The
idea of this being his 'first Petition' is logical, since he is to make
two requests, the first for knowledge, the second for quiet; but in
another sense this is strikingly belated for a 'first' petition, so late
into Dryden's career.

The terms in which Dryden conceives of poetic aspiration are
more spiritual than Virgil's, for in addition to astronomical knowledge Dryden seeks a more mystical understanding of 'The Depths
of Heav'n above, and Earth below' which may be rendered
impossible if

> my heavy Blood restrain the Flight
> Of my free Soul, aspiring to the Height
> Of Nature, and unclouded Fields of Light:[178]

where Virgil has:

> Sin, has ne possim naturae accedere partes,
> Frigidus obstiterit circum praecordia sanguis;[179]

---

[177] *Paradise Lost*, iii. 29.   [178] 'The Second Book of the *Georgics*', ll. 685–7.
[179] *Georgics*, ii. 483–4: 'unless the cold blood around my heart restrains me from attaining these parts of nature'.

Spiritual aspiration is slipped in as a supplement to Virgil's text, but it is a supplement which radically alters the tenor of the poem, confirming its dominant desire to understand how to possess a 'free Soul'.

Both for Virgil and for Dryden knowledge is essential to the life of the happy man:

> Felix, qui potuit rerum cognoscere causas,
> Atque metus omnes et inexorabile fatum
> Subjecit pedibus, strepitumque Acherontis avari!
> Fortunatus et ille, Deos qui novit agrestes,
> Panaque Sylvanumque senem, Nymphasque sorores!
> Illum non populi fasces, non purpura regum
> Flexit, et infidos agitans discordia fratres;[180]

> Happy the Man, who, studying Nature's Laws,
> Thro' known Effects can trace the secret Cause.
> His Mind possessing, in a quiet state,
> Fearless of Fortune, and resign'd to Fate.
> And happy too is he, who decks the Bow'rs
> Of Sylvans, and adores the Rural Pow'rs:
> Whose Mind, unmov'd, the Bribes of Courts can see;
> Their glitt'ring Baits, and Purple Slavery.
> Nor hopes the People's Praise, nor fears their Frown,
> Nor, when contending Kindred tear the crown,
> Will set up one, or pull another down.[181]

Virgil writes of knowing the causes of things (*rerum cognoscere causas*), while Dryden brings in 'Nature's Laws' and imagines following a chain of cause and effect back through an ordered and intelligible universe.[182] Knowledge, for Dryden here, is the pursuit of traces, the search for origins, for a cause which is not simply obscure but 'secret'. The happy man possesses his mind, is fully

---

[180] *Georgics*, ii. 490–6: 'Happy he who has been able to understand the causes of things, and has put underfoot all fears and inexorable fate and the clamour of voracious Acheron! Fortunate also is he who serves the country gods, and Pan and old Sylvanus, and the sister Nymphs! The *fasces* of the people and the purple of kings do not move him, and the discord which agitates faithless brothers.'

[181] 'The Second Book of the *Georgics*', ll. 698–708.

[182] For another instance of Dryden's interest in the laws of nature, this time in a translation from Ovid, see David Hopkins, 'Nature's Laws and Man's: The Story of Cinyras and Myrrha in Ovid and Dryden', *Modern Language Review*, 80 (1985) 786–801.

present to himself, without that self-possession being disturbed. Where Virgil's happy man has trampled underfoot all fear of death, Dryden's has overcome all fear of Fortune, and is calmly resigned to 'Fate', which in this instance probably means 'death' or 'the prospect of death'. There is an echo here of 'Horat. Ode 29. Book 3' where the speaker says of Fortune that 'The little or the much she gave, is quietly resign'd'.[183] Dryden's lines swerve away from Virgil's use of *Fortunatus*, seeing Fortune only as the force of alienation, the power which solicits man into accepting what she offers and then shakes that structure which he had been tempted to build on these foundations. Fortune . . . solicitation . . . *différance*. Against this Dryden attempts to set that humanist ideal, quiet of mind.

Twice in this passage Dryden adds the word 'mind', and in the second instance the happy man's mind is unmoved by the attractions or dangers of public life. Again there are verbal echoes here from Dryden's Horatian translations, this time from *Epode* II:

> Nor brib'd with hopes nor dar'd with awe
> To servile Salutations runs:[184]

Whereas Ruaeus interprets the opposition between *populi fasces* and *purpura regum* as a contrast between the Roman and the barbarian, Dryden makes both of them part of the English public scene, at once seductive and dangerous, drawing one into captivity. Then, when adapting *fratres* as 'Kindred' and the unspecific *discordia* as a struggle for the crown, Dryden implies that the political crisis of 1688–9 is another of those seductions from quiet of mind whose solicitations have to be resisted.

Throughout this passage Dryden has moved Virgil slightly towards Lucretius, as he had edged Lucretius towards Virgil in his earlier translations, shifting the focus here from a topography presided over by Pan and Sylvanus to a *topos* of moral thought, the search for peace of mind, freedom from agitation caused by anxiety and desire. These are some of the additions through which this emphasis is made:

---

[183] 'Horat. Ode 29. Book 3', l. 85.
[184] 'From Horace, *Epod.* 2d.', ll. 16–17.

Without Concern he hears, but hears from far

  . . . . . .

Nor with a Superstitious Fear is aw'd

  . . . . . .

Nor his own Peace disturbs . . .[185]

The first line repeats the point about distancing oneself from war which is the motif of the opening of *De Rerum Natura* Book II:

'Tis pleasant, also to behold from far
The moving Legions mingled in the war:[186]

The second quotation reminds us of Lucretius' concern to release man from a superstitious dread of punishments after death. And the third values Lucretian or Epicurean *ataraxia*, freedom from perturbation.[187] The effect of these interpolations into Virgil's account of the happy farmer is to make this part of the poem an account of how one takes possession of one's mind rather than one's farm.

Along with this shift of emphasis, Dryden rethinks the home. He adds to Virgil the idea that no money can draw the happy man 'From his lov'd Home'.[188] Where Virgil says that others may gain riches from war,

Hic petit excidiis urbem miserosque Penates[189]

Dryden has:

In foreign Countries others seek Renown,
With Wars and Taxes others waste their own.
And Houses burn, and houshold Gods deface.[190]

This accomplishes an unsettling turn within the idea of the home, for here it is their own country that these people are laying waste in wars and taxes. Dryden declines to accept Ruaeus' gloss here, which construes *Penates* as a metonym for *domus* ('home'): it is actually the household gods, the figurines themselves, which are

---

[185] 'The Second Book of the *Georgics*', ll. 709, 711, 714.
[186] 'Lucretius: The Beginning of the Second Book', ll. 5–6.
[187] This last line only achieved its Lucretian note in the process of revision, for the first edition had read 'Nor with a helpless Hand condoles'.
[188] 'The Second Book of the *Georgics*', l. 717; *Georgics*, ii. 502.
[189] *Georgics*, ii. 505: 'This man seeks to destroy the city and the wretched household gods'.   [190] 'The Second Book of the *Georgics*', ll. 722–4.

being defaced. (Does this suggest the destruction of Catholic images by Protestant iconoclasts? If so, it is a moment when Dryden holds together Catholic and pre-Christian cultic practices without embarrassment.) Contemporary references follow, or at least some phrases which invite a contemporary application, for William III was conducting an expensive war abroad which was requiring additional taxation at home. The allusion, or the invitation to make a connection, changes the level on which William's conduct can be seen if he becomes one of those who deface the household gods. This is more than a dynastic squabble, and is instead a battle for the preservation of that which gives the nation its identity, since our household gods are reminders of our origins and guardians of our future.

At the end of *Georgic* II, Virgil places this ideal rural life into a quasi-historical time; this was the life led by the Sabines and by Romulus and Remus:

> Hanc olim veteres vitam coluere Sabini,
> Hanc Remus et frater: sic fortis Etruria crevit,
> Scilicet et rerum facta est pulcherrima Roma,
> Septemque una sibi muro circumdedit arces.
> Ante etiam sceptrum Dictaei regis, et ante
> Impia quam caesis gens est epulata juvencis;
> Aureus hanc vitam in terris Saturnus agebat.[191]

> Such was the life the frugal *Sabines* led;
> So *Remus* and his Brother God were bred:
> From whom th' austere *Etrurian* Virtue rose,
> And this rude life our homely Fathers chose.
> Old *Rome* from such a Race deriv'd her birth,
> (The Seat of Empire, and the conquer'd Earth:)
> Which now on sev'n high Hills triumphant reigns,
> And in that compass all the World contains.
> E're *Saturn*'s Rebel Son usurp'd the Skies,
> When Beasts were only slain for Sacrifice:
> While peaceful *Crete* enjoy'd her ancient Lord.[192]

---

[191] *Georgics*, ii. 532–8: 'This was the life which the old Sabines once led, and Remus and his brother: thus strong Etruria arose, and thus also Rome was made the most beautiful of places, and enclosed for itself the seven hills within a single wall. Before the reign of Cretan Jove, and before the race impiously fed by killing cattle, the golden Saturn led this life on the earth.'   [192] 'The Second Book of the *Georgics*', ll. 777–87.

The Latin text has indications of time (*olim* ('once') ... *veteres* ('old')) which connect the Roman present to its past, albeit mythologically. Dryden removes these indicators of temporal connection and origin, and replaces them with a more complex set of tenses. He offers no equivalent for *olim* or *veteres*; even the rendering of *Remus et frater* ('Remus and his brother') as '*Remus* and his brother God' makes them mythological rather than historical figures. Dryden's phrase 'our homely Fathers', along with the addition of 'Old' and 'deriv'd her birth', focuses our attention on tracing origins. But whose origins? Who is referred to by 'our'? Can we, as late seventeenth-century readers, imagine this mythic history as, in part, our own mythic history? Is there a metonymic or a metaphorical link between the seventeenth-century present and the Roman past (which is itself a double past here, both the time of Remus—in so far as that is a time—and the time of Virgil)? The line in parentheses introduces an emphasis on empire which is not in the Latin, and implies that the security of a state is dependent upon its preserving its connection to its humble origins. The idea that all the world is contained within its compass expands Virgil's image of the seven hills encompassed by the wall to create an imagined world held within the embrace of Rome. Dryden's verbs ('reigns ... contains') are in the present tense (emphasized by 'now'), while Virgil again writes of a completed action in the perfect tense (*facta est ... circumdedit*). This was the Golden Age, a time in and out of time; a moment in history but also part of a mythology; a point of origin which we cannot quite own as ours.

FROM OVID: THE UNCANNY PLACE OF MANKIND IN THE UNIVERSE

Among the translations which Dryden made from Ovid's *Metamorphoses*,[193] two in particular provided him with an opportunity to contemplate the nature of the material universe, and the place of man in that universe. In 'The First Book of Ovid's

---

[193] For studies of other translations from Ovid see David Hopkins, 'Nature's Laws and Man's'; and his 'Dryden and Ovid's "Wit out of Season" ', in *Ovid Renewed*, ed. Charles Martindale (Cambridge, 1988), pp. 167–90.

Metamorphoses' and 'Of the Pythagorean Philosophy'[194] Dryden
explores the animation of the universe and the materiality of man,
and the strange links—sometimes disconcerting, sometimes
comforting—between the two. These Ovidian translations
continue the dialogue which Dryden had been conducting with
Lucretius and Virgil about the place of man in the natural world,
as if Dryden was never quite satisfied with any one viewpoint, and
needed always to be exploring other modes of being. The three
poets have different styles and different tones, which Dryden seeks
to match in his English: Lucretius' satirical didacticism, Virgil's
combination of melancholy and reverence, and Ovid's perpetual
wit and delight in paradox. But they all allow him to address the
central question of mutability. The opening of the *Metamorphoses*:

> In nova fert animus mutatas dicere formas
> Corpora.
>
> Of Bodies chang'd to various Forms I sing:[195]

could be a motto for Dryden's work as a whole, except that the
changes of the mind equally fascinated him, as did the intricate
relationship between body and mind:

As I am a Man, I must be changeable: and sometimes the gravest of us all
are so, even upon ridiculous accidents. Our minds are perpetually
wrought on by the temperament of our Bodies ... An ill Dream, or a
Cloudy day, has power to change this wretched Creature, who is so
proud of a reasonable Soul, and make him think what he thought not
yesterday.[196]

Ovid's capacity to represent nature, and particularly the mind, in
disorder, was one of the features which Dryden specially valued in
his writing, commenting that he images 'the movements and
affections of the mind, either combating between two contrary
passions, or extremely discompos'd by one ... he pictures Nature
in disorder'.[197] At the outset of his career as a translator Dryden
had tried his hand at representing the disorderly emotions of the

---

[194] First printed in *Examen Poeticum* (1693) and *Fables Ancient and Modern* (1700) respec-
tively.

[195] Ovid, *Metamorphoses*, i. 1–2; 'The First Book of Ovid's *Metamorphoses*', l. 1.

[196] Dedication to *Aureng-Zebe* (*Works*, xii. 157).

[197] 'An Account of the ensuing Poem' prefixed to *Annus Mirabilis*: *Poems*, p. 47.

heroines in *Ovid's Epistles*, while at the end of his life he rendered
'Cinyras and Myrrha' for *Fables Ancient and Modern*, in which he
showed the mind disordered by incestuous passion. But it was
perhaps to Ovid's vision of orderly and disorderly change in the
natural world that Dryden most responded.

Dryden is not usually thought of as a visionary poet—literary
histories are apt to contrast his mundane urbanity with the ecstatic
imagination of Vaughan or Traherne—and yet there is a repeated
visionary strain in Dryden's translations. In the opening passage from
Book I, describing the creation of the world from chaos, Dryden
stretches our imagination by means of some demanding formula-
tions which highlight the paradox of language engaged in describing a pre-linguistic, pre-human world. In this original state of chaos,

> One was the Face of Nature; if a Face,
> Rather a rude and undigested Mass:[198]

That self-corrective gesture ('if a Face') places under erasure
Ovid's *vultus*, alerting us to the approximate character of any
language which is used to describe a world without form. Similarly
when for Ovid's *Deus & melior . . . Natura* ('the god and better
nature') Dryden writes 'God or Nature',[199] his text hesitates over
how to name this creative power.

Dryden's material universe is animated, and often on the verge of
being anthropomorphized. So much of his language lost its alacrity
of perception through banal repetition in eighteenth-century poetic
diction that some effort is needed now to recover the freshness and
strangeness of Dryden's vocabulary for the natural world.[200] Certain
elements 'embrace' their 'next of kin', and the stars 'Exert their
Heads'.[201] The daring of Dryden's imagination, pushing language
beyond Ovidian paradox, had always been a feature of his style,[202]
a strongly baroque element in this classical poet, and this continues
to find expression here. He writes, for example, that

---

[198] 'The First Book of Ovid's *Metamorphoses*', ll. 9–10.

[199] 'The First Book of Ovid's *Metamorphoses*', l. 25; Ovid, *Metamorphoses*, i. 21.

[200] John Arthos, *The Language of Natural Description in Eighteenth-Century Poetry* (Ann
Arbor, 1949) is a valuable source of materials for recovering the imaginative precision and
richness of 17th-cent. poetic descriptions of the natural world.

[201] 'The First Book of Ovid's *Metamorphoses*', ll. 30, 89.

[202] See Harold Love, 'Dryden's "Unideal Vacancy"', *Eighteenth-Century Studies*, 12
(1978) 74–89, and 'Dryden's Rationale of Paradox', *ELH*, 51 (1984) 297–313.

> High o're the Clouds and empty Realms of wind,
> The God a clearer space for Heav'n design'd;
> Where Fields of Light, and liquid Æther flow;
> Purg'd from the pondrous dregs of Earth below.[203]

> Haec super imposuit liquidum & gravitate carentem
> Æthera, nec quicquam terrenae faecis habentem.[204]

Dryden's spatial vocabulary is more precise here than Ovid's, and the precision teases our imagination, especially in his third line. Ovid's *liquidum* means 'pure and unsullied' according to Cnipping,[205] but Dryden has chosen the meaning 'fluid' (*OLD* 1, 2), as we see from the unexpected verb 'flow', placed climactically at the end of the line. Realizing that the verb is plural, we re-read the line to establish its subject, and find that it is the 'Fields of Light' that are flowing, as well as the 'liquid Aether'. Or perhaps (disregarding the comma) they are fields made up of light and of aether. All is fluid, including the syntax.[206]

This opening book of the *Metamorphoses* includes one of the classic accounts of the Golden Age,

> when Man yet New,
> No Rule but uncorrupted Reason knew:
> And, with a Native bent, did Good pursue.
> Un-forc'd by Punishment, un-aw'd by fear,
> His words were simple, and his Soul sincere:
> Needless was written Law, where none opprest;
> The Law of Man, was written in his Breast:[207]

> Aurea prima sata est aetas, quae, vindice nullo,
> Sponte sua sine lege fidem rectumque colebat.
> Poena metusque aberant. nec verba minacia fixo
> Ære legebantur:[208]

---

[203] 'The First Book of Ovid's *Metamorphoses*', ll. 83–6.

[204] *Metamorphoses*, i. 67–8: 'Above these he placed the fluid and weightless aether, which has no earthy dregs.'

[205] *Purum, & ab omni faece remotum* (Cnipping *ad loc.*); corresponding to *OLD* 5, 'unclouded'.

[206] Cp. 'Of the Pythagorean Philosophy', l. 290: 'pure particles of *Æther* flow'; Ovid's verb is simply *est* ('is'): *Metamorphoses*, xv. 195.

[207] 'The First Book of Ovid's *Metamorphoses*', ll. 113–19.

[208] *Metamorphoses*, i. 89–92: 'Golden was the first age, which with no one to compel, of its own accord without a law kept faith and did right. There was no punishment or fear, no threatening words were read on brazen tablets.'

Distinctive interests have given Dryden's passage a special stamp. To Dryden, golden-age man possessed 'uncorrupted Reason', a faculty not mentioned by Ovid; he was naturally good, which may be implicit in Ovid's account, but is strongly emphasized by Dryden's.[209] Other elements which Dryden has introduced into this version of the state of nature are the idea that language was simple, the soul was sincere, and 'the Law of Man, was written in his Breast'. Moreover, 'all was safe, for Conscience was their Guard', says Dryden, in another addition to Ovid.[210] These ideas stand in contrast to the Hobbesian notion of man in a state of nature, where the absence of law means anarchy, and conscience is unable to restrain behaviour.[211] At the same time Dryden points out the difference from our own age by a series of negatives, 'uncorrupted . . . Un-forc'd . . . un-aw'd',[212] each of which is a trace referring forward to a later stage of human development—the present—which provides it with its definition, and is thereby judged.

After the corruption of mankind had been punished by Jupiter with a flood, Deucalion and Pyrrha were left to renew the race. They are the truly pious couple, reverential towards the gods and exemplary in their mutual love. They are described as a 'careful couple',[213] and this is true in a double sense: they are full of anxious cares, as the sole survivors of the flood, yet they are also full of reverential care to act rightly in the sight of the gods. Into his account of their pious efforts to understand the divine will Dryden has incorporated elements of Christian vocabulary. The pair make their way to the temple of the goddess Themis:

> The Stream was troubl'd, but the Foord they knew;
> With living Waters, in the Fountain bred,
> They sprinkle first, their Garments, and their Head,
> Then took the way, which to the Temple led.

[209] For other examples of Dryden imagining a primitive innocence see *1 Conquest of Granada*, I. i. 206–9, and Paul Hammond, *John Dryden: A Literary Life* (Basingstoke, 1991), pp. 62–3; 'Prologue to *The Indian Queen*', and notes *ad loc* in *Poems*, ed. Hammond.

[210] 'The First Book of Ovid's *Metamorphoses*', l. 122.

[211] Thomas Hobbes, *Leviathan*, ed. Richard Tuck (Cambridge, 1991), pp. 86–90, 48, 110. [212] This is the first example of 'unawed' recorded by the *OED*.

[213] 'The First Book of Ovid's *Metamorphoses*', l. 496.

> The Roofs were all defil'd with Moss, and Mire,
> The Desart Altars, void of Solemn Fire.
> Before the Gradual, prostrate they ador'd;
> The Pavement kiss'd, and thus the Saint implor'd.[214]

> Ut nondum liquidas, sic jam vada nota secantes.
> Inde ubi libatos irroravere liquores
> Vestibus & capiti; flectunt vestigia sanctae
> Ad delubra Deae: quorum fastigia turpi
> Squallebant musco; stabantque sine ignibus arae.
> Ut templi tetigere gradus; procumbit uterque
> Pronus humi, gelidoque pavens dedit oscula saxo.[215]

The lines which describe the temple emphasize its sorry state. Ovid's *Squallebant* means 'covered with a dirty layer', but Dryden's verb 'defil'd' implies religious as well as physical pollution. Ovid's *musco*, 'moss', becomes 'Moss, and Mire', the latter word being more than an emphatic addition, as it carries connotations of moral filth, of man abandoning God or abandoned by God. The apostle says that men who 'have escaped the pollutions of the world through the knowledge of the Lord' may be 'again entangled therein' like the washed sow returning to 'her wallowing in the mire'; while Job cries out despairingly that God 'hath cast me into the mire'.[216] The altars are also 'Desart', deserted, abandoned by men. Dryden is making sure that we present fully to our imaginations (visual and moral imaginations) the true image of the abandoned temple, the discontinued cult. A poignant example of such dereliction was close at hand in the Roman Catholic chapel which James II had built in Whitehall; sumptuously decorated in Italian style, it fell into disuse after 1688 and its furnishings disappeared; it would finally be destroyed by fire in 1698.[217]

That the waters were 'troubled' recalls the pool of Bethesda, where an angel periodically 'troubled the water' with the result

---

[214] 'The First Book of Ovid's *Metamorphoses*', ll. 501–8.

[215] *Metamorphoses*, i. 370–6: 'while not yet clear, it flowed within its familiar banks. When they had taken some drops from this and sprinkled them on their heads and clothes, they bent their steps to the goddess' sacred shrine, whose pediments were covered with foul moss, and whose altars were without fire. When they had reached the steps of the temple they each fell prone upon the ground, and with trembling lips kissed the cold stone.'

[216] 2 Peter 2: 22; Job 30: 19.

[217] See *The Hind and the Panther*, iii. 941; *The Survey of London*, ed. Montagu H. Cox and Philip Norman, vol. 13 (London, 1930), pp. 105–10.

that the next person to enter the pool was cured of their disease.[218] The phrase 'living Waters' is also biblical, being one of the images used by Jesus to describe the gift of the Spirit.[219] In both cases this is not so much a direct allusion as an indication that Deucalion and Pyrrha are on holy ground. Dryden's word 'Gradual' is the only example recorded by the *OED* in the sense of 'step': otherwise the noun always means the antiphon sung in the Mass before the reading of the gospel, at the steps of the altar. This nonce-usage seems to have been prompted by Dryden imagining the couple's approach to the goddess in terms of Catholic ritual. Themis is called 'the Saint' rather than the goddess, and described as 'righteous'—a term normally reserved for those Christians who act in a godly way.[220] The prayer which the couple address to Themis also leaves Ovid's classical language on one side and substitutes Christian terms: Ovid writes of prayers softening the gods (*remollescunt*), and their anger being turned aside (*flectitur ira*), whereas Dryden writes a language which is redolent of Christian theology: 'pity ... love ... forgive ... restore, by second birth'.[221] Deucalion and Pyrrha are told to cover their heads with their 'Vestments', and when Pyrrha objects to throwing her mother's bones over her shoulder in order to renew the human race, she refuses to 'tear | Those Holy Reliques from the Sepulchre'.[222] Dryden weaves the two worlds together here, not translating the classical world into Christian terms, but using Christian, and specifically Catholic, language because this is for him the appropriate way of indicating the religious significance of this episode. It also implies that in modern Rome the pieties of ancient Rome find not simply an echo but their fulfilment. This text, in orientating us towards one version of *archē*, the Ovidian creation myth, incorporates traces which allow (but do not compel) us to reorientate the story by reference to the Christian myth of *archē* and *telos*, and the contemporary manifestation of that myth in the Catholic church.

Book XV of the *Metamorphoses* begins, as Dryden says, with 'the

---

[218] John 5: 4.
[219] John 4: 10, 7: 38. The phrase is also an exact translation of Cnipping's gloss *aquae vivae*.   [220] 'The First Book of Ovid's *Metamorphoses*', l. 509.
[221] *Metamorphoses*, i. 378; 'The First Book of Ovid's *Metamorphoses*', ll. 510–13.
[222] 'The First Book of Ovid's *Metamorphoses*', ll. 516, 521–2.

Election of *Numa* to the crown of *Rome*'.[223] Numa, the enlight-
ened second king of Rome, and the appropriate successor to
Romulus, was a student of the philosopher Pythagoras, whom he
met at Crotona:

> Here dwelt the Man divine whom *Samos* bore,
> But now Self-banish'd from his Native Shore,
> Because he hated Tyrants, nor cou'd bear
> The Chains which none but servile Souls will wear:
> He, tho' from Heav'n remote, to Heav'n cou'd move,
> With Strength of Mind, and tread th' Abyss above;
> And penetrate with his interiour Light
> Those upper Depths, which Nature hid from Sight:
> And what he had observ'd, and learnt from thence,
> Lov'd in familiar Language to dispence.
> The Crowd with silent Admiration stand
> And heard him, as they heard their God's Command;
> While he discours'd of Heav'ns mysterious Laws,
> The World's Original, and Nature's Cause;[224]

> Vir fuit hic ortu Samius: sed fugerat una
> Et Samon & dominos; odioque tyrannidis exsul
> Sponte erat. isque, licet caeli regione remotos,
> Mente Deos adiit: &, quae natura negabat
> Visibus humanis, oculis ea pectoris hausit.
> Cumque animo, & vigili perspexerat omnia cura;
> In medium discenda dabat: coetumque silentum,
> Dictaque mirantum, magni primordia mundi,
> Et rerum caussas, & quid natura, docebat:[225]

The fourth line of this extract is Dryden's addition, emphasizing
not simply hatred of tyranny but the servility, the self-enslave-
ment, which the acceptance of tyranny produces. In the sixth line
we again meet Dryden's daring imagination formulating ideas on

---

[223] 'Of the Pythagorean Philosophy', headnote: *Poems*, p. 1717.
[224] Ibid., ll. 77–90.
[225] *Metamorphoses*, xv. 60–8: 'There was a man here, a Samian by birth, but he had fled
both from Samos and its rulers, and because of his hatred of tyranny was a voluntary exile.
Though he was far away from the heavenly region, he approached the gods in his mind,
and what nature denied to human sight he feasted on with his mind's eye. And when he
had surveyed all things in his mind by vigilant care, he would teach the public the things
which were worth learning, and they listened in wondering silence to his words—the
beginnings of the world, and the causes of things, and what nature was.'

the edge of what can be conceived: Pythagoras treads an abyss, and this abyss is actually above rather than below—a conceptual audacity repeated in the phrase 'upper Depths'. The crowd heard the words of Pythagoras as if they were the commands of a god, which is Dryden's addition. Pythagoras discourses of the 'Laws' of the universe, which is one of several points at which Dryden, sometime member of the Royal Society, writes into his translation the idea of nature having laws which are accessible to human knowledge. As Pythagoras' pupil, and as a wise king, Numa seeks to 'learn the Laws | Of Nature, and explore their hidden Cause'.[226] Ovid here had written that Numa sought *quae sit rerum natura*,[227] what the nature of things was. Pythagoras, the advocate of a vegetarian diet, denounces meat-eating as an 'impious use! to Nature's Laws oppos'd'—this again being Dryden's addition.[228] To kill other creatures in self-defence 'had been justify'd by Nature's Laws'.[229]

Much in human behaviour is impious, it seems, including religion, and in particular the conduct of priests. Destructive animals are 'to the bloody Priest resign'd', and 'In vengeance Laity, and Clergy join'. Both these points are Dryden's invention. In man's religious practices, 'Heav'n it self to bribe, | We to the Gods our impious Acts ascribe'. The animal which is prepared for sacrifice hears 'the murd'rous Pray'r the Priest prefers', where Ovid simply writes that it hears *precantem* ('the one who prays'). Then the victim 'broken up alive his Entrails sees, | Torn out for Priests t' inspect the God's Decrees'. There too Ovid had not mentioned priests, saying simply *inspiciunt . . . scrutantur* ('they inspect . . . they seek to discover').[230] Although as a Catholic Dryden would have been taught to regard priests as intermediaries between man and God, their classical predecessors have no such role in this poem. The existential mystery is not in their keeping.

At the heart of this book of the *Metamorphoses* is the idea that the human and the animal and the inanimate worlds are linked,

---

[226] 'Of the Pythagorean Philosophy', ll. 8–9.   [227] *Metamorphoses*, xv. 6.

[228] 'Of the Pythagorean Philosophy', l. 125. Ovid just has *scelus*, 'crime' (l. 88).

[229] 'Of the Pythagorean Philosophy', l. 150. Ovid has *pietate*, 'piously', or perhaps here 'without impiety' (l. 109).

[230] 'Of the Pythagorean Philosophy', ll. 161, 165, 186–7, 194, 200–1; *Metamorphoses*, xv. 132, 137.

and Dryden through a number of small touches responds to this philosophy, adding phrasing which clarifies the Pythagorean vision, often through a witty formulation worthy of Ovid himself. The inanimate world is given animation: as the landscape changes, the desert is inundated by unknown streams, 'Wondring to drink of Waters not her own'; and as nature changes she 'Seals up the Wombs' whence streams used to flow, so that the underground river whose course is altered 'blind in Earth | Runs on, and gropes his way to second Birth'. The river acquires, as it were, a new social status, 'Forgets his humble Birth, his Name forsakes, | And the proud Title of *Caicus* takes'.[231] Inundated fields are 'drunken', and hills suffer 'Cholick Pangs'.[232]

The passage in which Ovid describes the growth of the embryo sets before us the strange place of the human being in this material universe:

> Time was, when we were sow'd, and just began
> From some few fruitful Drops, the promise of a Man;
> Then Nature's Hand (fermented as it was)
> Moulded to Shape the soft, coagulated Mass;
> And when the little Man was fully form'd,
> The breathless Embryo with a Spirit warm'd;
> But when the Mothers Throws begin to come,
> The Creature, pent within the narrow Room,
> Breaks his blind Prison, pushing to repair
> His stifled Breath, and draw the living Air;
> Cast on the Margin of the World he lies,
> A helpless Babe, but by Instinct he cries.[233]

>   fuit illa dies, qua semina tantum,
> Spesque hominum primae materna habitavimus alvo.
> Artifices Natura manus admovit: & angi
> Corpora visceribus distentae condita matris
> Noluit; eque domo vacuas emisit in auras.
> Editus in lucem jacuit sine viribus infans:[234]

---

[231] 'Of the Pythagorean Philosophy', ll. 413, 415, 420–1, 426–7.
[232] Ibid., ll. 430, 455.   [233] Ibid., ll. 324–35.
[234] *Metamorphoses*, xv. 216–21: 'There was a time when we lay in our first mother's womb, only seeds and hopes of men. Nature worked with her skilful hands and did not wish that our bodies should lie cramped in our distended mother's body, and from our home sent us out into the empty air. Brought out into the light the infant lay without strength.'

The opening verb 'sow'd' is arresting, linking our conception to the processes of the natural world in a way which the more familiar noun 'seed' would not have done. Ovid offers no physical description of the embryo, but Dryden directs our attention to activity ('fermented') and texture ('soft'). The word 'coagulated', unusual in poetry, is placed at the point in the verse line where the expected pentameter is forced to turn into an Alexandrine: as we read we are momentarily thrown off balance by 'coagulated', linguistically and metrically, surprised into recognizing the materiality of the process. But then Dryden also adds the 'Spirit' which warms the embryo, and 'Spirit' is a word which moved between meaning 'animation' and 'divine soul'. The account of the birth continues to emphasize how we humans are constrained by our physical limitations, describing the narrowness of the womb, the darkness, and the lack of air, all of which are signalled in Ovid, but not so strongly. And without precedent in Ovid are the verbs which record the activity of the foetus as it struggles into the world: 'Breaks . . . pushing . . . draw . . . cast . . . cries'.

Man is, in Dryden's supplement to Ovid, 'Cast on the Margin of the World'.[235] The poetry registers the precarious, marginal place of man in the world's text, in this theatre of continual translation:

> Thus are their Figures never at a stand,
> But chang'd by Nature's innovating Hand;
> All Things are alter'd, nothing is destroy'd,
> The shifted Scene, for some new Show employ'd.
>
> .   .   .   .   .   .
>
> Those very Elements which we partake,
> Alive, when Dead some other Bodies make:
> Translated grow, have Sense, or can Discourse.[236]

Translation is the very condition of human life.

---

[235] This recalls the passage on the child which Dryden translated as 'From Lucretius: Book the Fifth' in *Sylvæ*.
[236] 'Of the Pythagorean Philosophy', ll. 386–9, 394–6.

4

THE EPIC OF EXILE

READING THE POLITICS OF VIRGIL'S *AENEID* AND
DRYDEN'S *AENEIS*

On the title page of *The Works of Virgil* (1697) Dryden placed this epigraph from Book II of the *Aeneid: Sequiturque Patrem non passibus Æquis.*[1] The quotation comes from the description of how Aeneas took his father Anchises on his shoulders, and, leading his son Ascanius by the hand, made his escape from Troy. Through this comparison Dryden puts himself in the place of the child Ascanius who follows his father with steps which cannot match the hero's strides. A humble image, yet one which also asserts a proper kind of pride, since Ascanius is the destined heir. In *Mac Flecknoe* Dryden had mocked Shadwell's pretensions to be a second Ascanius;[2] now he deftly stakes his own claim. Besides, this was a gesture which also identified Dryden with Virgil, since the designation of Ascanius as *magna spes altera Romae*[3] had been applied in antiquity to Virgil himself, as Dryden's own copy of Virgil's works recorded.[4]

But the relationship between Dryden and his Roman predecessors has changed. In the poems and essays from the early years of Charles II's reign, the acknowledgement of separation and repetition, and the tropes of deferral and inheritance, had been part of a rhetorical engagement with Rome which gave both form and substance to Dryden's contribution to the new Restoration culture. By the mid-1680s, with the poem on Oldham and the

[1] *Aeneid*, ii. 724: 'and he [Ascanius] follows his father with steps which are not equal [to those of Aeneas].'   [2] *Mac Flecknoe*, ll. 108–11.

[3] *Aeneid*, xii. 168: 'the second hope of great Rome'.

[4] See *Poems*, ed. Hammond, i. 324.

translations in *Sylvæ*, darker tones had emerged, with classical language being used to enable meditations on death and Fortune, on the instability of life and of selfhood. After the Revolution, satirical comments in the translations from Juvenal and Persius, and in the *Georgics*, contributed to a different mode of distancing the present through recourse to the classical past. And now in the *Aeneis* Dryden responds most strongly to the vein of tragedy which runs through Virgil's epic, as he faces up to the destruction of the homeland and meditates the possibility of finding or fashioning a new country. This summary oversimplifies, of course, in plotting such a trajectory, an ever-darker mood and a deepening disenchantment with his own times; for the variety of tone and voice in Dryden's translations continued throughout the period—and is, indeed, seen nowhere more wonderfully than in his final volume, the *Fables* of 1700. But it does seem that in composing his *Aeneis* Dryden responded with particular passion to several kinds of tragic loss and alienation, memorializing them in a monument which would be *aere perennius*.

In the 'Dedication of the *Aeneis*' addressed to the Marquess of Normanby, Dryden weaves a complex set of correspondences between himself and Virgil.[5] In part this is a way for Dryden to assert his own status in spite of his loss of public offices after the Revolution of 1688–9, and yet his text repeatedly resists any undue clarification of the relationship between the two poets or the dynamics of this reciprocal definition. When Dryden opens his account of Virgil's poem, he does so with a metaphor of warfare:

> I must now come closer to my present business: and not think of making more invasive Wars abroad, when like *Hannibal*, I am call'd back to the defence of my own Country. *Virgil* is attack'd by many Enemies: he has a whole Confederacy against him, and I must endeavour to defend him as well as I am able.[6]

This apparently straightforward image sets up multiple, problematic implications. Dryden's own position *vis-à-vis* Rome and its culture is complicated by his momentary alignment with Hannibal, Rome's quintessential enemy. The image is complicated further by

---

[5] There is a good discussion of this Dedication by Steven N. Zwicker in his *Politics and Language in Dryden's Poetry: The Arts of Disguise* (Princeton, 1984), pp. 178–88.

[6] *Poems*, p. 1011.

the implicit allusion to William III,[7] who after what Dryden would have regarded as an invasive war against England in 1688, had been called back in 1691 to the defence of Holland; at the time when Dryden was writing this essay in the spring or summer of 1697, the war was being concluded through negotiations for the Peace of Ryswyk. One implication of the comparison might be that William's own country is Holland rather than England, and that like Hannibal he will ultimately be unsuccessful in conquering the nation which he invaded. The allusion also suggests that while William is busy with the management of his empire, Dryden too has his own, no less important, territory to define and defend. The two men (both, in their way, rulers) are brought into an awkward, challenging proximity by this comparison, made to inhabit contingent but perhaps incompatible spaces. But the first sentence ends with the application of 'my own Country' indeterminate in Dryden's own case. What is this country which he is about to defend? In view of Dryden's discussion in the previous paragraph of the relative merits of epic and tragedy, we might expect this to be some aspect of his critical position or poetic practice; or (given 'my present business') it might be his own translation of Virgil; or from the political and martial imagery it might be England, perhaps more specifically the Stuart cause. What, for Dryden, is 'my own Country'? It turns out to be Virgil.

This surprising definition briefly constitutes Virgil as Dryden's territory, his *patria*. It appears as a metaphor constructed through asyndaton across the full stop, contrasting sharply with the explicit but unsettling simile which had linked Dryden with Hannibal. These two images, both difficult to handle, though difficult in different ways, prepare us to register disjunctions rather than simple likenesses in the subsequent account of Virgil's relation to the politics of his own day. If we have recognized incomplete, inexact resemblances, discontinuous parallels which provoke the reader into further reflection, we have recognized Dryden's mode of writing.

Contemporaries might well have expected a more straightforward and more explicit political deployment of the *Aeneid*. There was a tradition of translations of the *Aeneid* by Catholics and

---

[7] Noted in *Works*, vi. 944.

exiles.[8] Sir John Denham's translation of Book II as *The Destruction of Troy* (1656) had been angled towards royalists mourning the destruction of their kingdom.[9] After the Restoration, John Boys in his translation of Book III claims that Virgil 'in this wel-built fabrick of his gives us the full prospect of a well-order'd *Commonwealth*', and interprets the wanderings of Aeneas as an allegory of the troubles which beset the ship of state. When Aeneas finally landed in Italy, he laid 'the foundation of a never-declining *Monarchy*'. Boys then compares the wanderings of Aeneas with those of Charles II, and explains that the signal virtues of Aeneas— piety, wisdom, and valour—are equally exemplified in the new king.[10]

Dryden's own association of Virgil with contemporary history is more subtle. The moral of Virgil's epic, says Dryden, was shaped by the needs of his own community:

. . . we are to consider him as writing his Poem in a time when the Old Form of Government was subverted, and a new one just Established by *Octavius Caesar:* In effect by force of Arms, but seemingly by the Consent of the *Roman* People. The Commonwealth had receiv'd a deadly Wound in the former Civil Wars betwixt *Marius* and *Sylla*. The Commons, while the first prevail'd, had almost shaken off the Yoke of the Nobility; and *Marius* and *Cinna*, like the Captains of the Mobb, under the specious Pretence of the Publick Good, and of doing Justice on the Oppressours of their Liberty, reveng'd themselves, without Form of Law, on their private Enemies. *Sylla*, in his turn, proscrib'd the Heads of the adverse Party: He too had nothing but Liberty and Reformation in his Mouth; (for the Cause of Religion is but a Modern Motive to Rebellion, invented by the Christian Priesthood, refining on the Heathen:) *Sylla*, to be sure, meant no more good to the *Roman* People than *Marius* before him, whatever he declar'd; but Sacrific'd the Lives, and took the Estates of all his Enemies, to gratifie those who brought him into Power: Such was the Reformation of the Government by both Parties. The Senate

---

[8] Colin Burrow, 'Virgil in English Translation', in *The Cambridge Companion to Virgil*, ed. Charles Martindale (Cambridge, 1997), pp. 21–37, at pp. 23–4, 29, 35.

[9] See Lawrence Venuti, '*The Destruction of Troy*: Translation and Royalist Cultural Politics in the Interregnum', *Journal of Medieval and Renaissance Studies*, 23 (1993) 197–219; Nigel Smith, *Literature and Revolution in England 1640–1660* (New Haven, 1994), pp. 229–30.

[10] John Boys, *Aeneas his Errours, or his Voyage from Troy into Italy. An Essay upon the Third Book of Virgils Aeneis* (London, 1661), pp. 52–8. Boys's *Aeneas his Descent into Hell* (London, 1661), a version of Book VI, is dedicated to Lord Chancellor Hyde, and concludes with several speeches by Boys on the Restoration.

and the Commons were the two Bases on which it stood; and the two Champions of either Faction, each destroy'd the Foundations of the other side: So the Fabrique of consequence must fall betwixt them: And Tyranny must be built upon their Ruines. This comes of altering Fundamental Laws and Constitutions.[11]

This passage is, if not superfluous, at least elaborated beyond what is immediately relevant, in that Dryden's point is that the 'moral' of Virgil's poem was a response to contemporary experience. But the wars between Sulla and Marius were long over when Virgil was writing the *Aeneid*: Marius had died in 86 BCE, Sulla in 78. Virgil was not born until 70, began the *Aeneid* in 26, and died leaving the poem unfinished in 19. Dryden's summary of Roman history from the generation before Virgil's birth is not needed in order to establish the conditions which prevailed before the *Pax Augusta*, since the war which Octavius had ended was the later civil conflict which had followed the assassination of Julius Caesar in 44 BCE, and was brought to an end with the capture of Alexandria in 30. But what Dryden's detour does establish is a teasing interplay of similarity and difference between English and Roman history.[12] Much of the vocabulary in Dryden's account suggests a parallel with English history in the 1640s and 1650s: 'Commonwealth . . . Civil Wars . . . Commons . . . shaken off the Yoke . . . Nobility . . . Justice . . . Oppressours of their Liberty . . . without Form of Law . . . Liberty and Reformation . . . Cause of Religion . . . Rebellion . . . took the Estates . . . Reformation of the Government . . . Tyranny . . . altering Fundamental Laws and Constitutions.' It would not be difficult to construct a narrative of the English Civil Wars and Republic by taking those words and phrases in the same order and interpolating a few proper names. But no consistent parallel is possible, either between individuals or between causes: Sulla cannot be seen as a parallel for Cromwell except momentarily, for any further emplotment along these lines quickly breaks down; the constitutional, religious, and

---

[11] *Poems*, pp. 1012–13.

[12] Cp. Sir Richard Fanshawe's 'A Summary Discourse of the Civill Warres of Rome' (1648), which is patient of a contemporary political application. For a discussion of the contemporary political implications of the translation of Tacitus to which Dryden contributed, see Steven N. Zwicker and David Bywaters, 'Politics and Translation: The English Tacitus of 1698', *Huntington Library Quarterly*, 52 (1989) 319–46.

social issues are simply not comparable. Only the conclusion—that altering fundamental laws leads to ruin, and ruin to tyranny—seems to apply equally to Rome and to mid-century England. And to England after the Revolution of 1688–9. Yet however attractive it may be to read Octavius as William III (Octavius seen from a Tacitean viewpoint as one who subverted the old order and used the appearance of public and established forms to disguise the realities of a novel form of personal rule) the very awkwardness and fitfulness of the analogy protect Dryden from the charge of seditious writing.

The more firmly fashioned analogy between himself and Virgil might seem to place Dryden in the position of endorsing, or at least acquiescing in, the rule of William III, but the rhetoric of comparison once again proves complex, and to some degree self-deconstructing. When Dryden says that 'I may safely affirm for our great Author (as Men of good Sense are generally Honest) that he was still of Republican principles in his Heart'[13] he takes the responsibility of speaking for Virgil, of knowing his secret thoughts, on the basis of sharing some common ground with him, if only that of 'good Sense'. The idea of 'good Sense' makes the common ground between them not one of poetic insight or political principle, but civilized culture: the phrase, an English version of 'le bon sens',[14] implies a transhistorical, transnational community of the civilized to which intelligent readers of Dryden's translation are implicitly invited to belong.

Dryden then returns to the announced but deferred point, Virgil's design that the *Aeneid* should be a poem for his times:

> But to return from my long rambling: I say that *Virgil* having maturely weigh'd the Condition of the Times in which he liv'd: that an entire Liberty was not to be retriev'd: that the present Settlement had the prospect of a long continuance in the same Family, or those adopted into it: that he held his Paternal Estate from the Bounty of the Conqueror, by whom he was likewise enrich'd, esteem'd and cherished: that this Conquerour, though of a bad kind, was the very best of it: that the Arts of Peace flourish'd under him: that all Men might be happy if they would

---

[13] *Poems*, p. 1014.

[14] For examples of the currency of this idea in contemporary French criticism see Boileau, *L'Art poétique*, i. 28; Dominique Bouhours, *Les Entretiens d'Ariste et d'Eugène* [first published 1671] (Paris, 1962), pp. 125–6.

be quiet: that now he was in possession of the whole, yet he shar'd a great part of his Authority with the Senate: That he would be chosen into the Ancient Offices of the Commonwealth, and Rul'd by the Power which he deriv'd from them; and Prorogu'd his Government from time to time: Still, as it were, threatning to dismiss himself from Publick Cares, which he exercis'd more for the common Good, than for any delight he took in greatness: These things, I say, being consider'd by the Poet, he concluded it to be the Interest of his Country to be so Govern'd: To infuse an awful Respect into the People, towards such a Prince: By that respect to confirm their Obedience to him; and by that Obedience to make them Happy. This was the Moral of his Divine Poem: Honest in the Poet: Honourable to the Emperour, whom he derives from a Divine Extraction; and reflecting part of that Honour on the *Roman* People, whom he derives also from the *Trojans*; and not only profitable, but necessary to the present Age; and likely to be such to their Posterity.[15]

What is the time of this passage? Which is 'the present Age'— Virgil's time or Dryden's? After those detours and deferrals we reach a point in the 'Dedication' where we become conscious of several possible times. Most immediately we are aware of the temporality of our own reading, as the first sentence extends itself through that inordinately long series of clauses, and we wait for the conclusion to discover what Virgil had resolved about this (significantly unnamed) 'Conqueror'. When it arrives, the climax refers us back to the conditions which have just been spelt out, as we are told that Virgil decided that it was in his country's interests for it 'to be *so* Govern'd' and that the people should respect '*such* a Prince' (italics added). The focus here is on conduct not legitimacy. The previous paragraphs had sounded a stronger note of disapproval, with their references to 'despotick Power' in the hands of an 'Arbitrary Monarch', and their account of the aftermath of civil war: 'the Commonwealth was lost without ressource: The Heads of it destroy'd; the Senate new moulded, grown degenerate; and either bought off, or thrusting their own Necks into the Yoke, out of fear of being forc'd.'[16] After such a Tacitean analysis—and one which some of Dryden's readers could have applied without demur to the condition of England in 1688–9— the expansive, Clarendonian description of Octavius surprises by

[15] *Poems*, pp. 1014–15.   [16] *Poems*, pp. 1013–14.

its move into a new idiom. It becomes a meditation on possession. In these conditions it is conceded that 'an entire Liberty was not to be retriev'd', but even if such an original, complete freedom is lost (and when would that once have flourished? Dryden's account of Roman history has not posited such a time) certain valuable forms of possession are nevertheless confirmed: Virgil holds his paternal estates not by virtue of his inheritance but by the bounty of Octavius, who has besides 'enrich'd, esteem'd and cherish'd' the poet. Octavius himself possesses the whole power, yet shares it with the Senate; though a conqueror, he seeks to be elected into the ancient offices of state, wishing to be circumscribed by the very power which he derives from them. Octavius' possession is so complete that it allows bounty and self-limitation. But full self-possession—according to the moral tradition stemming from Horace, and revived in Cowley's *Essays* and Dryden's *Sylvæ*—requires retirement from public life, and Octavius is always on the point of renouncing the cares of public office which he has, of course, only undertaken out of disinterested concern for the common good, not from any delight in greatness.

But Dryden was well aware—and could rely on his readers being well aware—that the reputation of Octavius was at best mixed.[17] Moreover, regardless of the historical accuracy of this as a portrait of Virgil's patron, there is another time at work in this passage, which is the time of the 1690s, and thus the moment of Dryden and William III. We cannot avoid registering first the similarities between Augustus and William ('that an entire Liberty was not to be retriev'd: that the present Settlement had the prospect of a long continuance in the same Family, or those adopted into it'), and then the dissimilarities between them in their exercise of power, their hopes for retirement, and their treatment of great poets. Recognizing the ways in which William does *not* repeat the policies and achievements of Augustus, we recognize that Dryden cannot repeat Virgil's decision to accept the new order.

This lesson in interpretation, which invites us to recognize both similarity and difference, and to weigh discontinuous correspondences rather than seek a totalizing allegory, prepares us to read

---

[17] For the reputation of Augustus and its handling by English writers see Howard Erskine-Hill, *The Augustan Idea in English Literature* (London, 1983).

Dryden's account of the similarities between Aeneas and Augustus.[18] Aeneas is not '*Priam*'s Heir in a Lineal Succession', since he was only Priam's son-in-law and the King still had a son living, so he could only be 'an Elective King'. The similarities with William are obvious and uncomfortable; so too are the contrasts: '*Æneas*, tho' he Married the Heiress of the Crown, yet claim'd no Title to it during the Life of his Father-in-Law. *Pater arma Latinus habeto*,[19] &c. are *Virgil*'s Words. As for himself, he was contented to take care of his Country Gods, who were not those of *Latium*'. Augustus, says Dryden, was troubled by his lack of a lineal claim, and was tempted to assert his descent from Aeneas. As a way of consolidating his position, Augustus

had once resolv'd to re-build that City, and there to make the Seat of Empire: But *Horace* writes an Ode on purpose to deter him from that Thought; declaring the place to be accurs'd, and that the Gods would as often destroy it as it shou'd be rais'd. Hereupon the Emperour laid aside a Project so ungrateful to the *Roman* People.[20]

Here the poet has the role of counsellor, the one who knows that the present cannot be legitimized by the fabrication of a lineal claim or the rebuilding of Troy on its original site. One has to accept the real conditions of the present, the true nature and name of power. As for the possible addition of a third term to the comparison, making the parallel Aeneas/Augustus/William, that is neither proposed nor denied, but left as an open question. Dryden summarizes the character of Aeneas with an implicit question to his readers as to whether such a description would also fit William III:

the Manners which our Poet gives his Heroe . . . are the same which were eminently seen in his *Augustus*. Those Manners were Piety to the Gods, and a dutiful Affection to his Father; Love to his Relations; Care of his People; Courage and Conduct in the Wars; Gratitude to those who had oblig'd him; and Justice in general to Mankind.[21]

Could Dryden's readers honestly say this of William?

---

[18] *Poems*, pp. 1016–21.

[19] *Aeneid*, xii. 192: 'let father Latinus keep the sword'. As noted in *Works*, vi. 947, Dryden's quotation substitutes *pater* ('father') for Virgil's *socer* ('father-in-law'). This is peculiar, since Dryden's topical insinuation in 'father-in-law' (James II was William III's father-in-law) is no longer made safe by the immediate appearance of Virgil's word *socer*, instead we are aware of a disjunction between Dryden's term and *pater* which it supposedly translates.

[20] *Poems*, p. 1018. The ode is Horace, *Carmina*, III. iii.   [21] *Poems*, p. 1018.

One of the passages in which Dryden is most overt in his challenging of William through his definition of the qualities of the good ruler is protected from any interpretation of hostile intent in another way. This, according to Dryden, is Virgil's understanding of the virtues of his prince:

> *Virgil* had consider'd that the greatest Virtues of *Augustus* consisted in the perfect Art of Governing his People; which caus'd him to Reign for more than Forty Years in great Felicity. He consider'd that his Emperour was Valiant, Civil, Popular, Eloquent, Politick, and Religious. He has given all these Qualities to *Æneas*. But knowing that Piety alone comprehends the whole Duty of Man towards the Gods, towards his Country, and towards his Relations, he judg'd, that this ought to be his first Character, whom he would set for a Pattern of Perfection. In reality, they who believe that the Praises which arise from Valour, are superior to those, which proceed from any other Virtues, have not consider'd (as they ought,) that Valour, destitute of other Virtues, cannot render a Man worthy of any true esteem. That Quality which signifies no more than an intrepid Courage, may be separated from many others which are good, and accompany'd with many which are ill. A Man may be very Valiant, and yet Impious and Vicious. But the same cannot be said of Piety; which excludes all ill Qualities, and comprehends even Valour it self, with all other Qualities which are good. Can we, for example, give the praise of Valour to a Man who shou'd see his Gods prophan'd, and shou'd want the Courage to defend them? To a Man who shou'd abandon his Father, or desert his King in his last Necessity?[22]

This passage sails dangerously close to the wind. What praise can be given to a ruler who shows intrepid courage (as William did) but is impious and vicious? True piety demands that one defend one's gods, one's father, and one's king—a lesson for Mary as well as for William. And yet as Dryden says when introducing this paragraph, 'What follows is Translated literally from *Segrais*', and after it he carefully adds: 'Thus far *Segrais*'. He is right: the paragraph is an exact translation from the preface to Segrais' Virgil, and so difficult to object to—though not, therefore, innocent of political implications.[23]

[22] *Poems*, pp. 1020–1.
[23] *Traduction de L'Eneïde de Virgile par M^r. de Segrais* (Paris, 1668), p. 37. The rendering is virtually literal, except for the omission of the words 'imprudent' and 'menteur' in the sentence 'On peut fort bien estre vaillant, & estre impie, imprudent, menteur & vicieux', and the addition of the phrase 'in his last Necessity'.

   England in the 1690s was a political and literary culture in transition, in the process of re-formation, and in this respect provided
a close parallel with the conditions of Augustan Rome. It was to a
comparable sense of political and cultural endeavour in process
that the *Aeneid* responded,[24] with its evocation of 'one Empire
destroyed, and another rais'd from the Ruins of it'.[25] Dryden's
adroit handling of the possible parallels between Aeneas, Augustus,
and William demonstrates that the past cannot simply be appropriated in the interests of the present: its texts incorporate values
which judge us as we read. And if the culture of the present is to
be re-formed, that is the work of poets as well as kings. Dryden's
Aeneis is a politically engaged text, but not one which is merely
partisan. Dryden and Tonson planned the publication of *The
Works of Virgil* to appeal to a broad constituency in the nation,[26]
and the translation itself reshapes ideas of piety and nationhood in
ways which do not run smoothly along party lines but transpose
the issues of the day into a new, more demanding, imaginative
terrain.

   One of the plates for Dryden's *Aeneis* depicts Virgil reading the
Aeneid to Augustus, his scroll open at the passage which describes
the future Marcellus, the lost heir (see Plate 7). Both men are men
of power. Augustus sits elevated on his throne at the top of a flight
of steps, framed in a severely classical niche. But Virgil too has
power over the audience, for Octavia is fainting at his words. The
source of this powerful impression is the poet's open mouth and
the written scroll on which we can see the words *Tu Marcellus eris*.
There could be no equivalent for this relationship between poet,
ruler, and public in Dryden's own case. It is, then, symbolic (if
admittedly an accidental symbolism) that this plate has no fixed
location in *The Works of Virgil*. Too large for the ordinary-paper
editions, it is found only in the large-paper copies printed for
subscribers, and even then it is inserted at various different places
as seemed appropriate to the binder or the owner.[27] An image of
a mutually creative relationship between ruler and poet, this floating signifier cannot quite find its home in Dryden's text.

---

[24] Karl Galinsky, *Augustan Culture: An Interpretive Introduction* (Princeton, 1996), *passim*.
[25] *Poems*, p. 1016.
[26] As John Barnard shows in a forthcoming article on the subscription list for the 1697
Virgil.   [27] *Works*, vi. 940–1.

THE FALL OF TROY AND THE CONDITION OF EXILE

Virgil's *Aeneid* is an epic which tells of repeated displacements and deferrals.[28] Aeneas is forced to flee from the burning ruins of Troy, and his quest for the promised second homeland is frustrated by misrecognitions as he mistakes temporary havens for the site of the new city, and by his misinterpretations of oracles and prophecies. Despite being famously *pius Aeneas*, he has to contend throughout with the opposition of a powerful goddess, Juno. In translating this poem, Dryden could not fail to be drawn to the many kinds of suffering which attend the loss of Troy, and this epic of exile gave him the opportunity to accentuate certain moments when the condition of exile, its anguish and its responsibilities, press upon the reader. The *Aeneid* contemplates the destruction of the home, the most sacred hearth symbolized by Vesta, the Lares, and Penates, the point of origin which makes being human possible.[29] The destruction of the homeland is emphasized when Aeneas begins his narration in Book II, and tells of 'An Empire from its old Foundations rent' and 'A Peopl'd City made a Desart Place'.[30] But Aeneas is not the only exile, and the pathos of Dido's flight from her home is underscored when she tells Aeneas that she is 'Like you an Alien in a Land unknown'.[31] Dryden relates that she had fled 'with her household Gods, | To seek a Refuge in remote abodes'.[32] Nor is such pain confined only to humans, for even the stag shot by Ascanius belongs to a place which is sacred to him and which he tries to regain, as in his agony he 'seeks his known abodes; | His old familiar Hearth, and household Gods'.[33]

---

[28] For Virgil's emphasis on the difficulties of Aeneas see Galinsky, *Augustan Culture*, pp. 121–4. Pliny emphasized the difficulties and setbacks which Augustus faced throughout his career: *Naturalis Historia*, vii. 147–50.

[29] For the significance of Hestia/Vesta see Jean-Joseph Goux, 'Vesta, or the Place of Being', *Representations*, 1 (1983) 91–107.

[30] *Aeneis*, ii. 5, 7; no equivalent in Virgil.

[31] *Aeneis*, i. 890; there is no equivalent for 'Alien' or 'unknown' in *Aeneid*, i. 629.

[32] *Aeneis*, i. 491–2; Virgil in *Aeneid*, i. 357 has the less emotive *patriaque excedere* ('and leave her native land').

[33] *Aeneis*, vii. 696–7; Virgil in *Aeneid*, vii. 500 has no equivalent to the hearth and household gods: *nota intra tecta refugit* ('seeks refuge in the familiar building'). Dryden's addition here is a striking example of his compassionate interest in the animal world: cp. the simile of the dog and the hare in *Annus Mirabilis*, ll. 521–8, and, of course, the Hind in *The Hind and the Panther*.

When handling the question of what caused such exile, Dryden
had the opportunity to insert some definition of the political forces
at work. Aeneas says that he and his comrades were 'by Force
expell'd' from Troy.[34] In the case of Dido and her companions,
'all combine to leave the State, | Who hate the Tyrant, or who
fear his hate'.[35] This is a fairly close translation, providing no
grounds for any reader to suspect a political skewing of the text
through the use of 'Tyrant' (clearly justified by *tyranni*), but there
is a deft addition in that phrase 'to leave the State'. The word
'state' had a range of meanings at this date: as well as 'a nation and
its territory' (*OED* 30b), probably the primary meaning in this
context, and 'a particular form of government' (*OED* 28), it could
specifically mean 'republic' (*OED* 28b).[36] It is therefore a word in
which readers can, if they wish, see a reference to the kind of
political structure which good men might well hate and wish to
escape, though at the same time it can innocently mean no more
than 'territory'.

The poem shows us Aeneas searching for a home which (as it
turns out) is both a recovery of the point of origin and a new
beginning. Hesitations, reversals, and duplications abound.[37] This
quest is fraught with misunderstandings, for Apollo's oracle on
Delos is clear but unspecific, and too hasty a response to it leads
the Trojans to a disastrous sojourn on Crete. Only the appearance
of the household gods to Aeneas in a dream makes it apparent that
their home—both their point of origin and their goal—is in Italy:
'From thence we came, and thither must return.'[38] To Dryden's
contemporaries in the 1690s it would be impossible to read this
story of exile and return without being aware of parallels with
recent English history, but Dryden's translation does not make it

[34] *Aeneis*, i. 517; no equivalent in *Aeneid*, i. 375, though the repetition of *forte* ('by
chance') in 375 and 377 may have suggested 'force'.

[35] *Aeneis*, i. 497–8; translating *Aeneid*, i. 361–2: *Conveniunt, quibus odium crudele
tyranni | Aut metus acer erat* ('those come together whose hatred of the tyrant was fierce, or
whose fear intense').

[36] Cp. 'Prologue to *Amboyna*', l. 22. For the changing meanings of 'state' in the seventeenth century see Quentin Skinner, 'The State', in *Political Innovation and Conceptual
Change*, ed. Terence Ball, James Farr and Russell L. Hanson (Cambridge, 1989), pp.
90–131.

[37] See David Quint, *Epic and Empire: Politics and Generic Form from Virgil to Milton*
(Princeton, 1993), pp. 50–93.   [38] *Aeneis*, iii. 226.

into an allegory. The *Aeneid* is, anyway, not a poem about the restoration of a prince or a government, or even a way of life: it tells of how one comes to accept displacement, to resist the temptation to replicate the past (exemplified by Helenus and Andromache's miniature simulacrum of Troy[39]) and to start a new settlement on a new site, and with a new name. Dryden does indeed highlight some elements which provide a commentary on the recent revolution, but this is part of his invitation to reflect on a wider, common human experience—to find other forms of order in a world of chaos, to redefine what we hold sacred, to reconsider how we recover our past through difference rather than repetition.

That *translatio* which was at the core of Virgil's imagination is at the core of Dryden's also. For Virgil the *translatio imperii* involved the founding of Rome from Troy and the finding of modern Rome by a cultural translation of its sacred, original values. For Dryden the translation of Virgil was in part the translation of his contemporary cares into an imagined world, a textual space which enabled a reappraisal of them. The word *cura* echoes through the *Aeneid*, as 'care' does through Dryden's translation. Its ambiguity is important: the anxious cares which disturb the equanimity of the modern Englishman are addressed through that reverent care for life which this epic both enacts and enables.

Written in the 1690s, Dryden's *Aeneis* inevitably speaks to the political condition of England and of Dryden himself, but its politics—the way it rethinks nation and people and religion—is much more than a series of barbed allusions to William III and the revolution which had displaced James II.[40] Displacement, the search for the home, the gradual understanding of what 'restoration' might mean, become recurring themes in Dryden's translation, but as part of an imaginative philosophical and poetic engagement with Virgil's text, not as an appropriation of it in order to voice political resentments.

The *Aeneis* begins by mapping a textual world which is neither Virgil's Rome nor Dryden's England:

---

[39] *Aeneis*, iii. 448–51.

[40] For readings of the *Aeneis* which stress the Jacobite elements see Murray G. H. Pittock, *Poetry and Jacobite Politics in Eighteenth-Century Britain and Ireland* (Cambridge, 1994), pp. 94–107, and Howard Erskine-Hill, *Poetry and the Realm of Politics: Shakespeare to Dryden* (Oxford, 1996), pp. 201–15.

Arms, and the Man I sing, who, forc'd by Fate,
And haughty *Juno*'s unrelenting Hate;
Expell'd and exil'd, left the *Trojan* Shoar:
Long Labours, both by Sea and Land he bore;
And in the doubtful War, before he won
The *Latian* Realm, and built the destin'd Town:
His banish'd Gods restor'd to Rites Divine,
And setl'd sure Succession in his Line:
From whence the Race of *Alban* Fathers come,
And the long Glories of Majestick *Rome*.[41]

Arma, virumque cano, Trojae qui primus ab oris
Italiam, fato profugus, Lavinaque venit
Litora: multum ille et terris jactatus et alto,
Vi superum, saevae memorem Junonis ob iram.
Multa quoque et bello passus, dum conderet urbem,
Inferretque Deos Latio: genus unde Latinum,
Albanique patres, atque altae moenia Romae.[42]

While Dryden preserves the Roman proper names, some of the phrasing here invites us to recall the recent political history of England as we read. The phrase 'Expell'd and exil'd' is an addition to the Latin, and might prompt memories of the expelled and exiled James II, while line 7 is a curiously free translation of *Inferretque Deos* ('and brought in his gods'): the Latin verb does not mean 'brought *back*', so the idea of restoration is Dryden's own. Line 8 is entirely Dryden's addition, suggesting an allusion to the displacement of James II and his line from the English throne, and inviting us to imagine that displacement undone. '*Alban* Fathers' is an exact translation of *Albanique patres*, but readers who have by now been alerted to undercurrents of contemporary allusion in the text may remember that James had been Duke of Albany, and had been celebrated by Dryden under the allegorical title of Albanius

---

[41] *Aeneis*, i. 1–10. The opening of the *Aeneis* has often been commented on, e.g. by James Anderson Winn, *John Dryden and his World* (New Haven, 1987), p. 488. My discussion of the passage is adapted from my essay 'Classical Texts: Translations and Transformations', in *The Cambridge Companion to English Literature 1650–1740*, ed. Steven N. Zwicker (Cambridge, 1998), pp. 143–61.

[42] *Aeneid*, i. 1–7: 'Arms and the man I sing, who, driven by Fate, first came from the region of Troy to Italy, to the shores of Lavinum: he was greatly troubled on sea and land by the power of the gods, on account of the avenging anger of cruel Juno. He suffered much in war, before founding the city and bringing his gods into Latium: from whence arise the Latin people, and the Alban fathers, and the walls of lofty Rome.'

in the opera *Albion and Albanius* (1685). Ironically, it is this absolutely faithful translation of *Albanique patres* which permits a reading which leaves faithful interpretation far behind.

But then, keeping faith is exactly what both Virgil and Dryden, in their different ways, are concerned with. This teasingly unfaithful yet faithful opening to the *Aeneis* sets these issues working in the mind of the reader, and the irresolvable tensions of the initial paragraph initiate us into a complex mode of reading. Dryden is opening the poem out to include England, without making it an allegory of English history. The temporary association of Aeneas and James is quickly shown not to be allegorical as the poem itself rapidly deconstructs the rhetorical scheme which it had appeared to offer. Having suggested, and then placed under erasure, the possibility of associating Aeneas with William III in the 'Dedication', Dryden is not going to deliver a simple Jacobite alternative in the poem itself. The present tense in 'come' takes the poem into a present in which the long-established glories of Rome are still flourishing. Such a present tense would be appropriate for Virgil, writing when Rome was indeed still glorious, though in fact his Latin has no verb here and so does not specify a tense. It is Dryden's translation which, by creating this emphatic but impossible present—a time in which the Alban fathers and the glories of Rome are fully present—makes us recognize our own separation from such a time, and our exile from such a rich kind of nationhood. It establishes for the duration of the poem a milieu which is neither Rome nor England, but a placing and displacing of both.

Dryden's emphasis on Aeneas being expelled and exiled does more than suggest a link to James II. Engaging with this originary text, Dryden is led to meditate on what turns out to be a repeated condition of exile and displacement, a condition which also affects him personally, as there is an analogy between Aeneas' enforced displacement from Troy and his search for a safe home for himself and his gods, and Dryden's own form of internal exile as a Catholic in an aggressively Protestant land, dispossessed of his public offices and with his private worship ridiculed and harrassed. Yet Aeneas does not function as a precise parallel either for James or for Dryden: rather, the occasional emphasis on Aeneas' experience of loss and the deferral of his recovery of a homeland helps to shape a textual field into which readers can bring their own

experience. We recognize and reflect upon our own forms of exile and alienation all the more readily because Dryden has eased the poem away from its Roman origins, using a vocabulary which opens out a semiotic field which is English and seventeenth-century without prescribing exact modes of correspondence with the reader's experience.

In so doing he is, in fact, being faithful to one of Virgil's poetic characteristics, his imaginative movement between worlds.[43] Virgil did not write an *Augusteid*; instead his *Aeneid* is an imaginative translation of the values and anxieties of Augustan Rome into the world of epic struggle. The poem's first simile, in which the waves are likened to an unruly crowd before the appearance of an authoritative public figure calms them, is an early indication of the way that the *Aeneid* will move between the recognizably contemporary world of Rome and the imagined time of epic.[44] The textual field of the *Aeneid* is polysemic, rich in its intertextual allusions, often at a minute level,[45] but also exploiting the tendency of Latin to attach additional meanings to a fairly limited vocabulary rather than to coin new words. As Servius noted,[46] the poem's first verb, *cano*, is capable of several interpretations, 'sing', 'celebrate', 'prophesy'. The word thus points backwards and forwards in time, referring principally to a hero of the imagined past whose deeds can be recalled, but also implying the possibility of a future hero whose achievements the poet (*vates*) in his role as prophet (*vates* again) is able to celebrate in advance. Thus the first line of the *Aeneid* opens out its semiotic field to embrace epic past, present performance, and future glory, an implicitly Augustan glory which will be (but no—*may* be in the process of becoming) a repetition and fulfilment of the epic achievements of Aeneas. Dryden's polysemic mode follows that of his master, but without even his limited degree of political confidence.[47]

[43] In this paragraph I am indebted to various portions of Galinsky's *Augustan Culture*.

[44] For Virgil's complex representation of historical time and place see James E. G. Zetzel, 'Rome and its Traditions', in *The Cambridge Companion to Virgil*, pp. 188–203.

[45] See the commentaries by Austin; and Joseph Farrell, 'The Virgilian Intertext', in *The Cambridge Companion to Virgil*, pp. 222–38.

[46] *Servianorum in Vergilii Carmina Commentariorum Editionis Harvardianae Volumen II* (Lancaster, Pa., 1946), p. 7: 'CANO polysemus sermo est'.

[47] For Virgil's combination of imperialistic confidence and tragic recoil see the classic essay by Adam Parry, 'The Two Voices of Virgil's *Aeneid*', *Arion*, 2:4 (1963) 66–80.

Dryden's opening translation, or mistranslation—or perhaps 'Translation with Latitude', to use his own phrase[48]—is another instance of the troubling but creative solicitation of *différance* which keeps him always at some remove from Virgil, never quite assured of the succession. By the end of the first paragraph he has taken us into an impossible time and space whose very idiosyncrasy indicates that simple recovery, exact restoration, are unthinkable. And the first books of the *Aeneis* include repeated reminders that such a return is impossible. Though scrupulous in its attempt to provide a faithful rendering of Virgil's Latin, Dryden's account of the destruction of Troy is troubled by a recognition of separation from the hallowed source, and a special horror at the violation of that sacred place which it is compelled to describe. This fear solicits the English text, prizes it open, and separates it yet further from Virgil even as it seeks to keep faith with the Latin.

The murder of Priam is preceded by a preliminary violation when his house is broken open. The Greeks stand at his threshold. Virgil holds them there for a while, emphasizing the horror of this liminal moment which is observed from the top of a tower by Aeneas, who is close enough to see what is happening but too far away to intervene. Twice in this short passage Virgil uses the word *limen* ('threshold'; but also, in this polysemic language, 'door', 'entrance', 'house', 'beginning', and even—in post-classical Latin—'end'). First armed soldiers are seen standing on the outer threshold (*in limine primo*), and then, as our eyes become accustomed to the scene and we identify individuals in the crowd, we see that it is Pyrrhus and the two sons of Atreus who are standing there (*geminosque in limine Atridas*).[49] The broken door reveals that which had previously been kept secret:

> 'Apparet domus intus, et atria longa patescunt:
> 'Apparent Priami et veterum penetralia regum:
> 'Armatosque vident stantes in limine primo.[50]

---

[48] 'Preface to *Ovid's Epistles*', *Poems*, p. 182. [49] *Aeneid*, ii. 485, 500.

[50] *Aeneid*, ii. 483–5: 'The interior of the house appears and the long hall is revealed; the innermost rooms of Priam and the ancient kings appear, and they see armed men standing on the outer threshold.'

the Rooms conceal'd
Appear, and all the Palace is reveal'd.
The Halls of Audience, and of publick State,
And where the lonely Queen in secret sate.
Arm'd Souldiers now by trembling Maids are seen,
With not a Door, and scarce a Space between.[51]

To whom is this revelation made? Momentarily Dryden reverses
the viewpoint, changing Virgil's account of what the Greek
soldiers see as they peer through the splintered door, to show us
what the women inside the palace see as they look terror-stricken
at the enemy breaking in. Aeneas himself is speaking (and the
inverted commas at the beginning of each line in Ruaeus' edition
remind the reader that a particular illusion of presence is being
wrought here) but the secret places of the palace are being
revealed simultaneously to Aeneas and to Pyrrhus, to the pious
son and to the impious son. Which are we as we approach this
sight?

Pyrrhus kills one of Priam's sons in front of his father, and then
seizes the king himself:

'altaria ad ipsa trementem
'Traxit, et in multo lapsantem sanguine nati:
'Implicuitque comam laeva: dextraque coruscum
'Extulit, ac lateri capulo tenus abdidit ensem.
'Haec finis Priami fatorum: hic exitus illum
'Sorte tulit, Trojam incensam et prolapsa videntem
'Pergama, tot quondam populis terrisque superbum
'Regnatorem Asiae. Jacet ingens litore truncus,
'Avulsumque humeris caput, et sine nomine corpus.[52]

he dragg'd the trembling Sire,
Slidd'ring through clotter'd Blood, and holy Mire,
(The mingl'd Paste his murder'd Son had made,)
Haul'd from beneath the violated Shade;
And on the Sacred Pile, the Royal Victim laid.

---

[51] *Aeneis*, ii. 661–6.

[52] *Aeneid*, ii. 550–8: 'To the very altars Pyrrhus dragged him trembling, and slipping
in the copious blood of his son; and twisted his hair in his left hand, and with his right drew
out his flashing sword and buried it up to the hilt in his side. This was the end of Priam's
fall, this end overtook him by fate, seeing Troy in flames and Pergamon in ruins, once the
proud ruler of so many peoples and lands of Asia. The great trunk lies on the shore, the
head cut away from the shoulders, and the body without a name.'

His right Hand held his bloody Fauchion bare;
His left he twisted in his hoary Hair:
Then, with a speeding Thrust, his Heart he found:
The lukewarm Blood came rushing through the wound,
And sanguine Streams distain'd the sacred Ground.
Thus *Priam* fell: and shar'd one common Fate
With *Troy* in Ashes, and his ruin'd State:
He, who the Scepter of all *Asia* sway'd,
Whom Monarchs like domestick Slaves obey'd.
On the bleak Shoar now lies th' abandon'd King,
A headless Carcass, and a nameless thing.[53]

Dryden has added several important details to Virgil. The shade is violated; the king is a 'Royal Victim'; the sword-thrust goes to the heart of Priam; the blood gushes from the wound and stains the sacred ground. We are witnessing a parodic sacrifice. Most horrific is the emphasis on the young man's blood in which Priam slips. Virgil's vocabulary is simple—*in multo lapsantem sanguine nati*—and he achieves his effect through the crescendo as we move from one word to the next: 'in much sliding blood of his son', culminating in the one word, *nati*, which should never arrive, the possibility which should have remained hidden. Dryden by contrast tells us that Priam is dragged 'slidd'ring' through the 'clotter'd' blood. This word 'slidd'ring' is used nowhere else in Dryden's verse, and is not recorded by the *OED* in the previous two centuries. As for 'clotter'd', this variant form of 'clotted' seems to have been archaic by Dryden's day,[54] and the *OED*'s quotation of 'The clotter'd blood he sucks' from Chapman's *Iliad* suggests that Dryden may have chosen this variant because of its rarity and its epic associations: in any case, it is a word over which we stumble. Dryden's special horror at this point is signalled by his departure from Virgil's linguistic sobriety.

Was Dryden's response to Priam slipping on his son's blood informed partly by the memory of Nisus falling on the slippery place, on ground which was also wet with blood from a sacrifice? Intertextual echoes confirm the impression that in this passage

---

[53] *Aeneis*, ii. 748–63. For a good close reading of this passage see Eric Griffiths, 'Dryden's Past', *Proceedings of the British Academy*, 84 (1994) 113–49, at pp. 128–9. We arrived independently at some similar observations.

[54] There are no examples in the *OED* between 1640 and 1828, when Scott revived the word.

Dryden was returning to the site of deepest loss. (Unconscious, repeated return to a site which one would rather avoid is one of Freud's examples of the uncanny.) The phrase 'one common Fate' has no equivalent in Virgil, nor did it have any equivalent earlier in this episode when Hecuba said to Priam:

> With us, one common shelter thou shalt find,
> Or in one common Fate with us be join'd.[55]

But it does have a precedent when Dryden says of himself and Oldham:

> One common Note on either Lyre did strike.[56]

And there are other echoes in this passage from *Aeneis* II of that group of pieces (written in the same year as the poem on Oldham and printed in *Sylvæ*) in which Dryden had turned to a series of translations from Latin in order to imagine the loss of presence and the failure of succession: 'Nisus and Euryalus' and 'Mezentius and Lausus', both from Virgil, which mourn the loss of young men of promise, and 'Lucretius: Against the Fear of Death' in which Dryden temporarily adopted a Roman philosophy to write himself a consolation against the prospect of death. 'One common Fate' echoes 'One fate attends us; and one common Grave' in the translation from Lucretius;[57] the phrase 'holy mire' is without a precedent in Virgil, but echoes the 'holy gore' which made the place slippery in 'Nisus and Euryalus';[58] 'the fear of death'[59] has no equivalent in the Latin, but is part of the title of 'Lucretius: Against the Fear of Death'; while 'encompass round'[60] echoes the last line of 'To the Memory of Mr. Oldham'. The additional lines which stress the bloody death of Priam,

> The lukewarm Blood came rushing through the wound,
> And sanguine Streams distain'd the sacred Ground.

echo the description of the death of Mezentius:

> The Crimson stream distain'd his Arms around;
> And the distainful Soul came rushing through the wound.[61]

---

[55] *Aeneis*, ii. 714–15.   [56] 'To the Memory of Mr. Oldham', l. 5.
[57] 'Lucretius: Against the Fear of Death', l. 304.
[58] 'Nisus and Euryalus', l. 60.   [59] *Aeneis*, ii. 727.
[60] Ibid., 702.   [61] 'Mezentius and Lausus', ll. 240–1.

Mezentius is the king whose son Lausus has just died protecting him. Moreover, these lines are themselves echoed—indeed, virtually repeated—at the very end of the *Aeneis*:

> The streaming Blood distain'd his Arms around:
> And the disdainful Soul came rushing thro' the Wound.[62]

Here Aeneas kills Turnus, prompted by the sight of the golden belt which Turnus had taken from Pallas after killing him. Pallas is the last in the line of young men of promise, prospective heirs who have met an untimely death (Ossory, Oldham, Nisus, Euryalus, Lausus, Marcellus, Pallas) who haunted Dryden's memory. Aeneas dispatches Turnus with a blow which is explicitly given on Pallas' behalf:

> To his sad Soul a grateful Off'ring go;
> 'Tis *Pallas, Pallas* gives this deadly Blow.[63]

At last Pallas, the exemplary lost heir, is given the power to avenge his death. The concluding couplet echoes the earlier expressions of loss in a way which suggests that Dryden was making the last lines of his *Aeneis* a sign that this mourning is now, at length, completed. It is the point at which Dryden enters into his own inheritance by completing his translation of Virgil.

The final line of this episode in Book II recoils from the death of Priam in an unexpected way. 'A headless Carcass, and a nameless thing' is a quotation taken verbatim from Sir John Denham's translation in *The Destruction of Troy*, and is marked as such by Dryden in the only footnote anywhere in his translation. When he came to contemplate the headless body of the king and father, Dryden could find no words of his own; he was reduced to quoting Denham's version, entirely, exactly, with no difference, swerving away into using another man's words as if this were something too awful to say on his own account, too fearful to put his name to. Here, at the point where the father has been beheaded and made nameless, Dryden stumbles and finds himself momentarily displaced from the symbolic order over which the name of the father presides, incapable of utterance. But why choose Denham's words? Felicitous though the line is, it gains an

---

[62] *Aeneis*, xii. 1376–7.   [63] Ibid., 1373–4.

extra resonance from a sentence in Denham's preface, where he remarks that unless the translator adds some spirit of his own to the translation, he will be left with a '*Caput mortuum*'—a dead head.[64] If you do not supplement Virgil, you have only a lifeless body.

FORMS OF ORDER AND FORCES OF CHAOS

In this poem about the ruin and building of structures, much emphasis is placed upon fabrics.[65] In the 'Dedication of the *Aeneis*' Dryden figures the epic poem itself as a building whose every part should be properly constructed from good materials, and in the same essay the commonwealth is represented as a fabric ruined by civil war when each side undermined the other's foundations. In such circumstances, 'Tyranny must be built upon their Ruines'.[66] In the political sphere it may be tyranny which is built upon the ruins of ancient fabrics, but in the imagined terrain fashioned by poetry the fabric of the poem is a structure which can atone for the loss of the temporal building, taking its place.

The *Aeneis* includes many pointers towards the importance, and the vulnerability, of human constructions. At the climax of his prelude to Book I, Virgil's single line *Tantae molis erat Romanam condere gentem*[67] generates two lines in Dryden's translation:

> Such Time, such Toil requir'd the *Roman* Name,
> Such length of Labour for so vast a Frame.[68]

In effect Dryden translates *molis* three times, once as 'Toil', a second time as 'Labour' (these representing the sense *OLD* 8), and a third time as 'Frame', drawing on its other meaning of 'huge structure' (*OLD* 3). The word *gentem*, however, is not translated at all: Dryden seems uninterested at this point in the idea of a people or race (and his translation will show distrust of the people

---

[64] Sir John Denham, *The Poetical Works*, ed. Theodore Howard Banks, 2nd edn. (n.p., 1969), p. 159.

[65] For discussions of the importance of 'fabric' to Dryden's imagination see Richard Luckett, 'The Fabric of Dryden's Verse', *Proceedings of the British Academy*, 67 (1981) 289–305, and Robert W. McHenry, 'Dryden's Architectural Metaphors and Restoration Architecture', *Restoration*, 9 (1985) 61–74. [66] *Poems*, p. 1013.

[67] *Aeneid*, i. 33: 'so much labour did it cost [*or* such a great task it was] to found the Roman people.' [68] *Aeneis*, i. 48–9.

qua crowd when they have power to act politically); rather, it is the name and the frame which concern him, the word and reputation on the one hand, and the fabric of empire on the other. The implications of 'Frame' are left undefined: it could refer to the physical city of Rome or to the imperial structure which it established; but syntactically 'so vast a Frame' appears to refer back to 'Name', seeing the name itself, the reputation, as a construction, and so focusing not on the physical but on the conceptual structure of 'Rome'.

The structure of Troy, Troy as a fabric, often engages Dryden's imagination in Book II of the *Aeneis*. At the beginning of Aeneas' speech to Dido he says that the story will concern 'An Empire from its old Foundations rent',[69] which has no equivalent in Virgil. In Dryden's translation the Greeks construct 'a Fabrick ... | Which like a Steed of monstrous height appear'd', whereas Virgil says *Instar montis equum ... | Aedificant*: 'they build a horse as huge as a mountain'.[70] Where Virgil sees a horse which seems like a mountain, Dryden sees a fabric which seems like a horse. It is a 'Monster Fabrique',[71] a counter-structure which will bring about the destruction of Troy's own fabric. It is a 'hollow Fabrick' (where Virgil just has *ligno*, 'wood'[72]); and finally it is a 'fatal Fabrick' as it 'mounts the Walls'.[73]

In these instances the force of destruction is itself disconcertingly imagined as a solid structure, but elsewhere Dryden's imagination dwells upon the destructive movement of forces in the human world and in the natural. (The common people in the *Aeneis* often behave as if they were in a Hobbesian state of nature.) In many passages Dryden responds to opportunities to accentuate the liveliness of the natural world, often making forces of nature act with a quasi-human agency, and so calling our attention to the strange and difficult meetings of the human and the non-human, the irrational movements of humans, and the strangely animated world of nature; he shows us the precariousness

[69] *Aeneis*, ii. 5.   [70] *Aeneis*, ii. 19–20; *Aeneid*, ii. 15–16.
[71] *Aeneis*, ii. 45. This is Dryden's revision, as printed in the second edition (1698); in the first edition he calls it a 'fatal Engine'.   [72] *Aeneis*, ii. 58; *Aeneid*, ii. 45.
[73] *Aeneis*, ii. 311.

of human control over self, society, and nature. At the opening of Book I it is Juno who embodies the destructive force which is opposed to Troy. When Dryden tells us that 'The restless Regions of the Storms she sought'[74] there is an echo of *Absalom and Achitophel*, where Shaftesbury 'sought the Storms':[75] both goddess and politician actively seek to destroy the fabric of the state by embracing the forces of destruction. The chaos which would result from such a course of action is underlined by Dryden's emphasis on what the winds would do if they were not restrained by Aeolus:

> their unresisted Sway
> Wou'd sweep the World before them, in their Way:
> Earth, Air, and Seas through empty Space wou'd rowl,
> And Heav'n would fly before the driving Soul.[76]

> Ni faciat, maria ac terras coelumque profundum
> Quippe ferant rapidi secum, verrantque per auras.[77]

Not only is Dryden's passage longer and more vivid than Virgil's, it imagines the winds exercising a regal power ('Sway') of their own, which has to be resisted by Aeolus, here explicitly made their king, an 'undaunted Monarch'.[78]

Dryden's strong imaginative engagement with the forces of chaos is also evident when Aeneas, looking out over the city from his vantage point, first understands what it is that has happened to Troy while he has been sleeping:

> Thus when a flood of Fire by Wind is born,
> Crackling it rowls, and mows the standing Corn:
> Or Deluges, descending on the Plains,
> Sweep o're the yellow Year, destroy the pains
> Of lab'ring Oxen, and the Peasant's gains:
> Unroot the Forrest Oaks, and bear away
> Flocks, Folds, and Trees, an undistinguish'd Prey.
> The Shepherd climbs the Cliff, and sees from far,
> The wastful Ravage of the wat'ry War.[79]

---

[74] *Aeneis*, i. 77.   [75] *Absalom and Achitophel*, l. 161.

[76] *Aeneis*, i. 86–9.

[77] *Aeneid*, i. 62–3: 'If he did not, indeed, the rapid [winds] would carry off with them the seas and the lands and the uttermost sky, and drag them through the air.'

[78] *Aeneis*, ii. 84; no equivalent in Virgil.   [79] *Aeneis*, ii. 406–14.

'In segetem veluti cum flamma furentibus Austris
'Incidit; aut rapidus montano flumine torrens
'Sternit agros, sternit sata laeta boumque labores,
'Praecipitesque trahit sylvas: stupet inscius alto
'Accipiens sonitum saxi de vertice pastor.[80]

Dryden starts with 'a flood of Fire', a strong metaphor which boldly anticipates the second part of Virgil's simile, the oxymoron emphasizing the exceptional horror of the occurrence. He adds the idea that the fire crackles as it rolls, so linking sound and sight. As the scansion shows, Virgil's *incidit* comes from *incidere* (*OLD*[1]) meaning 'to fall upon' (Ruaeus' gloss here is *cecidit*), whereas Dryden translates it as if it came from *incīdere* (*OLD*[2]) meaning 'to cut through': hence his word 'mows'. This imaginative mistranslation makes the fire mow the standing corn in a striking fusion of human and non-human actions. Virgil's *sata laeta* ('thriving crops') become 'the yellow Year', an unusual extension of 'year' to mean 'the work or produce of the year'[81] which reifies time and so accentuates its waste. Where Virgil says that the water sweeps away the *sylvas* ('woods'), Dryden specifies 'Forrest Oaks' (weighty and venerable) and then 'Flocks, Folds, and Trees, an undistinguish'd Prey'.[82] The flood effaces distinctions, those geographical and conceptual boundaries which make the world a human, habitable space.

Dryden's handling of another simile, in which the raging sea calmed by Neptune is compared to a turbulent crowd soothed by the appearance of a grave statesman, illustrates both his fascination with the power of nature and his careful approach to passages which have political implications:

---

[80] *Aeneid*, ii. 304–8: 'As when fire falls into a field of corn when the south winds are raging, or a whirling torrent streaming from the mountain covers the fields and flattens the thriving crops and the work of the oxen, and carries away the woods headlong: the shepherd stands bewildered and uncomprehending high on the top of the rock as the sound reaches him.'

[81] *OED* 4b, citing only Wyclif's translation of Joel 2: 25 from 1382, but cp. the AV translation: 'I will restore to you the years that the locust hath eaten'. There is also a parallel usage in Latin, since *annus* can mean 'the produce of the year' (*OLD* 8).

[82] There may be an echo here of Dryden's translation of Horace's *Carmina*, III. xxix: 'Sheep and their Folds together drown' (l. 61), rendering *Stirpeisque raptas, & pecus, & domos* (l. 37). Lambinus' edition of Horace (p. 166 *bis*, *recte* 168) cites this passage in *Aeneid* II in the notes to Horace's description of the torrent.

As when in Tumults rise th' ignoble Crowd,
Mad are their Motions, and their Tongues are loud;
And Stones and Brands in ratling Vollies fly,
And all the Rustick Arms that Fury can supply:
If then some grave and Pious Man appear,
They hush their Noise, and lend a list'ning Ear;
He sooths with sober Words their angry Mood,
And quenches their innate Desire of Blood:
So when the Father of the Flood appears,
And o're the Seas his Sov'raign Trident rears,
Their Fury falls: He skims the liquid Plains,
High on his Chariot, and with loosen'd Reins,
Majestick moves along, and awful Peace maintains.[83]

Ac veluti magno in populo cum saepe coorta est
Seditio, saevitque animis ignobile vulgus;
Jamque faces et saxa volant; furor arma ministrat:
Tum, pietate gravem ac meritis si forte virum quem
Conspexere, silent, arrectisque auribus astant:
Ille regit dictis animos, et pectora mulcet.
Sic cunctus pelagi cecidit fragor: aequora postquam
Prospiciens genitor, coeloque invectus aperto,
Flectit equos, curruque volans dat lora secundo.[84]

Some aspects of Dryden's translation exhibit a degree of political caution. He avoids rendering *magno in populo* (is Virgil's *populus* a nation (*OLD* 1) or a crowd (*OLD* 4)?), and by translating *coorta est seditio* as 'in Tumults rise' he eschews such loaded contemporary words as 'plot' or 'rebellion'. The addition of the adjective 'Rustick' places the disturbance socially as the work of an unsophisticated group. The phrase 'ignoble Crowd' may be a carefully precise translation of *ignobile vulgus*, but even so it permits a recollection of the political influence of the London crowd during the street politics of the 1680s.[85] While Virgil says that the man whose

---

[83] *Aeneis*, i. 213–25.

[84] *Aeneid*, i. 148–56: 'As in a great crowd when, as often happens, a riot breaks out, and the ignoble mass is furious in its mind, and already firebrands and stones are flying, and madness provides arms: then, if by chance they have caught sight of a man of authoritative virtue and public service, they fall silent, and stand with their ears pricked up: he rules their minds with his words, and softens their hearts. Thus all the noise of the sea subsided: then looking out over the waters, the father [Neptune] having appeared in the clear skies turns his horses, and as he flies slackens the reins of his compliant chariot.'

[85] See Tim Harris, *London Crowds in the Reign of Charles II* (Cambridge, 1987).

appearance quells the disturbance is *pietate gravem ac meritis*, literally 'weighty in piety and meritorious public service', Dryden calls him 'grave and Pious'. By his omission of any translation of *meritis*, Dryden may be silently suggesting to those who know the original that it has become difficult to find a modern English equivalent for this word. Dryden's most striking departure from the Latin is in his addition of line 220, 'And quenches their innate Desire of Blood', which has no precedent in Virgil and suggests a radical distrust of the people. The arrival of Neptune brings the authoritative presence of sovereignty: Dryden's words 'Sov'raign' and 'Majestick' have no precedent in the Latin, neither does the phrase 'awful peace maintains'. Dryden emphasizes that the awesome presence which brings and maintains peace is monarchical.

This is one of several points where Dryden takes the opportunity to emphasize the unreliability of the people and their uninformed involvement in politics. When in Book I Aeneas catches sight of a herd of deer, Dryden makes the stags into 'a Lordly Train', while 'the more ignoble Throng | Attend their stately Steps'; Virgil says only that the stags wander while the herd follows (*cervos . . . errantes, . . . armenta sequuntur*).[86] Aeneas shoots the leaders first, and then 'the Vulgar', which may seem to be a close translation of *vulgus*,[87] but has a different charge: whereas Virgil almost always uses *vulgus* without contempt, meaning simply 'the ordinary people',[88] and in English 'the vulgar' can be neutrally descriptive,[89] Dryden tends to use the word with a pejorative force.[90] During the Civil War 'The Vulgar gull'd into Rebellion, arm'd'; James Duke of York is 'Opprest with Vulgar Spight' during the Exclusion Crisis; statesmen's statues the 'Effects of Vulgar Fury feel'; Turnus is 'with Vulgar hate oppress'd'; while even in the commonwealth of bees 'The vulgar in divided Factions jar'.[91] The

---

[86] *Aeneis*, i. 260–2; *Aeneid*, i. 184–6.   [87] *Aeneis*, i. 266; *Aeneid*, i. 190.

[88] *P. Vergili Maronis Aeneidos Liber Secundus*, ed. R. G. Austin (Oxford, 1964), pp. 44, 291.

[89] *OED* 3; and cp. Milton, *Samson Agonistes*, l. 1659: 'The vulgar only scap'd who stood without'.

[90] Of Dryden's 34 uses of 'vulgar' in his non-dramatic verse (as a noun or an adjective) roughly two thirds are pejorative and one third neutral.

[91] *Astræa Redux*, l. 33; *Absalom and Achitophel*, l. 353; 'The Tenth Satyr of Juvenal', l. 90; *Aeneis*, xii. 5; 'The Fourth Book of the *Georgics*', l. 94.

vulgar are gullible, irrational, and easily roused to vindictive violence. They are also poor judges of literature at whose mercy poets like Dryden find themselves,[92] and they maul the text of scripture.[93]

In *Aeneis* VII Dryden shows the dangers which arise when an ignorant and unruly people intervene in political matters and come under the sway of a skilful, opportunistic orator. Having landed in Italy, the Trojans are being opposed by 'The Clowns, a boist'rous, rude, ungovern'd Crew' who rush to battle 'With furious haste', which is a vigorous elaboration of Virgil's *Indomiti agricolae* ('wild [*or* ungoverned] countrymen').[94] They come under the influence of a madness incited by Juno and directed by Turnus:

> The Clowns return'd, from Battel bear the slain,
> Implore the Gods, and to their King complain.
> The Corps of *Almon* and the rest are shown,
> Shrieks, Clamours, Murmurs fill the frighted Town.
> Ambitious *Turnus* in the Press appears,
> And, aggravating Crimes, augments their Fears:
> Proclaims his Private Injuries aloud,
> A Solemn Promise made, and disavow'd;
> A foreign Son is sought, and a mix'd Mungril Brood.
> Then they, whose Mothers, frantick with their Fear,
> In Woods and Wilds the Flags of *Bacchus* bear,
> And lead his Dances with dishevell'd hair,
> Increase the Clamour, and the War demand,
> (Such was *Amata*'s Interest in the Land)
> Against the Public Sanctions of the Peace,
> Against all Omens of their ill Success;
> With Fates averse, the Rout in Arms resort,
> To Force their Monarch, and insult the Court.
> But like a Rock unmov'd, a Rock that braves
> The rageing Tempest and the rising Waves,
> Prop'd on himself he stands: His solid sides
> Wash off the Sea-weeds, and the sounding Tides:
> So stood the Pious Prince unmov'd: and long
> Sustain'd the madness of the noisie Throng.[95]

---

[92] 'Prologue to *1 Conquest of Granada*', l. 43; 'Prologue to *Circe*', l. 34; 'Epilogue to *Oedipus*', l. 11.   [93] *Religio Laici*, l. 400.
[94] *Aeneis*, vii. 724–5; *Aeneid*, vii. 521.   [95] *Aeneis*, vii. 791–814.

Ruit omnis in urbem
Pastorum ex acie numerus, caesosque reportant
Almonem puerum, foedatique ora Galaesi;
Implorantque Deos, obtestanturque Latinum.
Turnus adest, medioque in crimine, caedis et ignis
Terrorem ingeminat; Teucrosque in regna vocari,
Stirpem admisceri Phrygiam, se limine pelli.
Tum, quorum attonitae Baccho nemora avia matres
Insultant thiasis (neque enim leve nomen Amatae)
Undique collecti coeunt, Martemque fatigant.
Ilicet infandum cuncti contra omina bellum,
Contra fata Deum, perverso numine poscunt;
Certatim regis circumstant tecta Latini.
Ille, velut pelagi rupes immota, resistit:
Ut pelagi rupes, magno veniente fragore,
Quae sese, multis circum latrantibus undis,
Mole tenet: scopuli nequicquam et spumea circum
Saxa fremunt, laterique illisa refunditur alga.[96]

Dryden's passage opens with a translation of *pastorum . . . numerus*
(literally 'group of countrymen') which establishes the people's lack
of sophistication: they are mere 'Clowns'.[97] His version of the scene
where Turnus stirs up the crowd emphasizes the interaction
between leader and led: the bodies 'are shown', made part of a spec-
tacle, while 'Shrieks, Clamours, Murmurs fill the frighted Town', a
line which is Dryden's addition. In Virgil Turnus appears *in medio*
('in the midst') while in Dryden he appears 'in the Press', the latter
word conveying the physical presence of the densely-packed

---

[96] *Aeneid*, vii. 573–90: 'The whole group of countrymen rushes from the battle into
the city, and carries back the slain, the young Almon and the head of mutilated Galaesus;
and they invoke the gods and call upon Latinus. Turnus is present, in the midst of the
outcry at bloodshed and the blaze of passion he increases their fear; saying that the Trojans
are invited into the kingdom, that they will be mixed with Phrygian stock, and driven from
their home. Then they (whose mothers crazed by Bacchus run through the pathless woods
in their dance) assembled from all quarters come together and importune Mars—for the
name of Amata was held in no light regard. At once they all demand terrible war, contrary
to the oracles, contrary to the will of the gods, in defiance of divine power. Eagerly they
surround the house of King Latinus. He, like an unmoved rock in the sea, resists: like a rock
in the sea when a great crash comes, which stays on its foundation, as many waves roar
around it: in vain the billows and the foamy rocks rage and the seaweed is flung back as it
is dashed against its side.'

[97] 'Clown' originally meant 'countryman, rustic, peasant' (*OED* 1), but soon acquired
the implications of boorishness and ignorance which Dryden associates with the word
(*OED* 1b).

crowd. He is explicitly 'ambitious' as he incites the crowd (a characteristic which Dryden had associated with those two earlier manipulators of public opinion, Shaftesbury and Monmouth[98]), and Virgil's *ingeminat* ('increases') is rendered by two verbs, 'aggravating' and 'augments'. He makes his own personal cause an issue,[99] in a couplet which is Dryden's invention:

> Proclaims his Private Injuries aloud,
> A Solemn Promise made, and disavow'd;

Dryden gives a sample of the scurrilous language used by this speaker, for 'mix'd Mungril Brood' is derogatory whereas *Stirpem admisceri Phrygiam* ('to be mixed with Phrygian stock') is neutral in its vocabulary: Virgil reports the substance, but Dryden also reports the tone, deftly making Turnus a xenophobic demagogue. Then 'the Rout in Arms resort, | To Force their Monarch, and insult the Court'. Here Dryden brings out the threat of violence which the people pose to their own ruler. The word 'Rout' can simply mean a group or troop of people (*OED* 1), but is generally used to mean a tumultuous crowd bent on riot, with the technical sense of an unlawful assembly (*OED* 5); also—stressing the social origins of such a group—it is the common herd or rabble (*OED* 7). Virgil has no noun here. They are a violent mob ('in Arms' is also Dryden's addition) and they try 'To Force their Monarch'. Dryden has also introduced the idea that they 'insult the Court': 'insult' is a much stronger word than it would be in modern English: not only 'treat with scornful abuse or offensive disrespect, affront, outrage' (*OED* 2) but also 'attack, assault' militarily (*OED* 3, 4). But this attack is resolutely withstood by Latinus, as Dryden makes clear by adding the final couplet in this passage, contrasting the 'Pious Prince' with the 'madness' of the people.[100]

The extra detail in Dryden's scene testifies to his understanding

---

[98] *Absalom and Achitophel*, ll. 198, 304, 309, 479, 927; *The Medall*, ll. 30, 315. Turnus is again associated in Dryden's mind with Shaftesbury when in battle 'he takes the wish'd Occasion' (*Aeneis*, ix. 82), an echo of 'The wish'd occasion of the Plot he takes' (*Absalom and Achitophel*, l. 208). Both men are devotees of Fortuna/Occasio.

[99] For Dryden's disapproval of those who pursue public action for private motives cp. *Absalom and Achitophel*, ll. 180–1.

[100] Another passage where this theme emerges strongly is Laocoön's encounter with the crowd: *Aeneis*, ii. 50–5, *Aeneid*, ii. 39–42.

of the actual dynamics of street politics, and the practicalities of
how a crowd can be manipulated by an opportunistic politician.
But the vigour and intensity of the language also show us that this
is part of a larger combat between order and chaos which is
played out in the *Aeneis* both in the natural and the human
worlds. Here piety stands firm against madness, in a moment
which is not only a physical confrontation but also a reciprocal
definition of these two terms, and the social roles in which they
are embodied.

DREAMS OF RETURN AND RESTORATION

For men who are exiles in such a world of incipient chaos, what
kinds of recovery and restoration can the *Aeneis* envisage? At
several points Dryden imports the promise of restoration when
there is no warrant for this in the Latin. As we have already
seen, the opening lines envisage a restoration of the Trojan
gods. Anchises foresees that the patronal gods of Troy 'can yet
restore the ruin'd Town',[101] and Creüsa tells Aeneas that
'Fortune shall the *Trojan* Line restore'.[102] In Book IV Dido asks
Aeneas if he would leave her 'Were *Troy* restor'd, and *Priam*'s
happy Reign',[103] whereas in Virgil her hypothesis is that ancient
Troy still stood, *Troja antiqua maneret*: both the idea of restoration and the happiness of Priam's reign are Dryden's additions,
extending the pathos here with their quiet reminder that such a
restoration of such a happiness is impossible. Dryden again
replaces 'remain' (*manere*) with 'restore' when Aeneas replies to
Dido's challenge:

> For if indulgent Heav'n would leave me free,
> And not submit my Life to Fate's Decree,
> My Choice would lead me to the *Trojan* Shore,
> Those Reliques to review, their Dust adore;
> And *Priam*'s ruin'd Palace to restore.[104]

---

[101] *Aeneis*, ii. 955; for *servate domum* ('save the home', *Aeneid*, ii. 702).

[102] *Aeneis*, ii. 1066; an elaboration of Virgil's *res laetae* (*Aeneid*, ii. 783: 'a happy
state'—'state' in the sense 'state of affairs', i.e. both domestic and political arrangements).
Dryden's phrasing may have been influenced by Ruaeus' gloss *fortuna prospera* ('propitious
fortune').   [103] *Aeneis*, iv. 451; *Aeneid*, iv. 312.

[104] *Aeneis*, iv. 491–5.

'Me si fata meis paterentur ducere vitam
'Auspiciis, et sponte mea componere curas;
'Urbem Trojanam primum dulcesque meorum
'Relliquias colerem, Priami tecta alta manerent,
'Et recidiva manu posuissem Pergama victis.[105]

Dryden introduces the idea of an 'indulgent Heav'n' leaving Aeneas free, but the impossibility of such a blessing is underlined by the sad, ironic rhyme of 'free' and 'Decree'. Virgil's emphatically exposed word *Urbem* ('city') becomes Dryden's equally emphatically exposed 'Shore': if Aeneas were to return to Troy and land on its shore there would be no city, only the shore—that 'bleak Shoar'[106] where lay the headless body of Priam. Virgil's *Relliquias* (literally, 'those things which remain [*or* are left over]') could be the ruins of the buildings or the ashes of the dead; poignantly, it is also the word which Virgil uses elsewhere for Aeneas' band, the remnant of the Trojan race: *relliquias Danaum*.[107] Dryden's 'Dust' similarly does double duty, while his 'Reliques' echoes Aeneas' description of himself and his companions when praising Dido for her hospitality ('To save the Reliques of abandon'd *Troy*'[108]). The word 'relic' can also mean the surviving trace of some earlier quality or event:[109] men and rubble are alike traces of the destroyed city. 'Reliques' carries a sense of the sacred which is supported by the translation of *colerem* ('I would tend [*or* dwell]') as 'adore'. Once again *manerent* ('would remain') is rendered 'restore', this time under pressure from *recidiva* which means 'rebuilt after destruction' but more literally 'falling back into position'. The very idea of some restoration of Troy is thus made complex in Dryden's version, displaced into a conditional mood which we know to be an impossibility.

---

[105] *Aeneid*, iv. 340–4: 'If the fates allowed me to conduct my life on my own authority, and arrange according to my own will all that grieves me, I would tend the city of Troy first, and the dear relics of my people, the lofty palace of Priam would stand, and I would in person have established for the conquered a rebuilt Pergamon.' Austin's notes on this passage are characteristically sensitive and perceptive, and have been drawn upon in my discussion.   [106] *Aeneis*, ii. 762.

[107] *Aeneid*, i. 30, 598, iii. 87.

[108] *Aeneis*, i. 841. Anchises describes Ascanius as 'this Relick of the *Trojan* Race' (*Aeneis*, ii. 953), translating *nepotem* (*Aeneid*, ii. 702). Only a little later, Dryden has Anchises carry 'the Relicks' (ii. 974), translating *sacra* (ii. 716).

[109] *OED* 4: its quotation from Robert Barclay (1672) illustrates this usage well: 'There were some Reliques of the Heavenly Image left in Adam.'

When Aeneas does finally land in Italy, he is greeted by the god
of the Tiber who describes this as a homecoming; but it is a homecoming of some complexity:

> Thus, manifest to Sight, the God appear'd;
> And with these pleasing Words his Sorrow chear'd.
> Undoubted Off-spring of Etherial Race,
> O long expected in this promis'd Place,
> Who, thro the Foes, hast born thy banish'd Gods,
> Restor'd them to their Hearths, and old Abodes;
> This is thy happy Home! The Clime where Fate
> Ordains thee to restore the *Trojan* State.[110]

> Tum sic affari, et curas his demere dictis:
> 'O sate gente Deum, Trojanam ex hostibus urbem
> 'Qui revehis nobis, aeternaque Pergama servas,
> 'Expectate solo Laurenti arvisque Latinis:
> 'Hic tibi certa domus; certi (ne absiste) penates:[111]

It is an important moment when the god is 'manifest to sight'
(Dryden's addition), since several previous encounters which
Aeneas has had with the divine have been elusive or ambiguous,
with the god or the god's meaning not fully revealed—the meeting with his mother on the Libyan shore, the oracle of Apollo on
Delos, the appearance of the tutelary gods in a dream are all examples of such unsatisfactory theophanies. Dryden (as he often does)
omits the proper names to give his translation a wider reach, to
situate it in a slightly different terrain from Virgil's: here the territory to which Aeneas is welcomed is not specifically Laurentum or
Latium but—with biblical overtones—'this promis'd Place'. In a
choice of vocabulary which challenges our imagination, Virgil says
that it is the *urbem*, the city itself, which Aeneas has brought back;
Dryden focuses instead on the gods which have been 'banish'd'
and are now 'Restor'd', in a direct echo of the poem's opening
passage.[112] They are brought back to their 'Hearths, and old
Abodes', phrasing which directs our attention to the dwelling of

---

[110] *Aeneis*, viii. 49–56.
[111] *Aeneid*, viii. 35–9: 'Then thus he spoke, and removed his cares with these words:
"O offspring of divine race, who bring back to us the city of Troy from the enemy, and
keep immortal Pergamon safe for ever, you are welcome [or 'anxiously awaited, longed
for'] on Laurentan soil and the fields of Latium: here is your true home, your true household gods: do not leave." '   [112] *Aeneis*, i. 7.

the gods, and their return to their old, originary places. And this is where Aeneas will 'restore the *Trojan* State'; again we note that word 'State', which here implies a renewal of the political fabric. Twice within three lines Dryden uses the word 'restore', but we should not suppose that this word sounds a political imperative to English readers from a Jacobite sympathizer: this, mythologically, is the true form of restoration and thus the true task of the pious man.

One of the principal passages which deals with the question of how the Trojans may find a home occurs in Book I, when Venus, dismayed at the plight of the Trojans, asks Jupiter why he has neglected his promise to look after them and bring them safely to a new homeland. Venus reminds Jupiter that Aeneas has not failed in his obligations to the gods, and Dryden underlines the point by giving Aeneas the adjective 'Pious'[113]. This is one of the moments when Dryden contemplates the predicament of a man who has been faithful to his duties to the gods and the state, and yet is seemingly cast adrift. It is a passage which Dryden could have slanted in a Jacobite direction, but which he actually handles in such a way as to touch on the particular without losing sight of the multiple applications of the text: polysemic implications are once again brought into play. One instance where Dryden declines what could have been an attractive invitation from the Latin text occurs at the end of Venus' speech, where her concluding question to Jupiter is: *Sic nos in sceptra reponis?* ('Is this the way you restore us to our kingdom?').[114] But Dryden ignores the opportunity to write of restoration or restitution, and simply has Venus ask: 'Are these our Sceptres?'.[115]

But this does not mean that Dryden is uninterested in the contemporary resonances of Aeneas' plight, and there are indeed several moments in Jupiter's reply when small but significant additions or a telling choice of vocabulary alert readers to parallels with modern conditions. Jupiter foretells the fate of the Trojan exiles and the new city of Rome under a succession of leaders, and Dryden draws our attention to the importance of hereditary

---

[113] *Aeneis*, i. 317; no equivalent in Virgil.
[114] *Aeneid*, i. 253. My translation follows Ruaeus' gloss here, *Sic restituis nos in regna?*, which brings out the implications quite clearly.   [115] *Aeneis*, i. 344.

succession. First he makes Ascanius explicitly a king, saying that he 'the crown shall wear',[116] and that after him 'The Throne with his Succession shall be fill'd', where Virgil has the impersonal passive *regnabitur* ('there shall be kingly rule').[117] Then Dryden writes that '*Romulus* his Grandsire's Throne shall gain', where Virgil has *Romulus excipiet gentem* ('Romulus shall take over the people').[118] The reference to Romulus' grandfather is Dryden's own invention, and invites us to register the possibility of James II's grandson regaining the throne, for encoded in this brief interpolation is an allusion to a story of usurpation and its *nemesis*. The legend[119] runs that Numitor, king of Alba Longa, was deposed by his younger brother Amulius. To prevent Numitor's heirs seeking to depose him, Amulius compelled Numitor's daughter to become a vestal virgin. Nevertheless she was made pregnant by Mars and gave birth to the twins Romulus and Remus. When they grew up they led a rebellion against Amulius, killed him, and restored their grandfather Numitor to his throne. As we can see from the gloss provided here by Ruaeus (*succedet* in curam *gentis*, 'he succeeds to the care of the people'), *excipere* can mean 'succeed', but Virgil does not specify an office to which Romulus can succeed; rather, he is taking over responsibility for the people. Just as Ruaeus had to supply *in curam*, Dryden supplies 'Throne'. His verb 'gain' is another possible meaning of *excipere*, which can mean 'capture' or 'take', and so includes the implication of seizing something by an active intervention. Dryden's choice among the possible meanings of *excipiet* shows him imagining Romulus actively gaining a throne rather than succeeding naturally to rule over the people.

Jupiter also promises Venus that the time will come when the descendants of the refugees from Troy will turn the tables on their Greek vanquishers:

> An Age is ripening in revolving Fate,
> When *Troy* shall overturn the *Grecian* State:
> And sweet Revenge her conqu'ring Sons shall call,
> To crush the People that conspir'd her Fall.[120]

---

[116] *Aeneis*, i. 366; Virgil has *imperio* (*Aeneid*, i. 270; 'in power, in the office of ruler').
[117] *Aeneis*, i. 369; *Aeneid*, i. 272.   [118] *Aeneis*, i. 375; *Aeneid*, i. 276.
[119] Livy, *Ab Urbe Condita*, I. iii. 10–vi. 2.   [120] *Aeneis*, i. 386–9.

'Sic placitum. Veniet lustris labentibus aetas,
'Cum domus Assaraci Phthiam clarasque Mycenas
'Servitio premet, ac victis dominabitur Argis.[121]

Dryden imagines Greece not as the collection of separate cities
named by Virgil, but as a single state, a political entity which can
be overturned; and his second couplet (which draws out the implication of Virgil's text but is substantially an addition) makes a
general observation which is phrased so as to permit (but not
require) contemporary application. Virgil and Dryden imagine the
process of time differently. For Dryden the right time is 'ripening'
in a natural process; Fate comes round again as history moves in
cyclical fashion, whereas for Virgil time is linear (*labentibus* means
'sliding' or 'gliding') and events are subject to the will of Jupiter:
sic placitum he says with uncompromising brevity, 'this is my will'.
To Virgil the kind of time which is elapsing is special, for the
lustrum was the sacrifice made by the censors on behalf of the
whole people after the completion of the quinquennial census. To
measure time by *lustra* is thus to recognize man's dependence on
the gods for the successful continuation of civilized life.

Later in his speech Jupiter tells Venus that Rome will one day
enjoy a golden age under a Caesar who comes from Trojan stock.
Virgil's passage is at once hortatory, congratulatory, and prophetic,
a translation of his own times into mythological terms, and it is
given some significant emphases by Dryden. The great ruler is
Augustus,

> Whom, fraught with *Eastern* Spoils,
> Our Heav'n, the just Reward of Human Toyls,
> Securely shall repay with Rites Divine;
> And Incense shall ascend before his sacred Shrine.
> Then dire Debate, and impious War shall cease,
> And the stern Age be soften'd into Peace:
> Then banish'd Faith shall once again return,
> And Vestal Fires in hallow'd Temples burn;
> And *Remus* with *Quirinus* shall sustain
> The righteous Laws, and Fraud and Force restrain.

---

[121] *Aeneid*, i. 283–5: 'This is my will. The time will come, as the years pass, when the
house of Assaracus [great-grandfather of Aeneas] will crush Phthia and famous Mycenae in
slavery, and will lord it over conquered Argos.'

Janus himself before his Fane shall wait,
And keep the dreadful issues of his Gate,
With Bolts and Iron Bars: within remains
Imprison'd Fury, bound in brazen Chains:
High on a Trophie rais'd, of useless Arms,
He sits, and threats the World with vain Alarms.[122]

'Hunc tu olim coelo, spoliis Orientis onustum,
'Accipies secura: vocabitur hic quoque votis.
'Aspera tum positis mitescent saecula bellis.
'Cana Fides, et Vesta, Remo cum fratre Quirinus
'Jura dabunt: dirae ferro et compagibus arctis
'Claudentur belli portae: Furor impius intus
'Saeva sedens super arma, et centum vinctus ahenis
'Post tergum nodis, fremet horridus ore cruento.'[123]

This is a major passage for Virgil, presenting his vision of the
much-desired *Pax Augusta*.[124] The new order will be based upon
honoured ancient values. The first of these is *Fides*. One of the
striking features of Dryden's translation is his interpolation of the
idea that Faith (which for Virgil is *Cana*, 'grey', therefore ancient)
has been banished and will 'once again return'. *Fides* is one of
Rome's fundamental concepts, the guarantor of plain dealing and
in particular the guarantor of oaths. For Virgil, *Fides* will take part
in the making of laws: there may be an implication that she has
been absent from public life, but that is not made explicit. For
Dryden, by contrast, Faith has been banished. Dryden would have
considered many of his contemporaries to have broken faith by
abjuring their oaths of allegiance to James II, and to have taken
invalid oaths of allegiance to William III. But in Dryden's text
'Faith' must also imply Christian faith, and if banished, then the
Roman Catholic faith. And so Dryden is keeping faith with his
own household gods by making 'Faith' polysemic. For Virgil it

---

[122] *Aeneis*, i. 392–407.
[123] *Aeneid*, i. 289–96: 'Once you are secure you will accept him in heaven, weighed
down with eastern spoils; he too will be invoked in your prayers. Then harsh times shall
become mild as wars are abandoned. Grey Faith, and Vesta, and Quirinus [i.e. Romulus]
with his brother Remus shall give laws: the gates of war, in their close-wrought frame of
iron, shall be shut: inside impious Fury seated on savage arms, and bound with a hundred
brazen knots behind his back, shall roar hideously from his bloody mouth.'
[124] My discussion is indebted to the commentary in *P. Vergili Maronis Aeneidos Liber
Primus*, ed. R. G. Austin (Oxford, 1971).

suffices to name Vesta, while Dryden expands the reference to give us an image of vestal fires burning once again in hallowed temples: he locates this vision more precisely than Virgil needs to, making his verse delineate the sacred space which is once more inhabited by the sacred flame. This permits but does not require a hope for the restoration of Roman Catholic worship. So too, in the earlier reference to the cult of Augustus, 'incense' and 'shrine' might have connotations of Roman Catholic ritual for English readers, but if so they displace into this mythologized space the possibility of achieving an English equivalent to this Augustan state where the ruler is rewarded with divine honours by heaven itself. In Virgil's vision, Fides, Vesta, and the brothers Romulus and Remus all give laws, whereas for Dryden it is the brothers who 'sustain | The righteous Laws': sustain rather than innovate. The adjective 'righteous' is Dryden's addition, pointing to an alignment of human and divine law, in contrast to the kind of disjunction which he would have felt existed between them in the 1690s. Whereas Virgil is concerned that war should be ended, Dryden makes no explicit mention of war, and instead has Romulus and Remus restrain 'Fraud and Force', an addition which briefly creates two allegorical characters who are being held in check, and implies a verdict on the forces which had shaped the recent history of England. The movement towards personification continues in Dryden's striking introduction of Janus as gaoler outside his own temple. Responding to the archaic touches in Virgil's passage, Dryden has imbued his treatment of the subject with a touch of Spenserian allegory, a piece of Miltonic phrasing,[125] and a heightened poetic diction ('dire debate'; 'Fane'). The tense of Dryden's passage is a prophetic declarative future, with the word 'shall' occurring twenty-five times in the forty-four lines of Jupiter's speech, until the final sentence when the image of the imprisoned and vainly threatening Fury passes into the present tense, where Virgil is still using the future (*frement*). Dryden's vision of a harmony of human values and structures with divine law, with the ruler sanctioned by heaven, expands on Virgil's original to offer a prospect which is more *adunaton* than prophecy.

---

[125] 'High on a Trophie rais'd' echoes Milton's description of Satan 'High on a Throne of Royal State' (*Paradise Lost*, ii. 1); Dryden had previously described Flecknoe as 'High on a Throne of his own Labours rear'd' (*Mac Flecknoe*, l. 107) in a context with Virgilian allusions. All three examples are of threatening but ultimately powerless majesty.

This is one vision of the homeland. Another occurs in Book VIII when Aeneas visits the former Trojan Evander and hears about the origins of the settlement which he has founded in Latium. An uncanny sense of recognition will have affected Virgil's first readers at this point, since the description includes references forward to Roman sites from Virgil's own day. Dryden too writes the present into this account of the *archē* of Rome, chiefly through his handling of the religion rather than the geography. Evander explains that the religious ceremonies which Aeneas has just witnessed are not the result of superstition but an act of gratitude and reverence to Hercules, who had saved them from the monster Cacus:

> These Rites, these Altars, and this Feast, O King,
> From no vain Fears, or Superstition spring:
> Or blind Devotion, or from blinder Chance;
> Or heady Zeal, or brutal Ignorance:[126]

>   'Non haec solemnia nobis,
> 'Has ex more dapes, hanc tanti numinis aram,
> 'Vana superstitio veterumve ignara Deorum
> 'Imposuit:[127]

Dryden's translation, in seeking to define true religion against its multiple antitheses, brings into play some of the irreligious forces of his own day: fundamentalist Protestant 'Zeal', an atheistic adherence to the workings of blind chance, the 'brutal Ignorance' of the mob. Whereas 'Altars' is almost a straight translation of *aram*, it carries Catholic connotations, particularly when put into the plural: Catholic churches had several altars, whereas Protestant churches had what the 1662 Book of Common Prayer carefully calls 'the Lord's Table'. In a country suspicious of ceremonial rites at altars, Dryden is implying that true religion is often falsely regarded as superstition and blind devotion by those who look too hastily at the outward forms.

Then walking alongside Evander, Aeneas asks about the 'Acts and Monuments of Ancient Kings',[128] a phrase which makes a sly

---

[126] *Aeneis*, viii. 246–9.

[127] *Aeneid*, viii. 185–8: 'It is not empty superstition or ignorance of the old gods that has imposed upon us these rites, these customary feasts, and this altar to such divine power.'

[128] *Aeneis*, viii. 415, translating *virum monimenta priorum* (*Aeneid*, viii. 312: 'the monuments of earlier men').

reference to the title of John Foxe's catalogue of Catholic persecutions, *Actes and Monuments*, first published in 1563, but reprinted
as recently as 1684. There are, Dryden implies, other acts and
monuments than those established in Protestant historiography,
other ways of memorializing the past. Evander tells of the origins
of the settlement, for this was where Saturn came,

> who fled the Pow'r of *Jove*,
> Robb'd of his Realms, and banish'd from above.
> The Men, dispers'd on Hills, to Towns he brought;
> And Laws ordain'd, and Civil Customs taught:
> And *Latium* call'd the Land where safe he lay,
> From his Unduteous Son, and his Usurping Sway.
> With his mild Empire, Peace and Plenty came:
> And hence the Golden Times deriv'd their name.[129]

> 'Arma Jovis fugiens, et regnis exul ademptis.
> 'Is genus indocile ac dispersum montibus altis
> 'Composuit, legesque dedit; Latiumque vocari
> 'Maluit, his quoniam latuisset tutus in oris.
> 'Aurea, quae perhibent, illo sub rege fuerunt
> 'Saecula; sic placida populos in pace regebat.[130]

Dryden makes a tendentious addition to Virgil in the line 'From his
Unduteous Son, and his Usurping Sway'. The description of
Saturn's rule as 'mild' uses an adjective which Dryden had employed
on several occasions for the rule of the Stuart kings.[131] The rule of
Saturn is characterized (in a variation on Virgil's alliterative *placida
populos in pace*) by 'Peace and Plenty'.[132] After this golden age,
'Kings . . . | With Arbitrary Sway the Land oppress'd'.[133]

---

[129]　*Aeneis*, viii. 425–32.
[130]　*Aeneid*, viii. 320–5: ' "fleeing the weapons of Jupiter, an exile deprived of his king-
doms. He brought together this untaught race, dispersed over the high mountains, and gave
them laws; and chose that it should be called Latium, since he had been safely hidden in
that place. Golden were called the centuries which passed under that king; so he ruled the
peoples in quiet peace." ' There is a speculative etymology here deriving *Latium* from *latuis-
set*, 'he had been hidden'. Unable to replicate this etymological punning, Dryden uses alliteration instead: '*Latium* . . . Land . . . lay'.
[131]　*To My Lord Chancellor*, l. 57 (of Charles I); *Absalom and Achitophel*, l. 325 (of Charles
II); *Britannia Rediviva*, l. 221 (of the son of James II); and also of Christ in *The Hind and the
Panther*, i. 286.
[132]　Pope uses the phrase to make a political point in his vision of a golden age: 'Peace
and Plenty tell, a STUART reigns' (*Windsor-Forest*, l. 42).
[133]　*Aeneis*, viii. 438; no equivalent in Virgil, *Aeneid*, viii. 330.

A later account of the Golden Age also carries a clear political charge. The Latians send an envoy to request assistance from their neighbour Diomede, who as one of the Greek warriors at the siege of Troy might have been expected to be sympathetic to their desire to repel Aeneas. But Diomede has learnt the realities of war, and his reply reminds his visitors of their privileged heritage which they are in danger of destroying:

> *Ausonian* Race, of old
> Renown'd for Peace, and for an Age of Gold,
> What Madness has your alter'd Minds possess'd,
> To change for War hereditary Rest?
> Sollicite Arms unknown, and tempt the Sword,
> (A needless Ill your Ancestors abhorr'd?)

Then, emphasizing that the Greeks' victory over Troy was bought at a terrible cost, he proceeds to give a poignant account of his own sufferings as an exile. The speech is infused with all the rhythmic variety of Dryden's mature style to accentuate the emotion:

> Not one but suffer'd, and too dearly bought
> The Prize of Honour which in Arms he sought.
> Some doom'd to Death, and some in Exile driv'n,
> Out-casts, abandon'd by the Care of Heav'n:
> So worn, so wretched, so despis'd a Crew,
> As ev'n old *Priam* might with Pity view.
>
> .   .   .   .   .   .
>
> The Gods have envy'd me the sweets of Life,
> My much lov'd Country, and my more lov'd Wife:
> Banish'd from both, I mourn; while in the Sky
> Transform'd to Birds, my lost Companions fly:
> Hov'ring about the Coasts they make their Moan;
> And cuff the Cliffs with Pinions not their own.
>
> .   .   .   .   .   .
>
> Such Arms, this Hand shall never more employ;
> No Hate remains with me to ruin'd *Troy*.
> I war not with its Dust; nor am I glad
> To think of past Events, or good or bad.[134]

Diomede's speech is a rebuke to the Latians, first for not properly valuing their own condition, their age of gold. In Dryden's version

---

[134] *Aeneis*, xi. 386–432; cp. *Aeneid*, xi. 251–80.

they are more than *fortunatae*, they are 'Renown'd for peace'. But where Virgil has Diomede wonder what fortune could have solicited them to contemplate war (*quae vos fortuna quietos* | *Sollicitat*), Dryden phrases this more strongly: 'What Madness has your alter'd Minds possess'd, | To change for War hereditary rest?'.[135] The contemporary application is obvious. But more is at issue here than the opportunity for a passing allusion to England's rejection of strict hereditary succession, for this begins an extended passage on the evils of war, one which could be read as aimed at the warrior king William III, but which reaches far beyond that to remind readers of the actual human pain of war, and the real price of glory. Diomede says that in his experience the prize of honour was 'too dearly bought', and this passage is much more strongly worded than the equivalent in Virgil:

> 'infanda per orbem
> 'Supplicia, et scelerum poenas expendimus omnes,
> 'Vel Priamo miseranda manus.[136]

Dryden's lines, twice as many as Virgil's, with their emphasis on exile and abandonment, focus on the pain of the displaced soldiers instead of emphasizing as Virgil does the retribution (*supplicia . . . poenas*) which was exacted from the Greeks. Diomede has lost his country and his wife, while his soldiers have even lost their human identity. Typically, Dryden's imagination is drawn to the image of Diomede's companions turned into birds, and adds little details which enhance the poignancy of this displacement of human into animal, reading Virgil via Ovid: the birds 'cuff the Cliffs', noticing that the wings are 'not their own'. Where Virgil says that Diomede no longer has any quarrel with the Trojans (*nec mihi cum Teucris ullum . . . bellum*), Dryden says that 'No Hate remains', and, in a phrase which encapsulates the mutual tragedy, 'I war not with its Dust'. In Dryden's hands this rebuke to the thoughtless belligerence of the Latians has taken on an additional force. As Diomede reminds us, there is some pain for which there is no remedy, some changes which cannot be reversed, some exiles who cannot be restored.

---

[135] This echoes Laocoön's question to the crowd in *Aeneis*, ii. 55, and the image of Latinus withstanding the madness of the crowd in *Aeneis*, vii. 814.

[136] *Aeneid*, xi. 257–9: 'we have undergone terrible punishments through the world, and paid the price of our crimes, which even Priam himself might pity.'

PIETAS AGAINST FORTUNA

Piety, *pietas*, is one of the ideas which is recurrently associated with Aeneas.[137] He exemplifies this quintessentially Roman virtue which encompasses respect for one's obligations towards the gods, the state, and the family. It demands respect, devotion, responsibility, and compassion, and is therefore a mode of self-definition through attention to the needs and rights of others. It is also reciprocal, since *pietas* lays a moral obligation upon those to whom it is shown, expecting that they should respond in kind: thus *pietas* can be used of the gods' attitude towards human beings (*OLD* 2b). But while Aeneas may be *pius*, to act in accordance with *pietas* is often hard for him: this is a virtue whose demands are sometimes unclear or contradictory, and frequently difficult to implement. His homeland is destroyed and the promise of its restoration is enigmatic and elusive. Aeneas shows true *pietas* by carrying his father on his shoulders from certain death in Troy, while leading by the hand his little son whom the gods have marked out as the future hope of the race; and yet in this very moment he loses his wife. After finding love again in Carthage with Dido, he has to violate the obligations of a guest and of a husband (as she, at least, considers him to be) and slip away in secret because that is what his duty to the gods and his prospective homeland requires. Faithful to his household gods, Aeneas is nevertheless opposed by Juno, buffeted by Aeolus, and has to be warned twice by Mercury to leave Carthage and fulfil his destiny. He cannot follow his own desires when they conflict with *pietas* (as he admits to Dido, *Italiam non sponte sequor*[138]), since for a Roman to be *pius* is to have at once a psychological and a social identity. Because Virgil makes it difficult for Aeneas to cherish his homeland, his gods, and his family, *pietas* has to be defined through a process of trial and discovery, in struggle, against the odds. A way of placing the individual harmoniously in the universe and society, *pietas* actually has to be worked out in spite of the world which Aeneas faces. He has to find a way of being faithful to those values which would make the world

---

[137] See *OLD* for its range of meanings; also Austin *ad Aeneid*, i. 10; James D. Garrison, '*Pietas*' *from Vergil to Dryden* (University Park, Pa., 1992); Dryden's 'Dedication of the *Aeneis*', *Poems*, pp. 1018–21.

[138] *Aeneid*, iv. 361: 'It is not of my own free will that I seek Italy.'

cohere, in spite of all the signs that it no longer does cohere. Dryden in the 1690s would have understood that predicament.

Pietas is the summary term which acts to guarantee the coherence of that discourse which binds the public and the domestic, religion and nation, and yet for Dryden as he composed his translation of Virgil such a discourse was impossible. *Pietas* is reciprocal, and in earlier poems such as *Annus Mirabilis* he had used an English version of this vocabulary to define the mutual care of king and people. Now, however, it was hard for him to deploy the idea of *pietas* in respect of the current king and royal family. To keep faith would demand repeated efforts to think against the times, to set religion against the turns of fortune, to preserve public values through the private creation of an imaginative terrain whose horizons were wider than contemporary England. Now *pietas* needs redefinition, a new semiotic field and thus a freshly defined sphere of moral duty and imagined nationhood. To trace some of Dryden's uses of this concept is to see him rethinking this field of meaning.

The word *pius* reverberates through the *Aeneid*, as 'pious' does through Dryden's translation. But the occurrences do not always coincide, and Dryden particularly tends to introduce the idea of 'piety' at moments when someone is challenged to respond to adversity. (This had already characterized Dryden's usage of 'pious' in *Annus Mirabilis*.) To be pious does not mean that life will turn out easily and proffer one the rewards which one expects. Aeneas is described by Venus as 'my Pious Son'[139] when she is asking Jupiter why he has allowed Aeneas and his companions to be so harassed. In Book I Dryden adds the phrase 'Pious Prince' at the moment when Aeneas seems to be in the direst trouble, facing death in the storm which Aeolus has whipped up at Juno's behest:

> Thus while the Pious Prince his Fate bewails,
> Fierce *Boreas* drove against his flying Sails,
> And rent the Sheets:[140]

Dryden's first line here startles us with the connection which it makes between 'Pious Prince' and 'Fate bewails', challenging us to

---

[139] *Aeneis*, i. 317; there is no equivalent to 'pious' in Virgil, *Aeneid*, i. 231.
[140] *Aeneis*, i. 146–8; for Dryden's first line here Virgil has *talia jactanti* ('hurling such words', *Aeneid*, i. 102).

consider how it could be pious for Aeneas to rage against his fate. In fact Aeneas has been lamenting that he had not died in the siege of Troy:

> And thrice, and four times happy those, he cry'd,
> That under *Ilian* Walls before their Parents dy'd.
> *Tydides*, bravest of the *Grecian* Train,
> Why cou'd not I by that strong Arm be slain,
> And lye by noble *Hector* on the Plain,
> Or great *Sarpedon*, in those bloody Fields,
> Where *Simois* rouls the Bodies, and the Shields
> Of Heroes, whose dismember'd Hands yet bear
> The Dart aloft, and clench the pointed Spear?[141]

At this stage in his experience, *pietas* is backward-looking, leading Aeneas to regret that he had not been part of this tragic Trojan unity. To die before the walls of Troy, under the gaze of his parents and by the side of his comrades, would have fulfilled the demands of *pietas*. The emotion of the speech is conveyed by the enjambement which keeps spilling the sense over the line endings, even ignoring the expected pause at the end of the triplet, and in this way Dryden is fashioning an equivalent to Virgil's agitated word-order and rhythmic imbalances.[142] Dryden adds the thought of lying by the side of Hector, thus making Aeneas' longing for the physical proximity of sacrificial comrade-ship all the more poignant. Virgil writes that the river sweeps away shields, helmets, and bodies, but he has nothing which might suggest Dryden's gruesome image of the severed hands which are still clutching their spears. This scene which Aeneas imagines as the true scene of *pietas*—that unifying virtue—is characterized by dismemberment. For the moment, *pietas* can only be defined by means of the irrecoverable past, referred back to a site of terrible loss and fragmentation. Soon, however, Aeneas will learn to look forward and to find other ways of being *pius*. *Pietas* has to become polysemic.

The word 'pious' is used again when Aeneas tries to dispel the grief of his men after they have survived this storm and reached landfall. After shooting the deer to provide food, and opening the

---

[141] *Aeneis*, i. 137–45; rendering *Aeneid*, i. 94–101.
[142] See Austin *ad loc.*

wine, and serving out the venison in equal portions, 'the pious Chief, | With chearful Words, allay'd the common Grief'.[143] Here the actions of Aeneas begin to define *pietas* afresh. It is his care for the physical well-being of his companions and for their morale which makes him 'pious' here, and his speech of encouragement assumes that the gods will reciprocate and show *pietas* in their turn by fulfilling their promises:

> *Jove* will soon dispose
> To future Good, our past and present Woes.
>
> .   .   .   .
>
> Through various Hazards, and Events we move
> To *Latium*, and the Realms foredoom'd by *Jove*.
> Call'd to the Seat, (the Promise of the Skies,)
> Where *Trojan* Kingdoms once again may rise.[144]

This, as Virgil and Dryden make clear, is wishful thinking: Aeneas' heart does not go along with his words. But it is a necessary fiction, and this assertion of a belief in the value of *pietas* is his way of fulfilling his duty at this moment.

Aeneas is not the only character to display this virtue. Laocoön attracts the adjective when he runs 'with pious Haste' to aid his sons as they struggle with the sea-serpents.[145] He is, of course, showing *pietas* in trying to rescue his children, but it is noticeable that the word once again enters Dryden's text at a moment of desperate crisis; more specifically, at a moment when human beings are trying to fulfil their basic human duties in the face of inexplicably hostile supernatural forces. So too Aeneas, at another moment of great horror and fear, having just witnessed the murder of Priam, immediately thinks of his own father:

> Then, not before, I felt my crudled Blood
> Congeal with Fear; my Hair with horror stood:
> My Father's Image fill'd my pious Mind;
> Lest equal Years might equal Fortune find.[146]

---

[143] *Aeneis*, i. 275–6; there is no equivalent to 'pious' in Virgil, *Aeneid*, i. 197.

[144] *Aeneis*, i. 277–88.

[145] *Aeneis*, ii. 285; there is no equivalent to 'pious' in Virgil, *Aeneid*, ii. 216.

[146] *Aeneis*, ii. 764–7; there is no equivalent to 'pious' or 'Fortune' in Virgil, *Aeneid*, ii. 559–62.

Here *pietas* involves not only taking thought for his father, but also thinking against Fortune, that capricious power whose indifference to merit and morality makes her in some respects the antithesis of *pietas*.

In Book IV Aeneas is faced with the painful necessity of leaving Carthage and deserting Dido in order to fulfil his wider responsibilities. As Mercury leaves after imparting this message, Dryden marks the seriousness of this moment with the key word: 'The Pious Prince was seiz'd with sudden Fear.'[147] Here Dryden associates 'Pious' and 'Fear', because 'fear' in seventeenth-century usage includes not only fright but feelings of reverence and awe. After Mercury's second visitation Dryden again links piety and fear: 'The pious Prince arose with hasty fear.'[148] *Pietas* confronts a frightening universe with reverence, turning fear into fear. But the demands of *pietas* are complex and hard to live out, and so it is sadly unsurprising that Dido should use the word derisively of Aeneas:

> See now the promis'd Faith, the vaunted Name,
> The Pious Man, who, rushing through the Flame,
> Preserv'd his Gods; and to the *Phrygian* Shore
> The Burthen of his feeble Father bore![149]

But at the same time as using the near-equivalent English word 'pious', Dryden also rethinks *pietas* by exploring its semantic and moral field in other vocabularies. In his first description of Aeneas, Virgil's *pietate* is translated by two words, 'brave' and 'just'.[150] Later the same word is rendered by a whole phrase, as Ilioneus tells Dido:

> If our hard Fortune no Compassion draws,
> Nor hospitable Rights, nor human Laws,
> The Gods are just, and will revenge our Cause.
> *Æneas* was our Prince, a juster Lord,
> Or nobler Warriour, never drew a Sword:
> Observant of the Right, religious of his Word.[151]

---

[147] *Aeneis*, iv. 404.; there is no equivalent to 'pious' in Virgil, *Aeneid*, iv. 279.

[148] *Aeneis*, iv. 823; there is no equivalent to 'pious' in Virgil, *Aeneid*, iv. 571.

[149] *Aeneis*, iv. 857–60; there is no equivalent to 'pious' in Virgil, *Aeneid*, iv. 597, except *fides* ('faithful').   [150] *Aeneis*, i. 14.

[151] *Aeneis*, i. 764–9.

'Si genus humanum et mortalia temnitis arma;
'At sperate Deos memores fandi atque nefandi.
'Rex erat Æneas nobis, quo justior alter
'Nec pietate fuit, nec bello major et armis.[152]

Once again Dryden draws Fortune into a passage which defines *pietas*, making her a sign of the Trojans' unhappy displacement from a world in which justice prevails. Virgil's *justior . . . pietate* describes Aeneas as a man who is just in carrying out his duty; Dryden expands this into a line which marks him out as one who observed the right and religiously kept his word. Could one say the same of contemporary princes?[153]

In so far as *pietas* is an attempt to make the world cohere, it is engaged against Fortune, or works to mitigate the effects of her unpredictable, unprincipled actions. Dryden increases the number of references to Fortune from twenty-four in the Latin to ninety-two in his translation. Aeneas' plight is repeatedly attributed to Fortune. Although it would be wrong to suggest that Fortune is consistently imagined as a hostile power (Creüsa prophesies that Fortune will eventually restore Troy[154]) Dryden generally uses the term in ways which warn us against trusting ourselves to her. So in Book IV he signals the danger which attends the meeting of Dido and Aeneas in the cave by introducing the possibility that Fortune may be responsible:

> The Queen and Prince, as Love or Fortune guides,
> One common Cavern in her Bosom hides.[155]

For Aeneas to follow Love would be to follow Fortune rather than the gods, and so to frustrate his Roman destiny.

If sexual desire is Fortune's territory, as Dryden also implies in his translation from *De Rerum Natura* Book IV, so too is war. In the mêlée which follows the eruption of the Greek soldiers from inside their wooden horse, Aeneas gathers his comrades and tries

---

[152] *Aeneid*, i. 542–5: 'If you have no respect for the human race and the arms of mortals, yet you expect that the gods will remember good and evil acts. Aeneas was our king, than whom no one was more just in doing his duty, none greater in warfare.'

[153] James II had a reputation for keeping his word: see *Threnodia Augustalis*, ll. 484–7.

[154] *Aeneis*, ii. 1066; no equivalent in *Aeneid*, ii. 783.

[155] *Aeneis*, iv. 239–40; there is no equivalent to 'as Love or Fortune guides' in *Aeneid*, iv. 165–6.

to stem the tide of war, 'If Fortune favour'd, and repel the Foes'.[156] But Fortune does not favour. Instead, 'Confus'd the Fortune is, confus'd the Fight'.[157] Subsequently, the Trojans learn the cost of trusting to Fortune. At first things had seemed to go well, for when they encountered the Greek leader Androgeos he had mistaken them for allies and so was easily surrounded and killed:

> Thus Fortune on our first Endeavour smil'd:
> *Choroebus* then, with youthful Hopes beguil'd,
> Swoln with Success, and of a daring Mind,
> This new Invention fatally design'd.
> My Friends, said he, since Fortune shows the way,
> 'Tis fit we shou'd th' auspicious Guide obey.[158]

>   'aspirat primo fortuna labori.
>   'Atque hic exultans successu animisque Choroebus:
> "O socii, qua prima, inquit, fortuna salutis
> "Monstrat iter, quaque ostendit se dextra, sequamur.[159]

Dryden's text appears to offer a close translation of Virgil's repeated *fortuna*, but another form of translation is taking place here as Dryden rethinks the implications of the concept, making the hot-headed young Choroebus, elated with their first victory, propose a course of action which will turn out to be fatal. He urges his Trojan comrades to change their armour for Greek armour, and in this disguise to surprise their enemies. Unfortunately, this ruse leads to them being attacked by their own people. Choroebus follows Fortune, but does so because he is 'beguil'd', 'Swoln with Success', and over-daring. His 'new Invention' is a fatal innovation, as innovations often are in Dryden's mind.[160] To the man who restlessly seeks after novelty, Nature replies, 'I can invent, and can supply no more'.[161] Verbal echoes here of Dryden's description of the improper ambition of

---

[156] *Aeneis*, ii. 426; there is no equivalent to 'If Fortune favour'd' in *Aeneid*, ii. 317.

[157] *Aeneis*, ii. 497; there is no equivalent in *Aeneid*, ii. 368–9.

[158] *Aeneis*, ii. 518–23.

[159] *Aeneid*, ii. 385–8: 'Fortune favours our first effort [*or* at first favours our effort]. And Choroebus, heady and exulting in this success said: "O comrades, where Fortune first shows the way to safety and points with her right hand, let us follow." '

[160] Cp. *Absalom and Achitophel*, l. 800: 'Innovation is the Blow of Fate'.

[161] 'Lucretius: Against the Fear of Death', l. 139.

Absalom and Achitophel mark this out as a foolish reliance upon Fortune.[162]

As the tide turns against the Trojans, Aeneas tries to persuade his father Anchises not to stay and face death. It is a supreme challenge to Aeneas' *pietas*, for how can he leave his father? In desperation he resolves to seek death himself in the now futile defence of his city:

> Urg'd by Despair, again I go to try
> The fate of Arms, resolv'd in Fight to die.
> What hope remains, but what my Death must give?
> Can I without so dear a Father live?
> You term it Prudence, what I Baseness call:
> Cou'd such a Word from such a Parent fall?
> If Fortune please, and so the Gods ordain,
> That nothing shou'd of ruin'd *Troy* remain:
> And you conspire with Fortune, to be slain;
> The way to Death is wide, th' Approaches near:
> For soon relentless *Pyrrhus* will appear,
> Reeking with *Priam*'s Blood:[163]

In this crisis Dryden's Aeneas says that the only hope which remains to him is that which his death brings, whereas Virgil's Aeneas reflects that no scheme (*consilium*) or luck (*fortuna*) had come his way. Having removed this reference to Fortune (as a possible aid, though one which had not materialized) Dryden interpolates two other references when Aeneas turns to Anchises and says that he seems to wish to collaborate with Fortune in the destruction of the city and of himself. Fortune in Dryden's text has been made unambiguously destructive. She will soon be manifested again in the arrival of Pyrrhus, the ultimate example of impiety, who butchered the son in the sight of the father, and the father at his own altar.

References to Fortune also guide our reading of one of the most painful episodes in the poem, the killing of Pallas by Turnus. After trampling on the young lad's body, Turnus snatches his golden belt and puts it on:

---

[162] With 'daring' here cp. *Absalom and Achitophel*, l. 159 (and the note on this in *Poems*, ed. Hammond, i. 469) and l. 1008; with Choroebus' mistaken idea that Fortune is 'auspicious' cp. *Absalom and Achitophel*, l. 230, on which see Hammond, 'Dryden's Philosophy of Fortune', pp. 772–3.

[163] *Aeneis*, ii. 887–98; cp. *Aeneid*, ii. 655–62.

In an ill Hour insulting *Turnus* tore
Those Golden Spoils, and in a worse he wore.
O Mortals! blind in Fate, who never know
To bear high Fortune, or endure the low!
The Time shall come, when *Turnus*, but in vain,
Shall wish untouch'd the Trophies of the slain:
Shall wish the fatal Belt were far away;
And curse the dire Remembrance of the Day.[164]

If we know how this poem ends, we know that in its closing
lines Aeneas will reject Turnus' plea for mercy and kill him,
because he has caught sight of this very belt, now worn by
Turnus as a trophy. Even without that specific knowledge, we
understand that this is an ominous moment—a dark *kairos*—an
act of irreverent *hubris*. Turnus does not know how to cope
with his (very temporary) good Fortune, and is heedless of the
weight with which this moment is fraught. Before fighting
Turnus, Pallas had invoked the aid of Hercules, recalling his
father Evander's reception of the god, and so bringing into play
the mutual obligations of *pietas*. But there are times when
Fortune is triumphant, prayer is unavailing, and the gods themselves are powerless. Hercules can only turn away his eyes from
the battle.

When Evander laments the death of his son, he cries out that
their prayers have been fruitless. He can only find some bitter
consolation in the fact that his wife is no longer alive to know this
grief:

O curst Essay of Arms, disast'rous Doom,
Prelude of bloody Fields, and Fights to come!
Hard Elements of unauspicious War,
Vain Vows to Heav'n, and unavailing Care!
Thrice happy thou, dear Partner of my Bed,
Whose holy Soul the Stroke of Fortune fled:
Praescious of Ills, and leaving me behind,
To drink the Dregs of Life by Fate assign'd.
Beyond the Goal of Nature I have gon;
My *Pallas* late set out, but reach'd too soon.[165]

---

[164] *Aeneis*, x. 696–703, translating *Aeneid*, x. 501–4. Virgil has no reference to Fortune
here, though the word does occur in Ruaeus' prose paraphrase.
[165] *Aeneis*, xi. 236–45.

'Primitiae juvenis miserae, bellique propinqui
'Dura rudimenta, et nulla exaudita Deorum
'Vota, precesque meae! tuque, o sanctissima conjux,
'Felix morte tua, neque in hunc servata dolorem!
'Contra ego vivendo vici mea fata, superstes
'Restarem ut genitor.[166]

In this passage there are traces of other episodes in Dryden's *œuvre* where a father-figure mourns a lost youth, and with him a lost future. The word 'unavailing' leads us back to Anchises' 'unavailing Gift' of funeral flowers for Marcellus in Book VI.[167] The image in the closing couplet of Pallas reaching the goal before his father repeats the dominant image of 'To the Memory of Mr. Oldham'.[168] Evander says of his wife that her 'holy Soul the Stroke of Fortune fled', which is entirely Dryden's addition, setting up a spiritual opposition between the pure soul and Fortune. And there is a curious semantic overlap of English and Latin in the word 'Praescious', a rare word[169] whose spelling here alerts us to its Latin origins as *praescius* ('prescient'). It is no accident that Dryden should turn to Latin to signal the soul's apprehension of future ill, its troubled reading of *chronos* as a grim form of *kairos*.

When Aeneas leads the mourning for Pallas, Dryden adds descriptions of him as 'The Pious Chief'[170] and the 'Godlike Man'.[171] Then, when Aeneas sees the body of Pallas,

First, melting into Tears, the pious Man
Deplor'd so sad a sight, then thus began.
    Unhappy Youth! When Fortune gave the rest
Of my full Wishes, she refus'd the best![172]

---

[166] *Aeneid*, xi. 156–61: 'Wretched first fruits of a young man, and hard first experience of early war; no vows to the gods heard, nor prayers of mine! And you, O most holy wife, happy in your death, not preserved for this grief! I, however, in living on have outlasted my fate, and as the father will be left alive to survive him.'   [167] *Vide infra.*

[168] Virgil's *Primitiae*, 'first fruits', is an image which also recalls 'O early ripe' and 'Thy generous fruits' in 'To the Memory of Mr. Oldham', ll. 11, 19.

[169] See the *OED* (under the spelling 'prescious').

[170] *Aeneis*, xi. 3; no equivalent to 'Pious' in *Aeneid*, xi. 2–3.

[171] *Aeneis*, xi. 19; no equivalent in *Aeneid*, xi. 13.

[172] *Aeneis*, xi. 57–60, translating *Aeneid*, xi. 40–3. 'Deplore' was stronger in 17th-cent. usage than now: 'weep for, bewail' (*OED* 1), the sense of the Latin *deplorare*, which also means 'give up for lost' (*OLD* 2).

'Fortune' is there in Virgil, but 'pious' is not: Dryden is drawing out the association of piety with grief, and with a response to misfortune. And when Aeneas bids his last farewell to Pallas, he does so as 'the pious Chief' once again.[173] The whole episode represents the struggle of *Pietas* against *Fortuna*.

AENEAS IN THE UNDERWORLD: BETWEEN PAST AND FUTURE

Book VI of the *Aeneid* relates the one essential detour amongst the many detours which make up Aeneas' wanderings, for it is here that he leaves the upper world and encounters both the ghosts from his own past and the disembodied spirits who will be the principal actors in Roman history. Here Virgil provides a vision of the future generations of Rome, though this form of the future is deeply shadowed by a sense of lost possibilities. It is also the book in which Aeneas comes most clearly to understand how he can relate to the gods: the divine powers are very close here, very demanding, difficult to satisfy and yet ultimately ready to guard and guide him.

Having landed in Italy, Aeneas turns for guidance to the Sibyl, and at her prompting he addresses to Apollo a prayer which in Dryden's translation is instinct with a sense of the god's active care of him:

> Indulgent God, propitious Pow'r to *Troy*,
> Swift to relieve, unwilling to destroy;[174]

Virgil says simply that Apollo has always pitied the tribulations of the Trojans (*graves Trojae miserate labores*),[175] while Dryden's words 'Indulgent' and 'propitious' attribute to Apollo a more active, nurturing care.[176] But up to this point the Trojans have experienced few signs of divine care, for

> Thus far the Fate of *Troy*, from place to place,
> With Fury has pursu'd her wand'ring Race:[177]

---

[173] *Aeneis*, xi. 141; no equivalent in *Aeneid*, xi. 95.   [174] *Aeneis*, vi. 88–9.

[175] *Aeneid*, vi. 56.

[176] He had applied the adjective 'propitious' to Venus in 'Lucretius: The Beginning of the First Book', l. 2.

[177] *Aeneis*, vi. 96–7. Compare Virgil: *Hac Trojana tenus fuerit fortuna secuta* ('up to this point the ill-luck of Troy has followed us', *Aeneid*, vi. 62).

This adds to Virgil an emphasis on the exile and the repeated displacement of the Trojans, and the theme is repeated, with the same sad rhyme, when Aeneas prays that he may

> fix my wand'ring Gods; and find a place
> For the long Exiles of the *Trojan* Race.[178]

The phrase 'long Exiles' is Dryden's addition, as is the hope that they may ultimately find a place.

When the Sibyl speaks Apollo's reply, she advises Aeneas as to the frame of mind with which he should meet the trials which still lie ahead of him:

> But thou, secure of Soul, unbent with Woes,
> The more thy Fortune frowns, the more oppose.[179]

> 'Tu ne cede malis, sed contra audentior ito,
> 'Quam tua te fortuna sinet.[180]

Aeneas will triumph over frowning Fortune in so far as he is 'secure of Soul', a phrase without precedent in the Latin, but one which points to the need for spiritual self-possession.[181] The word 'secure' is part of the vocabulary which Dryden used in *Sylvæ* for the truly happy man. Aeneas in his reply says that 'The Fates, without my Pow'r, shall be without my Care'.[182] Here Dryden is expanding the expression of Stoic resolution which he found in Virgil: *Omnia praecepi, atque animo mecum ante peregi* ('I have taken thought for everything, and gone through it beforehand with myself in my mind').[183] But the particular inflection which Dryden gives to this attitude is that what is beyond ('without') our control should also be beyond our anxiety. There is a significant divergence here between Virgil and Dryden, for whereas Virgil's hero is facing up to the trials and terrors which await him in the underworld, and resolving to bear them unflinchingly, Dryden's hero resolves to expend no anxious care on those things which he is powerless to change. It is a note which Dryden had sounded in

---

[178] *Aeneis*, vi. 104–5.   [179] *Aeneis*, vi. 143–4.
[180] *Aeneid*, vi. 95–6: 'Do not give in to evils, but oppose them more boldly than your Fortune allows'. Ruaeus reads *quam*, but Austin *ad loc.* argues for *qua*.
[181] Cp. Nautes' advice to Aeneas: 'By suff'ring well, our Fortune we subdue; | Fly when she frowns, and when she calls pursue' (*Aeneis*, v. 930–1).
[182] *Aeneis*, vi. 158.
[183] *Aeneid*, vi. 105. For the Stoic expression here see Austin *ad loc.*

the Horatian poems in *Sylvæ*, and which he has absorbed partly from Raphael's message to Adam in *Paradise Lost*:

> nor with perplexing thoughts
> To interrupt the sweet of Life, from which
> God hath bid dwell farr off all anxious cares,
> And not molest us.[184]

The various encounters which Aeneas has in Book VI with the shades of the dead allow Dryden the opportunity to incorporate into his translation the moral and existential thinking which he had first worked out in his translations from Horace and Lucretius.

The first shades whom Aeneas meets in the underworld are his unburied comrades who met their death by drowning and are now stranded on the bank of the Styx unable to cross. Here Aeneas' progress is checked, as he stands 'Revolving anxious Thoughts within his Breast'.[185] In this case the anxious thoughts (Dryden's elaboration of *multa putans*: 'thinking many things') are not those selfish concerns which gnaw away fruitlessly, but a proper anxiety on behalf of the ghosts who have not received their due rites of burial, duties demanded by *pietas*. Among these is the helmsman Palinurus, and as Aeneas contemplates his fate he is moved to question the words and actions of the gods. He asks 'What envious Pow'r' was responsible for Palinurus' death, thereby suggesting that there may be some divine resentment at human happiness (Virgil just has *Quis . . . Deorum*, 'which one of the gods').[186] In this case alone Apollo has, it seems, deceived him by not delivering what he had promised: 'Is this th' unerring Pow'r?'.[187] The word 'unerring' was important in Dryden's theological vocabulary, for it signified the true church which provided believers with an infallible guide in matters of faith: as he exclaims in *The Hind and the Panther*,

> But, gratious God, how well dost thou provide
> For erring judgments an unerring Guide?[188]

---

[184] Milton, *Paradise Lost*, viii. 183–6.

[185] *Aeneis*, vi. 454; cp. *Aeneid*, vi. 332.

[186] *Aeneis*, vi. 467; cp. *Aeneid*, vi. 341.

[187] *Aeneis*, vi. 473; cp. *an haec promissa fides est?* ('is this his promised faithfulness?': *Aeneid*, vi. 346).   [188] *The Hind and the Panther*, i. 64–5.

The question mark in seventeenth-century punctuation often does duty for the modern exclamation mark, and in this case both seem required: this is an exclamation, prompted by secure faith ('how well does God provide!'); but it is also a question ('how well does God provide?') which needs an answer, and not simply an abstract and theological answer but one which has been informed by the trial of experience. That Dryden should use this word here in the *Aeneis* shows how he is engaged with contemporary theological problems during this journey through the classical world: here is a theology in process, and as Aeneas is moved to doubt divine providence and question the promises of Apollo, so Dryden's theology is being tested through these vividly imagined encounters with the displaced and the dispossessed. Palinurus begs Aeneas to help him over the Styx, but his plea is futile, and brings a stinging rebuke from the Sibyl: 'What Hopes delude thee, miserable Man?'. As he often does, Dryden has generalized the thought by omitting the proper noun: *Unde haec, o Palinure, tibi tam dira cupido?* ('whence, Palinurus, such dire desire?').[189] The focus has broadened from this one desperate man, to Man and his self-deluding hopes; and so to the reader. It is once again both exclamation and question.

If one of the thoughts which is guiding Dryden's translation of this book is the question of how one preserves a reverence for the gods, a reverence for life, in the face of misfortune, against the dispiriting flow of history, it is not surprising that he should be particularly engaged by the episode when Aeneas meets those who have committed suicide:

> The next in Place, and Punishment, are they
> Who prodigally throw their Souls away.
> Fools, who repining at their wretched State,
> And loathing anxious life, suborn'd their Fate.
> With late Repentance, now they wou'd retrieve
> The Bodies they forsook, and wish to live.
> Their Pains and Poverty desire to bear,
> To view the Light of Heav'n, and breath the vital Air:
> But Fate forbids; the *Stygian* Floods oppose;
> And, with nine circling Streams, the captive Souls inclose.[190]

---

[189] *Aeneis*, vi. 507; *Aeneid*, vi. 373.
[190] *Aeneis*, vi. 586–95; cp. *Aeneid*, vi. 434–8.

Following Christian teaching, Dryden is much fiercer in his account of the suicides than is Virgil, though 'prodigally' briefly gestures to an alternative narrative of repentance and forgiveness in the parable of the Prodigal Son. By contrast with Virgil's description of them as innocent (*insontes*), Dryden makes them foolish in their over-hasty escape from life's anxious cares, using language which echoes his own earlier translation of 'Lucretius: Against the Fear of Death'.[191] These are, it seems, two equally foolish attitudes: in Lucretius' characters a restless dissatisfaction with the present can result in an anxious grip on life, greedy for more and refusing to go along with the rhythms of nature when they lead towards death; in Virgil's, a desperate impatience and anxiety make suicide seem attractive. Both are solipsistic, neither is reverent. The suicides' belated change of mind is poignantly caught in the first Alexandrine, 'To view the Light of Heav'n, and breath the vital Air:' which is full of light, airy vowels, and stretches out to offer liberation (matching Virgil's line-ending *aethere in alto*, 'in the upper air'). But this long line is then capped and confined by a second Alexandrine, 'And, with nine circling Streams, the captive Souls inclose', a line which in sound and syntax moves slowly but firmly to enclose the captives.

Another group which, predictably, attracts Dryden's special interest are the usurpers and traitors. Here Aeneas meets those

> who Brothers better Claim disown,
> Expel their Parents, and usurp the Throne;[192]

> Hic quibus invisi fratres, dum vita manebat;
> Pulsatusve parens,[193]

Dryden clearly departs from Virgil in making this a political rather than a domestic crime, adding 'better Claim', and 'usurp the Throne', and interpreting *pulsatus* not as 'beaten, assaulted' (*OLD* 1, 5) but 'sent packing' (*OLD* 8). A few lines later we meet more villains:

---

[191] 'Lucretius: Against the Fear of Death', ll. 123, 132, 156.
[192] *Aeneis*, vi. 824–5.
[193] *Aeneid*, vi. 608–9: 'those to whom their brothers were hateful while they lived, or who beat their father'.

> To Tyrants others have their Country sold,
> Imposing Foreign Lords, for Foreign Gold:
> Some have old Laws repeal'd, new Statutes made;
> Not as the People pleas'd, but as they paid.[194]

> Vendidit hic auro patriam, dominumque potentem
> Imposuit: fixit leges pretio atque refixit.[195]

Though Dryden's 'Tyrants' has a precedent in Ruaeus' gloss *tyrannum*, there is no warrant in the Latin for 'Foreign', which is so emphatically repeated. (Rome was never threatened by foreign tyrants as much as it was by native ones.) The point of Virgil's second line is subtly but significantly modified through the idea that old statutes (for example, those governing the law of succession) have been repealed.

All these, and more, are examples of *pietas* violated; but when Aeneas finally meets the shade of his father Anchises we see *pietas* exemplified and rewarded. Anchises greets Aeneas as 'the Gods undoubted Race', confirming his place as the true heir.[196] When he replies, Aeneas is referred to not by a personal pronoun (like Virgil's *ille*) but instead by an abstract phrase which indicates that he is standing here primarily as an example of a particular virtue: 'To this, the Filial Duty thus replies'.[197] Where Virgil's hero sees his father's shade as sad (*tristis*), Dryden's Aeneas regards it as 'sacred'.[198]

At this point in Book VI Virgil moves into a vision of order and coherence imparted by the father to the son, albeit a pattern in which loss and pain have their part. Anchises explains how matter and spirit cohere in the universe, and then shows Aeneas the spirits of those who will fashion the Roman state. This is for Virgil a passage which is complex in its temporality, since it presents under the form of prophecy a series of episodes, some of which belong to Rome's distant and half-legendary past, some to its recent history, some to its present, and some to its imagined future: and

---

[194] *Aeneis*, vi. 845–8.

[195] *Aeneid*, vi. 621–2: 'Here is one who sold his country for gold, and imposed on it a powerful ruler; and made and remade laws for money.'

[196] *Aeneis*, vi. 931; no equivalent in *Aeneid*, vi. 687.

[197] There is an echo here of Dryden's description of Shadwell as 'the filial dulness' (*Mac Flecknoe*, l. 136), which itself had Miltonic connotations: see *Poems*, ed. Hammond, i. 136.

[198] *Aeneis*, vi. 943; *Aeneid*, vi. 695.

none of these times is quite distinct, since figures are introduced out of their actual historical sequence, and each episode is subtly informed by its neighbouring episodes and their own ideological inflections. As the poem reconfigures relationships between past, present, and future it establishes its own complex form of present time. And it is at this point in Book VI that the idea of restoration insistently re-enters Dryden's text, occurring four times within just seventy lines.

First there is the promise of a second Silvius, who is also a second Aeneas:

> A second *Silvius* after these appears;
> *Silvius Æneas*, for thy Name he bears.
> For Arms and Justice equally renown'd;
> Who, late restor'd, in *Alba* shall be crown'd.[199]

Ruaeus relates the story that Silvius Aeneas had been cheated out of his kingdom by his tutor, not gaining possession of it until the age of fifty-two, but then enjoying a reign of thirty-one years. Virgil makes Anchises hesitate over whether Silvius Aeneas will ever be king (*si unquam regnandam acceperit Albam*: 'if he will ever receive Alba to rule it'), while Dryden incorporates the gloss into the text by telling us that he will at length be restored and crowned. Both the idea of restoration and the regal imagery are Dryden's own, perhaps prompted by the recognition that Silvius Aeneas and James II came to the throne at the same age. Dryden has transposed the tense here from the conditional to an emphatically prophetic future. Just a few lines later he introduces Romulus:

> See *Romulus* the great, born to restore
> The Crown that once his injur'd Grandsire wore.[200]

In Virgil, Romulus is called the *comitem* of his grandfather, basically 'companion' (*OLD* 1); but *comes* is more strongly a comrade, a right-hand man, one who shares another's danger (*OLD* 2, 3, 5). Ruaeus offers the gloss *ultorem* ('avenger') explaining that Romulus' grandfather Numitor had been expelled from his kingdom by his

---

[199] *Aeneis*, vi. 1043–6; cp. *Aeneid*, vi. 768–70.
[200] *Aeneis*, vi. 1055; cp. *Aeneid*, vi. 777–9.

brother. Dryden had already expanded an earlier reference to Romulus with an allusion to the deposition of Numitor when translating Book I, and now he expands Virgil's reference by adding the ideas of restoration, of a crown, and the 'injur'd' grandfather, once again incorporating a gloss within his text.

Central to Virgil's list of Roman heroes is the figure of Augustus, for he is 'Born to restore a better Age of Gold'.[201] The word 'restore' is not an unfaithful translation of *condet . . . rursus*, for *condere* can mean either 'restore' (*OLD* 3) or 'found', 'originate' (*OLD* 10, 11), and *rursus* ('again') clearly makes this a re-establishment of the Saturnian age. But the echo of 'restore' through this passage is becoming insistent, particularly in the repeated phrase 'born to restore' with its emphasis on those duties which come by birthright.

The last instance of the word 'restore' occurs in the case of Brutus, who with his 'avenging Sword | . . . *Rome* restor'd' after the rule of the Tarquins. This phrase stands for the one word *ultoris* ('revenger'). Brutus' own sons seek to foment a new war (*nova bella moventes*), whereas in Dryden's rendering they 'seek the Tyrant to sustain, | And long for Arbitrary Lords again.'[202] Dryden's use of the word 'arbitrary' reuses vocabulary which had previously been applied by Whig writers to the Stuarts,[203] and in using it here Dryden is reminding his readers that there is more than one form of arbitrary government. But Dryden's rethinking of Virgil's text does not simply try to turn it into a contemporary allusion, for his most substantial addition here concerns the plight of Brutus when he is forced by his sense of public duty to condemn his own rebellious sons:

> Unhappy Man, to break the Pious Laws
> Of Nature, pleading in his Children's Cause![204]

Virgil is equally sensitive to this tragic dilemma, but Dryden's addition reminds us that underlying the paternal feelings in this

---

[201] *Aeneis*, vi. 1081; cp. *Aeneid*, vi. 792–3.

[202] *Aeneis*, vi. 1117–1122; cp. *Aeneid*, vi. 818–20.

[203] As in the title of Marvell's *An Account of the Growth of Popery and Arbitrary Government* (1677). Dryden had already contested Whig uses of the word in *Absalom and Achitophel*, ll. 212, 330, 701 and 762: see the notes *ad loc.* in *Poems*, ed. Hammond. He had also reminded his readers of what 'arbitrary' government was really like in *Aeneis*, i. 93, where 'arbitrary Sway' is imposed over the winds who are locked up and fettered.

[204] *Aeneis*, vi. 1126–7.

case are the general laws of nature which demand to be observed, the principles which we call *pietas*. But *pietas*, we know, should unify a man's duties to family and state, not set them in conflict, and Dryden's introduction of the word 'Pious' here sharpens our sense of the tragic dilemma of divergent duties which structures the *Aeneid* itself.

Different kinds of ruler are encountered in this part of Book VI. Julius Caesar is eager to seize the time, in language which echoes Marvell's reflections on the opportunistic seizing of the time in the 'Horatian Ode':

> The mighty *Caesar* waits his vital Hour;
> Impatient for the World, and grasps his promis'd Pow'r.[205]

The second line is Dryden's addition. Virgil returns to Julius Caesar later, when describing the civil wars between Caesar and Pompey.[206] He stresses that their relationship by marriage makes this conflict all the more impious, but whereas he uses the terms *socer* and *gener* ('father-in-law'; 'son-in-law') Dryden is more specific, and refers to 'His Daughter's Husband'—the relationship in which William III stood to James II. Virgil diplomatically suppresses proper names here, and so does Dryden, allowing the reference to reach contemporary events if readers so wish, while quietly prompting such an association by inserting the idea that one of the parties has a 'lawless claim'.

By contrast with these opportunistic rulers, there is the sacred figure of Numa.[207] In Virgil he carries the *sacra* ('sacred things', i.e. vessels or images), and in Dryden's translation this becomes 'a Censer', which is used only in Catholic ritual. Numa also wears 'holy Vestments' (without an equivalent in the Latin), which are

---

[205] *Aeneis*, vi. 1075–6; cp. *Aeneid*, vi. 790. There is a question as to whether Virgil is referring here to Julius Caesar or to Augustus; Dryden's interpretation follows Ruaeus. The rhyme here suggests a reminiscence of Marvell's lines: 'This was that memorable Hour | Which first assur'd the forced Pow'r' ('An Horatian Ode', ll. 65–6). Marvell's poem includes references to Caesar, and the lines immediately following these refer to the building of the Roman Capitol. There is another possible echo a little later, when Dryden writes: 'And scour his Armour from the Rust of Peace' (*Aeneis*, vi. 1124), with which compare Marvell: 'And oyl th' unused Armours rust' (l. 6; 'Peace' supplies a rhyme in l. 10). For Dryden's recollections of this poem elsewhere see Ch. 2.

[206] *Aeneis*, vi. 1140–5; cp. *Aeneid*, vi. 830–5.

[207] *Aeneis*, vi. 1103–8; cp. *Aeneid*, vi. 808–12.

again pointers to Catholic liturgy, thus associating classical and Catholic Rome. There is a haunting moment when Dryden translates *nosco* ('I recognize') by saying that these features 'bring | His lost Idea back': in this figure, at once regal and sacred, a lost idea of kingship is momentarily recovered.

But if this is one of the moments when the poem recognizes loss, its most poignant instance of loss is still to come, in the figure of the young Marcellus:

> Observe the Crowds that compass him around;
> All gaze, and all admire, and raise a shouting sound:
> But hov'ring Mists around his Brows are spread,
> And Night, with sable Shades, involves his Head.
> Seek not to know (the Ghost reply'd with Tears)
> The Sorrows of thy Sons, in future Years.
> This Youth (the blissful Vision of a day)
> Shall just be shown on Earth, and snatch'd away.
> The Gods too high had rais'd the *Roman* State;
> Were but their Gifts as permanent as great . . .
> No Youth shall equal hopes of Glory give:
> No Youth afford so great a Cause to grieve.
> The *Trojan* Honour, and the *Roman* Boast;
> Admir'd when living, and Ador'd when lost!
> Mirror of ancient Faith in early Youth!
> Undaunted Worth, Inviolable Truth! . . .
> Let me with Fun'ral Flow'rs his Body strow;
> This Gift which Parents to their Children owe,
> This unavailing Gift, at least I may bestow![208]

Into these lines Dryden has gathered some of the vocabulary which he used in 'To the Memory of Mr. Oldham', a poem which had addressed Oldham as the '*Marcellus* of our Tongue'.[209] Dryden has expanded into two lines the crowd's adulation of Marcellus, with the second line, an Alexandrine, marking a kind of excess which is abruptly cut short by what follows. A single line in Virgil describing the night which envelops Marcellus (*Sed nox atra caput tristi circumvolat umbra*[210]) is made into two lines by

---

[208] *Aeneis*, vi. 1196–1226; cp. *Aeneid*, vi. 865–86.
[209] In 'To the Memory of Mr. Oldham', 'Fate and gloomy Night encompass thee around' (l. 25), while here it is the crowds who 'compass him around'.
[210] *Aeneid*, vi. 866: 'but black night surrounds his sad head with darkness'.

Dryden. When Anchises advises Aeneas not to ask about the future, his *ne quaere* ('do not ask') becomes 'Seek not to know', a phrasing which connects this passage with Dryden's earlier injunctions against seeking out knowledge which God has wisely hidden from us. Marcellus is hailed as

> Mirror of ancient Faith in early Youth!
> Undaunted Worth, Inviolable Truth!

which translates *Heu pietas! heu prisca fides!*[211] This rethinks yet once more the semantic field of *pietas*.

At the heart of this vision is a discomforting dislocation of time, seen particularly in the strange temporality of this address to the spirit:

> Ah, cou'dst thou break through Fates severe Decree,
> A new *Marcellus* shall arise in thee!

> si qua fata aspera rumpas,
> Tu Marcellus eris.[212]

When Virgil read this book aloud in the presence of Augustus, it was at this moment, when she heard her son named, that Octavia fainted. The Latin here might mean 'if in some way you could escape your hard fate, you will be Marcellus' (thus Ruaeus): if the youth could somehow evade his fate, he might after all turn out to be the Marcellus, the great leader, for whom Rome hopes. But more probably it means 'if only, in some way, you could escape your hard fate—[but you cannot,] you will be Marcellus' (thus Austin): it is part of his hard fate to be Marcellus, and that includes dying young. Dryden's version seems to permit both readings. But the first one, the desperate wish, is itself a desperate wrenching of Virgil's Latin. The *si* ('if') is not conditional, but the mark of an unfulfilled, unfulfillable wish ('if only . . .'). The movement from the subjunctive in *rumpas* ('may you break', 'break free from', 'escape') to the indicative in *eris* ('you will be') seals the boy's fate. We know that *rumpas* will eternally remain subjunctive, for there is no way of escaping one's fate. The space between *rumpas* and *eris* is the purely fictional space, the impossible time, of unavailing longing.

---

[211] *Aeneid*, vi. 878: 'Alas piety! alas ancient faith!'
[212] *Aeneis*, vi. 1220–1; *Aeneid*, vi. 882–3.

As Anchises finally turns to strew the body with funeral flow-
ers, we are told that this is an 'unavailing Gift', *inane* | *Munere*
('empty gift'). It is, indeed, a strange, uncanny, gesture, a gesture
of mourning for one who is not yet dead, a ritual performed in an
impossible time and space over a body which is still a disembodied spirit, one as yet unborn. Virgil's placing of *Munere* at the
beginning of the line highlights it, and quietly shows us that this
gift has no place. Dryden makes the point differently, repeating the
word 'Gift', and the second time disabling it with the adjective
'unavailing', a word which is apparently his own coinage.[213] And
in a line added here to Virgil, Dryden calls it 'This Gift which
Parents to their Children owe', a generalization which opens out
its symbolic field.

We infer from the epigraph to Dryden's translation that he
thought of himself as a kind of son to Virgil. And he in turn imagined himself in a fatherly relationship to Oldham and to Congreve,
his two heirs. At this point in the *Aeneis* the son stands watching
his father mourn his own descendants, giving them an 'unavailing
Gift'. Unavailing, but not empty: Virgil's inheritance could never
be that. Through his *Aeneis* Dryden honoured his father with a
work which would be one of his richest gifts to his own posterity.
With the *Aeneis* Dryden finally brought into his own language the
Latin poem which had lived in his mind since childhood, and had
inhabited—as guest and as ghost—so much of his adult writing.
Like Aeneas at the site of Rome—that uncanny field which held
traces of both *archē* and *telos*—Dryden was taking possession of his
home ground.

---

[213] *OED*'s first example is from Dryden's *The Conquest of Granada*.

THEOXENY

In his *Fables Ancient and Modern* (1700), published two months before his death, Dryden included a translation from the *Metamorphoses* relating the story of Baucis and Philemon. The tale is offered by Lelex as a demonstration of the power of the gods and a rebuke to atheists and scoffers. Lelex has seen two trees which grow close together, an oak and a linden, and unlike the trees in Claude's painting these are the traces of a remarkable human couple. But like Delos, this too is holy ground, in this case because it has been the site of a theoxeny, the reception of a god.

During the degenerate age of mankind, Jupiter and Mercury travel in disguise through the world, and are refused hospitality at every door until they arrive at the poor cottage of Baucis and Philemon. Here they are welcomed with all the meagre fare which the old couple can muster. Though Dryden places the story 'in Phrygian Ground',[1] and has the hosts provide olives and wine for their visitors, he also includes in his text many details which are redolent of rural England: Baucis puts the kettle on the fire, serves coleworts, along with bacon which has been hanging from a sooty rafter, and places the food on a trivet-table which has been rubbed with mint; next come plums, apples, nuts, curds, cream, and honeycomb. The texture of this domestic milieu is recognizably English.

The meeting of humans and gods is instinct with comedy: the status of the visitors is not recognized until the bowls start dancing round the table and replenishing themselves with wine of a superior vintage. Then, not having a fatted calf to kill, Baucis and Philemon try to catch their goose for the pot, but the canny bird seeks protection from the gods:

---

[1] 'Baucis and Philemon', l. 15.

> But persecuted, to the Pow'rs she flies,
> And close between the Legs of *Jove* she lies:
> He with a gracious Ear the Suppliant heard,
> And sav'd her Life; then what he was declar'd,
> And own'd the God.[2]

Dryden relishes the comedy of this unequal encounter, but it is also a tale with serious consequences. Jupiter decides to flood the world in order to be rid of these wretched human beings, excepting only Baucis and Philemon. As the rising waters wipe out all trace of human life, their cottage is transformed into a temple, and they become guardians of the new shrine. When at last their own death approaches, in fulfilment of their wish that they should not be separated the two are transformed into trees.

The life of Baucis and Philemon has been one of harmony and reciprocity:

> Command was none, where equal Love was paid,
> Or rather both commanded, both obey'd.[3]

And this syntax of mutual love is repeated at their deaths:

> Old *Baucis* is by old *Philemon* seen
> Sprouting with sudden Leaves of spritely Green:
> Old *Baucis* look'd where old *Philemon* stood,
> And saw his lengthen'd Arms a sprouting Wood:[4]

The couple are, in effect, exemplars of *pietas* in their mutual love, their contented poverty, hospitality, and reverence for the gods. It is this which makes their cottage into sacred ground.[5]

The home of Baucis and Philemon is transformed by their reception of strangers, and becomes a space which is free from the surrounding flood. It is tempting to present this as a final image for Dryden's reception of the Latin poets, as the ground on which he could be free from the inundations of Restoration England. For Dryden's interest in the home, the hearth, and its gods is

---

[2] 'Baucis and Philemon', ll. 137–41.   [3] Ibid., ll. 39–40.

[4] Ibid., ll. 181–4.

[5] Indeed, Dryden incorporates into his description of their life some borrowings from Milton's account of Adam and Eve in *Paradise Lost*: see David Hopkins, 'Dryden's "Baucis and Philemon" and *Paradise Lost*', *Notes and Queries*, 227 (1982) 503–4; and J. R. Mason, 'To Milton through Dryden and Pope', unpublished PhD thesis, University of Cambridge, 1987.

characteristically played out on Roman ground. It is by standing on this ground that Dryden's work stands against several kinds of dislocation which his age had brought about, revolutions not so much in the political sphere (momentous though these were) as in the conceptual structure. One of these is the movement from a theory of language which holds that there is a necessary connection between the word and the thing, to one which asserts that the relationship between signifier and signified is purely conventional.[6] Another is the change from regarding monarchy as sacred, and embodied in the ruler, to seeing it as functional, as an office.[7] And a third is the decline in the belief in a supernaturally authenticated religion.[8] In all three areas there is a loss of the noumenal, of the idea of real presence. Dryden is often thought to stand with a stolid conservatism against these harbingers of the Enlightenment; but his poetry actually engages rigorously, imaginatively, in detail, with these changes, including within its fabric a deconstructive solicitation of its own conceptual structures, fashioning an inner dialogue. Dryden was making his own reformulation of language, majesty, and the sacred by his move onto a classic ground of his own definition. The second temple which his poetry constructed may have been a somewhat curious structure, more baroque than classical, the work not of an engineer but a *bricoleur*[9] who pieced together the fragments which came to hand, sometimes with passionate conviction, sometimes with ironic detachment. But inside that temple the sacred flame burned bright.

[6] See Brian Vickers, 'Analogy versus Identity: The Rejection of Occult Symbolism, 1580–1680', in *Occult and Scientific Mentalities in the Renaissance*, ed. Brian Vickers (Cambridge, 1984), pp. 95–163.

[7] See Quentin Skinner, 'The State' in *Political Innovation and Conceptual Change*, ed. Terence Ball, James Farr and Russell L. Hanson (Cambridge, 1989), pp. 90–131.

[8] In Dryden's lifetime this is already traceable in Hobbes and the Deists.

[9] Jacques Derrida, *L'Ecriture et la différence* (Paris, 1967, 1994), p. 418.

BIBLIOGRAPHY

PRIMARY SOURCES

Where more than one edition of a work is listed, quotations are taken from the one marked with an asterisk.

Dryden

Absalon et Achitophel. Carmine Latino Heroico [trans. William Coward] (Oxford, 1682).

Absalon et Achitophel. Poema Latino Carmine Donatum [trans. Francis Atterbury] (Oxford, 1682).

The Comedies, Tragedies, and Operas, written by John Dryden, Esq;, 2 vols. (London, 1701).

The Critical and Miscellaneous Prose Works of John Dryden, ed. Edmond Malone, 3 vols. (London, 1800).

★*The Poems of John Dryden,* ed. James Kinsley, 4 vols. (Oxford, 1958).

The Poems of John Dryden: Volume 1: 1649–1681 and *Volume 2: 1682–1685,* ed. Paul Hammond (London, 1995).

The Works of John Dryden, ed. Walter Scott, 18 vols. (London, 1808).

★*The Works of John Dryden,* ed. H. T. Swedenberg *et al.,* 20 vols. (Berkeley, 1956–). [For quotations from plays, and some prose works not included in Kinsley's edition.]

The Works of Virgil: Containing his Pastorals, Georgics, and Aeneis. Translated into English Verse; By Mr. Dryden (London, 1697).

Classical texts and commentaries

The principal Latin poets are cited from editions approximating to those which Dryden is known to have used (marked here with an asterisk). For other works the editions in the Loeb Library have been used, unless specific editions are listed.

CICERO
Cicero's Letters to Atticus, ed. D. R. Shackleton Bailey, vol. 2 (Cambridge, 1965).

HORACE

*Dionysius Lambinus, *In Q. Horatium Flaccum . . . Commentarius locupletissimus*, 6th edn. (Geneva, 1605).
Quinctus Horatius Flaccus, ed. Eilhardus Lubinus (Frankfurt, 1612).
Otho Van Veen [Vaenius], *Quinti Horatii Flacci Emblemata* (Antwerp, 1612).
Q. Horatius Flaccus cum commentariis selectissimis variorum, ed. Cornelius Schrevelius (Leiden, 1653).

JUVENAL AND PERSIUS

D. Junii Juvenalis, et Auli Persii Flacci Satyrae, ed. Cornelius Schrevelius (Leiden, 1664).
Juvenal: The Satires, ed. John Ferguson (Basingstoke, 1979).

LUCRETIUS

T. Lucretii Cari De Rerum Natura Libri VI, ed. Dionysius Lambinus (Paris, 1570).
Titi Lucretii Cari de Rerum Natura Libri Sex, ed. Thomas Creech (Oxford, 1695).

OVID

P. Ovidii Nasonis Opera Omnia, ed. Borchard Cnipping, 3 vols. (Leiden, 1670).

VIRGIL

P. Virgilii Maronis Opera, ed. Carolus Ruaeus (London, 1759; first published 1675).
P. Vergili Maronis Aeneidos Liber Primus, ed. R. G. Austin (Oxford, 1971).
P. Vergili Maronis Aeneidos Liber Secundus, ed. R. G. Austin (Oxford, 1964).
P. Vergili Maronis Aeneidos Liber Tertius, ed. R. D. Williams (Oxford, 1962).
P. Vergili Maronis Aeneidos Liber Quartus, ed. R. G. Austin (Oxford, 1955).
P. Vergili Maronis Aeneidos Liber Sextus, ed. R. G. Austin (Oxford, 1977).
Aeneid Book VIII, ed. K. W. Gransden (Cambridge, 1976).
Aeneid Book IX, ed. Philip Hardie (Cambridge, 1994).
Virgil: Georgics, ed. R. A. B. Mynors (Oxford, 1990).
Servianorum in Vergilii Carmina Commentariorum Editio Harvardiana, vols. 2 and 3 (Lancaster, Pa., 1946, and Oxford, 1965).

Renaissance and seventeenth-century texts

AMYOT, JACQUES, *Les Vies des hommes illustres*, 6 vols. (Paris, 1568).
Anglia Rediviva: Or, England Revived. An Heroick Poem (London, 1658).

ARINGHUS, PAULUS, *Roma Subterranea Novissima*, 2 vols. (Paris, 1659).

BACON, SIR FRANCIS, *The Essayes or Counsels, Civill and Morall*, ed. Michael Kiernan (Oxford, 1985).

BOILEAU-DESPRÉAUX, NICOLAS, *Œuvres complètes de Boileau*, ed. Charles-H. Boudhors, 7 vols. (Paris, 1934–43).

BOUHOURS, DOMINIQUE, *Les Entretiens d'Ariste et d'Eugène* (Paris, 1962).

BOYS, JOHN, *Aeneas his Errours, or his Voyage from Troy into Italy. An Essay upon the Third Book of Virgils Aeneis* (London, 1661).

—— *Aeneas his Descent into Hell* (London, 1661).

[BROME, ALEXANDER], (ed.), *The Poems of Horace, Consisting of Odes, Satyres, and Epistles, Rendered in English Verse by Several Persons* (London, 1666).

BROWN, TOM, *The Reasons of Mr Bays Changing his Religion* (London, 1688).

BUNYAN, JOHN, *Solomon's Temple Spiritualiz'd, or Gospel-Light Fetcht out of the Temple at Jerusalem, To let us more easily into the Glory of New-Testament-Truths* (London, 1688).

CAREW, THOMAS, *The Poems of Thomas Carew*, ed. Rhodes Dunlap (Oxford, 1949).

The Catholic Almanack for the Year 1687 (London, 1687).

CHARLES I, *Basilika: The Workes of King Charles the Martyr* (London, 1662).

CHARLETON, WALTER, *Epicurus's Morals* (London, 1656).

—— *The Immortality of the Human Soul, Demonstrated by the Light of Nature* (London, 1657).

CONGREVE, WILLIAM, *Comedies*, ed. Bonamy Dobrée (Oxford, 1925).

COWLEY, ABRAHAM, *Essays, Plays and Sundry Verses*, ed. A. R. Waller (Cambridge, 1906).

—— *Poems*, ed. A. R. Waller (Cambridge, 1905).

CREECH, THOMAS, *T. Lucretius Carus The Epicurean Philosopher, His Six Books De Natura Rerum Done into English Verse* (Oxford, 1682).

—— *T. Lucretius Carus, Of the Nature of Things*, ed. John Digby, 2 vols. (London, 1714).

DE LAUNE, THOMAS, *Eikon tou theriou, or The Image of the Beast, Shewing, by a Parallel Scheme, what a Conformist the Church of Rome is to the Pagan* (London, 1684).

DENHAM, SIR JOHN, *The Poetical Works*, ed. Theodore Howard Banks, 2nd edn. (n.p., 1969).

DONNE, JOHN, *The Elegies and The Songs and Sonnets*, ed. Helen Gardner (Oxford, 1965).

EVELYN, JOHN, *The Diary of John Evelyn*, ed. E. S. de Beer, 6 vols. (Oxford, 1955).

Examen Poeticum: Being the Third Part of Miscellany Poems (London, 1693).

FANSHAWE, SIR RICHARD, *The Poems and Translations of Sir Richard Fanshawe*, vol. 1, ed. Peter Davidson (Oxford, 1997).

FARLEY-HILLS, DAVID (ed.), *Rochester: The Critical Heritage* (London, 1972).

The Fatal Discovery; or, Love in Ruines (London, 1698).

FOWLER, ALASTAIR, (ed.), *The Country House Poem* (Edinburgh, 1994).

HIGDEN, HENRY, *A Modern Essay on the Tenth Satyr of Juvenal* (London, 1687).

HIGGONS, THOMAS, *A Panegyrick to the King* (1660).

HOBBES, THOMAS, *Leviathan*, ed. Richard Tuck (Cambridge, 1991).

HOOLE, CHARLES, *A New Discovery of the Old Art of Teaching Schoole* (London, 1660).

An Humble Remonstrance of the Batchelors, in and about London (London, 1693).

HUTCHINSON, LUCY, *Lucy Hutchinson's Translation of Lucretius: 'De Rerum Natura'*, ed. Hugh de Quehen (London, 1996).

INGELO, NATHANIEL, *Bentivolio and Urania: The Second Part*, 4th edn. (London, 1682; first published 1660).

*JONSON, BEN, *Ben Jonson*, ed. C. H. Herford, Percy and Evelyn Simpson, 11 vols. (Oxford, 1925–52).

—— *Poems*, ed. Ian Donaldson (Oxford, 1975).

KENNETT, BASIL, *Romae Antiquae Notitia: or, The Antiquities of Rome*, 7th edn. (London, 1721; first published 1696).

KITSON, MICHAEL, *Claude Lorrain: Liber Veritatis* (London, 1978).

LANGBAINE, GERARD, *An Account of the English Dramatick Poets* (Oxford, 1691).

LILY, WILLIAM, and JOHN COLET, *A Shorte Introduction of Grammar* (London, 1549).

Marcus Tullius Cicero: The Tragedy of that Famous Oratour (London, 1651).

MARVELL, ANDREW, *The Poems and Letters*, ed. H. M. Margoliouth, 3rd edn. revised by Pierre Legouis and E. E. Duncan-Jones, 2 vols. (Oxford, 1971).

*MILTON, JOHN, *The Poems*, ed. Helen Darbishire (Oxford, 1961).

—— *The Poems*, ed. John Carey and Alastair Fowler (London, 1968).

—— *The Complete Prose Works*, ed. Don M. Wolfe *et al.*, 8 vols. (New Haven, 1953–82).

Miscellany Poems (London, 1684).

MONTAIGNE, MICHEL DE, *Œuvres complètes*, ed. Maurice Rat (Paris, 1962).

MORE, HENRY, *Philosophical Poems* (Cambridge, 1647).

A New Session of the Poets, Occasion'd by the Death of Mr. Dryden (London, 1700).

The Nine Muses: Or, Poems Written by Nine Severall Ladies Upon the Death of the Late Famous John Dryden, Esq. (London, 1700).

ODEN, RICHARD L. (ed.), *Dryden and Shadwell* (Delmar, 1977).

OLDHAM, JOHN, *The Poems of John Oldham*, ed. Harold F. Brooks with the collaboration of Raman Selden (Oxord, 1987).

Oliva Pacis. Ad Illustrissimum Oliverum Reipub. Angliae Dominum Protectorem de Pace cum Faederatis Belgis feliciter sancita Carmen Cantabrigiense (Cambridge, 1654).

PATRIDES, C. A. (ed.), *The Cambridge Platonists* (London, 1969).

PEPYS, SAMUEL, *The Diary of Samuel Pepys*, ed. Robert Latham and William Matthews, 11 vols. (London, 1970–83).

Poems on Affairs of State, ed. George deF. Lord *et al.*, 7 vols. (New Haven, 1963–75).

POPE, ALEXANDER, *The Twickenham Edition of the Poems of Alexander Pope*, ed. John Butt *et al.*, 11 vols. (London, 1939–68).

ROCHESTER, JOHN WILMOT, EARL OF, *Poems, etc. On Several Occasions: With Valentinian; A Tragedy. Written by the Right Honourable John Late Earl of Rochester* (London, 1691).

★—— *The Poems of John Wilmot, Earl of Rochester*, ed. Keith Walker (Oxford, 1984).

ROSCOMMON, WENTWORTH DILLON, EARL OF, *Poems by the Earl of Roscomon [sic]*(London, 1717).

ROSS, ALEXANDER, *Mystagogus Poeticus, or The Muses Interpreter*, 5th edn. (London, 1672; first published 1647).

SEGRAIS, JEAN REGNAULT DE, *Traduction de L'Eneïde de Virgile par M^r. de Segrais* (Paris, 1668).

SHADWELL, THOMAS, *The Tenth Satyr of Juvenal, English and Latin* (London, 1687).

—— *The Virtuoso* (London, 1676).

Songes and Sonettes ['Tottel's Miscellany'] (London, 1557).

SPENSER, EDMUND, *Spenser's Faerie Queene*, ed. J. C. Smith, 2 vols. (Oxford, 1909).

—— *Spenser's Minor Poems*, ed. Ernest de Selincourt (Oxford, 1910).

STAPYLTON, SIR ROBERT (translator), *Juvenal's Sixteen Satyrs, or, A Survey of the Manners and Actions of Mankind* (London, 1647).

STILLINGFLEET, EDWARD, *Origines Sacrae* (London, 1663).

STOPFORD, JOSHUA, *Pagano-Papismus: or, An Exact Parallel between Rome-Pagan, and Rome-Christian, in their Doctrines and Ceremonies* (London, 1675).

Sylvæ: or The Second Part of Poetical Miscellanies (London, 1685).

VIDA, MARCO GIROLAMO, *The 'De Arte Poetica' of Marco Girolamo Vida*, ed. Ralph G. Williams (New York, 1976).
WOOD, THOMAS, *Juvenalis Redivivus, or The First Satyr of Juvenal taught to speak plain English* (London, 1683).

SECONDARY SOURCES

ANDERSON, JUDITH H., *Words that Matter: Linguistic Perception in Renaissance English* (Stanford, 1996).
ARMITAGE, DAVID, ARMAND HIMY, and QUENTIN SKINNER (eds.), *Milton and Republicanism* (Cambridge, 1995).
ARTHOS, JOHN, *The Language of Natural Description in Eighteenth-Century Poetry* (Ann Arbor, 1949).
BARNABY, ANDREW, ' "Another Rome in the West?": Milton and the Imperial Republic, 1654–1670', *Milton Studies*, 30 (1993) 67–84.
BARNARD, JOHN, 'Dryden: History and "The Mighty Government of the Nine" ', *University of Leeds Review*, 84 (1981) 13–42; repr. in *English*, 32 (1983) 129–53.
BARTHES, ROLAND, *Mythologies* (Paris, 1957, repr. 1970).
BATE, W. JACKSON, *The Burden of the Past and the English Poet* (London, 1971).
BEAL, PETER, *Index of English Literary Manuscripts*, ii: *1625–1700, Part 1: Behn–King* (London, 1987).
BENVENISTE, ÉMILE, *Le Vocabulaire des institutions indo-européennes*, 2 vols. (Paris, 1969).
BEUGNOT, BERNARD, *Le Discours de la retraite au XVIIe siècle* (Paris, 1996).
BINNS, J. W., *Intellectual Culture in Elizabethan and Jacobean England: The Latin Writings of the Age* (Leeds, 1990).
BLOOM, HAROLD, *The Anxiety of Influence: A Theory of Poetry* (New York, 1973).
BOTTKOL, J. McG., 'Dryden's Latin Scholarship', *Modern Philology*, 40 (1943) 241–54.
BRADY, JENNIFER, 'Dryden and Negotiations of Literary Succession and Precession', in *Literary Transmission and Authority: Dryden and Other Writers*, ed. Earl Miner and Jennifer Brady (Cambridge, 1993), pp. 27–54.
BROWER, RUBEN A., 'Dryden's Poetic Diction and Virgil', *Philological Quarterly*, 18 (1939) 211–17.
—— 'Dryden's Epic Manner and Virgil', *PMLA*, 55 (1940) 119–38.
CASEY, EDWARD S., *The Fate of Place: A Philosophical History* (Berkeley, 1997).

CLAUSEN, WENDELL, *A Commentary on Virgil, 'Eclogues'* (Oxford, 1994).

CLAUSS, SIDONIE, 'John Wilkins' Essay toward a Real Character: Its Place in the Seventeenth-Century Episteme', *Journal of the History of Ideas*, 43 (1982) 531–53.

CLAYTON, JAY, and ERIC ROTHSTEIN (eds.), *Influence and Intertextuality in Literary History* (Madison, 1991).

COMBE, KIRK, 'Clandestine Protest against William III in Dryden's Translations of Juvenal and Persius', *Modern Philology*, 87 (1989) 36–50.

COOLIDGE, JOHN S., 'Marvell and Horace', *Modern Philology*, 63 (1965–6) 111–20.

CORDNER, MICHAEL, 'Dryden's "Astræa Redux" and Fanshawe's "Ode" ', *Notes and Queries*, 229 (1984) 341–2.

COX, MONTAGU H., and PHILIP NORMAN, (eds.), *The Survey of London*, vol. 13 (London, 1930).

CURTIUS, ERNST ROBERT, *European Literature and the Latin Middle Ages* (London, 1953).

DE MAN, PAUL, *Allegories of Reading* (New Haven, 1979).

DERRIDA, JACQUES, *De La Grammatologie* (Paris, 1967); trans. Gayatri Chakravorty Spivak as *Of Grammatology* (Baltimore, 1976).

—— *L'Écriture et la différence* (Paris, 1967, repr. 1994); trans. Alan Bass as *Writing and Difference* (London, 1978).

—— *La Dissémination* (Paris, 1972); trans. Barbara Johnson as *Dissemination* (Chicago, 1981).

—— *Marges de la philosophie* (Paris, 1972); trans. Alan Bass as *Margins of Philosophy* (Hemel Hempstead, 1982).

—— *Apories: mourir—s'attendre aux «limites de la vérité»* (Paris, 1993, repr. 1996); trans. Thomas Dutoit as *Aporias* (Stanford, 1993).

—— *Le Monolinguisme de l'autre, ou la prothèse d'origine* (Paris, 1996).

DUMÉZIL, GEORGES, *Mythe et épopée: l'idéologie des trois fonctions dans les épopées des peuples indo-européens* (Paris, 1968).

EDWARDS, CATHERINE, *Writing Rome: Textual Approaches to the City* (Cambridge, 1996).

ERSKINE-HILL, HOWARD, 'Heirs of Vitruvius: Pope and the Idea of Architecture', in *The Art of Alexander Pope*, ed. Howard Erskine-Hill and Anne Smith (London, 1979), pp. 144–56.

—— *The Augustan Idea in English Literature* (London, 1983).

—— *Poetry and the Realm of Politics: Shakespeare to Dryden* (Oxford, 1996).

FERGUSON, ARTHUR B., *Utter Antiquity: Perceptions of Prehistory in Renaissance England* (Durham, NC, 1993).

FREUD, SIGMUND, *Gesammelte Werke*, ed. Anna Freud *et al.*, 18 vols. (London and Frankfurt, 1940–68); translated as *The Standard Edition of*

the Complete Psychological Works of Sigmund Freud, trans. James Strachey
et al., 24 vols. (London, 1953–74).

FROST, WILLIAM, *Dryden and the Art of Translation* (New Haven, 1955).

FUJIMURA, THOMAS H., *The Temper of John Dryden* (East Lansing, 1993).

GALINSKY, KARL, *Augustan Culture: An Interpretive Introduction* (Princeton, 1996).

GARRISON, JAMES D., *Dryden and the Tradition of Panegyric* (Berkeley, 1975).

—— *'Pietas' from Vergil to Dryden* (University Park, 1992).

GASTON, ROBERT W. (ed.), *Pirro Ligorio: Artist and Antiquarian* (Milan, 1988).

GENETTE, GÉRARD, *Palimpsestes: la littérature au second degré* (Paris, 1982).

—— *Seuils* (Paris, 1987).

GENT, LUCY (ed.), *Albion's Classicism: The Visual Arts in Britain, 1550–1660* (New Haven, 1995).

GILLESPIE, STUART, 'Dryden's *Sylvæ*: A Study of Dryden's Translations from the Latin in the Second Tonson Miscellany, 1685', unpublished PhD thesis, University of Cambridge, 1987.

—— 'The Early Years of the Dryden–Tonson Partnership: The Background to their Composite Translations and Miscellanies of the 1680s', *Restoration*, 12 (1988) 10–19.

—— 'A Checklist of Restoration English Translations and Adaptations of Classical Greek and Latin Poetry, 1660–1700', *Translation and Literature*, 1 (1991) 52–67.

—— 'Horace's *Ode* 3. 29: Dryden's "Masterpiece in English" ', in *Horace Made New*, ed. Charles Martindale and David Hopkins (Cambridge, 1993), pp. 148–58, 297–9.

GOUX, JEAN-JOSEPH, 'Vesta, or the Place of Being', *Representations*, 1 (1983) 91–107.

GREENE, THOMAS M., *The Light in Troy: Imitation and Discovery in Renaissance Poetry* (New Haven, 1982).

GRIFFIN, DUSTIN H., 'Dryden's "Oldham" and the Perils of Writing', *Modern Language Quarterly*, 37 (1976) 133–50.

—— *Literary Patronage in England, 1650–1800* (Cambridge, 1996).

GRIFFITHS, ERIC, 'Dryden's Past', *Proceedings of the British Academy*, 84 (1994) 113–49.

HALE, JOHN K., *Milton's Languages: The Impact of Multilingualism on Style* (Cambridge, 1997).

HAMMOND, PAUL, 'Dryden's Employment by Cromwell's Government', *Transactions of the Cambridge Bibliographical Society*, 8 (1981) 130–6.

—— 'The Integrity of Dryden's Lucretius', *Modern Language Review*, 78 (1983) 1–23.

HAMMOND, PAUL, *John Oldham and the Renewal of Classical Culture* (Cambridge, 1983).

—— 'Dryden's Library', *Notes and Queries*, 229 (1984) 344–5.

—— 'Dryden's Philosophy of Fortune', *Modern Language Review*, 80 (1985) 769–85.

—— 'Two echoes of Rochester's *A Satire Against Reason and Mankind* in Dryden', *Notes and Queries*, 233 (1988) 170–1.

—— 'John Dryden: The Classicist as Sceptic', *The Seventeenth Century*, 4 (1989) 165–87.

—— 'The King's Two Bodies: Representations of Charles II', in *Culture, Politics and Society in Britain, 1660–1800*, ed. Jeremy Black and Jeremy Gregory (Manchester, 1991), pp. 13–46.

—— *John Dryden: A Literary Life* (Basingstoke, 1991).

—— 'The Circulation of Dryden's Poetry', *Papers of the Bibliographical Society of America*, 86 (1992) 379–409.

—— 'Figures of Horace in Dryden's Literary Criticism', in *Horace Made New: Horatian Influences on British Writing from the Renaissance to the Twentieth Century*, ed. Charles Martindale and David Hopkins (Cambridge, 1993), pp. 127–47, 294–7.

—— 'Marvell's Sexuality', *The Seventeenth Century*, 11 (1996) 87–123.

—— 'Titus Oates and "Sodomy" ', in *Culture and Society in Britain 1660–1800*, ed. Jeremy Black (Manchester, 1997), pp. 85–101.

—— 'Classical Texts: Translations and Transformations', in *The Cambridge Companion to English Literature 1650–1740*, ed. Steven N. Zwicker (Cambridge, 1998), pp. 143–61.

HARDIE, PHILIP, *Virgil's 'Aeneid': Cosmos and Imperium* (Oxford, 1986).

—— 'After Rome: Renaissance Epic', in *Roman Epic*, ed. A. J. Boyle (London, 1993), pp. 294–313.

HARRIS, TIM, *London Crowds in the Reign of Charles II* (Cambridge, 1987).

HARRISON, JOHN, and PETER LASLETT, *The Library of John Locke*, 2nd edn. (Oxford, 1971).

HARTH, PHILLIP, *Contexts of Dryden's Thought* (Chicago, 1968).

—— *Pen for a Party: Dryden's Tory Propaganda in its Contexts* (Princeton, 1993).

HODGES, JOHN C., *The Library of William Congreve* (New York, 1955).

HOPKINS, DAVID, 'Dryden's "Baucis and Philemon" and *Paradise Lost*', *Notes and Queries*, 227 (1982) 503–4.

—— 'Nature's Laws and Man's: The Story of Cinyras and Myrrha in Ovid and Dryden', *Modern Language Review*, 80 (1985) 786–801.

—— *John Dryden* (Cambridge, 1986).

—— 'Dryden and Ovid's "Wit out of Season" ', in *Ovid Renewed*, ed. Charles Martindale (Cambridge, 1988), pp. 167–90.

—— 'Dryden and the Tenth Satire of Juvenal', *Translation and Literature*, 4 (1995) 31–60.

HORSFALL, NICHOLAS (ed.), *A Companion to the Study of Virgil*, Mnemosyne Supplementum 151 (Leiden, 1995).

KELSEY, SEAN, *Inventing a Republic* (Manchester, 1997).

KENNEDY, I. G., 'Claude and Architecture', *Journal of the Warburg and Courtauld Institutes*, 35 (1972) 260–83.

KIEFER, FREDERICK, 'The Conflation of Fortuna and Occasio in Renaissance Thought and Iconography', *Journal of Medieval and Renaissance Studies*, 9 (1979) 1–27.

KING, BRUCE (ed.), *Dryden's Mind and Art* (Edinburgh, 1969).

KRAMER, DAVID BRUCE, *The Imperial Dryden: The Poetics of Appropriation in Seventeenth-Century England* (Athens, Ga., 1994).

KROLL, RICHARD W. F., *The Material Word: Literate Culture in the Restoration and Early Eighteenth Century* (Baltimore, 1991).

LEWALSKI, BARBARA K., 'The Scope and Function of Biblical Allusion in *Absalom and Achitophel*', *English Language Notes*, 3 (1965) 29–35.

LOANE, GEORGE, 'Notes on the Globe "Dryden" ', *Notes and Queries*, 185 (1943) 272–81.

LOVE, HAROLD (ed.), *Restoration Literature: Critical Approaches* (London, 1972).

—— 'Dryden's "Unideal Vacancy" ', *Eighteenth-Century Studies*, 12 (1978) 74–89.

—— 'Dryden's Rationale of Paradox', *ELH*, 51 (1984) 297–313.

LUCKETT, RICHARD, 'The Fabric of Dryden's Verse', *Proceedings of the British Academy*, 67 (1981) 289–305.

LYNE, R. O. A. M., *Further Voices in Vergil's 'Aeneid'* (Oxford, 1987).

MACDONALD, HUGH, *John Dryden: A Bibliography of Early Editions and of Drydeniana* (Oxford, 1939).

MACDONALD, WILLIAM L., *The Pantheon: Design, Meaning, and Progeny* (Harmondsworth, 1976).

MCHENRY, ROBERT W., 'Dryden's Architectural Metaphors and Restoration Architecture', *Restoration*, 9 (1985) 61–74.

MCKENZIE, D. F., *The Integrity of William Congreve: The Clark Lectures for 1997* (Privately Printed, 1997). A copy is deposited in the library of Trinity College, Cambridge.

MCKEON, MICHAEL, *Poetry and Politics in Restoration England: The Case of Dryden's 'Annus Mirabilis'* (Cambridge, Mass., 1975).

MARTINDALE, CHARLES (ed.), *Virgil and his Influence: Bimillennial Studies* (Bristol, 1984).

—— *John Milton and the Transformation of Ancient Epic* (London, 1986).

—— (ed.), *The Cambridge Companion to Virgil* (Cambridge, 1997).

MASON, H. A., 'Is Juvenal a Classic?', in *Critical Essays on Roman Literature: Satire*, ed. J. P. Sullivan (London, 1963), pp. 93–176.

—— 'The Dream of Happiness', *Cambridge Quarterly*, 8 (1978) 11–55 and 9 (1980) 218–71. [On Dryden's translation of Horace's *Epode* ii.]

—— 'Living in the Present', *Cambridge Quarterly*, 10 (1981) 91–129. [On Dryden's translation of Horace's *Carmina* iii. 29.]

—— 'The Hallowed Hearth', *Cambridge Quarterly*, 14 (1985) 205–39. [On Dryden's translation of Horace's *Carmina* i. 9.]

MASON, J. R., 'To Milton through Dryden and Pope', unpublished PhD thesis, University of Cambridge, 1987.

MILLER, RACHEL, 'Physic for the Great: Dryden's Satiric Translations of Juvenal, Persius, and Boccaccio', *Philological Quarterly*, 68 (1989) 53–75.

MINER, EARL, and JENNIFER BRADY (eds.), *Literary Transmission and Authority: Dryden and other writers* (Cambridge, 1993).

MYERSON, GEORGE, *The Argumentative Imagination: Wordsworth, Dryden, Religious Dialogues* (Manchester, 1992).

NISBET, R. G. M., and MARGARET HUBBARD, *A Commentary on Horace, 'Odes', Book 1* (Oxford, 1970).

NORBROOK, DAVID, 'Marvell's "Horatian Ode" and the Politics of Genre', in *Literature and the English Civil War*, ed. Thomas Healy and Jonathan Sawday (Cambridge, 1990), pp. 147–69.

—— 'Lucan, Thomas May, and the Creation of a Republican Literary Culture', in *Culture and Politics in Early Stuart England*, ed. Kevin Sharpe and Peter Lake (Basingstoke, 1994), pp. 45–66.

—— 'Lucy Hutchinson versus Edmund Waller: An Unpublished Reply to Waller's *A Panegyrick to my Lord Protector*', *The Seventeenth Century*, 11 (1996) 61–86.

OGILVIE, R. M., 'Two Notes on Dryden's *Absalom and Achitophel*', *Notes and Queries*, 215 (1970) 415–16.

OSLER, MARGARET J. (ed.), *Atoms, 'Pneuma', and Tranquillity: Epicurean and Stoic Themes in European Thought* (Cambridge, 1991).

OTIS, BROOKS, 'Virgil and Clio: A Consideration of Virgil's Relation to History', *Phoenix*, 20 (1966) 59–75.

PARRY, ADAM, 'The Two Voices of Virgil's *Aeneid*', *Arion*, 2:4 (1963) 66–80.

PATCH, HOWARD R., *The Goddess Fortuna in Medieval Literature* (Cambridge, Mass., 1927).

PATRIDES, C. A., 'Renaissance and Modern Views on Hell', *Harvard Theological Review*, 57 (1964) 217–36.

PAVEL, THOMAS, *L'Art de l'éloignement: essai sur l'imagination classique* (Paris, 1996).

PIGMAN III, G. W., 'Versions of Imitation in the Renaissance', *Renaissance Quarterly*, 33 (1980) 1–32.

PITTOCK, MURRAY G. H., *Poetry and Jacobite Politics in Eighteenth-Century Britain and Ireland* (Cambridge, 1994).

PORTER, WILLIAM M., *Reading the Classics and 'Paradise Lost'* (Lincoln, Nebr., 1993).

QUINT, DAVID, *Origin and Originality in Renaissance Literature: Versions of the Source* (New Haven, 1983).

—— *Epic and Empire: Politics and Generic Form from Virgil to Milton* (Princeton, 1993).

RANDALL, DALE B. J., 'The Head and the Hands on the Rostra: *Marcus Tullius Cicero* as a Sign of its Time', *Connotations*, 1 (1991) 34–54.

REVERAND, CEDRIC D., *Dryden's Final Poetic Mode: The 'Fables'* (Philadelphia, 1988).

RICKS, CHRISTOPHER, 'Allusion: The Poet as Heir', in *Studies in the Eighteenth Century III*, ed. R. F. Brissenden and J. C. Eade (Toronto, 1976), pp. 209–40.

ROETHLISBERGER, MARCEL G., 'The Dimension of Time in the Art of Claude Lorrain', *Artibus et Historiae*, 20 (1989) 73–92.

RORTY, RICHARD, *Contingency, Irony, and Solidarity* (Cambridge, 1989).

RØSTVIG, MAREN-SOFIE, *The Happy Man: Studies in the Metamorphoses of a Classical Ideal, 1600–1700*, 2nd edn. (Oslo, 1962).

SASLOW, EDWARD L., 'Angelic "Fire-Works": The Background and Significance of *The Hind and the Panther*, II, 649–62', *Studies in English Literature 1500–1900*, 20 (1980) 373–84.

SIMONSUURI, KIRSTI, *Homer's Original Genius* (Cambridge, 1979).

SKINNER, QUENTIN, 'The State' in *Political Innovation and Conceptual Change*, ed. Terence Ball, James Farr, and Russell L. Hanson (Cambridge, 1989), pp. 90–131.

SLOMAN, JUDITH, *Dryden: The Poetics of Translation* (Toronto, 1985).

SMITH, CHARLES KAY, 'French Philosophy and English Politics in Interregnum Poetry', in *The Stuart Court and Europe: Essays in Politics and Political Culture*, ed. R. Malcolm Smuts (Cambridge, 1996), pp. 177–209.

SMITH, NIGEL, *Perfection Proclaimed: Language and Literature in English Radical Religion 1640–1660* (Oxford, 1989).

—— *Literature and Revolution in England 1640–1660* (New Haven, 1994).

SOWERBY, ROBIN, 'The Freedom of Dryden's Homer', *Translation and Literature*, 5 (1996) 26–50.

STRONG, ROY, *Britannia Triumphans: Inigo Jones, Rubens, and Whitehall Palace* (London, 1980).

SWEDENBERG, H. T., '*Astræa Redux* in its Setting', *Studies in Philology*, 50 (1953) 30–44.

SYFRET, R. H., 'Marvell's "Horatian Ode" ', *Review of English Studies*, 12 (1961) 160–71.

VENUTI, LAWRENCE, '*The Destruction of Troy*: Translation and Royalist Cultural Politics in the Interregnum', *Journal of Medieval and Renaissance Studies*, 23 (1993) 197–219.

VICKERS, BRIAN, 'Analogy versus Identity: The Rejection of Occult Symbolism, 1580–1680', in *Occult and Scientific Mentalities in the Renaissance*, ed. Brian Vickers (Cambridge, 1984), pp. 95–163.

WILDING, MICHAEL, 'Dryden and Satire: *Mac Flecknoe*, *Absalom and Achitophel*, *The Medall*, and Juvenal', in *John Dryden*, ed. Earl Miner (London, 1972), pp. 190–233.

WILSON, A. J. N., 'Andrew Marvell: *An Horatian Ode upon Cromwel's Return from Ireland*: the thread of the poem and its use of classical allusion', *Critical Quarterly*, 11 (1969) 325–41.

WILSON, G. E., 'Dryden and the Emblem of *Fortuna-Occasio*', *Papers in Language and Literature*, 11 (1975) 199–203.

WINE, HUMPHREY, *Claude: The Poetic Landscape* (London, 1994).

WINN, JAMES ANDERSON, *John Dryden and his World* (New Haven, 1987).

—— *"When Beauty Fires the Blood": Love and the Arts in the Age of Dryden* (Ann Arbor, 1992).

ZWICKER, STEVEN N., *Dryden's Political Poetry: The Typology of King and Nation* (Providence, 1972).

—— *Politics and Language in Dryden's Poetry: The Arts of Disguise* (Princeton, 1984).

ZWICKER, STEVEN N., and DAVID BYWATERS, 'Politics and Translation: The English Tacitus of 1698', *Huntington Library Quarterly*, 52 (1989) 319–46.

INDEX

This index does not cover place names, fictional or legendary characters, or entries in the bibliography.